# HILLFORTS
## of southern Scotland

AOC (Scotland) Ltd
*The Schoolhouse*
4 Lochend Road
Leith
Edinburgh
EH6 8BR

| | |
|---|---|
| **Publication** | First published in Great Britain 1992 by AOC (Scotland) Ltd |
| **Copyright** | 1992 Crown copyright |
| **Editorial** | John Barber |
| **Design** | Christina Unwin |
| **Typesetting** | Hewer Text Composition Services, Edinburgh |
| **Printing** | Burns and Harris Ltd, Dundee |
| **ISBN** | 0 9519344 1 4 |

# Forward

It can be difficult at times when excavating on a bleak exposed hilltop in the driving rain to remember that archaeology is fun. The enjoyment comes from the work itself and the companionship on an excavation. But it also comes from the experience of asking questions and solving problems. Hillforts offer many challenges to the archaeologist. Their purpose seems obvious 'defence' but is it as simple as that? Did prestige play a part in the strength and sophistication of the defences? Who lived in the hillforts? Were they occupied all year? How did they relate to the surrounding settlements? When were they built? When were they abandoned? Archaeologists have set themselves these questions. The answers are not easily won and the number of questions grows as we learn more. Within this volume many of these questions are addressed and some answers are offered.

Hillforts are part of our archaeological heritage, but they also help to make our landscape so diverse and attractive. Their loss would affect our view of the countryside, diminishing its richness and variety. Hillforts, like all other archaeological sites, are susceptible to a wide range of threats, represented in this volume by quarrying, the provision of modern facilities, in this case the improvement of radar installations and erosion. Threats to archaeological sites occur at random, and tend to lead to a haphazard extension of our knowledge; but sometimes, as in this volume, the fortunate combination of excavations can lead to the possibility of wider conclusions and feed into other archaeological investigations thus forming part of sustained research programmes. The value of such programmes is emphasised by the work of the late Professor George Jobey. Described as 'virtually a Commission in himself', George Jobey devoted his archaeological career to surveying, excavating and interpreting the archaeology of his native county of Northumberland. Central to his study was the relationship between later prehistoric settlement and Roman intrusion. In Scotland, hillforts, particularly the major hillforts or *oppida*, play a central role in the study of this relationship. It is appropriate for these reasons that this volume is dedicated to him.

The excavations reported in this volume were all undertaken by the Central Excavation Unit when an integral part of Historic Scotland. In welcoming the publication, I also take the opportunity to wish the newly formed AOC (Scotland) Ltd a successful archaeological career: *Hillforts of southern Scotland* is a sound base on which to build a new organisation.

*David J Breeze*
Chief Inspector of Ancient Monuments
Historic Scotland

# Acknowledgements

The excavations and post-excavation analyses of Eildon Hill North, The Dunion, Gillies Hill, Harpercroft and Wardlaw Hill were entirely funded by Historic Scotland. AOC (Scotland) Ltd would like to thank Historic Scotland for their grant towards the printing costs.

The authors are grateful to individual area Inspectors and various colleagues, both in the Inspectorate and elsewhere, for their advice during and after excavation, in particular Richard Feachem, Dr Noel Fojut, Professor Antony Harding, Peter Hill, A H Hogg, George Jobey, Dr Gordon Maxwell, Jack Stevenson and Robert Stevenson.

AOC (Scotland) Ltd are grateful to the Royal Commission on the Ancient and Historical Monuments of Scotland for their kind permission to use R W Feachem's survey results of the Dunion (1961) and the data from the 1939 survey (published 1956), also of the Dunion, and the 1956 survey results of Eildon Hill North. We are also grateful to the National Galleries of Scotland for their kind permission in allowing the reproduction of James Ward's painting of 'The Eildon Hills and the Tweed', 1807, and to Historic Scotland for permitting the reproduction of the cover photograph of Eildon Hill North, by Michael Brooks, photographic officer.

Many people have contributed to the production of the monograph and in particular the authors would like to thank the following: Christina Unwin (design); John Barber and Finbar McCormick (editing); Patrick Ashmore, Dr David Breeze and Dr Noel Fojut (refereeing); Dr Steven Carter, Dr Ann MacSween, Dr Coralie Mills and Dr Richard Tipping (specialist refereeing; soils, artefacts, environmental and pollen, respectively); Dilys Jones (copyediting); Sylvia Stevenson, Mary Kemp and Jim Rideout (line drawings); Nyree Finlay, Hilary McCallum, V J McLellan, Damian Robinson and Gill Walsh (assistants); Elizabeth Knox (wordprocessing).

None of the excavations would have been possible without the enthusiasm and hard work of the volunteers and site staff, who frequently experienced quite appalling extremes of climate and densities of Scottish insect life. Thanks also to the post-excavation staff – the writing up of these excavations is a testimonial to their organisational powers during the five moves of premises most of the excavation material has endured. In particular, the authors would like to thank Sheila Boardman (Gillies Hill macroplant assessment), Alan Duffy (Harpercroft & Wardlaw Hill), Norman Emery (Eildon), Eoin Halpin (The Dunion), Historic Scotland conservation laboratory services, Mike Rains (Eildon), Christopher Russell-White (The Dunion and Gillies Hill), Nick Tavener (The Dunion and Gillies Hill) and all the laboratory technicians, sievers and sorters.

Thanks also to the landowners and tenants who tolerated the sometimes annual seige of their land.

# Gazetteer

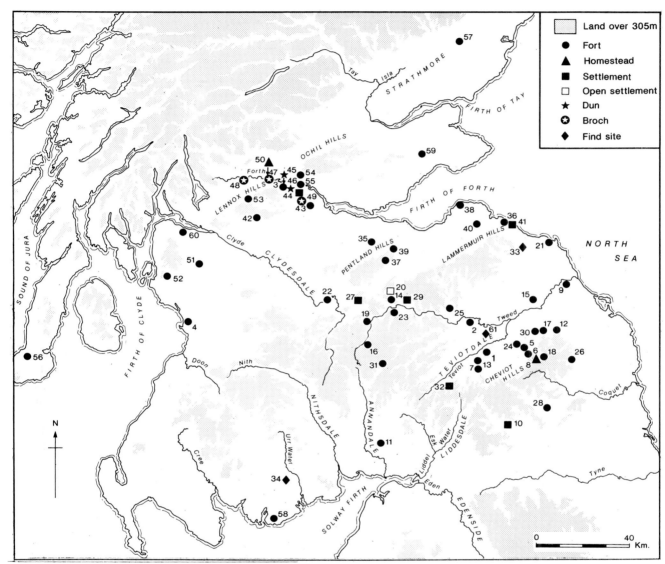

*Gazetteer of sites referred to in this monograph.*

1 The Dunion NT625190
2 Eildon Hill North NT555328
3 Gillies Hill NS768917
4 Wardlaw and Harperscroft
5 Hownam Law NT796220
6 Hownam Rings NT790194
7 Bonchester Hill NT595117
8 Crock Cleuch NT833176
9 Murton High Crags NT965496
10 Tower Knowe NY700871
11 Burnswark NY185786
12 Yeavering Bell NT928293
13 Rubers Law NT580155
14 White Meldon NT219428
15 Hirsel Law NT825416

16 Whiteside Rig NT112248
17 Humbleton Hill NT867283
18 Hayhope Knowe NT860176
19 Glenachan Rig NT106328
20 Green Knowe NT212434
21 Earn's Heugh NT892691
22 Cairngryffe Hill NS943411
23 Chester Hill, Hundleshope NT236360
24 Woden Law NT768125
25 Torwoodlee NT465384
26 Brough Law NT998164
27 Candyburn NT071411
28 Old Fawdon Camp NY897940
29 Horseburgh Castle Farm NT291400
30 Rings Plantation NT837284

# Archaeological background *J S Rideout*

Despite recent advances, the most useful distribution map of hillforts in northern Britain is still that produced in 1966 for *The Iron Age in Northern Britain* (Rivet 1966), upon which Figure 1.1 is based. Hogg's list of forts (1979) adds further sites, but does not materially alter the overall picture. Rivet's map shows a distinct concentration of forts in an area centred on the Tweed Basin between the Firth of Forth to the north, and the River Tyne to the south. A more dispersed group runs west from this concentration, through Nithsdale and Annandale and westwards to the Mull of Galloway. A third, even more dispersed group exists in the upper Forth Valley, Fife, and southern Tayside. Elsewhere in Lowland Scotland, northern Cumbria and Northumberland few forts have been identified. In the

Scottish Highlands and Islands, a few forts exist in an area dominated by duns in the south-west, and brochs in the north (*cf* map in Cunliffe 1983, 97, Figure 5).

The two larger sites reported upon here, The Dunion and Eildon Hill North, are only 14 km apart. They sit roughly centrally in the concentration of forts in the Tyne-Forth area. Gillies Hill is on the south-west edge of the group in the Forth Valley, Fife, Tayside area, and the two forts at Dundonald are part of a small dispersed group on the west coast of Ayrshire and Renfrewshire (Strathclyde).

Archaeological attention has, in the past, focused mainly on the forts of the Tyne-Forth province. Many of these forts were first identified at the end of the nineteenth century by David Christison (1887, 1888,

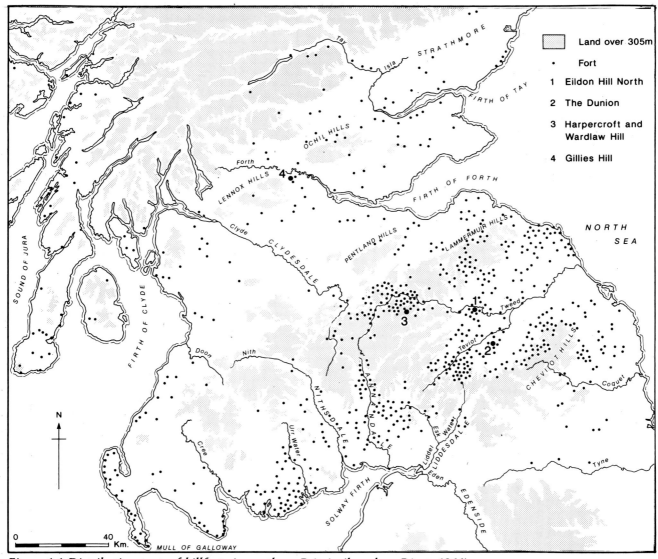

*Figure 1.1 Distribution map of hillforts in northern Britain (based on Rivet, 1966).*

1890, 1895 and 1898). Surveys of the area have been published in the RCAHMS *Inventories* for Berwickshire (1915), Midlothian (1929), East Lothian (1924), Roxburghshire (1956), Selkirkshire (1957), Peeblesshire (1967), and Lanarkshire (1978). The surveys of most of Berwickshire and Midlothian have recently been updated in *The Archaeological Sites and Monuments of Scotland* lists (respectively, *no* 10, 1980 and *no* 28, 1988).

Recorded excavation of the forts began with the relatively small-scale investigations by Curle on Eildon Hill North (Christison 1894, 119) and on the fort on the prominent hill, Rubers Law (Curle 1907), both in Roxburghshire. Larger-scale excavations, also by Curle, were undertaken on the fort at the equally prominent site of Bonchester Hill, some 4 km south-west of Rubers Law (Curle 1910). These small investigations were followed by fuller excavations at Traprain Law, East Lothian, jointly and severally by Curle and Cree (1915, 1916, 1920, 1921, 1922, 1923 and 1924). Despite later attempts by others (*eg* Jobey 1976), the results of the excavations at Traprain are still not fully understood. The 1930s saw excavations at Earn's Heugh, Berwickshire (Childe & Forde 1932) and Castlelaw Fort, Midlothian (Childe 1933), and further work was carried out at Traprain Law (Cruden 1940). Childe also undertook small excavations at Cairngryffe Hill, Lanarkshire (1941a) and Kaimes Hill, Midlothian (1941b). In the same period a small excavation was carried out at Chester Hill, Hundleshope, Peeblesshire (Keef 1946).

Between the late nineteenth century and the Second World War, understanding of the dating and cultural associations of southern Scottish hillforts changed. Initially identified as Roman 'camps', they were later attributed to the Iron Age period (Christison 1898, 352 and 381) and by the mid 1930s, Childe had developed a typology for forts and had identified cultural origins for the types (Childe 1935). Large forts like Eildon Hill North (The Dunion had not then been identified as a large fort), called Hill-Top Towns by Childe, were seen as native developments with roots in the Late Bronze Age. Other fort types were believed to have been introduced by invaders from outwith Scotland in the late first millennium BC.

In the years following the Second World War, hillfort excavations became more problem-oriented, as attempts were made to fit the forts of southern Scotland into the emerging British and European picture. To this end C M Piggott undertook a series of excavations in south-west Scotland. The results of the first of these, at Hownam Rings, Roxburghshire, gave rise to the Hownam sequence (Piggott C M 1948), which has since served as a model for the succession of settlement types in the area. The Hownam sequence was subsequently tested at Hayhope Knowe (Piggott C M 1949) and Bonchester Hill (Piggott C M 1950), both in Roxburghshire. The Hownam sequence indicates a development from palisaded settlement, to a fort defended by a single stone-built wall, and on to a multivallate fort with, later, a non-defensive settlement.

The excavator saw the palisaded phase, and possibly the stone-wall phase as being of native origin, with multivallation occasioned by an influx of a warrior aristocracy. The results of the excavations at Hayhope Knowe and Bonchester Hill did not contradict the Hownam sequence. Dating of such sites, following the trend in the south of Britain, was compressed into a few centuries before the arrival of the Romans.

In this same period of research, other forts were investigated in excavations of varying scale (Braidwood, Midlothian [Stevenson 1949]; Woden Law, Roxburghshire [excavated in 1950], [Richmond & St Joseph 1982]; Torwoodlee broch and fort, Selkirkshire [Piggott 1951]; Castle Law, Glencorse, Midlothian and Craig's Quarry, Dirleton, East Lothian [Piggott & Piggott C M 1952]; Braidwood and Craig's Quarry [Piggott 1958b]). This *floruit* of research in the southern Scottish Iron Age also included work on other site-types – palisaded homesteads and settlements, duns, and Unenclosed Platform Settlements, then believed transitional between the Late Bronze and Early Iron Ages. The culmination of this comparatively active period was a conference in 1961, the proceedings of which were published as *The Iron Age in Northern Britain* (Rivet 1966). The papers in the volume, amended to take into account the years between conference and publication, proved an invaluable summary of the period of research between the end of the Second World War and the early 1960s. Piggott's paper (*op cit*, 1–15) attempted to extend Hawkes' ABC scheme (1959) to the Iron Age in northern Britain. Feachem summarised and, to a certain extent, classified the hillforts of the area using this scheme (*ibid*, 59–97), while Jobey expanded the scheme to include Northumberland (*ibid*, 89–109). Aspects of artefact typologies and their cultural affinities were discussed by Stevenson (*ibid*, 17–44).

Following the conference there was a comparative lull in research into forts until the late 1970s. However, even during this period, forts were excavated, at Kaimes Hill, Midlothian (Simpson 1969), and Brough Law, Northumberland (Jobey 1971). By the late 1970s a simple model for the Iron Age in southern Scotland existed. Open settlement, continuing from the Late Bronze Age, was said to be replaced by palisaded sites in the Early Iron Age. Following the Hownam sequence, palisaded sites were followed by univallate stone-walled forts later superseded by multivallate forts. This progression was believed to have been interrupted by the Roman advance, and the vernacular architecture of the Roman and post-Roman periods was said to consist of open settlements and small enclosed homesteads, both containing stone-walled houses, overlying slighted hillfort defences. Some hillforts were re-used in the post-Roman/Dark Age period. The increasing number of available radiocarbon dates (*cf* MacKie 1969, Figure 2) forced a series of revisions to the chronology of the model.

The next milestone in Iron Age studies in south-east Scotland came in 1981 with a conference in Edinburgh on later prehistoric settlement in south-east Scotland, the proceedings of which were edited by Harding and published the following year (1982a). The conference was the result of another phase of field-work consisting of survey, rescue excavation and research work, and provided a vehicle for the publication of many interim reports (at the time of writing only one of the sites involved, Candyburn Enclosure, has been fully published [Lane 1986]). Amongst the sites then excavated, the fort at Broxmouth, East Lothian, is notable for being the first full excavation of a hillfort in southern Scotland (Hill 1982b). The results of this phase of field-work suggested that the development of Iron Age settlement was more complex than had been perceived, with different types of settlement sites in use contemporaneously and the reversal of the anticipated open-, to enclosed-settlement sequence observed on sites like Dryburn Bridge (Triscott 1982).

This conference did not explore the relationship between the forts and contemporaneous settlement types in south-east Scotland, with those to the north and west. The concentration of forts in the upper Forth Valley, Fife, and Tayside, within which Gillies Hill is located, is an area which also contains a significant number of duns and some brochs. Small numbers of brochs also occur in the main Tyne-Forth area, with two brochs within 15 km of Eildon Hill North.

Iron Age sites of the upper Forth area are relatively unexplored. RCAHMS *Inventories* exist for just two areas, West Lothian (1929) and Stirlingshire (1963). In the period before 1980 only two forts were excavated:

Meikle Reive in the Campsie Fells (Fairhurst 1956) and Camelon, a defended settlement near Falkirk, excavated in 1961 (Proudfoot 1978). Other forts have been investigated elsewhere in this area but these are too distant to warrant specific mention here. Other site types, however, have been investigated; West Plean palisaded homestead, Stirlingshire, the type-site for large ring-groove houses in south-east Scotland (Steer 1956); and duns at Castlehill Wood (Feachem 1957) and Wallstale (Thomson 1969), both within 2 km of Gillies Hill. Also excavated are brochs at Leckie (MacKie 1982), Buchlyvie (Main 1978) and Torwood (Dundas 1866; Hunter 1949), as well as a homestead at Keir Hill, Gargunnock (MacLaren 1958), all in Stirlingshire.

The Dundonald sites are among the few forts in an area dominated by duns. Excavated forts are, therefore, comparatively few and, with the exception of the small-scale excavation on the minor *oppidum* at Walls Hill, Renfrewshire (Newall 1960), most are not fully published. The only excavation of any scale was undertaken in 1978–9 at Carwinning Hill, *circa* 22 km north-north-west from Dundonald (Cowie forthcoming, *a*).

The areas within which Gillies Hill and the Dundonald sites exist, as well as other areas in south and east Scotland, have seen less excavation than the Tyne/Forth province. Consequently, while south-east Scotland has a well formulated model, the areas to the north and west suffer from poor development of the study of forts and other Iron Age settlement types.

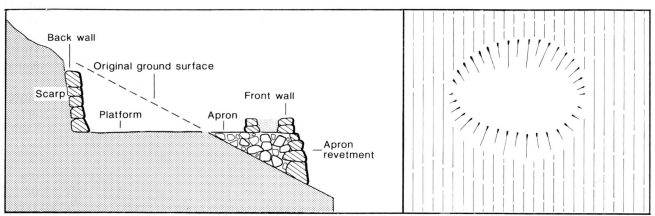

*Key to graphic conventions used in all plans and sections, except those for Gillies Hill.*

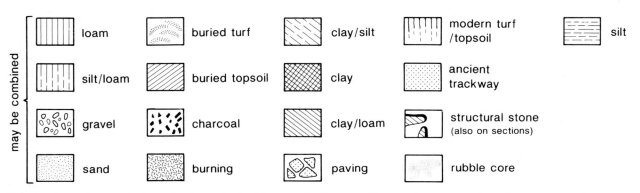

*Schematic section and plan of a hypothetical house platform to illustrate terms used in this monograph.*

# Vegetational history and land use  *S Butler*

With the aim of providing some information about regional landscape conditions for the two hillforts at Eildon and The Dunion, a pollen core was taken from a nearby infilled lake basin in the surrounding lowlands. This section presents the results from that core, together with a brief synopsis of existing pollen diagrams from south-east Scotland. Pollen analyses from on-site soils and deposits recovered during the course of excavations at Eildon and The Dunion are discussed in the relevant excavation reports (below).

## PRESENT ENVIRONMENT

In the broad context of south-east Scotland, the Eildon and The Dunion hillforts are situated in the foothill region along the eastern flank of the Southern Uplands. This region tends to have a 'corrugated relief' of closely spaced ridges and hollows (Ragg 1960), at a general altitude of 150–325 m OD. The climate is of a humid temperate variety and tends to be fairly warm and wet or moderately dry (Brown & Shipley 1982). Cooler and wetter conditions prevail in the uplands to the west, and warmer conditions in the Border lowlands to the east. Most of the soils have developed on glacial tills of varied texture, mostly derived from Lower Palaeozoic greywackes and shales. They tend to be either brown forest soils, often with some gleying, or noncalcareous gleys, but this foothill region is transitional to the more podsolised and peaty soils of the uplands.

The vegetation is now largely characterised by a range of rush, sedge and grass communities, of which sharp-flowered rush, soft rush, tussock grass and fescue are common elements. These pastures support sheep and cattle farming, but the land can also be used for short arable breaks. Forage crops such as rape are commonly grown in this manner. Some good quality arable land, capable of sustaining intensive cereal cultivation, is found in the eastern side of the region, roughly starting from a line drawn between the Eildon and The Dunion hillforts. However, arable farming becomes less viable towards the west of the region, where improved pastures can rapidly give way with increasing altitude to Atlantic heather moor, capable of sustaining only low density grazing. Forestry is concentrated in the less fertile uplands to the west, and woodlands are not dominant features of the foothill region. However, small coniferous plantations do occur, including that of the Eildon Estate on the southern slopes of the Eildon Hills. Broadleaved trees such as oak, beech, ash, sycamore and elm tend to occur as narrow shelter belts at the edges of agricultural land.

## PAST ENVIRONMENTS

Seven main pollen diagrams are currently available from south-east Scotland, plus two from just south of the Scottish border in Northumberland (Figure 1.2). The earliest work seems to have been that of Newey (1969) who published three pollen diagrams from raised bog and blanket peat in Midlothian and Peeblesshire. None of his three sites are radiocarbon dated, but two of the diagrams appear to cover the entire postglacial (Holocene) period, while one (Kitchen Moss) appears to date from the mid-Holocene (*circa* 5000 BP) onwards. All three diagrams show loss of woodland and development of heathland during the later prehistoric and historic periods. The woodland is represented largely by *Betula*, *Alnus*, Coryloid, *Quercus*, and *Ulmus* pollen. These same major woodland elements appear also in the diagrams from all the other sites shown in Figure 1.2, although the relative importance of individual taxa differs from site to site. Spatial variation in the composition of the woodland must have occurred in response to altitude, exposure, soils, hydrology and other ecological factors, and it is difficult to make generalisations from the available data. The Coryloid pollen category includes both *Corylus avellana* (hazel) and *Myrica gale* (sweet gale), but Birks (1989, 508) refers to evidence from northern England and south-west Scotland that the pollen type here largely represents *Corylus avellana*. Rackham (1976; 1988) regards the native woodland of south-east Scotland as belonging to an oak-hazel province, in which hazelwoods characterised the better soils and oakwoods the worse. Coryloid pollen certainly features strongly in all the existing pollen diagrams from the region, while *Betula* and *Alnus* may have been particularly competitive at more exposed sites and on damper soils respectively.

In so far as any general trend can be identified, an overall tendency towards progressive deforestation from about 5000 BP onwards seems to be evidenced. Although stressing the need for caution, Morrison (1983, 13) suggests that in Scotland as a whole deforestation 'seems to have been greater in the Bronze Age than in the Neolithic, and very much greater in the Iron Age than previously'. The radiocarbon dated pollen diagrams from Northumberland (Davies & Turner 1979), display a classic sequence of temporary clearance and regeneration phases during the Neolithic and Bronze Ages. At Steng Moss there are substantial but temporary peaks in herbaceous pollen at *circa* 1065 BC and *circa* 636 BC (uncalibrated), followed by more permanent clearance at *circa* 20 BC (uncalibrated). At Fellend Moss

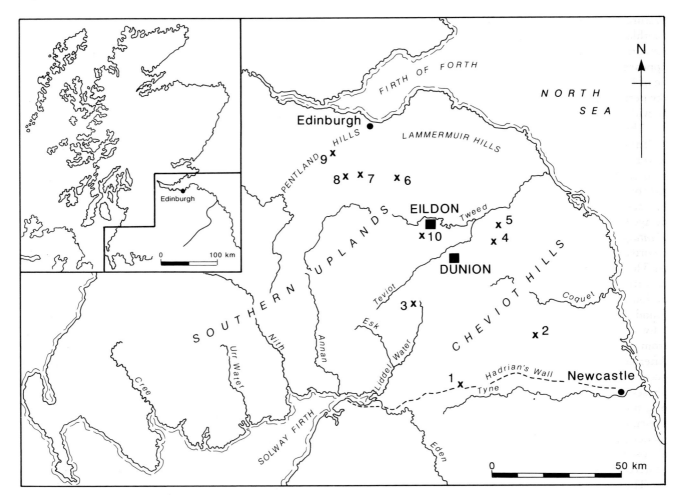

*Figure 1.2 Location of pollen sites.*
1 *Fellend Moss NY679658, 200 m OD (Davies & Turner 1979).*
2 *Steng Moss NY965913, 305 m OD (Davies and Turner 1979).*
3 *The Dod NT472060, 220 m OD (Shennan & Innes 1987).*
4 *Linton Loch NT793254, 91 m OD (Mannion 1978a).*
5 *Din Moss NT805318, 170 m OD (Hibbert & Switsur 1976).*
6 *Threepwood Moss NT425515, 290 m OD (Mannion 1978B).*
7 *Side Moss NT285555, 274 m OD (Newey 1969).*
8 *Upper Eddleston Valley NT242537, 260 m OD (Newey 1969).*
9 *Kitchen Moss NT165608, 411 m OD (Newey 1969).*
10 *Blackpool Moss NT517289, 260 m OD (Webb & Moore 1982; also present study).*

there is a Bronze Age clearance episode at *circa* 1700 BC (uncalibrated), followed by a long period of low herb pollen representation until extensive clearance beginning at *circa* ad 2 (uncalibrated). The greater evidence for arable farming that accompanies the apparently more permanent clearances of the later Iron Age and Romano-British periods (see Turner 1983) might reinforce Piggott's (1958a) impression that the prehistoric economy of northern Britain was largely based on nomadic pastoralism, although it is clear from Steng Moss and Fellend Moss that major changes took place just before, rather than with, the arrival of the Roman army in this area. After comparison of nine pollen diagrams from north-east England, Turner (1979, 289) states: 'It is apparent then, that the native British populations of the two centuries before and early first century after Christ cleared woodland, maintained

pasture and grew crops on a totally different scale from that of their predecessors in both the uplands and the lowlands, and that the cleared land remained in use throughout the Roman occupation'. Wilson's (1983) summary of the pollen evidence from north-east England suggests that permanent clearance began from the mid-third millennium BP onwards, and intensified towards the end of that millennium.

The seven pollen diagrams from south-east Scotland lack the detail and dating control of the English sites. There is some evidence for episodes of clearance and regeneration of woodland at Newey's (1969) sites, but here it is Ericaceae rather than Gramineae that dominates the non-arboreal pollen, indicating the role of heathland. The presence of *Plantago* pollen might suggest that these heaths were used for grazing. Mannion (1978b) also points to the role of heathland pasture at Threepwood Moss. The clear extension of heathland shown in her pollen sequence from here remains undated but occurs well after the first appearance of *Plantago lanceolata*, and might therefore be of later prehistoric or historic date. A similar delay in the permanent extension of heath and reduction in forest is evidenced at Din Moss (Hibbert & Switsur 1976).

The pollen sequences from Linton Loch (Mannion 1978a) contain little Ericaceae pollen, perhaps due to the lower altitude of the site. Interpretation of regional landscape changes is here complicated by local hydroseral developments and lack of radiocarbon dates, but here again the main expansion of open ground is delayed until some time after the first appearance of *Plantago lanceolata*. Mannion points to the numerous records of Bronze Age finds in and around Linton Loch. At The Dod (Shennan & Innes 1987) there is unfortunately a hiatus in the peat profile covering the period *circa* 5000 BP to *circa* 1650 BP, but the authors found evidence under the associated earthwork for hillwash deposits which they reason may have resulted from woodland clearance during the Neolithic period. After *circa* 1650 BP 'peaks of open habitat herb grains occur at intervals in the pollen record . . . representing phases of increased clearance activity within the context of a progressively deforested landscape . . . Clearance pressure seems to have increased in intensity up to modern times, and by the uppermost pollen levels an almost totally cleared landscape seems to have been achieved' (23).

Thus it is possible, in the absence of radiocarbon dates, to read the pollen record from south-east Scotland as generally concurring with the evidence from north-east England for only minor landscape changes until about the mid first millennium BC or later. However, Wilson (1983) makes the interesting point that during the first millennium BC farmers may have begun to exploit the lower-lying clay lands, and that a previous concentration of settlement on higher ground has been under-represented in the pollen record due to the distribution of pollen sites. Young (1987) makes out a strong case for this in his analysis of barrows and cairns in Co. Durham, suggesting that arable cultivation and large areas of already cleared land existed there at an earlier date than the pollen records indicate. Whittington (1980) has pointed to the growing body of evidence for arable and mixed farming during the Neolithic, Bronze and Iron Ages in Scotland, suggesting that Piggott overstated his case and that the Highland-Lowland division now seen in Scottish agriculture did not come into existence until the early centuries AD.

## Blackpool Moss, Whitlaw

Reconnaissance of numerous small waterlogged basins in the region around the Eildon and The Dunion hillforts revealed that the potential of most sites to provide later prehistoric deposits had been destroyed by subsequent human interference, through drainage, peat cutting or clay digging. However, the possible existence of an intact postglacial sediment sequence at Blackpool Moss, Whitlaw, was suggested by the work of Webb and Moore (1982) and this site was selected for further investigation. The site lies 4 km south-west of the Eildon hillfort complex at NT517289 (Figure 1.2). It forms one of a group of five small mosses or fens which, at heights of between 245 m and 275 m OD, collectively cover an area of some 1.5 km².

Lithostratigraphic work by Webb and Moore (1982) indicates that the Whitlaw group of small basins probably remained as small open lakes throughout prehistory, until finally overgrown completely in historic times to form the eutrophic basin fens of today. Blackpool Moss, which occupies a basin of approximately 300 x 150 m in size, is fed by surface run-off and groundwater seepage. Webb and Moore (1982) report that groundwater is base-rich, and this is probably related to the occurrence of limestone nodules in local bands of rock (Birse 1980). The fen is now characterised by closed willow carr (*Salix atrocinerea*) in its central and eastern portion, with areas of reedswamp (*Phragmites communis*), wet meadow (*Filipendula ulmaria*) and sedge swamp and mire (*Carex* spp.) in the western and northern portions. The present day vegetation of the Whitlaw fens has been described by Birse (1980).

### Field and laboratory methods

In the centre of Blackpool Moss the post-glacial sediment thickness reaches just over 7 m (Webb & Moore 1982). However, working unaided, the author was able only to retrieve the topmost 3 m of sediment using an 8 cm diameter Russian corer. Three samples of surface sediment from different places in Blackpool Moss were also collected with the aim of examining the modern relationship between pollen deposition and vegetation at the site. The sample points are located *circa* 50 m apart; one from the centrally located coring site, now under closed willow carr, one to the west of this in *Phragmites* reedswamp, and one to the north-east in an area of sedge mire and wet meadow.

The processing of sub-samples for pollen analysis followed standard alkali digestion and acetolysis treatments, but involved the use of microfiltration at 150 microns and 10 microns, rather than hydrofluoric acid, to deal with the minerogenic component (Cwynar *et al* 1979; Hunt 1985). Processed samples were mounted in silicone oil for microscopic examination at x400 magnification. Pollen identifications were made with the aid of a reference collection and the pollen keys in Moore and Webb (1978), Andrew (1984) and Faegri and Iversen (1975). Cereal type pollen was identified according to the size categories of Andersen (1979), which include some non-cultivated wild grass species. Analysis of each sample continued until at least 250 total land pollen (excludes aquatics and spores) had been identified (range = 265–398). For presentation of the fossil pollen results (Figures 1.3 and 1.4) 95% confidence limits have been calculated for all percentage and

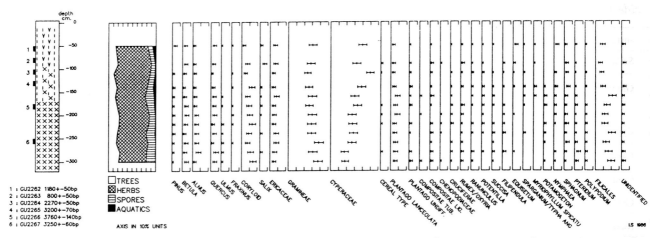

*Figure 1.3   Percentage pollen diagram for Blackpool Moss (main taxa). Values are expressed as percentages of either total pollen and spores or total pollen and aquatics. Total pollen excludes spores and aquatics. The bars indicate 95% confidence limits. (Diagram generated by the* Newplot 10 *plotting program, devised by E Shennan).*

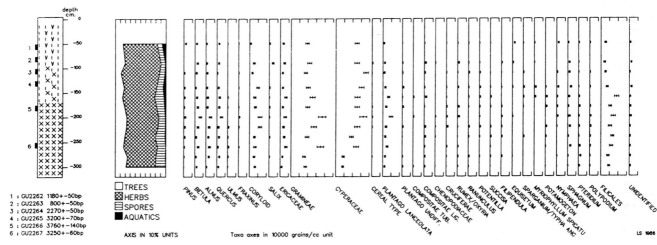

*Figure 1.4   Pollen concentration diagram from Blackpool Moss (main taxa). The bars indicate 95% confidence limits. (Diagram generated by the* Newplot 10 *plotting program, devised by E Shennan).*

concentration estimates. These confidence limits allow assessment of the statistical significance of the observed fluctuations in the taxa curves at different depths in the profile. Only the more frequently recorded taxa are included in the diagrams; rarer taxa are shown as presence/absence data in Table 1.1. The surface pollen results are presented in Table 1.2 as standard percentage estimates.

### SURFACE POLLEN SAMPLES

A total of twenty-nine different taxa were recorded. Of these, fifteen can be related to fen plant types recorded by Birse (1980) as occurring in Blackpool Moss or adjacent mosses. The remaining fourteen are not mentioned in Birse's floristic tables but derive instead from outside the fen plant communities. In this respect they might be described as 'non-local' (ie extra-local and regional) rather than 'local' pollen elements. In each sample this non-local pollen component comprises 14%–18% of the total pollen sum. It is comprised in itself mainly of tree pollen, amongst which the

Table 1.1   Blackpool Moss rarer pollen taxa.

|  | 50 | 90 | 110 | 140 | 160 | 180 | 200 | 220 | 240 | 260 | 280 | 300 |
|---|---|---|---|---|---|---|---|---|---|---|---|---|
| *Artemisia* |  |  |  |  |  |  |  |  |  |  | + |  |
| *Astragalus* cf *danicus* |  |  |  |  |  |  | + |  |  |  |  |  |
| *Caltha* type |  |  |  |  |  |  |  | + |  |  |  |  |
| *Centaurea cyanus* | + |  |  |  |  |  |  |  |  |  |  |  |
| *Fagus* |  |  |  |  | + |  |  |  |  |  |  |  |
| cf *Geum* | + |  |  |  |  |  |  |  |  |  |  |  |
| *Leguminosae* |  |  |  |  |  |  |  |  |  |  |  | + |
| *Mercurialis perennis* |  |  |  |  |  |  |  | + |  |  |  |  |
| *Nuphar* |  |  |  |  |  |  |  |  |  |  | + |  |
| cf *Prunus* |  |  |  |  |  | + |  |  |  |  |  |  |
| cf *Papaver* |  |  |  |  |  | + |  |  |  |  |  |  |
| *Stachys* type | + |  |  |  |  |  |  |  |  |  |  |  |

*Table 1.2  Surface pollen results. Values are expressed as percentages of total pollen and spores.*

| surface pollen taxa | willow carr | reed swamp | sedge/meadow | local fen species (after Birse 1980) |
|---|---|---|---|---|
| *Salix* | 24.05 | 2.17 | 5.59 | *Salix atrocinerea, S pentandra* |
| Gramineae | 33.68 | 57.76 | 24.34 | *Phragmites communis, Molinea caerulea, Hierochloe odorata,* and others |
| Cyperaceae | 1.37 | 4.04 | 20.07 | *Carex* spp, *Eriophorum angustifolium* |
| Caryophyllaceae | 0.34 | 0.62 | 0 | *Lychnis flos-cuculi* |
| Compositae lig | 4.81 | 0.62 | 0.66 | *Crepis paludosa* |
| Compositae tub | 0.34 | 0 | 0.33 | *Cirsium* spp, *Achillea ptarmica* |
| *Rumex* | 3.44 | 1.24 | 0 | *Rumex acetosa* |
| Rosaceae undiff | 0 | 0 | 0.33 | *Potentilla* spp, *Crategus monogyna* |
| *Potentilla* type | 0 | 0.62 | 0.33 | *Potentilla erecta, P palustris* |
| *Galium* type | 0 | 0 | 0.99 | *Galium palustre, G aparine, G uliginos* |
| *Filipendula* | 9.97 | 10.87 | 25.99 | *Filipendula ulmaria* |
| Umbelliferae | 0.34 | 0 | 0 | *Angelica sylvestris* |
| Filicales | 1.37 | 5.28 | 1.32 | *Dryopteris* spp |
| *Equisetum* | 0 | 0 | 0.99 | *Equisetum palustre, E fluviatile* |
| *Sphagnum* | 0.69 | 0.62 | 0 | *Sphagnum* spp |
| *Pinus* | 13.75 | 6.21 | 7.89 | non-local |
| *Fagus* | 0.34 | 0 | 0 | |
| *Taxus* | 0 | 0.62 | 0 | |
| *Fraxinus* | 0.69 | 1.24 | 1.64 | |
| *Alnus* | 0.34 | 1.24 | 0 | |
| *Quercus* | 0.69 | 0.62 | 1.64 | |
| *Ulmus* | 0.34 | 0.93 | 0.33 | |
| Coryloid | 0.34 | 1.55 | 0.99 | |
| Ericaceae *cf Calluna* | 0.69 | 0 | 0.66 | |
| Cereal type | 0.69 | 0 | 0.66 | |
| Chenopodiaceae | 0 | 0 | 0.66 | |
| *Plantago* undiff | 0.34 | 0.62 | 0.66 | |
| *Plantago lanceolata* | 0.34 | 0.62 | 0 | |
| *Pteridium* | 0.34 | 0.31 | 0.33 | |

| | | | |
|---|---|---|---|
| trees | 17.53 | 11.49 | 15.46 |
| shrubs | 24.40 | 3.73 | 6.58 |
| herbs | 55.67 | 78.57 | 75.33 |
| spores | 2.41 | 6.21 | 2.63 |
| non-local element | 18.2 | 15.2 | 14.1 |

importance of *Pinus* reflects the nature of present day woodland in the area. Examples of all the tree types recorded can be found within an approximate 2 km radius of the sampling site, which indicates that some pollen from these distances is represented. Of the non-local herb pollen taxa, cereal type and Chenopodiaceae may both derive from the arable fields now found in the vicinity. It is noteworthy that only traces of both occur in the easternmost sample, which is located only some 20 m from the corner of a cultivated field. *Plantago lanceolata* occurs in the grassy pastures which surround the fens, and the presence of small amounts of its pollen in the surface samples might suggest that some of the Gramineae pollen is also derived from this source, although a large amount must relate to local moss grasses and reeds.

Clearly, all three spectra are dominated by local pollen producers, and inter-sample variation can largely be explained as a function of sample location relative to local plant communities. It would therefore appear that the rich local vegetation has had a screening or swamping effect on more regional pollen input. Prior to development of the rich fen, however, such local effects on pollen deposition must have been less significant, so that regional pollen representation might be expected to be higher in the underlying lake sediment than in the overlying fen peat and surface samples. It is also significant that lakes, in contrast to peats, can receive large amounts of their pollen from inflowing streams (Pennington 1979; Jacobson & Bradshaw 1981). The present drainage system at Whitlaw might suggest that, for the lake sediment, a stream (and therefore pollen) catchment area of some 2 km radius was augmented by an aerial catchment that may have reached distances of up to 5 or 10 km, although representation of the more distant elements is likely to be low.

### Stratigraphy and dating

The 3 m sediment profile passed down from a light brown, herbaceous and woody peat at the surface to a darker, orange-brown fine detrital mud at the base. The

transition is very diffuse, and takes place gradually through a silty peat or coarse detrital mud between *circa* 60 cm depth and *circa* 160 cm depth. An idealised stratigraphic column is shown on the pollen diagrams. Readers are referred to Webb and Moore (1982) for a more detailed analysis of the general stratigraphy at Blackpool Moss. The stratigraphy is considered to represent the infilling of a small lake, with the peaty deposit in the topmost *circa* 60–160 cm representing development of the swamp and fen environment still seen today.

Six radiocarbon dating samples were obtained and the uncalibrated results are shown on the pollen diagrams. Dendrochronological calibration of these dates, using Stuiver and Reimer (1986), gives the date ranges plotted on Figure 1.5 as a time-depth graph. Age inversions occur at the top and bottom of the profile, and this makes it impossible to fit a meaningful time-depth curve to the distribution of points. The solid lines drawn on the graph joining the individual dates enclose an area within which the time-depth curve could lie, assuming that some of the mid-profile dates are correct. However, the reverse situation could apply; that is, the mid-profile dates could be incorrect while GU-2263 and GU-2267 are correct. This would lead to the very different time-depth curve shown as a dashed line. It is difficult to argue which of the two situations is the more likely, since samples could be contaminated by either younger or older carbon. Hard water error from the lime-rich drainage waters might be expected to produce dates that are too old, but why this should affect the mid-profile dates more than GU-2263 and GU-2267 is not clear. Indeed, the mid-profile dates appear fairly consistent with one another, while GU-2267 appears too young, but this forces us to accept contamination of the latter lake sediment sample with younger carbon from above. In view of these problems no firm core chronology can be proposed.

### Vegetational history

The pollen record is dominated throughout by herbaceous taxa, of which Gramineae and Cyperaceae are the main contributors. Gramineae pollen representation at 25-40% TLP compares favourably with values obtained from the present day sediment surface under both willow carr and sedge mire/wet meadow vegetation. Cyperaceae pollen representation tends to be much higher than that found in the surface sediment, even under present sedge mire/wet meadow vegetation. A local source for much of the pollen of both Gramineae and Cyperaceae in lake fringe or fen vegetation seems likely. The high frequencies for Cyperaceae pollen suggest that sedge mire was more extensive in the past than it is today, except in the basal levels of the profile. Fen development in this central part of the lake basin could have got under way as early as the second millennium BC, depending on how one interprets the radiocarbon dates and the litho-stratigraphy. The later increase in *Salix* pollen at 90 cm

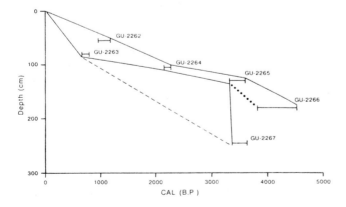

*Figure 1.5  Blackpool Moss calibrated radiocarbon dates. The solid lines enclose the area within which a time-curve may lie, but age inversions at the top and base of the profile extend the area to the broken line.*

depth records the local succession to willow carr still found at the site today, and perhaps dating from the early centuries AD. Examination of Birse's (1980) floristic tables for present day fen taxa in the Whitlaw group of fens reveals that, as well as Gramineae and Cyperaceae, the majority of other herbaceous pollen in the profile could also derive from fen or lake fringe vegetation. The only clear exceptions are *Plantago lanceolata*, *Plantago* undifferentiated, cereal type and Chenopodiaceae, together with most of the rarer taxa recorded in Table 1.1. *Plantago lanceolata* is commonly found as a ruderal plant in grassland pastures, and can also play an important part in the recolonisation of fallow land, perhaps itself grazed (Behre 1981). Indeed, Groenman-van Waateringe (1986) has suggested the possibility that it may in fact have occurred partly as an arable weed in prehistory. Cereal type pollen is recorded sporadically in low amounts throughout the profile, suggesting a history of arable agriculture within the pollen catchment area of the site. The poor dispersal and hence under-representation of cereal pollen in pollen diagrams is well known (Vourela 1973), and the surface pollen samples from Blackpool Moss have highlighted how cultivated fields adjacent to the fen can produce only traces of cereal type pollen on the fen surface less than 30 m away. It should be borne in mind that Andersen's (1979) cereal type categories include some wild grasses, but none of those named by Andersen are recorded as occurring in the present day fen vegetation at Whitlaw (Birse 1980).

Chenopodiaceae is a large family of plants, but does include the chickweed, *Stellaria media*, which is primarily an arable weed. Its association with cereal type pollen in both the surface samples and the profile samples, and its absence from the present fen vegetation tends to argue for an arable source. It is difficult to be certain that phases of cultivation separated by lacunae are represented, but there are some indications of increased agricultural activity between *circa* 150 cm and *circa* 220 cm depth in the profile. Here *Plantago lanceolata* pollen frequencies rise and both cereal-type and Chenopodiaceae occur. The presence of *cf Papaver* pollen at 180 cm tends to reinforce this impression, since species such as *Papaver rhoeas* are characteristic of arable ground. According to Figure 1.4 this section of the profile could date from as early as the second or third millennia BC.

The preponderance of possible local fen and lake fringe pollen types causes difficulties for the recognition of wider landscape changes. This problem is compounded by uncertainties over the source area for Gramineae, the pollen of which could represent both local and non-local grasses. The same is true of Cyperaceae, since sedges are today a common feature of the surrounding pastures. Of the tree and shrub pollen, *Salix* and *Betula* may well have been local wet ground types, since these taxa are characteristic of the present day fen. It is possible that *Alnus* and *Myrica gale* (Coryloid pollen category) also favoured the fens and

former lake shores, but these taxa do not occur in Birse's (1980) floristic tables. The Coryloid pollen category includes *Corylus* spp. as well as *Myrica gale*, and Rackham (1988) has suggested that *Corylus avellana* was a common tree in the native woodland of south-east Scotland. Total tree or shrub pollen values (excluding *Salix* and *Betula*) of 10–25% TLP compare with values of 13–17% TLP in the surface pollen samples. Thus, in gross terms, the extent of woodland within the pollen catchment area of Blackpool Moss may have remained quite similar throughout the length of time represented by the profile, apparently *circa* 3500–4500 years according to the radiocarbon dates.

There is a general trend towards decreasing non-local tree and shrub pollen values from the base to the top of the profile, but plentiful open ground occurred throughout, and the presence of *Plantago lanceolata* and occasional arable indicators suggests agricultural use of the land. There are hints of possible clearance and regeneration phases within the overall trend towards woodland decline, but they are difficult to pick out with certainty and have not, for this reason, been used to define local pollen assemblage zones. Thus, at *circa* 220–280 cm depth, clearance might be evidenced in the decline of non-local tree and shrub pollen values from 25.5%–15% and the increase in Gramineae pollen. Subsequent regeneration involved ferns (Filicales) and then hazel (Coryloid). Subsequently, between *circa* 140 cm and 220 cm there is another and more gradual decline in tree and shrub pollen values from 21.6%–15.2% and an increase in *Plantago lanceolata*, followed again by regeneration involving ferns and then hazel. The final decline in Coryloid pollen above 140 cm is quite clear in both the percentage and concentration estimates, indicating that it is not purely a statistical effect of the associated rise in Cyperaceae pollen. This appears to date from the early first millennium BC, and therefore interestingly coincides in time with the first phase of occupation at Eildon.

## Conclusion

Whilst the 3 m profile from Blackpool Moss undoubtedly covers the Iron Age period, the radiocarbon dates have failed to provide a firm chronology and the pollen record has been heavily influenced by local vegetation. As a result only limited conclusions can be drawn from the analysis. The general lack of pollen data for south-east Scotland makes any contribution both potentially useful and potentially misleading in terms of regional landscape developments. One of the most interesting conclusions from Blackpool Moss is the apparently long history of arable agriculture and diminished woodland in the vicinity of the site, stretching back well into the prehistoric period. Further support for this interpretation is provided by an outline pollen diagram from deeper sediment at Blackpool Moss, retrieved during a subsequent visit to the site (Figure 1.6). This second profile comes from 3m

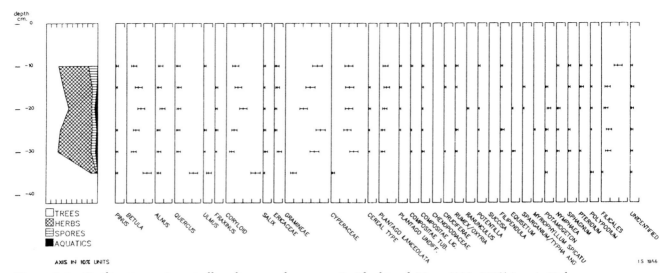

*Figure 1.6 Outline percentage pollen diagram from core 2, Blackpool Moss (300–550%) cm). Values are expressed as percentages of either total pollen and spores or total pollen and aquatics. Total pollen excludes spores and aquatics. The bars indicate 95% confidence limits. (Diagram generated by the* Newplot 10 *plotting program, devised by E Shennan.)*

to 5.5 m depth, thus ranging back beyond the period covered by the first profile, although it is not itself directly dated.

The basal sample of this second profile has tree and shrub pollen values of 90% TLP, clearly representing a heavily forested landscape around the small lake which then existed at Blackpool Moss. The dominant trees were *Corylus*, *Quercus* and *Betula*, while *Ulmus* was also present. At 5.5 m depth this spectrum presumably represents the native, probably pre-elm decline, wildwood of the region. The subsequent massive fall in tree and shrub pollen values to less than 40% TLP is most striking. The high representation of Gramineae and Cyperaceae might point to an interpretation in terms of reedswamp or mire expansion around the edges of the lake, but there are also good grounds for postulating regional woodland clearance and agriculture. Thus, appearance of the pollen of the light-demanding ash (*Fraxinus*) is consistent with the creation of more open conditions, as is the appearance of *Plantago lanceolata*, another shade intolerant plant and a common agricultural indicator. The occurrence of cereal type pollen reinforces the argument for human activity.

Although the figures are not presented in this report, total pollen concentration values fall dramatically at this horizon. This might be explained as resulting from woodland clearance and arable agriculture, which would cause both a change from a high to a low pollen productivity landscape, and increased surface run-off, soil erosion and sediment yields. The subsequent temporary increase in Coryloid, *Betula* and *Alnus* pollen frequencies higher up the profile, and the associated fall in Gramineae, suggests regeneration of secondary woodland after the initial clearance phase. *Quercus* and *Ulmus*, however, never fully recovered; and the

secondary woodland was itself gradually re-cleared, apparently from about the third millennium BC according to the first profile age estimates for the sediment at *circa* 3 m depth.

Seen in this longer historical context, there is little evidence to suggest that major landscape changes around Blackpool Moss were delayed until the mid first millennium BC or later. They appear to have taken place much earlier, during the Neolithic or Bronze Age periods. This is contradictory to the cultural landscape developments postulated for north-east England, and should caution us against making too generalised regional scale statements in the absence of a network of closely spaced pollen sites. The representation of regional pollen elements at Blackpool Moss may be low, and it is possible that the extent and history of regional woodland recorded in the pollen spectra has been masked by local pollen input. Nonetheless, the immediate area does appear to have been used for arable agriculture from an early date, if we can rely on the cereal type pollen curve. There is some evidence for increased clearance of woodland in the early first millennium BC, coinciding with Later Bronze Age occupation at Eildon *circa* 4 km away, but the chronology is insecure.

## ACKNOWLEDGEMENTS

The author is grateful to the Borders Region Nature Conservancy Council for allowing access to Blackpool Moss and other sites, and to Dr Ian Shennan for allowing access to his *Newplot 10* pollen diagram plotting program. Thanks are also due to A Duffy and D Jordan for fieldwork assistance, and to Dr R Tipping and Dr C Mills for much needed comments on an earlier draft of this report.

# 2 Excavations

# Eildon Hill North, Roxburgh, Borders  *O A Owen*

## Contributors

Geology, geomorphology and soils *D Jordan*
Defensive systems *M J Rains*
Coarse stone *A Clarke*
Chipped stone *S McCartan*
Jet armlets *M M B Kemp*
Glass *J Henderson · M M B Kemp*
Metalwork *F M Ashmore*
Metalworking and vitrified debris *R M Spearman ·*
*P Wilthew*
Roman pottery *J N Dore · J Senior*

Coarse wares *V J McLellan*
Routine soil analyses *S Carter*
Animal bones *F McCormick*
Pollen *S Butler*
Carbonised material *R P J McCullagh*
Radiocarbon calibration *M Dalland*
Igneous rocks *G Collins*
Thermoluminescence dates *D C W Sanderson*
Line drawings *S Stevenson*

## Abstract

*Small-scale excavations on Eildon Hill North were undertaken in 1986 in advance of remedial work on the western approaches to the fort. Although only a tiny proportion of the interior of the fort was excavated, the seven trenches examined all three postulated defensive systems, one entrance and two complete house platforms and part of a third. Occupation activities on the hill dated to the Late Bronze Age and the Roman Iron Age.*

The consolidation of tracks on the western approaches to Eildon Hill North was proposed in October 1985 as part of a recreational management strategy for the Eildon Hills, which lie on the Buccleuch Estates. The strategy was drafted by the Borders Regional Council in consultation with other interested bodies. The proposed works involved minor disturbances to the well-known hillfort on Eildon Hill North (RCAHMS 1956, *no* 597, 306–310). In response, Historic Buildings and Monuments (SDD), (now *Historic Scotland*), conducted small-scale excavations of the threatened areas within the fort. The excavations were undertaken by the then Central Excavation Unit for Scotland, over six weeks in August–September 1986.

Eildon Hill North (NGR NT 555 328; Figure 2.1) lies in Ettrick and Lauderdale District, Borders Region, within the old county of Roxburghshire, immediately south of Melrose. The triple summits of the Eildon Hills, known as Wester Hill (371 m OD), Mid Hill (422 m), and Hill North (404 m), dominate the skyline from almost any viewpoint in the Middle Tweed Basin. Eildon Hill North occupies a commanding position over the important natural routeways along the valleys of the Tweed to the south and west and the Leader Water to the north, and over the fords across the Tweed above and below the angle in the river by Old Melrose. 'The Eildon Hills cannot be equalled as a viewpoint in the Border Country' and they are visible from over 40 kilometres away (Whittow 1977, 39).

## GEOLOGY, GEOMORPHOLOGY AND SOILS
*D Jordan*

The Eildon Hills are composed primarily of hard igneous rock, which represents the remains of an enormous composite laccolith where magma, forced upwards, pushed apart the bedding planes of the overlying Old Red Sandstone and then cooled in thick sheets between them (Greig 1971, 89). Erosion subsequently removed the overlying rocks to reveal the igneous core covering and, at its margins, incorporating some of the sandstone in which it was emplaced. The rock itself is a trachyte, basic and fine-grained, rich in potassium, feldspar and quartz, and it breaks into large, angular blocks along lines of cleavage. It has suffered frost shattering, and decays to release quantities of clay and sesquioxides of which Iron III Oxyhydroxides dominate the soil colour and Aluminium Oxyhydroxides the soil texture.

Superimposed on the solid geology are drift deposits which consist mainly of indurated till on the upper slopes, and fluvio-glacial outwash overlapped extensively by more modern alluvium on the lower slopes and in the valleys. The thickness of these deposits varies considerably from a proven maximum of 5 m of fluvio-glacial sand and gravel near Melrose, to a few centimetres on the upper hillslopes where till is often confined to cracks in the broken bedrock surface. On the upper slopes it has been subject to solifluction. Till

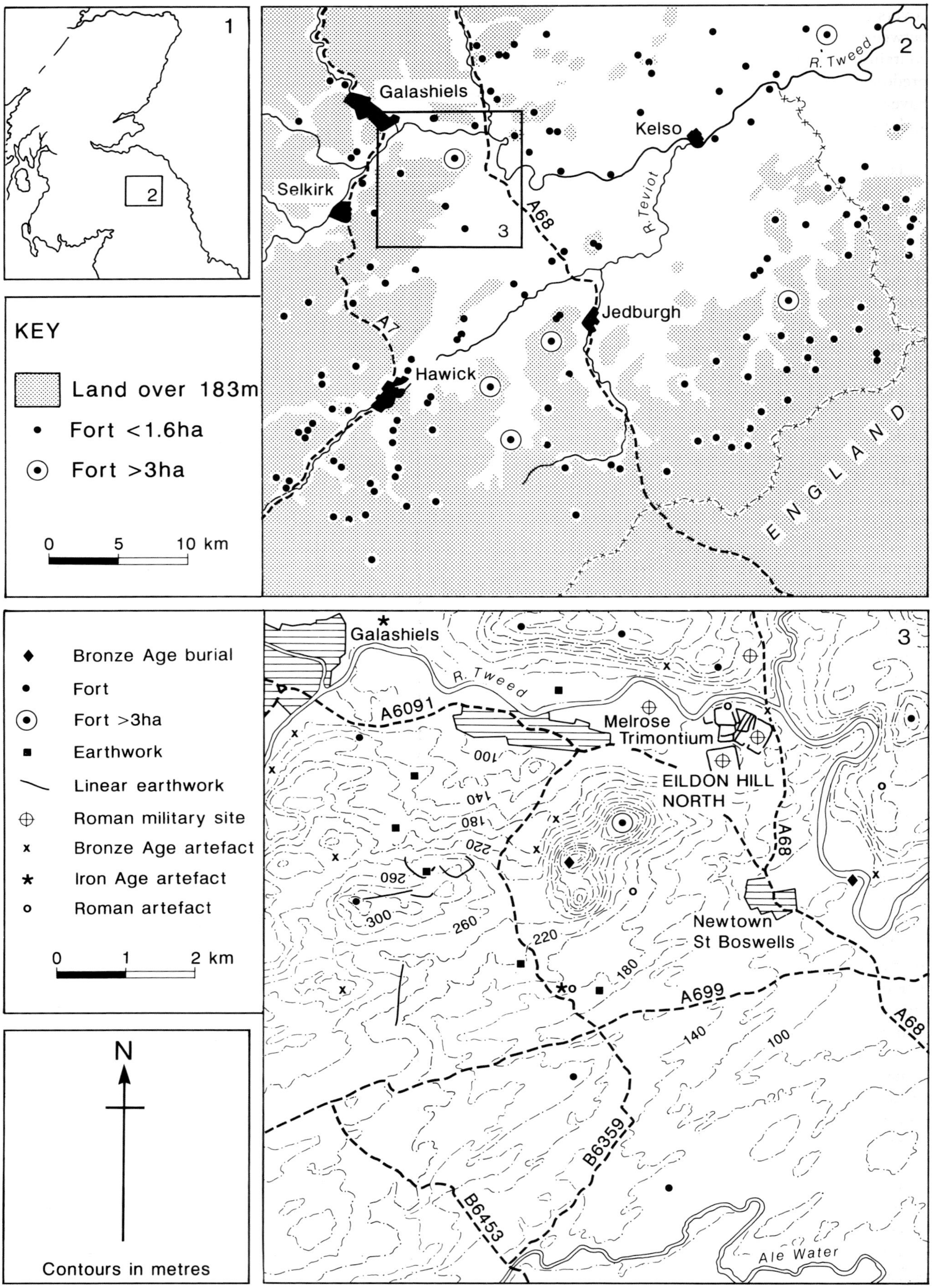

**KEY**

- [ ] Land over 183m
- • Fort <1.6ha
- ⊙ Fort >3ha

0    5    10 km

- ◆ Bronze Age burial
- • Fort
- ⊙ Fort >3ha
- ■ Earthwork
- ⁄ Linear earthwork
- ⊕ Roman military site
- x Bronze Age artefact
- * Iron Age artefact
- o Roman artefact

0    1    2 km

N

Contours in metres

*Figure 2.1   Map composite to show the location of Eildon Hill North.*

covers a high proportion of the surrounding landscape, between approximately 100 m and 250 m OD. It contains erratics from rocks to the west, carried by predominantly east-north-east flowing ice which would have met the hill on its west side, and which flowed over and around it.

## Soils

The Eildon Hills support skeletal soils of the Bemersyde Association, that is, soils developed on intrusive trachyte (Ragg 1960). Angular trachyte blocks are always present at the surface and solid rock, if not visible, is seldom more than 0.3 m below the surface. Beyond the ramparts on Eildon Hill North, and covering large areas to the north, south and east, there are Brown Forest Soils of the Kedslie Series (Ettrick Association), with gleyed B-, and C-horizons, found on gentle or moderate slopes and developed on a till of fine texture derived from Ordovician and Silurian greywackes and shales. To the west are found poorly drained soils of the Ettrick Series (Ettrick Association), gleys derived from Ordovician and Silurian greywackes and shales, developed on till of fine texture on flat or gently sloping sites.

The skeletal soils of the Bemersyde Association encountered during excavation are characterised by their stoniness and by the reddish colour of the $B_2$-horizon, possibly caused by thermal metamorphism (Ragg 1960, 73). Bare rock and scree give way to thin Brown Forest Soils with occasionally podsolising upper parts overlying B-, and B/C-horizons of moderate base status. Lithologies in the top 0.2 m comprise both local and exotic types; below this, stones are increasingly derived from the bedrock. Areas of podsolisation, with ericaceous vegetation, support up to 0.1 m of organic material and a slight, thin, eluviated $A_2$-horizon. These occur even in soils of only 0.15 m total depth. The soil structure tends to be well developed, fine crumb, with textures ranging from clay to clay loam. It is firm, with little intact organic matter, many pores, a high proportion of pore space, and frequent to abundant roots.

The hillslopes on which the archaeological features are found are in a state of physical and chemical decay. The chemical decay, facilitated by the characteristics of the bedrock, has caused the release of bright orange-red iron oxyhydroxides and the formation of a strong soil structure, which has been re-arranged by bioturbation to produce a homogeneous soil. These natural soil processes tend to mask the archaeological stratigraphy and, ultimately, to bring about its irreversible destruction. Consequently, all soil boundaries are diffuse and all the matrices encountered are fairly homogeneous.

Level or near level areas on the hill, such as house platforms, do not seem to have undergone much erosion. Archaeological strata survive, albeit with indistinct boundaries, in relatively stable sequences in such areas. In some cases anthropic deposits are marked only by differential stone distributions in otherwise homogeneous soil profiles (*eg* Figure 2.9). Similarly, charcoal concentrations, detectable as zones of grey colour tones, and the presence of artefactual and other inclusions, also indicate anthropic deposits. However, these level areas also appear to have been areas of net soil accumulation. Indeed, some of the deposits on them may have derived entirely from hillwash, and the masking of stratigraphic boundaries by chemical soil processes sometimes obscures the distinctions between anthropic and hillwash deposits. Nevertheless, it seems that the location of materials within the anthropic deposits has not altered significantly. This is a crucial factor in considering the validity of the radiocarbon results (below).

The vegetation cover on Eildon Hill North is dominated by ericaceous species and grasses. Bilberry (*Vaccinium myrtillus*) is common. Where erosion is severe, the vegetation cover has been removed to reveal bare rock and scree.

The Land Capability map for south-east Scotland (Brown & Shipley 1982; 1:250,000, sheet 7) shows that the higher reaches of the Eildon Hills fall into Land Capability Class 6, Division 2, that is land capable of use only as rough grazings. The area around the Eildon Hills includes the very fertile Class 3, Division 1 lands to the north, south and east. These are lands capable of producing consistently high yields from a narrow range of crops (principally cereals and grass) or moderate yields of a wider range (including field beans and other vegetables and root crops), and short grass leys are common. Clearly then, Eildon is centred in and overlooks some of the most favoured land in Scotland.

## ARCHAEOLOGICAL BACKGROUND

The Eildon Hills have long attracted interest from antiquarians and other observers, both because of their topographical prominence and because of the clearly visible nature of the archaeological remains on Hill North. In 1768, Milne wrote:

'On the top of the north-east hill are plain vestiges of a Roman Camp well fortified with two fosses and mounds of earth, more than 1½ mile in circuit, with a large plain near the top of the hill, on which may be seen the *praetorium* or the General's Quarter, surrounded with many houses. It has all the properties of a well chosen camp . . .' (Milne 1768, 2).

The Statistical Account of Scotland quotes extensively from Milne, but also makes the ambiguous statement: 'On the north side of the middle hill, Mr Milne seems to place a second camp from which he says is a large ditch for 2 miles to the west' (SAS 1793, 92). No traces of such a feature can be seen today. In the New Statistical Account, Thomson dismisses Milne's claims for a Roman fort on top of Eildon: 'What he calls a Roman encampment on the top of the Eildons may easily have been a border fastness, to which the cattle of the neighbourhood might be driven on the approach of

Plate 2.1  *'The Eildon Hills and the Tweed' by James Ward, 1807. (Printed by permission of the National Galleries of Scotland).*

the enemy; for there are no distinct indications observable from which it can be inferred that it was Roman' (NSA 1845, 55). In 1793, Roy mentioned Eildon in connection with the Roman fort of *Trimontium*, which he identified as Newstead (Roy 1793, 116). However, no fortifications are marked on the 'Aildon Hills' on his military map (Roy 1744/5, map 8/3). By 1807 (Plate 2.1), the allocation of the hillfort to native peoples had become more widely accepted, with Chalmers' reference to the 'Eldon Hills, on the summit whereof there was a very strong fort of the Britons with a Roman station in its vicinity' (Chalmers 1807, 140).

The first detailed survey work was undertaken by Christison in 1893, who stated that 'Eildon appears to have been defended by palisaded terraces, enclosing huts of some easily perishable material' (Christison 1894, 111). He reported that Curle had made 'some exploratory excavations' on three house platforms and proposed to undertake more (Christison 1894, 119). Curle apparently found charcoal on all three and a sherd of coarse pottery on one, but did not produce a fuller account and it was not possible to identify the three platforms which he examined. Christison's work was full, accurate and well-illustrated although, surprisingly, he made no mention of a circular, ditched enclosure, 10.75 m in internal diameter, which is situated amongst the house platforms at the west end of the summit-plateau. This feature formed the subject of the only other excavation on Eildon Hill North prior to 1986.

The fort was fully surveyed in 1950 by the RCAHMS, in preparation of the *Inventory* for Roxburghshire. Subsequently, Steer and Feachem undertook partial excavation of the circular, ditched-enclosure to determine its nature (Steer & Feachem

1952, 202–5). They interpreted the features uncovered as the remains of a Roman signal station. The indications are that it was originally a two-storeyed building, roughly 3.4 m square, with a stone paved floor and a tiled roof. Coins of ad 116 and 120 were found, but the excavators prefer to see the station dated to approximately ad 80 when Julius Agricola first crossed the border and advanced as far north as the Tay. It would have served the Roman fort of Newstead (*Trimontium*), at the north-east foot of Eildon Hill North, which has been shown by excavation to have had two Flavian occupations, the first beginning with Agricola in ad 80, and two Antonine occupations, the last terminating not later than ad 196 (Curle 1911; Hartley 1972).

In 1966, a number of surface finds were made on Eildon Hill North (*PSAS* 1967, 266). These included a whetstone, stone discs, five sherds of Roman coarse ware, four sherds of native ware, an oval bronze ring and part of a bone pin. The Roman pottery is likely to be second century AD or later, and two fragments of black jar date to the third or fourth century AD (Robertson 1970, 212, Table vi).

## Site description

Eildon Hill North (404 m OD) has a summit-plateau and terraces, and affords a better strategic vantage point than does its higher but steeper neighbour, Mid Hill. The summit-plateau is roughly rectangular in shape, measuring approximately 255 m east-west by 108 m north-south. It is highest along the southern edge, slopes gently towards the north and more sharply towards the east. From its edges, the summit-plateau falls away abruptly to the north and south, and steeply to the east and west. A series of natural terraces leads from the south-west corner of the summit-plateau in the direction of the col linking Eildon Hill North to Mid Hill. Except on the east side, the flanks of the summit-plateau are separated from the main slopes of the hill by contiguous shelves, either flat or gently inclined, whose outer edges unite to form a continuous lower shoulder. The largest of these shelves is on the south side of the summit and 80 m below it. Cultivation rigs of unknown date cover its surface and the greater part of it has subsequently been enclosed, probably for a plantation, by an earthen bank faced with drystone walling.

The 1950 RCAHMS survey has provided the basis for all subsequent research (RCAHMS 1956, *no* 597, 306–310). Figure 2.2 is based on their plan and shows the positions of the 1986 excavation trenches. The RCAHMS identified three defensive systems, five entrances and 296 platforms; their nomenclature for the defensive systems and entrances is followed throughout this text. The three house platforms examined have been arbitrarily numbered 1–3.

Defensive System A comprises triple ramparts, roughly circular in plan and nearly a mile in circumference. These enclose 39 acres of the hilltop and are clearly visible for miles around. Defensive System B encloses the whole of the summit-plateau, together with a naturally terraced area on the east side, but it has left only slight traces on the ground in the form of a fragment of wasted rampart near the south-east corner of the summit-plateau. The course of Defensive System C was 'plainly visible' (RCAHMS 1956, 310) on aerial photographs taken in 1948 (CPE/SCOT 315, 3184–5), but cannot now be discerned on the ground. It encloses an elliptical area on the summit-plateau, some 180 m east–west by 51 m north–south.

Entrances 1 to 5 are irregularly spaced and pierce the triple defences of System A. Of the 296 house platforms identified by the RCAHMS, exactly half are concentrated on the summit-plateau. The RCAHMS surveyors postulated that the original total was substantially higher, since many may have been obliterated by the cultivation on the south shelf. In addition, since only the platforms survive as evidence of early houses, it is probable that houses erected on naturally level ground would leave little or no trace. In several cases, platforms appear to overlie the courses of Defensive Systems B and C, and the RCAHMS go so far as to suggest that the line of System C 'has been largely destroyed by the construction of huts' (RCAHMS 1956, 310). At least one platform is overlain by the plantation enclosure wall on the south shelf.

## Project design and excavation strategy

Stevenson's comment of 1966 highlights the underlying but persistent sense of enigma associated with Eildon:

'Another *oppidum* is rarely mentioned although its extent is 39 acres: this is the one on Eildon overlooking the major Roman site of Newstead near Melrose, and, whether or not its main occupation was pre-Roman, no real understanding of the Iron Age in Southern Scotland is surely possible until Eildon can be brought into the story' (Stevenson 1966, 28).

On the evidence of Ptolemy (*Geographia*, Book ii, Ch. ii), the fort at *Trimontium* has been assumed to represent the chief 'town' of the four attributed to the Selgovae. Until recently, this assumption has underpinned studies of the place of Eildon among Scottish hillforts (*cf* Feachem 1966, 79). The relationship of the Romans to the occupants of the fort has long concerned specialists, the Ptolemaic reference prompting visions of the sacking of the Selgovian hilltop *oppidum* by the Romans.

Since the publication of the 1950 survey (RCAHMS 1956), many hypotheses have been advanced by students of this type of monument as to the fort's likely date, function and, especially, its political significance. The identification of three separate defensive systems (RCAHMS 1956, 306–10) has been interpreted as representing a sequence of successive structural phases: 'At Eildon Hill North, after a primary enclosure of about 2 acres [Defensive System C] there followed an expansion to about 9 acres [Defensive System B] before the final enlargement to 40 acres [Defensive System A]' (Feachem 1966, 77). Feachem goes on to suggest that Eildon is the 'capital settlement . . . of the various bands of native peoples and immigrants who eventually merged into the historical Selgovae'; and that the fort may have accommodated a 'population amounting to perhaps two or three thousand', not all of whom 'would have been engaged upon the production of food' (*ibid*, 79). Doubt has recently been cast on the attribution of the hillfort to the Selgovae, with all that implies for local political geography and the relationship between Romans and natives (Breeze 1982, 28–9; Mann & Breeze 1987, 88–9).

In reality, and in the absence of any major excavation, no solid evidence exists to test any of these theories. Curle's investigation of three platforms confirmed, to Christison's satisfaction at least, '. . . the origin and purpose of these levelled surfaces . . .' (Christison 1894, 119). He believed that they represent the stances of several hundred huts built '. . . of some easily perishable material . . .' for which no other structural evidence survived. The 1952/3 excavation showed beyond reasonable doubt that the hilltop had been used in the early Roman period, possibly from about ad 80, to accommodate a signal station serving the Roman fort of Newstead, located at the foot of the hill. In addition, finds of 'native' pottery and a 'pitching', or rough paving, of stones containing a scatter of animal bones '. . . doubtless represent the destruction . . . of an earlier, native occupation-floor . . .' (Steer & Feachem 1952, 203). Archaeological evidence thus indicates that, on the hilltop at least, one platform was superseded by a Roman construction dating to about ad 80. It does not prove conclusively

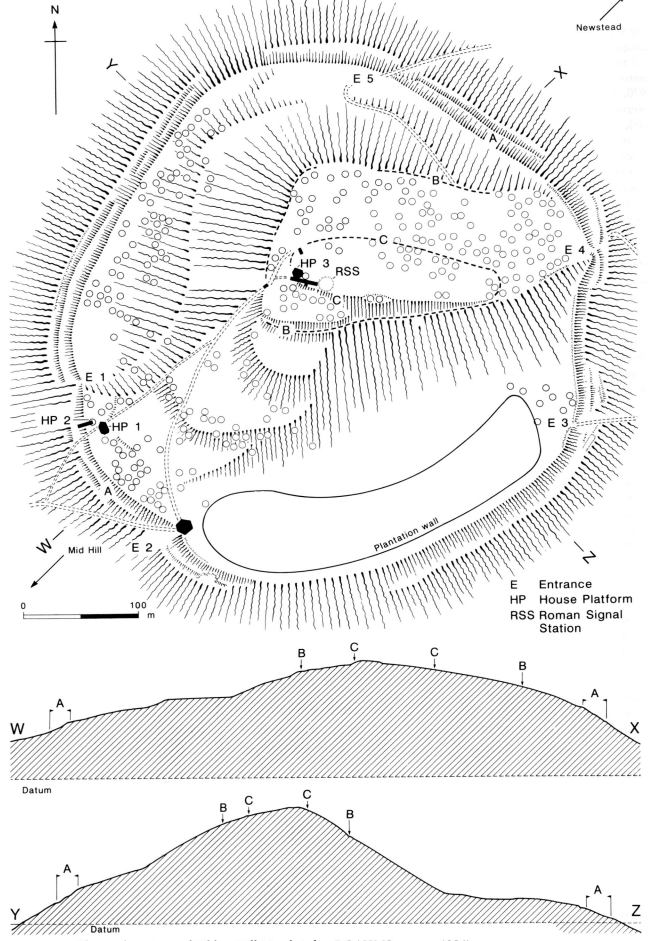

N

Newstead

E 5

X

Y

A

B

C

E 4

HP 3    RSS

C

B

C

E 1

HP 2

HP 1

A

E 3

W

Mid Hill    E 2

Plantation wall

Z

0        100
         m

E    Entrance
HP   House Platform
RSS  Roman Signal
     Station

B        C        C        B
                                    A
W                                        X

Datum

B    C    C    B
         A              A
Y                           Z
         Datum

*Figure 2.2   Plan and sections of Eildon Hill North (after RCAHMS survey, 1956).*

that the entire site had been abandoned by its native occupants at that date. Surface finds of second-, third-, and fourth-century AD Roman pottery indicate some continued Roman period activity on the hill (Robertson 1970, 212), although these may onlyrepresent intermittent visits from individuals rather than settlement of the hilltop.

In view of the number and variety of hypotheses raised about the site in the past, it seems useful to re-state the basic premises on which the current excavation strategy was built. These were, that:

*i* there exist at least two, and possibly three, defensive systems of unknown date, relative or absolute, which confirm that the site is a hillfort;

*ii* there exist a minimum of 296 levelled platforms which, on the available archaeological evidence, represent house stances; and

*iii* a Roman signal station, on the summit of the hill, overlies one platform.

Given that only three relatively secure statements could be made about the monument, it was clear from the outset that the excavation strategy should be devised to address the fundamental issues, namely absolute dating, relative chronology and the nature of the site's structures. It was also clear that many attendant issues which have been discussed previously would fall outwith the scope and remit of the 1986 enquiry. These included social and administrative organisation of the settlement, and the relationship between inhabitants of the monument and those of sites in its vicinity. The 1986 work was intended to lay the foundations for such broader enquiries as these, which might one day be explored in more extensive excavations of the fort defences and interior.

### Archaeological aims and methods

*Defences*

*i* To examine the construction of Defensive Systems A and B;

*ii* to establish the existence or otherwise of Defensive System C;

*iii* to retrieve datable material from all defensive systems;

*iv* to establish the defence arrangements and/or structural sequence at one entrance.

*Structures*

*i* To investigate and compare the structural nature of one or two platforms;

*ii* to retrieve datable material from a selection of platforms.

In all, seven areas were opened, of which three were open area excavations and four were trenches (Figure 2.2). Open area excavations were undertaken:

*i* at Entrance 2 (Area 1). The opened area encompassed the entrance, small segments of the inner rampart of Defensive System A and a small area immediately within the entrance;

*ii* on a house platform in the south-west quadrant of the fort, immediately within the inner circuit of Defensive System A (Area 2, House Platform 1);

*iii* on a house platform located within the area of Defensive System C, just below and west of the summit of the hill (Area 7, House Platform 3).

Trenches were excavated:

*i* across the inner circuit of Defensive System A in the south-west quadrant of the fort and into the centre of a house platform which appeared to be backed against it (Area 3, House Platform 2);

*ii* along the site of a dispersed narrow track leading up to the summit-plateau from the west, across the line of Defensive System C (Area 4);

*iii* adjacent to the main track to the summit-plateau, also crossing the line of Defensive System C (Area 5);

*iv* adjacent to the main track to the summit-plateau across the line of Defensive System B (Area 6).

### THE DEFENSIVE SYSTEMS　*O A Owen · with M J Rains*

#### Defensive System A: Entrance 2

The main track to the summit passes through Defensive System A at Entrance 2 and its erosion by the passage of pedestrian, equine and vehicular traffic had revealed bedrock at several points on the track, where the thin soil and vegetation cover had been completely removed. The track had been widened at this point in recent times to allow vehicular access to the summit. The excavation aims here were fourfold:

*i* to examine the construction of the rampart both north and south of Entrance 2;

*ii* to obtain evidence of gateway construction, if any;

*iii* to locate and investigate any structures or areas of activity lying immediately within the entrance; and

*iv* to retrieve dating material for the construction of Defensive System A.

To these ends, a hexagonal area with maximum dimensions of 13 by 13.5 m was investigated.

*Pre-rampart activity (Figure 2.3)*

Partially underlying the slumped material of the south rampart and on a slightly different, but generally north to south alignment, a large, elongated, oval pit (Pit 1), measuring approximately 2 by 1 m, was cut into bedrock to a depth of some 0.75 m. The original cutting of the pit would have been aided by the generally fractured and shattered nature of the bedrock across the site. During excavation, the pit was tentatively interpreted as a quarry pit for the south rampart. Subsequent analysis of a series of samples, taken at regular intervals along the profile of the pit, has revealed abnormally high phosphate levels indicative of other functions (Carter, below).

A probable hearth (Figure 2.3) underlay the south rampart terminal, west of Pit 1. A spread of compact red-brown clayey silt containing much charcoal overlay a rough setting of sub-angular stones, each up to 0.2 m

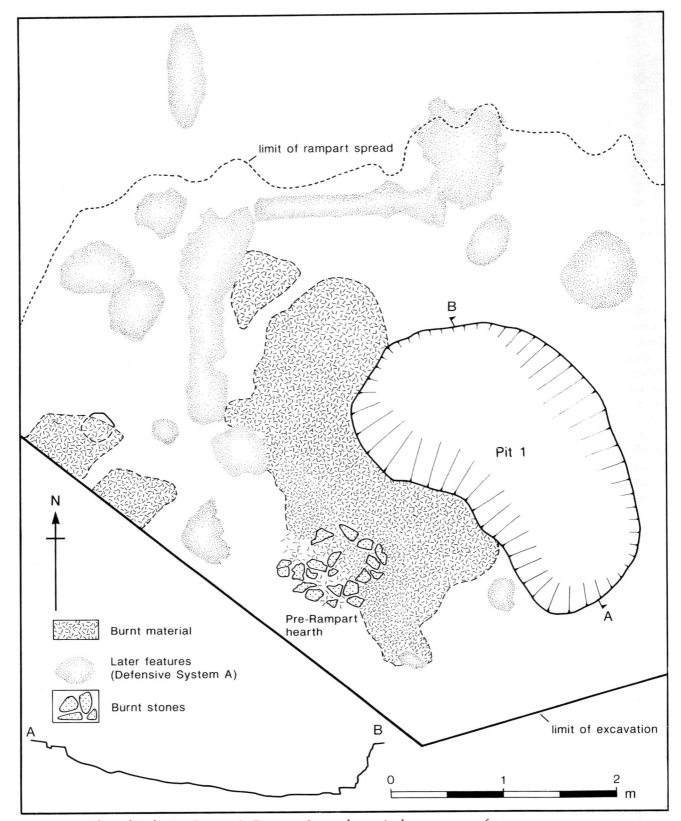

*Figure 2.3    Plan of Defensive System A, Entrance 2, south terminal: pre-rampart features.*

in diameter, laid flat and mostly burnt on their upper surfaces. The charcoal, consisting of a wide range of species (alder, elm, birch, hazel, Pomoideae, wild cherry or blackthorn, and oak), all came from small diameter roundwood. It gave radiocarbon dates of $2760 \pm 50$ bp (810 bc; GU-2190) and $2870 \pm 50$ bp (920 bc, GU-2370).

*North rampart terminal (Figure 2.4 & 2.5; Plate 2.2 & 2.3)*

The north rampart took advantage of, and was built on the lip of, a slight, natural scarp in the bedrock. On the summit of the scarp, a series of seven rock-cut post-holes was found, apparently delimiting the rampart terminal

*Plate 2.2   Rock-cut post-holes beneath the north rampart terminal.*

*Plate 2.3   The north rampart terminal.*

(Plate 2.2). These varied in size and depth but, on average, were *circa* 0.4 by 0.45 by 0.2 m deep. They were filled with mid-brown clayey silt with some small angular stones and variable, but generally small, amounts of charcoal, contained within a ring of medium sized, sub-angular packing stones. No traces of the original posts remained, the charcoal consisting of small diameter roundwood with sometimes more than one species represented, indicating that it is not primary to the post-holes. The original posts may have formed revetments to contain the material of the rampart.

The rampart core consisted of largely undifferentiated, red and reddish-brown clayey silts, with rubble and small amounts of charcoal. Isolated, decomposed turves were present in this material but did

not form a continuous turf-line nor did they constitute turf walling. In places along the outer face and on the butt end of the north rampart, medium and large stones, 0.25 m across on average, appeared to have been pressed into the rampart material (Plate 2.3). The material of both ramparts was considerably collapsed and slumped and, in the case of the north rampart, it had spread well beyond the area delimited by the post-holes, particularly, down the natural scarp face.

*South rampart terminal (Figure 2.4 & 2.5; Plate 2.4 & 2.5)*

On the south rampart, stonework was roughly stepped up the gently inclining slope and the top courses were pressed back into the rampart core (Plate 2.4). In this

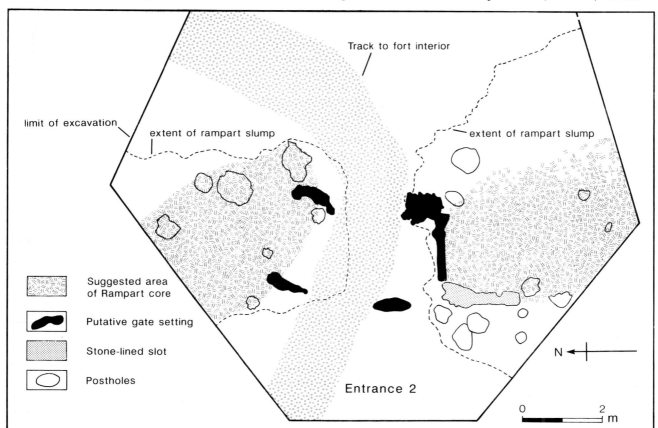

*Figure 2.4   Plan of Defensive System A, Entrance 2.*

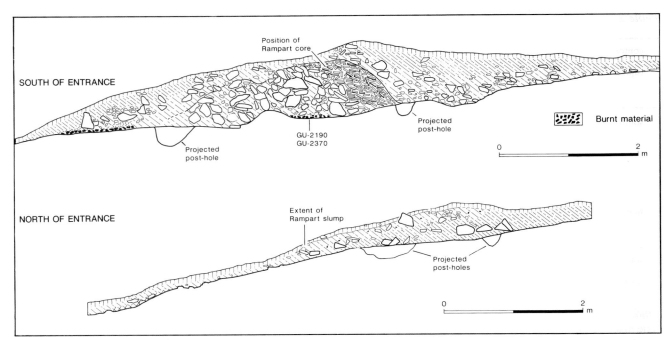

*Figure 2.5    Sections of Defensive System A, Entrance 2.*

way, a plinth was created to match the natural scarp on which the northern rampart had been built. Apart from the stone plinth, no clear wall construction was apparent. A group of ten post-holes was discovered, again apparently outlining the original shape of the rampart terminal (Plate 2.5). They varied in size and depth but were generally similar to those of the north terminal. Four of these, as well as a stone-lined slot, approximately 1.5 m long and located parallel to the east (front) face of the rampart, were excavated into the plinth courses and were not rock-cut.

A deposit, 0.45 m thick, of very loose brash, full of voids and with almost no soil content, had been dumped behind and above the stonework (Figure 2.5). Behind this and perpendicular to it, a short stretch (0.6 m long) of very tumbled but possibly coursed stonework may represent an attempt at buttressing the rampart. A rock-cut slot, *circa* 1 m long and aligned east to west, was found at the north end of the south rampart. It may have been a bedding trench for timbers revetting the rampart terminal. Above and behind the brash dump was an

extensive but severely slumped deposit of reddish-brown clayey silt similar to the material of the north rampart but containing a higher proportion of stone and gravel. East of this and spreading over the surface of bedrock, an extensive deposit of red silty clay occurred.

*Gateway (Figure 2.4)*
Bedrock was visible in the entrance in many places prior to excavation and is only covered by a very thin layer of soil and vegetation elsewhere. Positive structural features indicative of a gateway have not survived. However, four negative features, rock-cut slots each *circa* 0.7 m long, 0.2 m wide and 0.07 m deep, were discovered. They were aligned north to south and arranged in pairs, approximately 2.5 m apart, on either side of the track. Two, possibly related, roughly circular post-holes (each *circa* 0.5 m across by 0.12 m deep) were located adjacent to the inner slots. Taken together, these may be tentatively interpreted as the footings for a timber gateway structure.

*Plate 2.4    The stonework plinth beneath the southern rampart.*

*Plate 2.5    Post-holes beneath the south rampart terminal.*

*Table 2.1   Artefacts from Defensive System A, Entrance 2 (excluding modern).*

| context | coarse pottery | stone | other |
|---|---|---|---|
| topsoil and unstratified | 143 | 32  flint<br>26  pebble<br>101  vitrified | 76  bloomery waste |
| south rampart core | 121–2  (Roman)<br>129–42<br>144 | 9  whetstone<br>14–16  hammerstone<br>33–8  flint<br>58  quartz<br>47  chert arrowhead<br>99, 102  vitrified | 65  glass armlet<br><br>86–98  crucible frags |
| north rampart core | 128 | 48  chert<br>61  jet armlet<br>39  flint | 61  jet armlet<br>64  glass bead<br>75  bloomery waste |
| south rampart post-holes | | 103  vitrified | |
| north rampart post-holes | | 62  jet armlet | 74  iron nail |

*Finds (Table 2.1)*

The artefactual assemblage comprises almost sixty items (excluding modern finds), most of which were retrieved from the disturbed and spread bodies of the ramparts. The pre-rampart hearth produced fragments of burnt bone as well as much charcoal, but no artefacts; and no finds were recovered from Pit 1. Similarly, very little material was recovered from the post-holes and slots below the ramparts, a fragment of jet armlet and part of an iron nail being the only items of note.

The north and south rampart cores produced a diverse range of artefactual debris amongst which no material type is dominant. Notable finds include a chert, barbed and tanged arrowhead, jet and glass armlet fragments, a glass bead and a number of crucible fragments. The south rampart produced a larger and more varied assemblage than did the north rampart. Elsewhere in the area, several ancient and modern items were found incorporated in deposits overlying the shattered bedrock surface, immediately beneath the turf. These have clearly been conflated by bioturbation.

**Defensive System A, adjacent to House Platform 2 (Figure 2.6)**

A trench, measuring 10 m by 1.5 m and aligned roughly west to east, was opened on the west side of the fort, crossing the inner circuit of Defensive System A about 35 m south of Entrance 1 (Figure 2.2). The trench extended into the centre of House Platform 2, which appeared to be backed against the rampart. An army range-warning sign had been inserted into the centre of the platform and a narrow footpath traversed the rampart. The aims of the excavation here were threefold:

*i* to examine in section the rampart construction;
*ii* to ascertain the relationship between House Platform 2 and the rampart; and
*iii* to retrieve dating material from both.

*Pre-rampart activity*

A shallow pit (Pit 2) was found immediately below the rampart, cut into glacial till. No old ground surface was

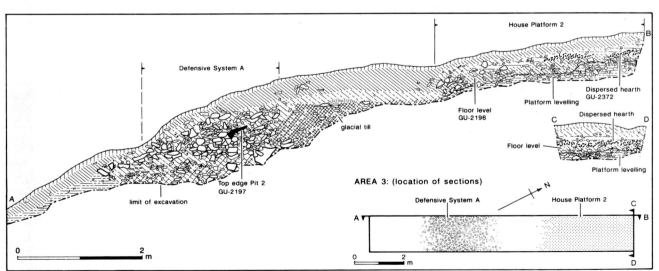

*Figure 2.6   Sections of Defensive System A and adjacent House Platform 2.*

*Table 2.2    Artefacts from Defensive System A, adjacent to House Platform 2.*

| context | coarse pottery | stone | bronze |
|---------|----------------|-------|--------|
| rampart base | 163<br>165 | 3  pounder<br>10  whetstone<br>40  flint | |
| pre-rampart (Pit 2) | | | 69  tool |

discernible between the top of the pit and the base of the rampart. The (incompletely excavated) pit extended beyond the south margin of the trench. It appeared oval in shape with a rounded base and was at least 0.4 m wide and 0.25 m deep. It was filled with loose, angular, small stones, till and some mid-brown silt. However, it also contained abundant charcoal, and burnt and unburnt fragments of mammal bone, including ten teeth from a mature horse. The wood species represented among the charcoal include hazel, alder, birch, ash and willow, almost all of which derived from small diameter roundwood. Radiocarbon assay of charcoal from this pit gave a date of $2680 \pm 130$ bp (730 bc, GU-2197).

### Rampart

The rampart was insubstantial, built of angular stones of mixed sizes, set in a matrix of reddish silty clay. It was positioned on the lip of a natural scarp and many of the stones had subsequently slipped down the slope. No evidence of facing or wall construction was discerned. It was overlain by similar red silty clay, which also lapped up behind the rampart. No evidence of post-holes, slots or other constructional features was discovered below the rampart.

### Finds (Table 2.2)

A bronze tool was recovered from the upper levels of Pit 2 beneath the rampart. Finds from the rampart itself were sparse. At its base were found two stone tools.

## Defensive System B

Defensive System B was examined in a trench measuring 6 m by 1.5 m, aligned roughly south-west to north-east, immediately adjacent to the eroding main track on the western approach to the summit (not illustrated in section). The surface was heather-covered and no features were visible before excavation; but the trench crossed the pronounced edge of the intermittent terrace which marks the boundary of the summit-plateau, and represents the line of Defensive System B. The terrace edge was accentuated by the presence of a sheep track which had cut a groove into the ground surface. The aims of the excavation were twofold:
*i* to examine the structure of Defensive System B; and
*ii* to retrieve dating material from it.

### Results

Immediately below the thick heather cover, a haphazard spread of angular stones, mostly 0.2–0.3 m across, occurred in a band *circa* 2 m wide along the top edge of the terrace. In places, there were superimposed levels of stones. They tended to be slightly larger where they occurred along the lip of the natural scarp, although no structure was discernible. These overlay a stone-free, reddish silty clay deposit, *circa* 0.6 m thick, which in turn overlay glacial till. There was, therefore, only minimal evidence of a rampart at this point, the spread of stones perhaps representing the vestiges of a rampart base. No finds were recovered.

### Defensive System C (Figure 2.7)

Two trenches were opened on the line of Defensive System C, as identified by the RCAHMS survey. The first, 25 m long by 1 m wide and aligned roughly west to east, was positioned on the final western ascent to the signal station on the summit-plateau. The second, 6 m long by 1.5 m wide and aligned roughly north-west to south-east, was located adjacent to the main track just below the summit of the hill. The first trench was opened along a 25 m stretch to allow for possible inaccuracies in locating the line of System C on the ground. In positioning the second, an attempt was made to determine the crossing point of System C and the main track (as illustrated by the RCAHMS), using conventional survey techniques. The aims of both excavations were as follows:
*i* to establish the existence or otherwise of Defensive System C; and
*ii* if so established, to ascertain its character and to retrieve dating material.

### Results

In both trenches, the irregular, badly weathered surface of bedrock was exposed immediately beneath the turf, heather and subsoil, although the soil deposits were slightly deeper in the second trench than the first. The rock surface was broken with cavities formed along lines of cleavage, obscuring all but the most substantial rock-cut features.

In the 25 m long trench, one rock-cut post-hole was discovered towards the top of the slope. It was 0.35 m in diameter and 0.28 m deep, with near vertical sides and a pointed base, and was filled with reddish-brown silty clay and small, angular, re-deposited stones. However, extensions to the trench on either side of it failed to locate any further features.

At the north-west end of the second trench (Figure 2.7), a discontinuous shallow groove or slot of roughly rectangular section was found in the rock surface. The upslope edge of the groove may, perhaps, have been cut

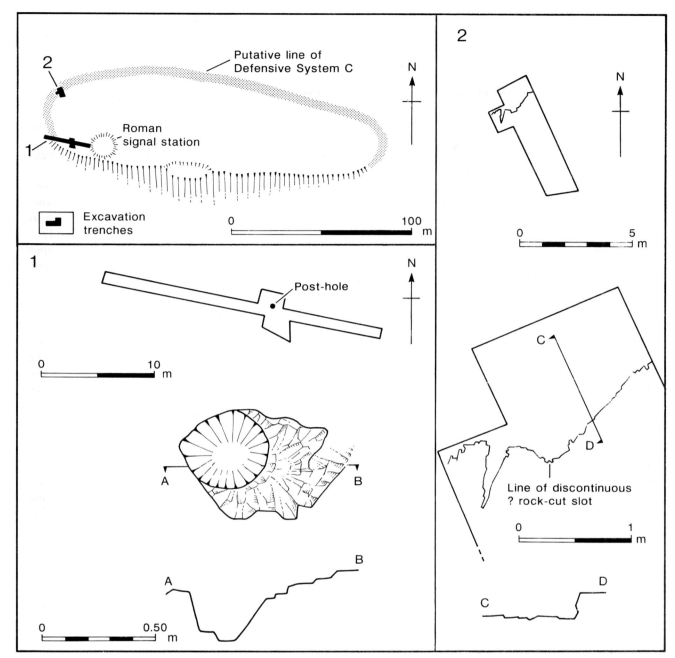

*Figure 2.7   Trench plans of Defensive System C.*

but, downslope, the edge was imprecise. The groove was *circa* 0.45 m wide and of variable depth, up to 0.18 m. It was traced over a length of 1.4 m but extensions to either side of the trench failed to locate any continuation of the feature.

Clearly, no trace of any rampart structure has been recovered from these trenches. Nor does it seem likely that either the discontinuous groove or the single post-hole represent a vestigial palisade.

*Finds*
An assortment of modern glass shards was recovered from immediately beneath the turf of both trenches. One retouched chert flake [49] was found in the first trench excavated, and one sherd of pottery of uncertain origin [127] in the second.

**Summary**

Defensive System A is more impressive in plan than in section. Its inner circuit comprises a stone and earth bank which has suffered disturbance in antiquity and more recently. The rampart terminals at Entrance 2 appear to have been outlined by posts. The north terminal may have had a rounded end and turned inwards; the south terminal may have been slightly more pointed and turned outwards. Scant traces of possible footings for a timber gate construction were found. No evidence of activities inside the entrance had survived. No material suitable for radiocarbon dating was retrieved and artefactual debris, dating from probably the Late Bronze Age to modern, was mixed within the cores, signifying both incorporation of early material into the ramparts and post-constructional disturbance of them.

No constructional, artefactual or dating evidence was retrieved from Defensive System B, although its existence is not in serious doubt. The very existence of Defensive System C, however, is very much in question.

HOUSE PLATFORMS

Three house platforms were investigated, two fully and one partially. All three had suffered some erosion. House Platform 1 was located in the south-west quadrant of the fort (Figure 2.2), immediately within Defensive System A, and it was cut by a narrow footpath leading up to the summit. House Platform 2 was immediately north-east of House Platform 1, and adjacent to it. Before excavation, it appeared to be backed against the rampart forming the inner circuit of Defensive System A. It was affected by the same footpath as House Platform 1 and had also had an army range-warning sign erected at its centre. House Platform 3 was located on the eroding scree slope on the final western approach to the summit-plateau, within the area of Defensive System C. Here,

severe erosion had affected the whole of the front edge of the platform.

All the Eildon platforms look broadly similar, consisting of roughly level surfaces which have been constructed by excavating into a moderate slope at the rear and by banking up the downhill side to form a terrace. The terminology employed in the platform descriptions is defined elsewhere in this report (p 5).

**House Platform 1 (Figure 2.8, 2.9 & 2.10; Plate 2.6)**

Before excavation, thick heather cover obscured the perimeter of House Platform 1, but it appeared roughly sub-oval in shape. It sat in the hollow of a partly natural shelf which had apparently been exploited by deepening and steepening the back scarp and levelling up the front. Because of the shape of the platform and the difficult nature of the terrain, an irregular, heptagonal cutting, with maximum dimensions of 12.5 by 9 m, was opened.

Excavation revealed that the site consisted of two platforms, one superimposed on the other. Clear evidence of this was provided by two episodes of rock cutting at the back of the platform, the later of which

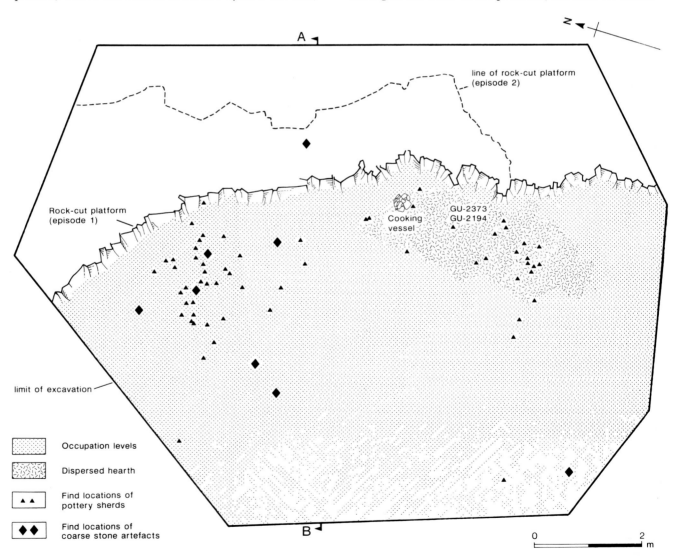

*Figure 2.8   Plan of House Platform 1, Episode 1.*

also saw a slight re-orientation of the house site. The two main constructional episodes are described separately below. The associated soil matrices had been chemically weathered (Jordan, above) and it was not possible to distinguish floor and other deposits unambiguously. However, although the soil boundaries were diffuse and their matrices fairly homogeneous, broad division into periods was possible and the interpretation of less ambiguous contexts is discussed below.

*Episode 1: the earliest platform (Figure 2.8 & 2.9; Plate 2.6)*

*Construction*  An almost vertical cut had been made into the rock scarp upslope of the site. The cut, which survived to a maximum height of 0.5 m, was detected over a length of 8.5 m, curving round the sides of the platform and flattened at the back, to form a roughly oval shape. The jagged rock surface thus produced at the foot of the cut was hewn roughly level, and surfaced with rock chippings and gravel in till-derived, red-brown, silty clay. Similar material was used to level up the front of the platform, and excess rock and gravel was found heaped around its sides.

*Overlying stratigraphy (Figure 2.8)*  The soil deposits were remarkably uniform with horizons indicative of former stratigraphy characterised by spreads of varying stone content and, occasionally, by colour or textural differences. A deposit of reddish-brown sandy clay with abundant small stones and gravel was found over the whole platform but was thickest in the centre and towards the north. A slightly darker grey band of similar material overlay this and ran across the

*Plate 2.6   House Platform 1, Episode 1.*

back half of the platform, while a better defined spread of markedly darker, grey-brown sandy clay also overlay the reddish-brown deposit in the south half of the platform, at the foot of the cut rock scarp. It was not clear during excavation that these deposits were significantly different from each other, or from the underlying reddish-brown deposit. Rather, they appeared to be discoloured areas within an otherwise homogeneous deposit. Both of the dark bands contained charcoal, fragments of burnt bone and significant quantities of coarse pottery (*circa* seventy sherds altogether). The markedly darker band, which produced one almost intact cooking vessel, may represent the spread of a hearth, dispersed over an area of *circa* 4.5 by 1.75 m.

The two dark bands are interpreted as vestigial occupation deposits on the original house floor. Radiocarbon assay, on small diameter roundwood of

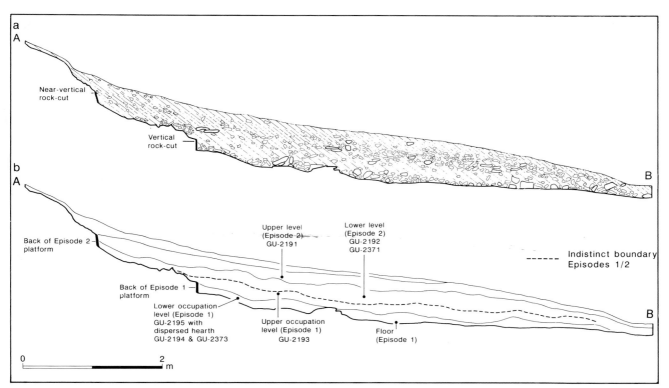

*Figure 2.9   Section of House Platform 1.*

alder, birch, hazel, willow and *Prunus* species from the
dark spread at the back of the platform, gave a date of
2750 ± 50 bp (800 bc; GU-2195); while charcoal samples
of birch, ash, oak and willow from the dispersed hearth
gave a date of 3020 ± 60 bp (GU-2194), and of
2600 ± 50 bp (650 bc; GU-2373) when oak was excluded.

A deposit of homogeneous, reddish-brown, silty
clay, 0.15 m thick, containing abundant stones and
gravel, overlay the dark bands. It contained occasional
patches of charcoal and small areas of darker soil.
Several sherds of coarse pottery were recovered but,
generally, finds were few. This deposit filled the
platform site up to the level of the second phase of
constructional rock-cutting, and its upper levels, at least,
must represent an abandonment horizon. Radiocarbon
assay, on alder, birch, hazel and willow charcoal from
the darker patches within this material, gave a date of
2650 ± 60 bp (700 bc; GU-2193).

*Episode 2: the later platform (Figure 2.9 & 2.10)*
The vertical, cut face at the back of the early platform
was subsequently re-cut on a slightly different alignment
and up to 2.5 m further back into the rock. In the south
half, the curving line of the later rock-cut face crossed
and completely destroyed the remains of the earlier cut,
so that in plan the two cuts appear almost as two
intersecting arcs. The later face sloped steeply; the rock
surface at the foot of the secondary face survived as a
crescentic ledge, the front edge of which is defined by the
line of the earlier cut.

Plate 2.7   Rock-cut slots in House Platform 1,
Episode 1.

On this rock ledge, four rock-cut, roughly
rectangular slots were discovered (Plate 2.7). All four
occurred in the north half of the ledge, two along the
base of the back scarp, one in the centre of the ledge, and
one on the edge of the Episode 1 face. Together, they
appeared to form part of a curving line of rock-cut
features (Figure 2.10). Their dimensions varied between

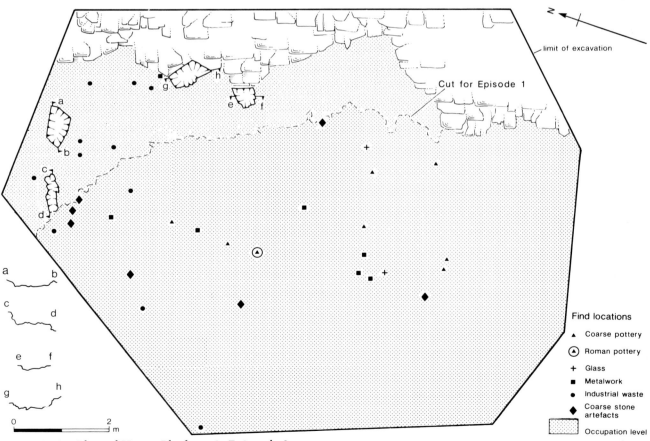

Figure 2.10   Plan of House Platform 1, Epiosode 2.

0.6–0.8 m long by 0.2–0.4 m wide; and they vary in depth from 0.1–0.25 m. Their bases were jagged and uneven. These features are likely to have been constructional and may have housed the ends of timbers.

Broken stone and gravel were used to level up the front and sides of the platform, and a roughly level surface of broken stones and gravel in reddish-brown silty clay had been formed over both the rocky ledge and the earlier deposits in front of the ledge. However, despite generally increased stoniness, the boundary (between the Episode 1 abandonment horizon and this, Episode 2, levelling horizon) was far from distinct, except on the rocky ledge.

*Overlying stratigraphy (Figure 2.9)* A series of poorly defined, homogeneous, less stony, sandy clay layers accumulated over the stony surface. In general, the upper strata were less distinct than the lower, presumably as a result of post-depositional processes (Jordan, above). However, the original stone-packed surface and the sandy clay immediately above it produced more artefactual debris than overlying deposits, and probably represent vestigial occupation levels.

This assemblage is distinguished by its paucity of coarse pottery fragments and its relative richness of bronze artefacts and metalworking debris. Chief among these was part of a dragonesque fibula of probably first to second century AD date (Owen & Ashmore below).

Carbonised samples from the stony surface and the sandy clay above it were submitted for radiocarbon assay. The lower samples, comprising alder, birch, hazel, Pomoideae, willow and heather charcoal, gave dates of $2220 \pm 60$ bp (270 bc; GU-2192) and $2000 \pm 130$ bp (50 bc; GU-2371); and the upper one, comprising the same species excluding Pomoideae, gave a date of $1760 \pm 50$ bp (ad 190; GU-2191). Abandonment and decay of the Episode 2 site could not be discerned in the overlying stratigraphy, which comprised a series of reddish to reddish-brown, fine, silty to sandy clays, with abundant roots and frequent stones. The disturbed nature of this upper material is evidenced by the discovery of a small quantity of assorted artefactual debris in all layers, including the topsoil. The platform is in an area of net soil accumulation, and it is likely that some of this material and debris has washed onto the site from the higher reaches of the hill.

*Finds (Table 2.3)*
The Episode 1 assemblage is dominated by sherds of coarse pottery, totalling about seventy individual finds and one almost intact cooking pot (Plate 2.8). In contrast, the Episode 2 assemblage is dominated by fragments of bronze artefacts and by metalworking debris. Small assemblages of stone tools and fragments of glass also survive. The disturbed deposits above the Episode 2 platform produced a small, mixed assemblage.

*Table 2.3 Artefacts from House Platform 1.*

| Episode | context | pottery | glass | bronze | metalworking debris | stone |
|---|---|---|---|---|---|---|
| 1 | floor and vestigial occupation | 125–6<br>149–50<br>152–4<br>157<br>161–2 | | | | 1 flake<br>5 pounder<br>13 whetstone<br>18 hammer |
| 1 | dispersed hearth | 147–8<br>151–2<br>155–7 | | | | 27 pecked stone |
| 1 | upper occupation, ?abandoned | 145<br>149–50<br>159–60 | | | 107 clinker | 12 whetstone<br>4 pounder |
| 2 | ?floor surface | 146–7<br>149<br>157–8 | 66 armlet | 71 fibula, dragonesque<br>72 fibula, pin<br>73 bronze sheet | 78–82 bloomery waste<br>83–5 run metal<br>104–6 clinker | 17 hammer<br>114–7 vitrified |
| 2 | ?abandoned | 123 Roman | | | | 11 whetstone<br>28 sharpener<br>42 flint chunk<br>50–4 chert<br>108, vitrified<br>112–3 |
| | topsoil | 118 baked clay | 67 melted armlet | | | 41 flint flake<br>59 chalcedony<br>109–11 vitrified |

*Plate 2.8   Cooking-pot* in situ *from House Platform 1, Episode 1.*

**House Platform 2 (Figure 2.6)**

House Platform 2 was located less than 15 m north-east of House Platform 1 and approximately 35 m south of Entrance 1 (Figure 2.2). It was turf covered, with clumps of heather and bilberry, and was situated on a natural flat terrace immediately within the inner circuit of Defensive System A, apparently backed against it. Surface indications of its outline were imprecise. A trench, measuring 10 by 1.5 m and aligned roughly west to east, was cut across the adjacent rampart and into the centre of the platform. The aims were:

*i* to ascertain the relationship between the house platform and the rampart; and
*ii* to retrieve dating material from both.

*Construction (Figure 2.6)*   The platform was cut into glacial till, covered by a compact, largely till-derived, stone-packed layer of reddish sandy clay, which served to level the site. This overlay red, comparatively stone-free, sandy clay, possibly hillwash, which itself overlay the rampart core, indicating that the platform post-dates the rampart.

*Overlying stratigraphy*   The levelling layer was covered with a compacted, stone-packed deposit of medium-brown sandy clay which may represent the original floor surface. Charcoal flecks and burnt bone fragments were present but few artefacts. Radiocarbon assay on a sample of alder, hazel and willow charcoal, all from small diameter roundwood, gave a date of 1820±60 bp (ad 130; GU-2196). Above this, a 0.1 m thick deposit of dark brown to black sandy clay, containing abundant charcoal and burnt bone fragments, may represent the remains of a dispersed hearth, similar to that found on House Platform 1, Episode 1. Its roughly central position on the platform

supports this hypothesis. Radiocarbon assay, on small diameter roundwood of alder, birch, hazel, ash, cherry and willow, gave a date of 1780±50 bp (ad 170; GU-2372). No clear abandonment level was discernible, the overlying stratigraphy comprising homogeneous, reddish-brown clay loam with some small stones.

*Finds (Table 2.4)*
Comparatively few artefacts were recovered from the platform and, since only a small portion of it was excavated, they may not be representative of the total assemblage. The coarse pot sherd, found in the levelling layer, is likely to have been re-deposited. The only finds of note were fragments of glass and jet armlets.

**House Platform 3 (Figure 2.11; Plate 2.9)**

House Platform 3 was located on a west-facing slope, immediately below the summit-plateau, within the area of Defensive System C (Figure 2.2). The slope has been severely eroded and the footpaths marked on the RCAHMS survey undertaken in 1950 (published as Figure 417 in RCAHMS 1956) are no longer present. Much of the slope is now covered with loose scree and gravel, and the front edge of the platform was badly damaged and undercut. Before excavation, the platform appeared gently inclined from back to front. It was mostly grass-covered with scree at the front, while the back slope and immediate surrounds had thick heather cover. A heptagonal trench was opened, encompassing the whole platform and part of the back scarp. It had maximum dimensions of 10.5 by 9 m.

*Construction*   The natural rock scarp behind the platform defines its back limit, in front of which the slightly inclining surface of bedrock had been used without major alteration. However, the slope at the front of the platform had been levelled with a deposit of shattered stones and coarse gravel, much of which has subsequently been lost over the eroded front edge. Similar material was heaped around the sides and towards the front of the platform. Burnt bone fragments, one flint flake and two sherds of coarse pottery found in this material are probably re-deposited.

In all the hilltop excavation areas, rock-cut features were often poorly defined because the bedrock was severely weathered and its surface insecure. The back scarp and the front edge of House Platform 3 were particularly badly affected but several rock-cut constructional features were identified. These comprised a curvilinear slot at the back of the platform, two rock-cut post-holes and one smaller post-hole cut into the

*Table 2.4   Artefacts from House Platform 2.*

| context | coarse pottery | stone | other |
|---|---|---|---|
| hearth | | | 68   glass armlet |
| floor | | 21   anvil | |
| levelling layer | 164 | 63   jet armlet | |

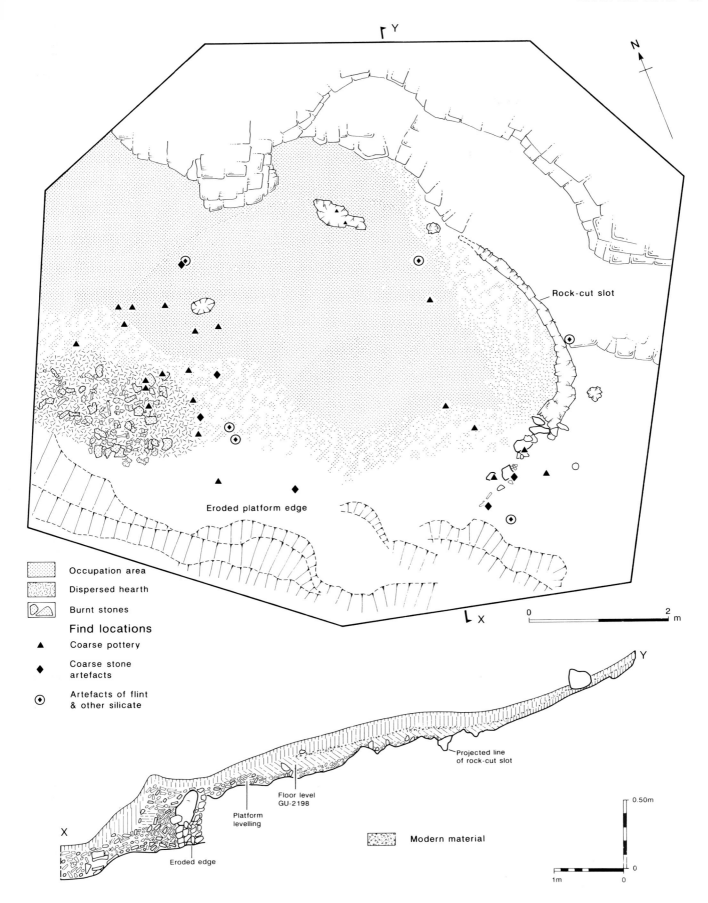

*Figure 2.11   Plan and section of House Platform 3.*

*Plate 2.9  House Platform 3.*

gravel make-up at the front of the platform, and one other isolated feature halfway up the scarp behind the platform.

The curvilinear slot (Figure 2.11) was rectangular in section, some 0.15 m deep and between 0.12–0.2 m wide. It survived intact for a length of nearly 3.5 m in the south half of the platform, where the rock surface was slightly better preserved, and was traced intermittently for another 2 m in the north half. No trace of it was found in the gravels which made up the front and sides of the platform. Its fill, light brown, silty clay, produced a sherd of coarse pottery. In its best preserved section, the course of the slot was marked by a line of protruding stones, one of which was a pounder or grinder and another, a quern rubber.

A circular post-hole, 0.2 m wide and 0.1 m deep, was situated adjacent to the outer curving edge of the rock-cut slot in the south half of the platform. Another, partially stone-lined, oval post-hole, 0.25 m by 0.2 m across and 0.17 m deep, lay roughly on the projected line of the slot in the north half of the platform; its fill contained a piece of flint. A smaller (0.1 m in diameter and 0.15 m deep), circular post-, or stake-hole was found cut into the gravel at the front of the platform, outwith the line of the slot. Finally, a less regular, possible rock-cut feature was identified on the sloping back scarp, 1.5 m outwith the line of the slot, roughly opposite the centre of the platform area. It had maximum dimensions of 0.24 m across by 0.16 m deep. The fills, variable brown silty clays flecked with charcoal, were uninformative, but all these features may once have housed the ends of timbers.

The roughly level, stone base of a putative hearth was found in the north half towards the front of the platform. The setting of locally derived, angular stones, several fire-reddened, was *circa* 0.6 m square. It was situated close to, but probably still within, the north edge of the putative house, if the course of the slot is projected round to the north. The overlying matrix was disturbed but concentrations of charcoal, burnt bone and sherds of coarse pottery were found in the immediate vicinity of the fire base.

*Overlying stratigraphy*  House Platform 3 was set in an area of considerable soil erosion, unlike House Platforms 1 and 2, and the archaeological stratigraphy

**Table 2.5  *Artefacts from House Platform 3.***

| context | coarse pottery | stone |
|---|---|---|
| post-abandonment | 124  (Roman)<br>166–7<br>170 | 2  flake<br>6  pounder<br>19  hammerstone<br>25  quern<br>29–30  polished<br>43  flint<br>55–7  chert<br>60  chalcedony<br>119–20  vitrified |
| *occupation* | | |
| floor | 166–9 | 7  pounder<br>20  hammerstone<br>22  anvil<br>23  quern rubber<br>44  flint |
| curvilinear slot fill | 166 | 8  pounder<br>24  quern rubber<br>31  cobble |
| post-hole fill | | 46  flint |
| *construction* | | |
| gravel make-up | | 45  flint<br>55  chert |

had not survived. All soil deposits were disturbed and no, even vestigial, occupation levels could be distinguished. However, a dark, reddish-brown, gravelly clay, noted over the whole platform and roughly on a level with the putative fire base, contained artefactual debris, notably coarse pottery and stone implements. Radiocarbon assay, on roundwood charcoal of alder, birch, hazel, ash, elm, willow, oak and *Prunus*, collected from the vicinity of the fire base, gave a date of $2620 \pm 60$ bp(670 bc; GU-2198). Very few finds were retrieved from above this level.

An extensive spread of burnt material containing lumps of charred wood, bottle glass and two coins overlay the back half of the platform and covered the back scarp. The intense heat had affected the underlying contexts. This may have been the site of a beacon fire, lit several times and as recently as early this century on coin evidence.

*Finds (Table 2.5)*
The Platform 3 assemblage consists primarily of coarse pottery sherds and stone implements, mostly found on a level with, and most frequent in the area of, the fire base. A Roman period rim sherd comes from an overlying context. A small but varied stone assemblage, vitrified stones, burnt bone fragments and charcoal were also recovered.

## ARTEFACTUAL EVIDENCE

The artefacts have been numbered in a single sequence, organised by material type. Within material types, the artefacts have been ordered by area, as follows: Defensive Systems A, B and C (DS-A, DS-B or DS-C); followed by House Platforms 1, 2 and 3 (HP-1, HP-2 and HP-3). Detailed descriptions are included here only for those artefacts which have undergone further analysis, or which are chronologically sensitive. The full finds catalogues are presented in the appendices (Appendix 1–12). Catalogue numbers are presented in text in square brackets.

Standard catalogue abbreviations have been used as follows:
L – length; W – width; D – depth; T – thickness; dia – diameter; mm – millimetres; g – grammes; kg – kilograms. All measurements are given in millimetres and all weights in grammes, unless otherwise stated.

## Coarse stone (Appendix 1) *A Clarke*

The coarse stone assemblage comprises thirty-one items, most of which can be identified as either pounders/grinders, whetstones, hammerstones, anvils or quern rubbers. A (probable) quern fragment was also recovered. Two of the pieces are flakes whilst the rest are made of water-worn cobbles or unworn fragments. The artefacts are mostly made of sandstone, ranging from fine-, to coarse-grained, but quartzite and igneous rocks, usually trachyte, also served as raw materials. These are all local to the Eildon Hill area (Appendix 2).

Most of the pieces were not modified before use, their selection being based on original cobble shape and raw material. Thus, flat, fine-grained pebbles have been selected for the whetstones since they provide a useful edge for sharpening. The wear on whetstones of this type is less distinctive than on fashioned examples, which often have shallow concave areas worn into their surfaces. Although less worn, the Eildon whetstones display, perhaps, more polish than fashioned examples.

In contrast, the pounders are made of coarse-grained sandstone or quartzite and are more rounded. The use-wear on these pieces takes the form of pecking and grinding, which causes facets over their surfaces. The hammerstones exhibit only small amounts of wear in the form of pecking and flaking. This wear is not standardised and probably indicates a variety of functions.

The shapes of certain pieces were modified, by pecking, before use. A possible pounder and/or pestle [3] is a fine example; it had been pecked over its whole surface to form a cylinder and both ends were pecked hollow. Two other items [26–27] have been made into oblate spheres by pecking. The quern rubbers have been made from slabs of igneous rock. It is not possible to determine how much working of the raw material was necessary to form these items.

In conclusion, the coarse stone artefacts from the Eildon assemblage represent a variety of types of use-wear, which indicate several different, intended functions. Unfortunately, without experimental replication, it is not possible to clarify all the types of use represented by the observed wear patterns.

## Chipped stone (Appendix 3) *S McCartan*

The assemblage comprises twenty-nine pieces, fifteen of which are flint, eleven are chert, one is quartz and two are chalcedony. The small number of pieces and their poorly stratified contexts means that only limited information can be derived from the assemblage. Furthermore, some of the assemblage may not have been associated with the main occupation phases of the site; indeed a barbed and tanged arrowhead [47] must pre-date the earliest dated occupation phase by up to 500 years (below).

Flint and chert were the main raw materials used. There are no *in situ* deposits of flint in Scotland, although flint pebbles are derived from glacial and other deposits. Chert outcrops are, however, known from the Roxburghshire region (Wickham-Jones & Collins 1977–8, 17–18); but the evidence from Eildon Hill suggests that a pebble source of chert as well as pebble flint was exploited. During excavation, some small, weathered and flawed chert pebbles were collected; their condition suggests that chert (and flint) may have been gathered from the nearby riverbanks of the Tweed.

There is no evidence that knapping was carried out on site. No cores, core trimming flakes or core rejuvenation flakes are present. Only two flakes provide enough detail for any analysis of primary technology. Both have small platforms with diffused bulbs suggestive of direct percussion with a soft hammer (Ohnuma & Bergman 1982). However, there is insufficient evidence to enable any general conclusions to be drawn about primary knapping technology for the site as a whole. Only four of the pieces have been retouched and two of these are broken, so their original morphology is unclear. Three flakes have edge damage and, while this may be indicative of use, it can also be caused by other, pre-, and post-depositional processes.

The barbed and tanged chert arrowhead ([47] Figure 2.12) is the most notable of the retouched pieces. The original flake has been modified by careful retouch to produce a finely shaped distal end and a 'square' barb. Unfortunately, the tang and one of the barbs are broken. On the basis of size, weight and the 'square' barb the arrowhead is of the Conygar Hill type as recognised by Green (1980) and dated by him to the Early Bronze Age. Such an artefact would have normally functioned as an object of war and display (Pitts & Jacobi 1979, 173–4). The remaining retouched tool is a broken awl [53], also made of chert. The piece has been modified by irregular retouch to form a point, broken perhaps in use. This awl is not diagnostic of a particular culture or chronological period but is a common form, used through many cultural traditions.

[47]

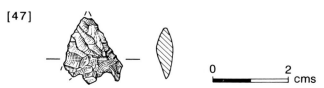

*Figure 2.12 Chert arrowhead.*

To summarise, pebble flint and chert was used at Eildon, supplemented by the exploitation of chalcedonic material and quartz. There are four retouched pieces, two of which are recognisable tool forms. The assemblage is composed mainly of irregular chunks and flakes, doubtless a reflection of the poor raw material.

### Acknowledgements

Sinéad McCartan would like to thank Caroline Wickham-Jones and Ann Clarke for their advice and assistance on the chipped stone assemblage; and the Royal Museum of Scotland for the use of its facilities in the Artefact Research Unit.

### Jet armlets (Appendix 4) *M M B Kemp*

Three fragments of jet armlet were recovered, two from the ramparts of Defensive System A at Entrance 2 [61–2], and one from House Platform 2 [63]. The latter comprises two adjoining pieces, broken in antiquity, from an armlet measuring some 84 mm in diameter and 10 mm thick. One third of the circuit of [61] survives; it is D-shaped in cross section with an estimated diameter of 68 mm (surviving L 70 mm, T 7 mm). Only a small fragment of [62] survives (L 12 mm), from which neither section form nor diameter can be deduced. Jet is a generic term used, archaeologically, to describe a range of related materials including shale and cannel coal. The actual raw material used for any particular armlet cannot be distinguished by visual inspection alone. There is a wide variety of sources for these materials in lowland Scotland. Callander (1916, 234–7) drew attention to the fact that partly finished jet ornaments have been found throughout Scotland, including the south-east, and there seems no reason to assume anything but local manufacture for the Eildon pieces.

Jet armlet fragments occur in Late Bronze Age contexts at Heathery Burn, Co. Durham (Britton & Longworth 1968) and Staple Howe, Yorkshire (Brewster 1963, 118–20), and are among finds, probably of post-Roman date, from the crannog at Buiston, Ayrshire (Munro 1882, 232). The majority of these finds, however, are from sites conventionally assumed to have been occupied during Iron Age and Roman times. By far the largest collection comes from Traprain Law (Curle 1915, 175–76; Curle & Cree 1916, 104; Curle 1920, 71; Curle & Cree 1921, 173, 180, 191; Cree & Curle 1922, 227, 228–31, 235, 237, 248, 252; Cree 1923, 19–96, 202, 212; Cree 1924, 254, 269–71). Although this site was probably occupied in the Late Bronze Age, it is clear that these armlets were in use throughout most, if not all, of the main Iron Age and Roman periods of occupation.

Although termed armlets, bracelets or anklets, many are clearly too small in diameter to have served as any of these things. Three size ranges were recognised among the armlets from Roman York: internal diameters of 76–63 mm, 63–44 mm and less than 38 mm, with a suggestion that the smaller examples might be hair-rings (RCHME 1962, 144). However, the Eildon fragments fall within the larger class and are interpreted as armlets.

### Acknowledgements

Mary Kemp would like to acknowledge Professor Robert Stevenson and Dr David Clarke for their help with the glass and jet armlets.

### Glass (Figure 2.13; Appendix 5) *J Henderson · comments M M B Kemp*

The excavations produced three glass armlet fragments and a single glass bead. The bead [64] and one armlet [65] were found in disturbed levels in the ramparts of

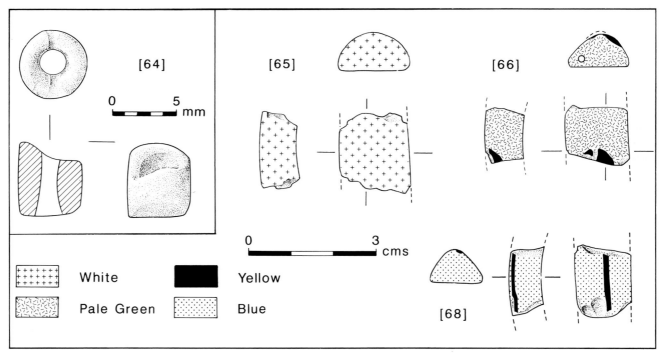

*Figure 2.13   Glass bead [64] and armlet fragments.*

Defensive System A at Entrance 2; one armlet [66] was found on House Platform 1 (Episode 2); the other [68] was found in the occupation level of House Platform 2. The original character of a second glass fragment from House Platform 1 [67] cannot be ascertained because of heat damage. The armlet fragments are all sub-triangular in cross section. One fragment [65], made of opaque white glass, has an estimated diameter of 52 mm. Another [66], of transparent green glass decorated with an opaque yellow blob on its apex, has an estimated diameter of 64 mm. The third [68], of opaque blue glass decorated with a thin opaque yellow trail along its apex, has an estimated diameter of 80 mm. The bead is cylindrical, 5 mm across with a 2 mm diameter perforation, and made of transparent green glass. It is of Guido's Roman cylindrical bead type (1978, 95, 208).

The armlet fragments are of Romano-British types commonly accepted as dating mainly to the first to second centuries AD (Kilbride-Jones 1938: [65] is Kilbride-Jones type 3A; [66] is type 3H; and [68], type 3G). The bead is also of a Romano-British type, similar beads having been found in Scotland at Newstead (Curle 1911, 337, Plate *xci*, 25) and at Traprain Law (Curle & Cree 1915, 109, Figure 25, 7–8). Guido notes that this type of bead ranges in date from the first century BC, through Roman times into the post-Roman period (1978, 95 and 92, Figure 37, 5).

Kilbride-Jones' initial study of the armlet series (1938) concentrated on the Scottish material. Later publications have shown that their distribution extends further south (Stevenson 1976; Price 1988). Visual inspection of the Eildon examples has added little to the study of glass armlets. Therefore, chemical analysis was undertaken to characterise the properties of the glass and to test the hypothesis that they were manufactured in Scotland; only a small number of Romano-British glass armlets had previously been chemically analysed.

*Chemical analysis*
The technique used was electron-probe microanalysis. A micro-sample of *circa* 1 mm diameter was removed from each colour of glass on each artefact, mounted in epoxy resin, highly polished and coated with carbon to prevent distortion of the electron beam. Each sample was analysed at least three times to assess the degree of compositional variation, and the results averaged. A full description of the methodology is published elsewhere (Henderson 1988).

Analysis of the armlets (Table 2.6) shows that a basic soda-lime-silica composition with a low magnesia content was used in their manufacture. Various opacifiers, clarifiers and colorants were added to this glass to achieve the desired colouring effects. The opaque white glass (analysis *no* 1) contains 1.4% antimony oxide (as analysed), which probably formed part of calcium antimonate crystals (Henderson 1985), liberally distributed through the glass. Otherwise, the composition of this glass has the normal levels of manganese and iron oxides encountered in glass of this age (see below). Stevenson (1954, 218) suggested that the

opacity of these armlets was formed by the mechanical introduction of masses of gas bubbles into the glass. In this case, the glass is certainly bubbled (which would contribute to the opacity), but the chemical means of opacification is caused by calcium antimonate crystals.

The colour of the translucent, green glass armlet matrix [66] is very similar to that of many Roman Period glass vessels and one can postulate that melted down scrap vessel glass (cullet) was used in its manufacture; the antimony in this case can be regarded as an impurity. The principal colorant is iron oxide which is probably present in mixed higher (ferric) and lower (ferrous) oxide states, imparting a green colour to the glass in the presence of manganese oxide.

The opaque yellow decoration of armlet [66] has, again, a basic soda-lime-silica composition, but this has been modified by the addition of 11.5% lead oxide which would lower its melting and softening temperatures (analysis *no* 3). This would allow the glass to be applied as decoration to the green armlet matrix without distorting it. The opacity of the glass is probably caused by the presence of lead antimonate crystals modified, and given a more orange hue, by just over 1% of iron oxide.

An antimonate was also used for colouring the blue matrix of armlet [68]. Again, opacity appears to be caused by a dispersion of white calcium antimonate crystals in an overall translucent blue glass providing an opaque blue colour. The glass is of the soda-lime-silica composition; the blue colour is almost certainly due to iron in a reduced (ferrous) state or, just conceivably, due to very low (undetected) levels of cobalt. The lead oxide should also be considered as an impurity.

The green glass bead (analysis *no* 5) also has the soda-lime-silica type of composition. It has a different impurity pattern from the armlet glasses, with levels of manganese, iron and copper oxides at above 1% which would provide the green colour, probably dominated by copper. The relatively high levels of titanium oxide (0.2%) and lead oxide (1.8%) also distinguish this glass from that used in the armlets. The tin and possibly the lead oxides are likely to have formed scrap bronze possibly used in colouring the glass.

*Archaeological conclusions*
The soda-lime-silica composition of these glass armlets is similar to that of much Roman vessel glass in western Europe in the first and second centuries AD although, in the absence of a serious analytical study of such glass, precise correlations between vessel form and composition are lacking.

The armlet with the green matrix [66] may have been produced from re-melting cullet. However, in the absence of positive industrial evidence, for example melted and malformed armlets and armlet fragments, this cannot be proven. One possible example of the former was recovered from Eildon [67], but none of the latter. The one to one ratio of manganese oxide to iron oxide in the green armlet glass (and in the blue and white armlets), is often found in analysed Roman vessel

*Table 2.6   Electron-probe microanalysis of the glass.*

| analysis | 1 | 2 | 3 | 4 | 5 |
|---|---|---|---|---|---|
| artefact number | 65 | 66 | 66 | 68 | 64 |
| colour | opaque white | transp green | opaque yellow | opaque blue | transp green |
| element oxide | | | | | |
| NaO | 14.9 | 18.8 | 14.6 | 15.1 | 18.1 |
| MgO | 0.5 | 0.6 | 0.7 | 0.5 | 0.9 |
| $Al_2O_3$ | 2.6 | 2.4 | 2.5 | 2.3 | 2.5 |
| $SiO_2$ | 70.5 | 68.0 | 61.1 | 70.1 | 63.7 |
| $P_2O_5$ | 0.1 | 0.1 | 0.1 | 0.1 | ND |
| $SO_3$ | 0.2 | 0.2 | 0.1 | 0.2 | 0.2 |
| Cl | 0.8 | 0.9 | 0.7 | 1.1 | 1.2 |
| $K_2O$ | 0.5 | 0.7 | 0.6 | 0.5 | 0.4 |
| CaO | 6.9 | 6.0 | 5.3 | 7.5 | 5.9 |
| $TiO_2$ | ND | 0.1 | 0.1 | 0.1 | 0.2 |
| CrO | ND | ND | ND | ND | ND |
| MnO | 0.2 | 0.6 | 0.5 | 0.5 | 1.2 |
| $Fe_2O_3$ | 0.3 | 0.6 | 1.2 | 0.5 | 1.5 |
| $Cr_2O_3$ | ND | ND | ND | ND | ND |
| NiO | ND | ND | ND | ND | ND |
| CuO | ND | ND | MDL | ND | 1.2 |
| ZnO | ND | ND | 0.1 | ND | ND |
| $As_2O_3$ | 0.2 | ND | ND | ND | ND |
| $SnO_2$ | ND | 0.1 | 0.2 | MDL | 0.4 |
| $Sb_2O_3$ | 1.4 | 0.3 | 0.8 | 0.7 | ND |
| BaO | ND | ND | ND | ND | 0.2 |
| PbO | ND | ND | 11.5 | 0.4 | 1.8 |

| | |
|---|---|
| transp green | transparent green |
| ND | not detected |
| MDL | minimum detectable level |

glasses, indicating that a very similar stock of glass was used in both vessel and armlet production. Had the armlets been manufactured in Scotland from locally occurring raw materials, they would probably show different compositional characteristics.

Thus, while glass may have been worked into armlets, it is most unlikely that the primary raw materials were formed into glass at sites in Scotland. There is evidence for the shipment of scrap Roman glass in Europe but, as yet, no evidence for trade or movement of the primary raw materials into Scotland. The primary raw materials would include a mineral-based alkali, like natron, which would introduce *circa* 1% chlorine into the glass and a relatively low magnesia level; a clean

sand for silica; a lime source, though this may have been in the sand as shell fragments; and lead for the decorative glass. To the best of the writer's knowledge, there are no suitable alkali sources in Scotland which would provide the glass composition found in Roman glass – the plant ash as a source of alkali would produce a different composition.

The concentration of glass armlets in Scotland, however, indicates that they were probably manufactured there. The site of Traprain Law has produced large numbers of glass armlets, yet there is no proven manufacturing location. The only other site which has produced possible industrial evidence, perhaps relating to armlet production, but with no suitable glass vessel fragments, is Culbin Sands, Morayshire (Henderson, 1989a and 1989b). Glass beads were probably manufactured here, and the presence of melted armlet fragments may indicate that these also were manufactured at the site. No vessels in which glass would have been softened were discovered.

## Metalwork (Appendix 6) O A Owen · F M Ashmore

The metalwork assemblage consists of one complete and five fragmentary items of bronze; one complete and six fragmentary iron nails; and two modern coins.

### Bronze artefacts

The assemblage comprises one small chisel or metalworker's tool, two fragments of Roman Iron Age fibulae and four tiny fragments of sheet, the last found together. The remaining two fragmentary artefacts are unidentifiable.

The small tool ([69], Figure 2.14) found in Pit 2 is complete and in good condition. It is a tanged, chisel-shaped implement, and tool or file marks are visible at the tanged end where it originally fitted into a shaft or handle. X-Ray fluorescence showed the metal to be a leaded bronze (P Wilthew and A O'Berg, pers comm). The object is possibly a metalworker's tool, perhaps a tracer used for incising a pattern of straight or curved lines (Maryon 1938, 243), although it is smaller than most other examples (L 27 mm; W 7 mm; T 3.8 mm). The tool can be compared with five similar implements from the lowest levels of Traprain Law (Curle 1920, Figure 7.33–8, Figure 8.11–15), attributed to the Late Bronze Age (Burley 1955–6, 149).

One of the fragmentary Roman Iron Age brooches [71] is part of an unenamelled dragonesque fibula. All that survives is part of the central section of the body and the adjoining head, snout and ear, which are now bent at right angles to the better preserved body portion (Figure 2.15; Plate 2.10). The fragment is from a fibula exactly parallelled at Traprain Law (Cree & Curle 1921–2, Figure 28.4), which has a broken ear but is otherwise complete. The two objects are so similar that it is conceivable that they came from the same mould.

Such brooches are believed to date from the mid-first century to the later part of the second century AD, on the basis of the excavated examples (Bulmer 1938, 146–53; Feachem 1951, 32–44); and Collingwood & Richmond also postulate that the dragonesque fibula had a very short life (1969, 295), as did Burley in her re-examination of the Traprain Law evidence (1956, 159).

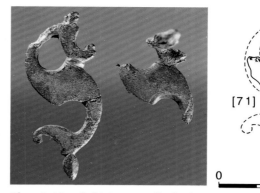

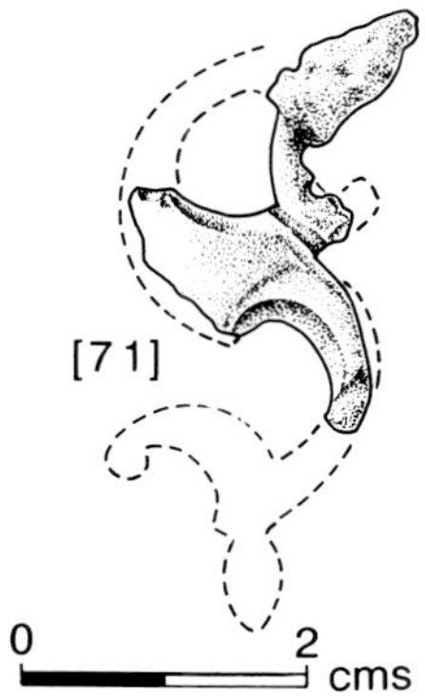

Plate 2.10 (left) Bronze fibula from Traprain Law (left) compared with the fragment from Eildon Hill North (right).
Figure 2.15 (right) The Eildon Hill North brooch fragment reconstructed.

The second putative fibula fragment from Eildon Hill comprises part of a pin with the remnants of the hinge still in place [72]. Unfortunately, the object is too fragmentary to allow the fibula type to be ascertained. Both fibula fragments were recovered from House Platform 1 (Episode 2) as were the fragments of sheet [73], the smallest of the two unidentifiable pieces, and three stones stained with bronze, probably from a completely corroded object (not catalogued). The larger of the two unidentifiable objects [70] was found in the disturbed upper levels of the south rampart at Entrance 2. Its original form and date are not ascertainable.

### Iron artefacts

The iron assemblage comprises seven complete or fragmentary nails. Five were found in the topsoil and the extensive area of modern burning overlying House Platform 3 and are not considered further. The two remaining nail fragments were found during excavation of the ramparts on either side of Entrance 2; one in the disturbed top levels of rampart core and one in the fill of a post-hole below the north rampart. Only this latter fragment may be *in situ* and it is poorly preserved [74]. A 'great many' iron nails were found on Traprain Law but most have corroded away or been lost (Burley 1955–6, 215).

### Modern coins (not catalogued)

Two coins were found in modern contexts, overlying House Platform 3; both in poor condition. One is a 'much abused and corroded' halfpenny of Edward VII, probably dating to 1902 (D Bateson, pers comm). The other is a silver threepenny coin of George V.

### Acknowledgements

Olwyn Owen and Fionna Ashmore wish to acknowledge the advice of Dr Mike Spearman, Richard Welander and Paul Wilthew on aspects of the bronze objects; and Donal Bateson, of the Hunterian Museum, Glasgow, for his help with the coins.

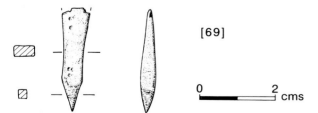

[69]

Figure 2.14 Bronze tool.

## Metalworking and vitrified debris (Appendix 7)
*R M Spearman · XRF analyses and comment P Wilthew)*

Metalworking debris from the site included ironworking slags, copper alloy scrap and coarse ceramic crucibles. The vitrified debris comprised both stones and clinker. One piece of baked clay lining was also found. The assemblage was examined visually at x10 magnification and checked for magnetic attraction. X-Ray Fluorescence analysis (XRF) of crucible rims and a selection of other non-ferrous metalwork and debris was undertaken in the Conservation and Analytical Research Department of the Royal Museum of Scotland.

### Ironworking slags
Metalworking slags from the site are all of the same type: dark brown, iron-rich, vesicular bloomworking or smithing slags. The production of bloomery iron is essentially a two-stage operation. Unlike non-ferrous metals, iron, with a melting point of 1525°C, was not produced in a molten form in simple low temperature bloomery furnaces. Instead, a fused mass of slag, metal, fuel and cinder was separated from the furnace and forged at temperatures around 1115°C. At this temperature, the slag and cinder softens and can be squeezed out to leave a purer, workable iron. The debris from these two separate operations is understandably similar and it is not clear from the small quantity of slag recovered whether only the first, or both processes were undertaken at Eildon Hill North.

There is no remaining evidence of artefactual smithing at the site although some iron nails were recovered. Ironworking debris was recovered from two locations on the hill, in the ramparts of Defensive System A at Entrance 2 and on House Platform 1 (Episode 2).

### Copper alloy scrap
A few pieces of run copper alloy were recovered from the upper occupation level of House Platform 1 (Episode 2). The larger pieces, one of which weighed 84.8 g, had evidently dripped onto and round the edges of flat stones.

### Coarse ceramic crucibles (Figure 2.16)
Seven fragments, five of them rim sherds, from coarse, large crucibles were recovered from the ramparts of Defensive System A at Entrance 2. In addition, there are seven, small, body sherds which have been strongly heated but, as these show no sign of vitrification, they may be from pots rather than crucibles. In general, only the inner surfaces and rims of the crucibles show any substantial signs of heat damage and vitrification, while their exteriors appear to be relatively lightly baked. Both coarse pottery and crucibles from Eildon Hill North were made from a clay tempered with poorly mixed grog and angular-grit, prone to angular fractures. There are no complete crucible profiles. However, all the rims are flattened and 14-18 mm thick. Three rim sherds [88, 89 and 90] retain sufficient form to indicate that at least some of these heavier crucibles were pieces of shallow bowls measuring *circa* 70 mm in internal diameter by 15–20 mm deep. The basal corner of another rim sherd [86] shallows to the rim in what may be the beginning of a spout. Two of the remaining fragments [91–92] appear to come from flat 'tiles' rather than bowls.

There is little indication of how these heavy shallow crucibles were used. It has been suggested (in connection with similar crucibles from Garranes and Garryduff I in Ireland) that they had been embedded in either sand or some form of container which could be used to help in pouring out their contents and that they were heated from above by a blow-pipe (O'Riordain 1942, 138, Figure 24; O'Kelly 1964, 96–8, Figure 21). This interpretation is applicable to the Eildon Hill North crucibles as their lower surfaces are relatively friable and show no signs of having been heated directly. Their poor fabric and low strength may have necessitated their being heated in this way.

The function of these crucibles has been little considered although O'Riordain has tentatively suggested that they were used for glass working (O'Riordain 1942, 138). However, XRF analysis of four of the Eildon Hill North crucible rims and one 'tile' fragment indicated that they had all contained a copper-lead-tin bronze; and antimony and/or nickel were present in most cases. These results indicate that the crucibles were used to melt bronze, and that the metal contained lead and perhaps low levels of antimony and/or nickel. The vitrification was consistent with a reaction between the metal and the clay fabric of the crucible. There was no evidence that glass rather than metal had been worked. Similar, open shallow crucibles have been found on a small number of sites, in contexts dating from the Late Bronze Age to the early historic period (Tylecote 1986, 96–100, 233–7; below). Thick bodied coarse fabric crucibles with flattened rims and similar areas of internal vitrification were found at Traprain Law, associated with mould fragments for Late Bronze Age metalwork (Burley 1956, 154 cat T53; NMS reg GVB 53 and 54a). Crucibles of this type were also found in the Late Bronze Age smith's workshop at Jarlshof (Hamilton 1956, 29; NMS reg HSA 3984, 3985). The Eildon Hill crucible fragments may also be Late Bronze Age artefacts. Other examples regarded as potentially Late Bronze Age include several fragments from shallow crucibles found at Green Castle, Portknockie (Spearman forthcoming), as well as a complete example found at Banchory in 1988 (NMS reg EC 28).

Similar crucibles have been recovered from a number of Late Iron Age/early historic sites. However, these are usually made of the more refractory clay which is also used to form the more normal, small and triangular crucibles of this period. Published examples of these include five fragments of what are described as 'dishes of uncertain purpose', found in the Pictish horizon at the Brough of Birsay (Curle 1982, 42, Figure 25; 413, cat 413–7). There are also examples of large thick-walled

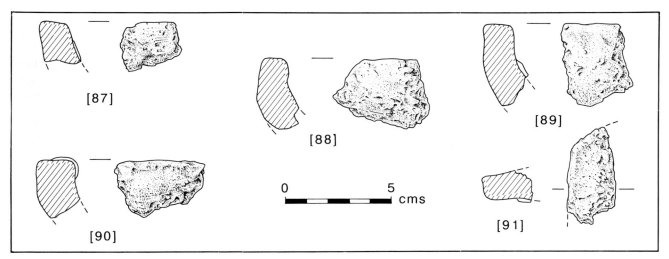

*Figure 2.16 Coarse ceramic crucibles.*

crucibles with internal vitrification from both Dunadd (NMS reg GP 228) and Dunollie (Duncan 1982, ii, 59–60).

### Vitrified stone and miscellaneous

There are two main types of vitrified debris from the site: a light, highly vesicular clinker, and lightly vitrified stone. All of the pieces are small, abraded and robust, and there are no indications of *in situ* vitrification. Some of this debris may have been produced in an industrial furnace, but a more likely explanation is a major fire. The majority of the pieces were found on House Platform 1 (Episode 2) or in its disturbed upper levels. Two pieces came from House Platform 3 and a few pieces were found in the ramparts of Defensive System A. A fragment of baked clay lining was also discovered overlying House Platform 1.

### Summary

The recovered debris mainly consists of vitrified stone and clinker, ironworking slags, copper-based alloy scrap and coarse ceramic crucibles. No mould fragments were recovered from the site but analysis of the crucibles from Defensive System A would suggest that bronze-working had taken place on Eildon Hill North. Unfortunately, these were found in disturbed contexts but may date to the Late Bronze Age on typological grounds. Metalworking activities are apparently confirmed by the discovery of droplets and run copper alloy scrap from House Platform 1 (Episode 2). The fragments of vitrified stone and ironworking slag are also predominantly from House Platform 1 (Episode 2). It is, however, unlikely that the vitrification or any metalworking took place in the immediate vicinity of the excavated areas. The quantity of debris is extremely small and no evidence of *in situ* vitrification or of any industrial features was recovered.

### Acknowledgements

Mike Spearman and Paul Wilthew wish to thank the Royal Museum of Scotland for the use of facilities in its Conservation and Analytical Research Department.

### Roman Pottery (Appendix 8) *J N Dore · thin-section petrology J Senior*

Seven fragments of pottery were examined, of which only four can be confidently pronounced Roman. Of these, one was found overlying House Platform 1 and another overlay House Platform 3. The remaining two were found in disturbed contexts in the ramparts of Defensive System A at Entrance 2. These four sherds date from the second to the fourth centuries AD with one of them [124] specifically dating to the fourth century. Provenances are suggested for two of them: an abraded fragment of a samian vessel [123] probably came from Central Gaul; and a rim sherd from a small mortarium [124] was almost certainly produced in the Oxford region, England. This latter is similar to Young's Oxford Ware vessel type, C100 (1977, 123, Figure 67); an example of the same type was also found on Traprain Law (Curle & Cree 1916). The unprovenanced wall sherds [121–122] perhaps both derive from a single vessel, a large, narrow-mouthed jar.

Of the other three sherds, one was found overlying House Platform 1, and two were recovered in levels associated with House Platform 1 (Episode 1). Only one sherd [125] is of sufficient size to merit further comment. It is a hand-made sherd, black throughout, with a well burnished outer surface. Its inclusions are angular, mostly under 0.5 mm diameter, but occasionally up to 2 mm diameter.

This sherd has been thin-sectioned and its petrology studied, in an attempt to ascertain its source and thence, possibly, its date. This has revealed that its fabric contained quartz, (small quantities only), feldspar, (mostly orthoclase, some plagioclase), biotite mica, and composite grains containing pyroxene and iron oxide. The angularity of the inclusions, combined with the presence of biotite mica, suggests that they were obtained by crushing rock. The minerals present are likely to have derived from an intermediate igneous rock, probably of non-local origin.

There are no features of the vessel which can be regarded as intrinsically 'Roman' although vessels of generally similar form are known from contexts of Roman period date at other sites (for example Murton High Crags, see Jobey & Jobey 1987; Figure 11, nos 12–14). The sherd is of particular significance in analysing the excavation results: it was found in apparently Late Bronze Age levels but, in fabric type, is quite unlike the coarse pottery assemblage which dominates these levels. All that can be said here is that it cannot unequivocally be declared not to be Roman.

*Acknowledgements*
John Dore would like to thank Dr J Senior of the Department of Continuing Education, University of Durham, for his comments on the thin section of pottery sherd [125].

## Coarse wares (Appendix 9) *V J McLellan*

The coarse pottery assemblage is comprised entirely of sherds which, on present evidence, are common to the Late Bronze and Iron Ages in lowland Scotland. There are 166 pieces (weighing 1.6 kg) in addition to the substantial remains of a large, flat-bottomed, coil-built, upright vessel [148] (3.7 kg). The bulk of the material comes from House Platform 1 (Episode 1), with a handful of sherds from overlying levels; the remainder was recovered from House Platforms 2 and 3, and from the ramparts of Defensive System A at Entrance 2.

Almost all the sherds from Defensive System A at Entrance 2 were found in the rampart cores which, from the mixed nature of their artefactual assemblages, had clearly suffered disturbance in antiquity and more recently. Thus, this material is both derived and conflated. All the sherds are abraded and measure less than 5 cm across (maximum); some two-thirds of this group measure less than 3 cm. Given that the average sherd size for the assemblage as a whole is *circa* 6 cm (excluding the almost complete vessel: [148]), coarse wares from Defensive System A at Entrance 2 had been exposed and worn, either before incorporation into the rampart matrix, or during its subsequent disturbance.

The pot sherds from the platforms are, in general, larger and less abraded. In particular, the large sherds from House Platform 1 (Episode 1), including a large rim section [147] and the largely complete vessel [148], indicate by their size and lack of abrasion that they had been abandoned *in situ*, or deposited there after the structure had fallen out of regular use.

Of the handful of sherds recorded from the Episode 2 levels of House Platform 1, all but two were found to join sherds from the Episode 1 levels. The remaining two sherds are indistinguishable in type from the rest of the coarse wares from this platform. This calls into question the stratigraphic integrity of the deposits. Given that none of the range of metal and other artefacts of the Episode 2 levels have found their way into the Episode 1 deposits, the presence of a few coarse wares in the Episode 2 levels is, perhaps, best explained by their having been brought up into the higher levels during the construction or use of the Episode 2 platform.

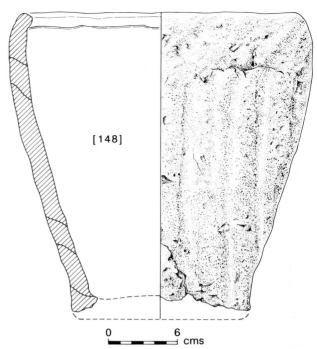

[148]

0        6  cms

*Figure 2.17   Coarse ware vessel from House Platform 1.*

Interpreted thus, it becomes clear that coarse wares were in common use during the Episode 1 use of the platform but may not have been used at all during the Episode 2 phase.

No decorated pieces were identified in the assemblage. One rim section [147] is dimpled with a neat row of fingertip impressions, but these are more likely to have resulted from rim formation than from deliberate decoration.

*Fabric descriptions*
The assemblage divides into four main fabric types:
Type 1: dark to very dark grey (10YR 3/4, 10YR 4/1), robust and tempered with angular grits;
Type 2: grey/light grey (7.5YR N6/0), easily abraded and tempered with angular grits;
Type 3: dark grey (2.5Y N4/0), very hard and tempered with small angular grits;
Type 4: grey (5Y 5/1) with no visible grits and quite robust.

A few sherds do not fall into any of the above categories (*eg* [160–161]). They are red (2.5YR 5/8), or burnt with powdery white surfaces.

The bulk of the assemblage is tempered with angular grits which are generally no larger than 10 mm and are well sorted throughout the fabric. Their presence gives the pottery a rather coarse appearance as they tend to protrude through the surfaces of the sherds. On House Platform 1, some 56% of the pottery is of fabric Type 1; the remainder is represented by thirty-seven sherds of Type 2 fabric, twenty-nine of which represent one vessel. The sherds from House Platform 3 are predominantly Type 3 fabric, with the remaining sherds appearing to have been burnt. Only eight sherds (all from Defensive System A at Entrance 2) are of fabric Type 4. These are thinner than the rest of the pottery, with no visible grits, although this does not necessarily imply that they have been more finely finished.

## Vessel shape (Figure 2.17)

All those sherds which were large enough to indicate angle and curvature were from flat-based vessels. From the base, the walls rose straight, or with a slight angle, for example [170]. The most complete example is [148] from House Platform 1. It stands 29 cm tall with a maximum diameter at the shoulder of 26 cm and a minimum of 15 cm at the base. The body of the vessel rises from an expanded base up to a gently inward curving shoulder and a rounded lip.

## Rim variations

Six different rim forms were identified: everted with either a rounded or flattened lip; inturned with either a rounded or flattened or obliquely flattened lip; or upright with a flattened lip. The sample is too small to detect reliable correlations between rim variation and fabric. Many rims have sooty residues on both interior and exterior surfaces.

## Discussion

The coarse ware assemblage from Eildon Hill North is not chronologically sensitive and relies on the radiocarbon determinations for its dating. On this basis, the majority of the pottery (from House Platforms 1 and 3) is apparently Late Bronze Age in date, *circa* ninth century BC. On the basis of their rim forms and fabrics, the sherds from Defensive System A could be ascribed to a similar period. Likewise, the few sherds recovered from House Platform 2 and House Platform 1 (Episode 2) may also be Late Bronze Age in date.

Even without radiocarbon dates, and allowing for variations due to regional differences of source material which will have influenced the refinements of the final product (Yarrington 1982, 176–177), the Eildon pottery, on the basis of vessel form, can be compared with assemblages from sites as diverse in location and type as Wardlaw Hill (Halpin below), Craighead (Rideout, forthcoming), Dalrulzion (Thorneycroft 1933, 196–206), Dalnaglar (Coles 1962, 153–4) and the native pottery from the lower levels at Traprain Law. Sherds 1–4, 6–7 and 10–11 from the Unenclosed Platform Settlement at Green Knowe, Peeblesshire (Jobey 1978, 85–87) are almost indistinguishable from those from Eildon although they are some 600 years earlier in date. This type of coarse pottery is thinner and finer than that described for the Middle and Late Iron Age by Cool (1982, 93).

To summarise, this ubiquitous pottery type does not seem to be diagnostic of any precise period. It seems likely that the open-necked, solid, sturdy shape and the relative coarseness of the vessels, were functionally appropriate and long-lived. This pottery tradition survived with little variation over the course of centuries and may even have had its roots in earlier urn production, as hinted at by Jobey (1980, 87).

## Acknowledgements

V J McLellan would like to thank Peter Hill, Olwyn Owen, John Barber and Finbar McCormick for comments on an earlier draft.

# PEDOLOGICAL AND PALAEOENVIRONMENTAL EVIDENCE

## Routine soil analyses *S Carter*

A soil sample was collected from every excavated context and analysed for pH, Loss on Ignition and phosphorus. In addition more detailed analyses of phosphorus content were carried out on a limited number of samples by the Department of Soil Fertility, Macaulay Land Use Research Institute.

*Results and discussion (see Appendix 10 for methods)*
Soil pH in distilled water was in the range 3.5–5.5 with most values between 4–5; these compare well with published values for soils of the Bemersyde Association (Ragg 1960). High values for Loss on Ignition (greater than 20%) were almost limited to modern surface soil horizons, with a maximum of 55% recorded from topsoil just below the summit-plateau. The only exceptions were three contexts in the ramparts of Defensive System A at Entrance 2. The field interpretation of these deposits was that they had been turves incorporated into the rampart construction; high Loss on Ignition values (of 31%, 25% and 40%), due to a high organic matter content, support this interpretation.

Spot Test phosphate analyses produced a low rating for easily available phosphate in the majority of samples (104), most of which were recorded in the collapsed ramparts of Defensive System A. Some five samples had a medium rating and fifteen had a high rating (Table 2.7). Of these twenty, five were modern surface contexts in which the enhancement of phosphate levels was probably the result of recent enrichment. The remaining fifteen include the hearth and three post-holes beneath Defensive System A, the floors and dispersed hearths of House Platform 1 (Episode 1) and House Platform 2, and Pit 2. Thus, the medium and high results correlate reasonably well with the better preserved features, floor and hearth deposits, and probably reflect the presence of decayed bone and other detritus. The only exception was material interpreted as undisturbed glacial till (beneath Defensive System A adjacent to House Platform 2); this also returned a high phosphate value which, if correct, suggests that phosphate must have been derived from overlying horizons.

Pit 1 showed increased levels of easily available phosphate. Initially interpreted as a quarry pit, no artefacts or ecofacts were recovered from the fill; thus, further analysis of the phosphorus content was undertaken in an attempt to discover the nature of the enhancement. Seven samples collected across the base fill of the pit were analysed for total phosphorus and acetic acid extractable phosphate. For comparison, seven other

*Table 2.7   Contexts with medium (M) or high (H) ratings for easily available phosphate.*

| context | rating |
|---|---|
| pre-rampart (DS-A) | |
| hearth material | H |
| stone hearth-base material | H |
| burnt material | M |
| clay and silt at rampart base | M |
| Pit 2, fill | H |
| Defensive System A, At Entrance 2 | |
| post-hole fill | H |
| post-hole fill | H |
| post-hole fill | M |
| turf in rampart core | H |
| House Platform 1, Episode 1 | |
| floor level | H |
| dispersed hearth | H |
| House Platform 2 | |
| glacial till (beneath) | H |
| platform preparation | M |
| floor level | H |
| dispersed hearth | H |
| modern | |
| topsoil (various areas) | H |
| | M |
| | H |
| burnt material | H |
| | H |

samples, which had not shown phosphate enhancement, were also selected for analysis. The results of the analyses are presented in Table 2.8.

Published data for subsurface soil horizons in the Bemersyde Association (Ragg 1960, 152, 158) give total phosphorus values in the range 1240–1920 mg/kg and acetic acid extractable in the range 10–39 mg/kg. This suggests that, for the archaeological samples, total phosphorus is not significantly high but the acetic acid extractable fraction is. There is a close correlation between the acetic acid and spot test results but neither of these correlate with total phosphorus. The acetic acid extraction data are therefore a quantified version of the spot test data and must be identifying the same fraction of the total phosphorus in the soil. Those samples with high levels of acetic acid extractable phosphate also have a higher percentage of their total phosphate in this form.

Therefore, enrichment of the easily available fraction has occurred, rather than an overall increase in all phosphate fractions. This result confirms that Pit 1 is most unlikely to have been a quarry pit; and is more likely to have contained detritus, or perhaps an animal burial (like Pit 2), or even a human burial. Thus, although the precise identity and source of the Pit 1 enrichment is unknown, it is clearly anthropic.

*Conclusion*

The overall characteristics of these samples are typical of soils of the Bemersyde Association. High phosphate spot test ratings appear to correctly identify areas with enhanced levels of easily available phosphate. It is not clear what human activity has caused this enrichment but for floors and hearths, normal food preparation and occupation activities would account for its presence.

**Animal bones (Appendix 11)** *F McCormick*

Only calcified bone or, to a lesser extent, animal teeth survived on Eildon Hill North, due to the acidity of the soil. In all cases, the calcified bone was extremely denuded and survived only as tiny unidentifiable fragments. The largest fragments came from Pit 2. Only here does the inner, spongy cancellous bone survive as well as the outer compact surface of some of the fragments. This implies that at least some of the material did not undergo surface abrasion prior to deposition as seems to be the case with the burnt material from other areas.

The identifiable material consisted of cattle teeth from the ramparts of Defensive System A, at both points examined; as well as ten teeth from a mature horse in Pit 2. The horse teeth consist of five premolars and five molars from two matching mandibulae. No incisors or canines were present. Since there is no reason why the absent teeth should have preferentially decayed, this indicates that the anterior part of the mandibulae had been removed prior to deposition. However, the pit was not fully excavated and the missing teeth may lie in the undisturbed deposit. More than 260 small, burnt and unburnt fragments were also found in Pit 2. None were identifiable to species, but a small number were from the skull of a large animal. On the basis of the extant evidence, horse is the only species known to be represented in the pit and, therefore, the burial of a partly cremated, mature horse is tentatively suggested. However, the value of this observation is reduced by the poor preservation of the excavated fragments and the incompleteness of the excavation.

Burnt bones, even if identifiable, usually represent such a small proportion of a faunal assemblage that where they alone survive, they are likely to mislead rather than inform. This was clearly demonstrated at the site of Haughey's Fort, a hillfort in Co. Armagh, Ireland. Soil conditions in that site's interior were such that 98% of the surviving bone was burnt while, in the waterlogged bottom of the enclosing ditch, burnt bone accounted for less than 5% of the well-preserved

*Table 2.8  Total phosphorous, acetic acid extractable and easily extractable phosphate content of selected samples (mg P per kg of air-dried soil).*

| context | 1 | 2 | 3 | 4 |
|---|---|---|---|---|
| Pit 1; samples collected longitudinally across rock-cut profile | | | | |
| sample    1 | 9<br>136 | 860<br>1940 | 1.0<br>7.0 | H<br>H |
| 2 | 84 | 1060 | 7.9 | H |
| 3 | 110 | 990 | 11.1 | H |
| 4 | 109 | 1090 | 10.0 | H |
| 5 | 134<br>179 | 870<br>910 | 15.4<br>19.7 | H<br>H |
| 6 | 128 | 1090 | 11.7 | H |
| 7 | 150 | 1430 | 10.5 | H |
| Defensive System A, at Entrance 2 | | | | |
| post-hole fill | 6 | 610 | 1.0 | L |
| north rampart core | 30 | 750 | 4.0 | L |
| south rampart core | 8 | 1170 | 0.7 | L |
| bedrock surface | 13 | 880 | 1.5 | L |
| House Platform 1, bedrock surface | | | | |
| sample    1 | 89 | 890 | 10.0 | L |
| 2 | 50 | 1230 | 4.1 | L |
| 3 | 21 | 760 | 2.8 | L |

1  acetic acid extractable
2  total
3  1 as a percentage of 2
4  easily extractable (spot test rating)

assemblage (McCormick 1988, 24). At Eildon, where only fifteen of the 2357 recovered fragments are identifiable (to horse and cattle), no reliable conclusion can be reached on the animal husbandry practices of the site or on the role of domesticated animals in its economy.

## Pollen record *S Butler*

The shallow, aerated mineral soils and archaeological deposits on Eildon Hill do not readily appear as material suitable for pollen analysis. In general terms the depositional and post-depositional characteristics of such deposits differ significantly from the waterlogged peat and lake sediments that pollen analysts normally seek, but their value lies in their direct association with archaeological features. Their pollen content might thus relate to the local vegetation of the settlement area and to the human use of plants within that settlement. The palynology of archaeological sites and soils is discussed by Dimbleby (1985), and there has recently been

growing interest in the palynology of on-site, excavated contexts, much of the methodology deriving from North American research (Bryant & Holloway 1983; Holloway & Bryant 1986; Schoenwetter 1987; Pearsall 1989). The analysis of Eildon presented here took place in 1986 as a pilot study aimed primarily at assessing pollen preservation and concentration in excavated contexts as a preliminary exploration of the site's archaeopalynological potential. Samples were collected routinely by the excavation team, and a selection of fifteen samples was submitted for pilot analysis after excavation was complete. It must therefore be stressed that the study is not based on a fully integrated specialist archaeopalynological research design.

### Results
From each sample a sub-sample of 2 ml wet sediment volume was processed using alkali digestion, microfiltration and swirling (Funkhouser & Evitt 1959; Cwynar *et al* 1979; Hunt 1985). The preservation and concentration of pollen was found to be highly variable,

*Table 2.9  Pollen record. Values are expressed as percentages of total pollen. Total pollen excludes ferns (Filicales) and unidentified.*

| | DSA | | | | HP1 | | | | | | | | HP2 | | HP3 |
|---|---|---|---|---|---|---|---|---|---|---|---|---|---|---|---|
| context *no* | 318 | 143 | 192 | 109 | 216 | 214 | 213.1 | 213.2 | 212 | 208 | 207 | 201 | 303 | 319 | 705 |
| *Pinus* | | | | 0.34 | | | | | | | | | | | 3.90 |
| *Tilia* | | | | | | | | 1.10 | | | | | | | |
| *Quercus* | 4.35 | 3.29 | 2.37 | | 7.02 | 1.43 | | 1.10 | | | | 0.49 | | | |
| *Betula* | | | 0.95 | 2.04 | | | | | 0.90 | | 0.61 | 0.98 | | | 1.30 |
| *Alnus* | | 8.45 | 6.16 | 0.68 | 22.81 | 10.00 | 2.94 | 2.20 | 1.35 | 3.79 | 1.22 | 2.94 | | 2.27 | 2.60 |
| Coryloid | 2.61 | 38.03 | 29.86 | 12.59 | 15.79 | 10.00 | 7.35 | 5.49 | 13.90 | 9.00 | 25.00 | 15.69 | 16.13 | 11.36 | 16.88 |
| *Salix* | | | | 0.68 | | | | | 0.45 | | | | | | |
| Ericaceae | 17.31 | 2.82 | 31.28 | 12.59 | 15.79 | 25.71 | 32.35 | 9.89 | 42.60 | 40.28 | 30.49 | 44.61 | 14.52 | 17.05 | 35.06 |
| Gramineae | 62.61 | 24.41 | 20.85 | 0.68 | 24.56 | 21.43 | 29.41 | 31.87 | 24.22 | 35.07 | 22.56 | 15.69 | 33.87 | 37.50 | 22.08 |
| Cyperaceae | | | | 54.42 | | 4.29 | 4.41 | 1.10 | 3.59 | 0.95 | 0.61 | 0.49 | | | |
| *Plantago* undiff | 1.74 | 7.04 | 4.27 | 11.56 | 3.51 | 1.43 | 2.94 | 1.10 | 3.59 | 3.32 | 4.27 | 9.80 | 8.06 | 7.95 | 2.60 |
| Compositae lig | 0.87 | 0.47 | 0.95 | 0.34 | | 10.00 | 5.88 | 14.29 | 3.59 | 1.42 | 1.83 | 3.92 | 9.68 | 14.77 | 3.90 |
| Compositae tub | 0.87 | 3.76 | 1.42 | 8.50 | 3.51 | | | 2.20 | 1.79 | 0.95 | 0.61 | 1.47 | | | 1.30 |
| Caryophyllaceae | | 5.63 | | 3.06 | | | 1.47 | 2.20 | | 0.47 | 2.44 | | 3.23 | 2.27 | |
| Chenopodiaceae | | 2.82 | | 2.38 | | | | | | | 0.61 | | | | |
| Cruciferae | | | | 0.68 | | 1.47 | | | | | 0.61 | | | | 1.30 |
| Labiatae | | | | 0.68 | | | | | | 1.42 | 1.22 | | | | |
| Rumex | | | | | | | | | | | 0.61 | | | | |
| Filipendula | | | | | | | | | 0.45 | | | | 1.61 | | 1.30 |
| Umbelliferae | | | | | | | | | | | | | 1.61 | 1.14 | |
| *Urtica* | 1.74 | | | | | | | | | | 1.83 | | | | |
| Succissa | | | | | | | | | | 0.47 | | | | | |
| Potentilla type | | | | | | | | | | 0.47 | | 2.45 | | | |
| *Galium* type | 0.87 | | | | | | | | | 1.42 | | 1.47 | 1.61 | 1.14 | 5.19 |
| *Sphagnum* | | | | | | | | | | 0.47 | 3.05 | | | | |
| *Pteridium* | 3.48 | | | | | | | | | | 1,83 | | 9.68 | 4.55 | 1.30 |
| Filicales | 36.52 | | | | | | | | | 2.37 | 6.71 | 1.96 | 16.13 | 2.27 | |
| unidentified | 4.35 | | | | | | | | | 13.27 | 4.88 | 8.82 | 56.45 | 13.64 | 35.06 |
| trees and shrubs | 6.96 | | | | | | | | | 12.79 | 26.83 | 20.10 | 16.13 | 13.63 | 24.67 |
| herbs | 89.57 | | | | | | | | | 86.26 | 67.68 | 79.90 | 74.19 | 81.82 | 72.73 |
| pollen sum (number of grains) | 115.00 | | | | | | | | | 211.00 | 164.00 | 204.00 | 62.00 | 89.00 | 77.00 |
| total concentration ($10^3$ grains/ml) | 16.27 | | | | | | | | | 170.20 | 116.72 | 137.13 | 14.56 | 18.20 | 88.73 |

Defensive System A (DSA)

318   fill of Pit 2, beneath DSA
143   pre-rampart hearth, at Entrance 2
192   post-hole fill, south rampart, at Entrance 2
109   core material, north rampart, at Entrance 2

House Platform 1 (HP1), Episode 1
216   levelling horizon
214   vestigial occupation deposit
213.1   dispersed hearth
213.2   dispersed hearth
212   upper occupation/abandonment level

House Platform 1 (HP1), Episode 2
208   ?levelling horizon
207   vestigial occupation level
201   ?abandonment

House Platform (HP2)
303   floor level
319   dispersed hearth

House Platform 3 (HP3)
705   floor level

in some cases exceptionally poor, and it was often difficult to achieve substantial pollen counts (Table 2.9). Some of the samples are characterised by large amounts of fern spores or large amounts of deteriorated and unidentifiable pollen. These fern spores and unidentified types have been excluded from the sum used for percentage calculations because they tend to mask variations in other taxa when included in the sum. As a result, only six of the fifteen samples have pollen sums greater than 200 grains, and a further two have sums greater than 100 grains. The samples with low pollen sums tend to be those with large numbers of unidentifiable grains, and this is a clear warning that post-depositional decay of pollen has significantly devalued their information content, probably biasing these spectra in favour of more resistant pollen types.

In the discussion which follows, an attempt is made to interpret those samples with good pollen preservation and concentration, and hence higher pollen sums. The interpretations are limited and very tentative because, as a pilot analysis, the data set provides scant coverage of the site, and lacks the replication and controls advocated by Bryant and Holloway (1983). Furthermore, post-depositional movement of pollen down through the deposits has probably occurred with soil leaching, and the effects of this are impossible to evaluate without a more comprehensive data set incorporating stratigraphic sampling down selected soil profiles.

## Discussion

*Pre-rampart hearth, beneath Defensive System A at Entrance 2*   This spread of hearth material was found beneath, and hence pre-dates, the inner rampart of Defensive System A. Tree and shrub pollen comprise *circa* 50% TLP, with Coryloid the main contributor. This suggests that some woodland or scrub dominated by hazel or sweet gale existed on Eildon Hill prior to the building of the ramparts. The large amounts of fern spores (Filicales) would be consistent with a woody or scrubby environment. The value of *circa* 50% for tree and shrub pollen suggests a light, fairly open woodland, or a local clearing on the hilltop with generally quite well wooded hillsides, and the occurrence of *Plantago* pollen at 7% TLP further suggests the local existence of open ground. As a hearth deposit, the possibility has to be considered that some of the pollen derives from fuel supplies. Woodland pollen adhering to the bark and twigs of firewood collected from further afield would, for example, give a distorted spectrum unrepresentative of the local environment. In this respect it is interesting that charcoal fragments of *Corylus*, *Alnus* and *Quercus* occur in this hearth material (McCullagh, below).

*Post-hole fill, south rampart, Defensive System A at Entrance 2*   Interpretation of pollen from such contexts is complicated by uncertainty over the age and derivation of the fill material itself. For example, more cohesive subsoil rather than loose topsoil may have been preferred for supporting the post, so that older pollen would be incorporated, while later material may also have collapsed into the hole after disuse. Tree and shrub pollen representation is less than in the pre-rampart hearth (above), but still attains a value of *circa* 40% TLP and fern spores are still abundant. The main difference between the two spectra occurs in the Ericaceae values, which are much higher (31.3%) in the post-hole fill and indicate some heathland vegetation. This suggests either: *i* different environments and perhaps different dates for the post-hole and the hearth, or *ii* contamination of the post-hole pollen with younger or older material representing a different (heathland) environment.

*North rampart terminal core material, Defensive System A at Entrance 2*   This material was comprised

partly of clearly recognisable turves and had apparently slumped downslope some time after construction. Thus it is again difficult to be sure of the age of the pollen, since it may derive from pre-rampart soils used in construction, and/or from vegetation growing over the ramparts either during or after use. The spectrum is dominated by Ericaceae pollen at 54.4%, while tree and shrub pollen and fern spore values are rather low at 16.3% and 5.4% respectively. The material thus contains more heathland and less woodland pollen than both the hearth and the post-hole. A *Plantago* value of 8.5% suggests quite open conditions but it is surprising that the Gramineae value is only 11.5%, and it may be that *Plantago* was growing as a settlement ground ruderal rather than in grassy pasture. Heathland and woodland environments are not particularly favoured by *Plantago* species where grassy places are as limited as the Gramineae pollen value suggests.

*House Platform 1, Episode 1, upper occupation/ abandonment level*   The origin of the pollen, which is mostly Ericaceae and Gramineae, is correspondingly uncertain. If we assume that all the pollen is contemporary and relates to the temporary period of abandonment of House Platform 1, then a local heath-grass association is probably represented. Although specific level determination of Ericaceae pollen was not made, it is thought that *Calluna vulgaris* is mainly represented. Work by Evans and Moore (1985) indicates that in a grass/heather moorland values of *circa* 40% TLP for *Calluna* pollen are quite common even from the more grassy patches where *Calluna* itself is absent from the immediate (1 m radius) locality. Thus it may be that the abandoned house platform was a grassy patch within a more general heath-grass mosaic on Eildon hill. Tree and shrub pollen at 16.5% indicates insubstantial local woodland, but certainly a regional (hillside or beyond) presence.

*House Platform 1, Episode 2 ?levelling horizon*   Pollen transport mechanisms to such a deposit as this may include wind-blown pollen arriving from the surrounding vegetation but some concentration of certain taxa by the house inhabitants may also have come into play. There is however no anomalous concentration of a particular taxon in the pollen spectrum, and it seems to more simply reflect the local hilltop vegetation. Ericaceae (40%) and Gramineae (35%) are again the best represented taxa, but Gramineae pollen representation is higher than found in the abandonment phase material (above), and it would seem that grasses were locally dominant. Grasses, together with most of the other recorded herb taxa, would perhaps be expected to characterise the settlement area vegetation, either as gardens, pasture or waste ground beside houses and paths. A value of 40% Ericaceae pollen reminds us, however, that heathland was never very far away, while 12.8% tree and shrub pollen suggests that trees were sparse or more distant components of the vegetation.

*House Platform 1, Episode 2 ?abandonment*   Again, the origin of the material is not clear and it may be a disturbed soil (Jordan, above). If the pollen is contemporary with abandonment then it seems to register a decrease in grasses and an increase in *Plantago*, Compositae liguliflorae, and *Potentilla* since the prior occupation. This could be a reflection of a spread of 'weeds' and ruderals with abandonment of the house, and it is tempting also to point at the increase in tree and shrub pollen from 12.8% to 20.1% as a reflection of a more general decline in occupation at the site, allowing some regeneration of woodland or scrub in the area.

*Other contexts*    Interpretation of the other nine contexts is hampered by low pollen sums and high numbers of deteriorated pollen grains. In five of these, the unidentified pollen count exceeds 35% of the total pollen content, but in the remaining four contexts unidentified pollen is less than 13.5%. These latter four spectra therefore seem to have been less heavily influenced by post-depositional decay of pollen. The discussion ends with consideration of these four spectra, but it must be borne in mind that their pollen sums comprise less than 200 grains.

*Fill of Pit 2, beneath Defensive System A*    The derivation of this pit fill is uncertain, and similar problems to those of the post-hole fill apply (see above). The pollen spectrum is, however, noticeably different to that of the post-hole fill and is dominated by Gramineae pollen at 62.6% TLP. Tree and shrub pollen representation is low (*circa* 7%) and fern spores are not particularly abundant (36.5%) compared to some other contexts. If all this pollen is contemporary then a grassland flora seems to be indicated, together with some heathland (Ericaceae 17.4%). The relative abundance of grass pollen contrasts with all other contexts examined, including those also occurring beneath the ramparts. Without more secure dating and depositional information and more comprehensive pollen sampling, it is not known whether this variation reflects temporal or spatial variation in the extent of grassland, heathland and woodland. Further taphonomic considerations raise questions such as whether there is an association between the abundance of Gramineae pollen in this pit fill and the presence of a partial horse skeleton in the same context (McCormick, above).

*House Platform 1, Episode 1, dispersed hearth*    Pollen analysis was undertaken of the soil matrix surrounding a pot sherd on which an organic residue was found. However, the pot residue yielded only a single, corroded grass grain (non-cereal type) together with some unknown fungal and algal remains, and was found to consist largely of heavily blackened organic fragments. The blackening is probably due to burning, although there was little complete charring. The pollen spectrum from the soil matrix is dominated by grass pollen (*circa* 32%), but also contains significant proportions of Compositae liguliflorae and *Urtica* type pollen. Fern and bracken spore representation is also significant at *circa* 60% and *circa* 19% respectively. It is possible that the plants of all these taxa had specific uses to the house inhabitants, but it is equally easy to

envisage grasses, ferns, bracken, dandelions and nettles growing round about the settlement area.

*House Platform 1, Episode 2, vestigial occupation level*    The pollen spectrum from this putative later occupation level in House Platform 1 differs from both the underlying and overlying spectra, and this tends to reinforce its designation as a separate context. At 25% TLP, Coryloid pollen is well represented and is roughly on par with the representation of Ericaceae (*circa* 30%) and Gramineae (22.5%). As with all these Eildon samples, taphonomic questions remain unresolved, but it would appear that the extent of woodland was greater than that evidenced palynologically in the levelling horizon. It would be interesting to test the idea, through further pollen sampling, of a possible pattern of higher woodland pollen representation occurring in abandonment rather than occupation deposits from the house platforms.

*House Platform 2, dispersed hearth*    Although the pollen spectrum from the floor surface itself is in much poorer condition, the relative representation of identified taxa is quite similar in both samples. Local, presumably settlement area, grasses are represented together with *Plantago* and Compositae liguliflorae herbs, but heathland pollen is less well represented than in the House Platform 1 floor surfaces. Again it is not known, however, whether this difference reflects temporal, spatial or other taphonomic influences.

*Conclusion*
Pilot analysis of the Eildon on-site contexts has shown that archaeopalynological data can be obtained from these deposits, but the preservation and concentration of fossil pollen is highly variable. The data certainly contains information about the vegetation of the settlement and summit area, and this information is relevant to the phasing, occupational history and environmental conditions of the settlement, and to the activities of its inhabitants. Three or four main vegetational units appear to be evidenced in the samples so far analysed; woodland, heathland/heath-grass, and grassland/settlement ground flora, and these provide some parameters for an initial reconstruction.

However, lack of contextual and taphonomic information currently prevents detailed interpretations and firm conclusions, and the interpretations discussed above are presented as preliminary hypotheses, developed from an exploratory analysis and now requiring critical evaluation through a more comprehensive archaeopalynological research design. This research design should pay attention to understanding the varying temporal and spatial scales, taphonomic characteristics and interpretive relevance of pollen deposition and survival in different types of context.

**Carbonised material *R P J McCullagh***

Analysis of the carbonised material was undertaken in two stages. In the first, samples were selected from specific deposits for radiocarbon dating. These were identified to guard against the inclusion of exotic or introduced species. Nine samples were subsequently submitted for dating.

In the second stage, a series of twelve hypotheses about the nature of specific contexts, or groups of contexts, were proposed by the excavator. These questions were addressed by analysis of the state of preservation of the charcoal and the species diversity of each of the samples. A further four samples were submitted for dating.

### Methodology

Carbonised material was collected by hand during excavation, either from discrete patches or from diffuse spreads within specific contexts, and by flotation of bulk soil samples in post-excavation. All the material recovered from a single context, by whichever means, was amalgamated.

The samples were dried, then washed or sieved as appropriate, and the flots recovered in 1 mm and 0.3 mm sieves. They were re-dried and stored in aluminium foil. The 1 mm retent usually produced identifiable fragments of carbonised wood. The 0.3 mm retent commonly contained rounded soil masses and comminuted wood charcoal, too small to identify to species. It was examined for the presence of carbonised seeds and fruits. The non-floating retent was also examined to check for carbonised material which had not been released from the soil in the elutriator.

Identifications were made using a binocular microscope at magnifications up to x190. Specimens with transverse cross-sectional areas of as little as 5 by 5 mm can be identified. The term 'roundwood' is used to describe any wood which does not display signs of working. However, almost all the charcoal survived as small angular pieces and no tool marks or cut facets were observed.

### Results (Table 2.10)

### Defensive System A, Entrance 2

The pre-rampart hearth contained a wide range of species represented by a mixture of angular and rounded fragments. With the exception of oak, the charcoal all came from small diameter roundwood. About half the oak specimens came from more mature wood with tyloses in the vessels indicating that heartwood was present. Some of the oak may have been root wood, the ring boundaries being indistinct; the remaining oak component consisted entirely of angular, radially split fragments. Only two small fragments of elm were recovered, one from the hearth and one from House Platform 3, suggesting that, even if growing locally, elm was not commonly used as firewood. This hearth material also contained carbonised fragments of grass stems, small twigs and some sclerotia, the over-wintering bodies of the fungus, *Cenococcum geophilum*.

The fills of the post-holes beneath the north and south rampart terminals each contained charcoal of a single species, either alder or hazel, and two features also contained heather. However, as none of the charcoal seemed to have derived from wood greater in diameter than *circa* 20 mm, it cannot represent the remains of posts. It is likely to have been residual, or re-deposited, in the post-holes.

The samples from the south rampart terminal produced more charcoal than those from the north, but neither produced significant amounts and the material was highly abraded, in the main. In general, specimens consisted of small fragments of small diameter roundwood, with few of the slower grown timbers present. Several pieces retained the bark and one clear branch node of hazel was noted. Again, hazel is preponderant. This charcoal is likely to be firewood-derived and residual in the contexts from which it was recovered.

### Defensive System A, adjacent to House Platform 2

Pit 2 (beneath the rampart of Defensive System A) produced a wide range of species, shapes and sizes, most specimens being angular, radial fragments of roundwood, originally 20–50 mm in diameter. The 0.3 mm sieve also produced burnt bone fragments (McCormick, above), and three carbonised barley grains.

### House Platform 1, Episode 1

The sample from the floor surface contained a relative abundance of charcoal representing a range of species. It included numerous large fragments with angular facets, mostly from 30–50 mm roundwood. It is likely to represent the debris of firewood. Unusually, oak charcoal is absent from this assemblage.

The samples from the dispersed hearth produced an abundance of charcoal, of a wide range of species, in a mixture of rounded and angular fragments usually of 20–50 mm diameter roundwood, with a few pieces of larger diameter roundwood present. One or two fragments retain the bark, while some are highly glossed suggesting that they may have been reburnt. Fragments of burnt bone and carbonised barley grains were recovered. This material is likely to be derived from firewood and food preparation activities.

Charcoal from the upper, 'abandonment' levels was mostly angular fragments of small diameter roundwood, but some specimens came from timber of 50–100 mm diameter. It occurred as relatively large, unabraded fragments and there was very little comminuted charcoal in the sieve and no burnt bone or other domestic refuse. This implies a different, though still local, origin for this charcoal from that in underlying horizons.

### House Platform 1, Episode 2

Charcoal retrieved from the putative floor level shows a wide range of species but the suite is dominated by hazel. The samples contained a mix of rounded and angular fragments of small diameter (40 mm) roundwood. Sieving produced much comminuted charcoal and burnt bone fragments, and some small

*Table 2.10   Carbonised wood identification. The number of identified fragments is given in parentheses. Weights are expressed in grammes.*

| context | | species | total weight |
|---|---|---|---|
| Defensive System A, Entrance 2 | | | |
| pre-rampart | hearth base | hazel (5) | 1.6 |
| GU-2190 GU-2370 | hearth material | alder (15), birch (10), hazel (32), Pomoideae (2), *Prunus* (21), oak (23), willow (1), elm (1) | 73.9 |
| | hearth material | oak (10) | 18.6 |
| north rampart | post-hole fill | alder (1) | 0.1 |
| | post-hole fill | alder (1), heather (1) | 0.4 |
| | post-hole fill | hazel (1) | 0.2 |
| south rampart | post-hole fill | hazel (4), heather (1) | 6.3 |
| | gateway feature | alder (1) | 0.1 |
| north rampart | core | hazel (4) | 0.7 |
| | core | hazel (5) | 1.6 |
| south rampart | core | hazel (3) | 1.4 |
| | core | birch (2), hazel (5), *Prunus* (1), oak (2) | 38.8 |
| | core | alder (1), birch (3), hazel (24), willow (12), heather (1) | 27.4 |
| Defensive System A, adjacent to House Platform 2 | | | |
| Pre-rampart, fill of Pit 2 GU-2197 | | alder (8), birch (7), hazel (9), ash (4), *Prunus* (1), willow (14), heather (1), barley (3) | 98.7 |
| House Platform 1,  Episode 1 | | | |
| floor surface GU-2195 | | alder (5), birch (8), hazel (4), *Prunus* (2), willow (1) | 32.1 |
| dispersed hearth GU-2194 | | alder (3), birch (26), hazel (13), ash (1), *Prunus* (7), oak (6), willow (20), heather (1), barley (2) | 22.5 |
| abandonment *i* GU-2193 | | alder (5), birch (6), hazel (1), willow (8) | 23.3 |
| *ii* | | alder (1), hazel (9) | 10.6 |
| House Platform 1, Episode 2 | | | |
| Level 1 GU-2192 GU-2371 | | alder (4), birch (10), hazel (32), ash (2), Pomoideae (2), oak (1), *Prunus* (4), willow (10), heather (4) | 42.2 |
| Level 2 GU-2191 | | alder (5), birch (6), hazel (4), willow (1), heather (1) | 13.2 |
| abandonment | | alder (1), birch (4), hazel (3) | 3.4 |
| House Platform 2 | | | |
| floor surface GU-2196 | | alder (6), hazel (26), willow (4), barley (3) | 24.8 |
| dispersed hearth GU-2372 | | alder (2), birch (3), hazel (25), ash (1), *Prunus* (1), oak (4), willow (4), heather (2), seeds (3) | 32.7 |

| House Platform 3 | | |
|---|---|---|
| fill of curvilinear slot | hazel (10), *Prunus* sp (2) | 3.4 |
| fill of post-hole | hazel (6) | 1.9 |
| floor level (mostly from fire-base area) GU-2198 | alder (4), birch (4), hazel (10), ash (8), *Prunus* sp (2), oak (10), willow (6), elm (1) | 60.0 |

carbonised twigs and stems, probably of heather, were also noted. It is interesting to note that this suite is similar to that from the dispersed hearth of the Episode 1 platform, rather than its floor. The sample from the upper level produced smaller quantities of charcoal of small diameter roundwood, and two fragments of birch representing wood of perhaps 100 mm diameter. Generally, the fragments are angular and unabraded, some retaining their bark. Carbonised twigs and heather stems were observed. It is possible that some of these fragments, particularly the birch, may have derived from wood used in the house structure.

Only eight specimens were identified from the 'abandonment' level, all of which were rounded, fragile and in small pieces.

*House Platform 2*
The samples from the floor surface produced small amounts of abraded charcoal, all of small diameter roundwood. The dispersed hearth contained a much larger assemblage with a wide range of species represented but hazel predominant. Most fragments were rounded, abraded and fragile, and came from small diameter roundwood. Sieving produced carbonised twigs, barley grains and burnt bone fragments. Again, this is likely to be firewood-derived with other food preparation debris incorporated.

*House Platform 3*
All the fills of features on Platform 3 were analysed for charcoal but what little was found was, in the main, finely comminuted. Two fragments of cherry were identified from the curvilinear slot; the other pieces were hazel. The source of the charcoal cannot be ascertained.

The relict floor surface produced a small assemblage but a wide range of species, hazel and oak being most often identified. The fragments were a mix of angular and rounded pieces of both fast and slow grown roundwood of 20–50 mm diameter. The oak was derived from mature wood, and the presence of a single specimen of elm is noteworthy. Comminuted charcoal was present in the 0.3 mm sieve.

*Conclusion*
The conversion of wood to charcoal is a selective process and seldom preserves more than a fraction of the original wood used on the site. Furthermore, the link between the morphology of the charcoal and the original function of the wood may not be a strong one. The taphonomy of the charcoal-bearing contexts needs

careful consideration if the possibility for mixing of non-contemporaneous fragments exists on the site.

The dispersed hearths on House Platforms 1 and 2 produced considerably more, and a wider range of species of charcoal than their associated floor deposits, although the suites were generally similar. Analysis of charcoal recovered from the exceptionally poorly defined stratigraphic units perceived on House Platform 1 (Episode 2) seems to confirm the distinction made on site between occupation and abandonment levels. The dubious origins of charcoal retrieved from the fills of rock-cut features has been noted, indicating that nothing of the original posts has survived.

The majority of the assemblage derives from probable hearth contexts, in which unworked roundwood was often used for fuel, which was probably consumed in the form of faggots or slender rods. There is a preponderance of hazel in the samples with alder and birch appearing persistently and, to a lesser extent, willow and oak.

DATING EVIDENCE   *O Owen · with M Dalland*

The provision of a reliable dating framework for settlement on Eildon Hill North was one of the primary aims of the excavation strategy. Dating evidence was restricted to radiocarbon assays and diagnostic artefacts. Ambient radioactivity on the hilltop was high and rather variable (D Sanderson, pers comm), and it was considered inadvisable to undertake thermoluminescence dating (Appendix 12). The radiocarbon dates are calibrated and discussed below, and then compared with the chronological evidence of the artefactual assemblages. The calibration is based on Dalland (forthcoming).

**Radiocarbon calibration** *M Dalland*

The calibration was based on data from Pearson *et al* (1986). The calibration data, usually at twenty dendro-year intervals, were interpolated to five-year intervals. From this data, calibration matrices were calculated which show the probabilities that radiocarbon concentrations (age BP) stem from samples of known (dendro) ages. The calibrated probability distribution for each date was then calculated from its uncalibrated normal probability distribution, using the calibration matrices. The probability distributions of the Eildon dates are presented in Figure 2.18.

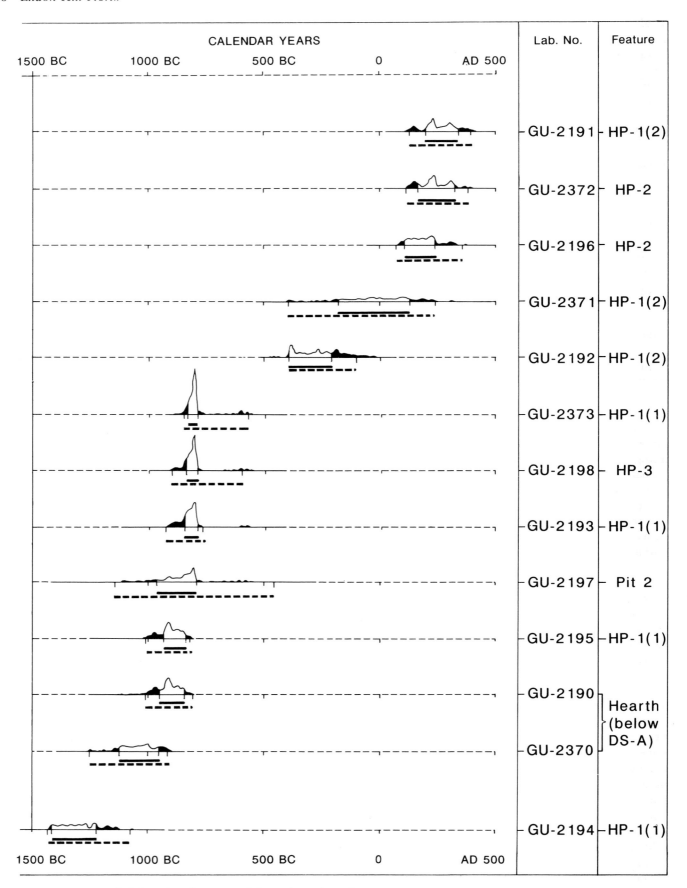

*Figure 2.18    Probability distributions of the radiocarbon dates.*

Table 2.11  *Radiocarbon calibration: pre-rampart hearth at Entrance 2.*

| lab *no* | uncalibrated age BP | calibrated SCR | calibrated LCR |
|---|---|---|---|
| GU-2190 | 2760 ± 50 | 950–840 BC | 1010–810 BC |
| GU-2370 | 2870 ± 50 | 1125–950 BC | 1255–920 BC |
| combined | 2815 ± 35 | 1005–915 BC | 1115–900 BC |

Table 2.12  *Radiocarbon calibration: House Platform 1, Episode 1.*

| lab *no* | uncalibrated age BP | calibrated SCR | calibrated LCR |
|---|---|---|---|
| GU-2373 | 2600 ± 50 | 830–790 BC | 850–570 BC |
| GU-2193 | 2650 ± 60 | 850–795 BC | 930–770 BC |
| GU-2195 | 2750 ± 50 | 930–830 BC | 1005–815 BC |
| GU-2194 | 3020 ± 60 | 1415–1225 BC | 1430–1080 BC |

Table 2.13  *Radiocarbon calibration: House Platform 3.*

| lab *no* | uncalibrated age BP | calibrated SCR | calibrated LCR |
|---|---|---|---|
| GU-2198 | 2620 ± 60 | 840–795 BC | 905–600 BC |

Since the calibration is based on data at five-year intervals, the calibrated distributions appear as histograms where the heights of the bars reflect the probability that the age of the sample lies within the five-year bar-interval.

It is therefore possible to calculate the probability that the date falls within any specified period. Based on such calculations, the probabilities that a date would fall within specific centuries are sometimes quoted in the text.

The tabular summaries (Table 2.11–2.16) show the shortest continuous calibrated range which adds up to probabilities equal to or greater than 68.26%, the Short Continuous Range (SCR), and 95.45%, the Long Continuous Range (LCR). These values are the same as those for the 1σ and 2σ ranges of normal probability distributions.

*Late Bronze Age (Table 2.11–2.14)*

*Pre-rampart hearth at Entrance 2 (Table 2.11)*  The two samples, of mixed wood species, derive from the same sealed and undisturbed archaeological deposit and therefore date the same event. The combined uncalibrated dates cannot be assumed to be different at the 95% confidence level; they are therefore best represented by their weighted mean and standard deviation. This shows that it is 72% probable that the calibrated date of this hearth falls within the tenth century BC, and 92.4% probable that it lies within the eleventh to tenth centuries BC.

*House Platform 1, Episode 1 (Table 2.12)*  Taphonomically, material from the lower dark band, interpreted as a vestigial floor horizon was, by Eildon standards, relatively secure, as was carbonised material

from the dispersed hearth. Of the four samples submitted, the upper level of 'floor' deposit was considered the most vulnerable to possible contamination. However, given the rare survival of visible stratigraphy at this level, it was hoped that, together, the four samples would furnish evidence of the date of this episode of platform use with, perhaps, some indication of the duration of its occupation. In fact, the Episode 1 floor and one of the two uncalibrated dates from the dispersed hearth, cannot be said to be different at the 95% confidence level. Their weighted mean is 2669 ± 30, giving calibrated ranges of 850–810 BC (SCR) and 895–805 BC (LCR).

The remaining House Platform 1 (Episode 1) date, also from the hearth, is significantly different from the other three Episode 1 dates (3020 ± 60 uncalibrated). Given the high degree of correspondence between the other three results, it seems likely that this date is aberrant and it is not considered further here.

Thus, there is a 99% probability that House Platform 1 (Episode 1) dates to the ninth century BC and a 77% probability that it dates to the first half of the ninth century BC.

*House Platform 3 (Table 2.13)*  Stratification on this platform was less well-preserved and less securely sealed than that on House Platform 1 (Episode 1). Material was carefully collected from a discrete area in the vicinity of the fire base. The resulting date correlates remarkably well with that for House Platform 1 (Episode 1), a corroboration which strengthens confidence in its accuracy. It is 81% probable that the calibrated date of House Platform 3 falls between 850 and 750 BC; it is 69% probable that it lies between 840 and 795 BC. The hypothesis that House Platforms 1

*Table 2.14    Radiocarbon calibration: Pit 2.*

| lab *no* | uncalibrated age BP | calibrated SCR | calibrated LCR |
|---|---|---|---|
| GU-2197 | 2680 ± 130 | 960–790 BC | 1145–455 BC |

*Table 2.15    Radiocarbon calibration: House Platform 1, Episode 2.*

| lab *no* | uncalibrated age BP | calibrated SCR | calibrated LCR |
|---|---|---|---|
| GU-2191 | 1760 ± 50 | AD 200–345 | AD 130–400 |
| GU-2371 | 2000 ± 130 | 175 BC–AD 130 | 395 BC–AD 240 |
| GU-2192 | 2200 ± 60 | 400–210 BC | 400–105 BC |

*Table 2.16    Radiocarbon calibration: House Platform 2.*

| lab *no* | uncalibrated age BP | calibrated SCR | calibrated LCR |
|---|---|---|---|
| GU-2372 | 1780 + 50 | AD 165–325 | AD 115–380 |
| GU-2196 | 1820 + 60 | AD 110–240 | AD 75–360 |
| combined | 1796 + 38 | AD 135–245 | AD 120–330 |

(Episode 1) and 3 are broadly contemporary was examined. Comparison between this date and the dates of the floor levels and dispersed hearth of House Platform 1 (Episode 1) shows that there is a 68.5% probability that the two platforms were in use within 30 years of each other.

*Pit 2 (Table 2.14)*    Pit 2 was sealed beneath the rampart of Defensive System A and, thus, the dated material from its fill was securely stratified. Unfortunately, the uncalibrated date of Pit 2 has a standard deviation of 130 years which is reflected in the calibrated ranges (170 years at SCR and 690 years at LCR). The statistical comparisons between this and other dates in the sequence are not possible. However, it is 68% probable that Pit 2 dates to the tenth to ninth centuries BC and, 95% probable that it dates to the Later Bronze Age (1200 to 500 BC).

*Iron Age (Table 2.15 & 2.16)*

*House Platform 1, Episode 2 (Table 2.15)*    The dates from House Platform 1 (Episode 2) have proved difficult to reconcile internally, falling, as they do, within an unfavourable area of the calibration curve. Stratigraphically, the Episode 2 platform was poorly preserved, even by Eildon standards, and no hearth site was identified. With hindsight, it was perhaps folly to attempt to date this episode, given the nature of the deposits from which the samples were collected. However, the two earlier dates derive from a single recorded context which was interpreted as the relict floor horizon; the later date derives from the deposit immediately above this. The boundaries between these deposits, and between these and others above and below them, were indistinct but the dates do reflect the stratigraphy as recorded in the field. Both deposits produced a significant quantity of artefactual debris,

unlike those higher up the profile, the diagnostic components of which seem to be Roman Iron Age in type and to correlate better with the younger date (below).

The two older dates from the lower, recorded level are significantly different from the date from the upper, Episode 2 level. There is a 69% probability that the calibrated difference between the two levels is 355–600 years, which is not explicable on stratigraphic grounds and must raise some doubt about the taphonomy of the material used for radiocarbon dating. This is supported by examination of the artefactual inclusions, particularly coarse pottery (below), which indicate mixing of the lower floor deposit with material from the underlying Episode 1 platform. Given the clear (Episode 2) evidence of a major re-cutting of the rock at the back of the platform, it seems reasonable to assume that some mixing must have occurred during construction of the later platform and, specifically, during levelling of the surface in front of the rock-cut scarp to form the floor of the later platform. Therefore, despite the fact that the two older dates cannot be said to be different at the 95% confidence level, the results are at best ambiguous. Equally, given the lack of clear horizonation, it seems inadvisable to reject the earlier dates in favour of the later date which may also have been contaminated, perhaps in this case by material washed onto the platform following its abandonment. Two courses are open to us, either to discount the dates as unreliable; or to interpret them together, but cautiously, as representing a maximum date range. On this basis, House Platform 1 (Episode 2) dates to some period between the third century BC and the fourth century AD.

*House Platform 2 (Table 2.16)*    Stratification on House Platform 2 was better preserved, with occupation levels and a dispersed hearth site interpreted in the field with reasonable confidence. The two dates, one from the hearth material and the other from the dark band interpreted as an occupation level are only 40 radiocarbon years apart. They were therefore combined on archaeological and statistical grounds. The result shows that the platform is almost certainly Roman Iron Age in date; it is 99% probable that it dates to the second to mid-fourth century AD, and 63% probable that it dates to the mid-second to mid-third century AD.

*Acknowledgement*
Magnar Dalland would like to thank John Barber for his advice during calibration and analysis of the radiocarbon dating results.

## Artefactual dating

The usefulness of the Eildon artefactual assemblages for dating varies. The stone tools, for example, are undiagnostic while the pottery and jet are of types which were in use over several centuries. None of the assemblages are large enough to trace the development of a specific type over the life of the site. Added to this is the problem that many of the finds which can be more closely dated have come from contexts which were disturbed in antiquity, or more recently. In general terms, the timespan represented by the artefacts is the Early Bronze Age to the fourth century AD, although certain groups of artefacts can be dated more specifically within this range.

The only datable chipped stone find from Eildon is the barbed and tanged arrowhead [47] from the rampart of Defensive System A. This artefact was derived in the context in which it was found. It falls into the Conygar Hill type (Green 1980, 192), which is found throughout Britain and is commonly associated with Food Vessel pottery of the Early Bronze Age (McCartan, above).

The coarse, heavy crucible fragments [86–98] recovered from the rampart core of Defensive System A at Entrance 2 are comparable with fragments found at Traprain Law, associated with fragments of Late Bronze Age moulds (Burley 1956, 154, cat T 53; NMS reg GVB 53 and 54a). Other, less well-dated, examples are also regarded as potentially Late Bronze Age (Spearman, above). These are also derived in the context from which they were retrieved.

A small bronze tool [69] from the top of Pit 2, beneath the rampart of Defensive System A, is similar in type to a group of small chisels retrieved from the lowest levels at Traprain Law (Curle & Cree 1921, 164–5, Figure 10.5–14). These have been designated Late Bronze Age by analogy with four implements in the hoard from Loch Trool, Kirkcudbrightshire and one from Heathery Burn Cave, Durham (Curle & Cree 1920–1, 165; followed by Burley 1956, 146–9; Owen & Ashmore, above).

The fragment of unenamelled dragonesque fibula [71] is from a type dated from the mid-first century to the later part of the second century AD, and is exactly

paralleled by a find from Traprain Law (Cree & Curle 1921–2, Figure 28.4; above). The fibula pin (cat *no* 72), too fragmentary to permit identification of the fibula type, is probably also Roman Iron Age. Both fibula fragments were found on House Platform 1 (Episode 2).

Jet armlets seem to have been in common use from the Late Bronze Age (Heathery Burn Cave, Durham; Britton & Longworth 1968) to the eighth century AD (Buiston Crannog, Ayrshire; Munro 1882, 232; Stevenson 1976, 50; Kemp above). They add little to our understanding of the chronology of this site.

The coarse pottery assemblage is not diagnostic to a specific period in itself but, at Eildon, it occurs overwhelmingly in contexts radiocarbon dated to the Late Bronze Age. The few sherds which do not derive from House Platforms 1 (Episode 1) and 3 mostly occurred in contexts where they are likely to have been re-deposited, for example levelling for House Platform 2, and the rampart core of Defensive System A at Entrance 2. The value of this observation is strengthened by the fact that, of the handful of sherds from House Platform 1 (Episode 2), only two did not join sherds from the better preserved Episode 1 levels. This evidence suggests that coarse wares are absent from the areas examined, in levels post-dating the Late Bronze Age.

Three glass armlet fragments are somewhat more diagnostic. Found on House Platform 1 (Episode 2), on House Platform 2 and in the upper levels of the rampart of Defensive System A at Entrance 2, they are all likely to have been manufactured in the first to second centuries AD (Henderson & Kemp, above; Stevenson 1976). The glass bead, also from the upper levels of the rampart of Defensive System A at Entrance 2, is of a type current from the first century BC through Roman times into the post-Roman period (Guido 1978, 92, 95, Figure 37.5).

Four sherds of Roman pottery were recovered. Two [121–2], found in the rampart core of Defensive System A at Entrance 2, may derive from the same vessel and are dated to the second to fourth century AD (Dore, above). A fragment of samian [123], which overlay House Platform 1, dates from the first half of the second century AD; and part of the rim of a small mortarium [124], which overlay House Platform 3, is from the fourth century AD. Previously recovered stray finds of Roman pottery are similarly dated. These include fragments of fine fumed grey platter (second century AD, or later), red Nene Valley ware (third century AD) and two fragments of black jar (third or fourth century AD) (Robertson 1970, Table vi).

A number of the finds are modern (not catalogued). These include iron nails, glass vessel sherds and two twentieth-century coins. They derive primarily from the ramparts of Defensive System A at Entrance 2 and from burnt deposits overlying House Platform 3.

## Integrating the chronologies

Table 2.17 illustrates a degree of corroboration between the radiocarbon dates and the dates indicated by the

*Table 2.17  Correlation of dating evidence.*

| period | feature | radiocarbon dating | artefactual dating |
|---|---|---|---|
| EBA | Defensive System A, rampart core | none | chert arrowhead |
| LBA | Pre-rampart hearth | 810 bc ± 50<br>920 bc ± 50 | none<br>bronze tool |
| | Pre-rampart, Pit 2 | 730 bc ± 130 | bronze tool |
| | Defensive System A, rampart core | none | crucible fragments; coarse pottery |
| | House Platform 1, Episode 1 | 700 bc ± 50<br>1070 bc ± 60<br>800 bc ± 50<br>650 bc ± 50 | coarse pottery |
| | House Platform 3 | 670 bc ± 50 | coarse pottery |
| RIA | Defensive System A, rampart core | none | glass armlet; glass bead; Roman pottery |
| | House Platform 1, Episode 2 | ad 190 ± 50<br>250 bc ± 60<br>50 bc ± 130 | two fibula glass fragments; glass armlet |
| | House Platform 1, post-abandonment | none | Roman pottery |
| | House Platform 2 | ad 130 ± 60<br>ad 170 ± 50 | glass armlet |
| | House Platform 3, post-abandonment | none | Roman pottery |
| modern | rampart core | none | iron nails; glass vessels |
| | House Platform 1, topsoil | none | glass vessels |
| | House Platform 3, topsoil | none | glass vessels; 20th-century coins |

EBA   Early Bronze Age
LBA   Late Bronze Age
RIA   Roman Iron Age

artefacts. Both indicate that there are at least two, distinct phases of activity on Eildon Hill North, one in the Late Bronze Age and one in the Roman Iron Age.

Most importantly, the internal consistency of the chronological indicators suggests that the destructuring of the soil stratigraphy has not markedly affected the distribution of artefactual and other debris. It seems that the natural processes which have caused masking of the soil stratigraphy (Jordan, above) have not, in the majority of cases, caused its total destruction.

Thus, the two Pre-Roman Iron Age radiocarbon dates, initially thought to have come from an uncontaminated, Episode 2 floor level, may in fact derive from mixing carbonised material from Late Bronze Age and Roman Iron Age levels. There is no evidence for an intermediate Episode 1/2 level. The balance of the evidence is, therefore, that House Platform 1 (Episode 2) is more likely to date to the Roman Iron Age. A fragment of samian, dating to the first half of the second century AD (Dore, above), was found in the deposit immediately above the dated, upper 'floor' level (calibrated date: 130–400 ad at the 2σ confidence level). It is interesting to note in this respect that the better stratified, Roman Iron Age House Platform 2 produced radiocarbon dates which closely correlate with the

uppermost, House Platform 1 (Episode 2) date; and the two platforms are immediately adjacent to each other.

**Summary of chronology**

*Phase 1: Early Bronze Age*
Early Bronze Age activity on the hill is represented by a single, uncontexted barbed and tanged arrowhead.

*Phase 2 (Periods 1 and 2): Late Bronze Age*
The features attributed to this period include the hearth and Pit 2 beneath the rampart of Defensive System A, House Platform 1 (Episode 1) and House Platform 3. To these may be added the Late Bronze Age artefacts. Furthermore, analysis of the radiocarbon dates indicates that two, Late Bronze Age periods may be represented among the dated features. The hearth probably dates to the early first millennium BC; Pit 2 may be slightly later and is, perhaps, roughly contemporary with the ninth-century BC house platforms (above).

*Phase 3: Late Bronze Age to Roman Iron Age*
The ambiguous dating of House Platform 1 (Episode 2) suggests that the apparently pre-Roman Iron Age radiocarbon dates from that site should be discounted.

Defensive System A has not been closely dated but it is stratigraphically later than two Late Bronze Age features (the pre-rampart hearth and Pit 2); and pre-dates House Platform 2, which dates to the Roman Iron Age. A Late Bronze Age or Early Iron Age date is probable but not proven, at least for the inner circuit of Defensive System A at the points examined.

*Phase 4: Roman Iron Age*

House Platform 2 was occupied during the Roman Iron Age. Additionally, it has been very tentatively suggested that House Platform 1 (Episode 2) was in use during the Roman Iron Age (above).

### Interpretation of excavated features

No Early Bronze Age features were excavated. An Early Bronze Age presence on the hill has been inferred from the discovery of the barbed and tanged arrowhead alone.

Three, probably unrelated, pre-rampart features are ascribed to the Late Bronze Age; the hearth and Pit 1 below the south rampart of Defensive System A at Entrance 2; and Pit 2, below the same Defensive System, some 130 m north of Entrance 2. The hearth has been radiocarbon dated to the tenth century BC; while Pit 2 has been dated to probably slightly later, in the early first millennium BC, indicating that the feature may be closer in date to House Platforms 1 (Episode 1) and 3 (Phase 2; below). Fragments of burnt bone from the hearth indicate that it was used for cooking. The attribution of Pit 1 to this period is not certain and no datable material was recovered. However, its proximity to the hearth and its similar stratigraphic relationship to the overlying rampart may indicate their rough contemporaneity. The dating and character of the hearth and Pit 1 indicate that there are probably contemporary settlements on the hill which have yet to be identified.

Pit 1 has unusually high phosphate levels, at its base. These may have derived from domestic rubbish or excreta dumped in the pit; however, its brashy fill contained no anthropic material. The irregular profile of the pit and its location indicate that it is unlikely to have contained a human burial. It may, however, have contained a ritual burial of animal or, indeed, of human remains.

Among the artefacts incorporated into the later rampart cores at Entrance 2, of Defensive System A, was a group of probably Late Bronze Age crucible fragments. Their presence here indicates that Late Bronze Age metalworking may have taken place in the vicinity of the hearth and Pit 1 since the rampart core material was almost certainly collected locally (above).

Pit 2 is slightly later than the hearth. Bone and charcoal inclusions within its fills indicate that at least the partial remains of one mature horse were deposited in this pit, probably partly cremated. Like Pit 1, this also may have been a rubbish pit, but it is possible that the deposition of horse bones was a ritual act. A bronze metalworking tool [69], recovered from its topmost fill, was probably an accidental inclusion. If the horse

remains in Pit 2 were a ritual deposit associated with the establishment of the rampart this would imply that the rampart also is Late Bronze Age in date.

House Platforms 1 (Episode 1) and 3 are roughly contemporary, radiocarbon dated to approximately the ninth century BC. They share a common artefactual assemblage dominated by coarse pottery and small groups of stone artefacts.

On Platform 1 (Episode 1), a considerable effort was expended in quarrying out the platform. That the excavated area probably embraced the majority of the platform is supported by the distribution pattern of the finds (Figure 2.8). An oval platform was created, its long axis parallel with the contours. The finished platform offered considerably more shelter from the elements than was readily available in the vicinity.

Re-use of the platform (in Episode 2) had obliterated the upper part of the original, rock-cut back face, but this may have stood more than 1 m high. Given its conjectured height and verticality, the rock-cut back face might have obviated the need for walling here. It is notable that the burnt material of the dispersed hearth spreads almost to the base of the cut face, precluding the insertion of house walling along the rear of the platform.

On the platform, the floor surface and vestigial occupation deposits were significantly firmer than other stratigraphic units; the greater compaction of these layers tends to support their interpretation. Charcoal from the dispersed hearth and associated levels, all from small diameter roundwood, probably derives from firewood. The presence of two carbonised barley grains and burnt bone fragments indicates food preparation and consumption on the site.

The artefactual assemblage comprised a small number of stone objects, and *circa* seventy sherds of coarse pottery, probably from cooking vessels. The almost complete cooking vessel [148] from the hearth area may have been abandoned *in situ*. Pollen analysis of its residues was uninformative. Pottery sherds were found distributed in a broad band across the centre of the excavated area, but two concentrations appear to be present, one around the hearth area and one on the north half of the platform (Fig 2.8).

On House Platform 3, there was little evidence of platform preparation, in spite of its exposed west-facing, location on the hilltop. The platform was backed against an insubstantial rock scarp and the gently sloping bedrock was used as a floor, without major alteration. The front of the platform had been levelled with a deposit of shattered stones and coarse gravel. Over this, lay the artefact-rich floor deposit.

It is probable that the rock-cut features once housed the ends of timbers, or perhaps wattle walling in the case of the curvilinear slot. There is insufficient evidence to permit detailed reconstruction, although a building some 7 m in diameter is indicated. The presence of two carbonised barley grains and of quantities of burnt bone, in the hearth deposit, indicate that cooking took place within this structure.

A setting of stones, mostly burnt, located towards the front of Platform 3, has been interpreted as a hearth base. A reddish-brown gravelly clay covered the platform on a level with the hearth and contained artefactual debris; this has been interpreted as a relict 'floor' level. Charcoal from this level probably represents firewood. Burnt bone fragments were also recovered. Amongst the artefacts a quern rubber, quern and pounder were found in the fill of the curvilinear slot, and a further quern rubber was found in the floor level. These indicate that the grinding of grain occurred at this site. The coarse pottery sherds probably derive from cooking vessels.

Thus, a range of domestic activities appear to have taken place on both of the excavated Late Bronze Age platforms. Despite the virtual absence of indications of a superstructure on either platform, these activities are likely to have taken place within the shelter of buildings of some type.

Defensive System A is stratigraphically later than the pre-rampart hearth and Pit 2 (Late Bronze Age features of the tenth and ninth centuries BC), and earlier than Platform 2, which dates to the Roman Iron Age. In the absence of evidence for settlement in the interval between these periods, Defensive System A is likely to be either Late Bronze Age or Pre-Roman Iron Age. The absence of A- and B-horizon development between the pre-rampart features and the rampart base indicates that the rampart was probably erected in the earlier part of the interval, *ie* that it is a Late Bronze Age rampart. The slender basis, and tentative nature of this chronological interpretation must be emphasised.

Only the inner circuit of the triple ramparts of Defensive System A was examined. It appeared to stand more than 1.5 m above the general hill slope before excavation but proved to be more impressive in plan than in section, having suffered considerable disturbance and erosion. This was equally true of the rampart terminals at Entrance 2 and the rampart adjacent to House Platform 2.

At Entrance 2, differences of constructional detail between the rampart terminals north and south of the entrance are at least partly attributable to differences in topography. The north rampart took advantage of a natural scarp, while the builders of the south rampart employed greater quantities of stonework and core, presumably to achieve height and stability. The core material was dominated in all the examined sections by homogeneous, reddish clayey loam and stones. However, it contained varying amounts of rubble, more on the south than the north; decomposed turves were included in places on the north; and quantities of loose brash with little soil were incorporated into the core on the south. The impression is one of exploitation of whatever materials were at hand to form the earth and stone bank, rather than any specific seeking out of particular kinds of core materials. This, combined with a deliberate effort to exploit the underlying topography wherever possible, would have reduced the amount of construction work required, and must, to some extent, have determined the detailed siting of the ramparts.

The rampart core had slumped and spread in all the examined sections and its original width, height and appearance cannot be determined. From the amount of spread core material, it seems unlikely that the ramparts were substantial constructions.

There is some inconclusive evidence that both the north and south terminals of Entrance 2 may have been outlined by posts whose precise function is not clear (Figure 2.4). If so, the north rampart terminal had a rounded end and turned slightly inwards, while the south terminal had a more pointed end and turned slightly outwards. The rock-cut slots and post-holes arranged in pairs across the track through the entrance have been interpreted as the scant remains of footings for a timber gate construction. This interpretation is based on their relative positions. Defensive System B, at least at the point examined, revealed negligible structural evidence. Its course coincides with the pronounced edge of the intermittent terrace which marks the boundary of the summit-plateau. This line marks a natural point of defence, the ground falling away steeply on all sides especially to the north, west and south, and, in places, its ascent is extremely difficult today. The occupants of the fort may have had to do little more than rely on the hill's natural topography in order to defend or enclose themselves adequately along the line of System B. There are some surface indications of a bank construction along its less well naturally defended south-west sector; the RCAHMS notes the existence of a '. . . fragment of a wasted rampart, 8 ft thick and only 1 ft high, near the east end of the south margin of the plateau . . .' (RCAHMS 1956, 309). This might, on excavation, yield more structural and datable evidence than was recovered in 1986.

The two rock-cut features on the line of Defensive System C were ambiguous and discontinuous, and they provide insufficient evidence to either substantiate or refute the earlier identification of this System on aerial photographs. Both features may equally well be interpreted as traces of non-defensive structures, particularly houses. The poor condition of the rock surface on the hill, combined with the possibly insubstantial character of any original enclosure, may also frustrate future attempts to recover more conclusive evidence unless large areas are opened.

House Platform 2 is dated to between the second and fourth centuries AD and, at the 67% confidence level, may have been in use sometime between the early second and mid third centuries AD. With considerably less certainty, it has been suggested that House Platform 1 (Episode 2) is also Roman Iron Age in date (above). Its attribution to the Roman Iron Age should be treated cautiously.

House Platform 1 (Episode 2) was superimposed on the Episode 1 platform and faced roughly south-west. The vertical cut face at the back of the early platform was re-cut on a slightly different alignment and up to 2.5

m further back into the rock. At the foot of the new rock face a level rock surface was created which was truncated by the earlier cut in front (Figure 2.9). On this rock ledge four roughly rectangular slots were discovered. These are interpreted as scant structural remains which may have once housed the ends of timbers. Whether this is sufficient evidence to confirm the presence of a structure on the platform is debatable.

The presumed abandonment and, perhaps, hillwash levels which had accumulated over the Episode 1 platform were used to form an earthen floor for the Episode 2 platform. Here, archaeological stratigraphy was particularly difficult to discern, a problem highlighted by the ambiguous nature of two of the radiocarbon dates, the samples for which may have been retrieved from the mixed and indistinct interface between the two platform levels (above). The consistent presence of artefacts and increased charcoal inclusions in a particularly stony level was interpreted as evidence of a relict 'floor', but no hearth area was distinguished. It was equally difficult to locate precisely the level at which the Episode 2 platform fell out of use and hillwash began to accumulate again.

The artefactual assemblage was notable for metalworking debris (run metal masses, bronze fragments, vitrified stones and clinker, a hammerstone *etc.*) and some bronze artefacts of Roman Iron Age type. It is likely that metalworking activities had taken place in the vicinity, although there is insufficient evidence to postulate that the Episode 2 platform functioned specifically as a metalworking area. The preponderance of metalworking debris, almost to the exclusion of other artefact types, militates against the argument that this material had washed on to the platform after its abandonment. Had the assemblage derived from hillwash, a greater mix of materials would be anticipated.

All but two of the few sherds of coarse pottery recovered from the lower level proved to be parts of vessels from the Episode 1 platform (fabric Types 1 and 2). This evidence corroborates the radiocarbon evidence of the post-depositional mixing of materials at an intermediate Episode 1 abandonment/Episode 2 establishment level. Furthermore, it may indicate that coarse wares are absent from the Episode 2 phase of platform use, since the non-joining two sherds are of the same type as the large quantity of Episode 1 pottery. No pottery was found in the perhaps less disturbed, upper dated horizon whose inclusions consisted entirely of metal fragments and metalworking debris.

It seems likely that the Episode 2 builders were unaware of the existence of the earlier rock-cut platform since it would certainly have been easier to have excavated and re-used the original site. Given the time span ranging from more than half a millennium, at a minimum, to more than a millennium, between the two episodes of use of the same site, this is hardly surprising.

Although House Platform 2 was only examined in a 1.5 m wide trench, the charcoal-rich hearth area was located roughly centrally on the platform. The charcoal was probably derived from small diameter kindling. Three carbonised barley grains were recovered. The only diagnostic artefact was part of a glass armlet of probable first- to second-century AD date [68]; part of a jet armlet [63] was also recovered. Three sherds of coarse pottery (fabric Type 1) were probably re-deposited in platform preparation levels. No pottery was found in the darker, occupation and dispersed hearth deposits, which tends to support the contention that coarse wares are absent from excavated features post-dating the Late Bronze Age. The platform appears to have had a domestic function but, again, no structural evidence for a house was found although, here, this may be at least partly due to the limited scale of excavation.

Apart from the metalwork and glass armlet fragments found on Platforms 1 (Episode 2) and 2, four sherds of Roman pottery were recovered, all re-deposited, dating to the second to fourth centuries AD [121–4]. These, together with earlier stray finds of Roman pottery, testify to probable Roman connections (below).

Modern disturbance of the ramparts of Defensive System A at Entrance 2 was evidenced in the mixed artefactual assemblage. A local informant believed that the entrance may have been slightly widened in the relatively recent past to facilitate vehicular access.

The site of a large fire overlay House Platform 3 on the hilltop. This may have been a beacon fire, lit as recently as earlier this century on coin evidence. The hill is popular with walkers, horse-riders and motorbike scramblers, and a variety of modern glass and other debris was found in all topsoils.

## GENERAL DISCUSSION

### Nature of the house platforms

Despite the marked differences in date between the platforms they are broadly similar in type, reflecting a common response to topography. They yielded negligible structural evidence other than platform preparation. This was particularly well attested on House Platform 1. An oval platform is indicated, on which a house 7 to 8 m in diameter could have been erected. However, there is insufficient surviving evidence to reconstruct the house shapes, dimensions, construction or internal arrangements. Given this paucity of structural evidence, it seems likely that houses were, indeed, '. . . made of some easily perishable material . . .' (Christison 1894, 111) such as, perhaps, turf, wood or wattle. Post-abandonment robbing of materials might have taken place, although this would not account for the relative rarity of rock-cut features, such as post-holes or ring-ditches. Another possible interpretation is that the platforms were used as bases for temporary, or even portable accommodation such as tents, a hypothesis which it is difficult to test.

Pottery was recovered predominantly in Late Bronze Age levels. Where it occurs in later levels, it appears to have been re-deposited. The varied stone assemblages are not sufficiently numerous to examine patterning of distribution, but it is clear that chipped and other stone tools played a limited part in the everyday life of the inhabitants.

Burnt bone fragments were recovered from all platforms except Platform 1 (Episode 2) but, as they represent only a tiny sample of what must have once been present, no dietary or economic conclusions can be drawn from them. Cattle teeth were found on Platforms 1 (Episode 1) and 2. Identifiable charcoal fragments, probably derived from firewood, do not indicate any change in the types of wood selected for this purpose, from the Late Bronze Age to the Roman Iron Age. Hazel charcoal was predominant in all the samples examined. Barley grains from Pit 2, Platform 1 (Episode 1) and Platform 2 indicate that barley was grown in both periods.

The platforms appear to have served a range of common domestic functions, with the possible exception of House Platform 1 (Episode 2) in whose vicinity Roman Iron Age metalworking may have taken place.

### Nature of the hilltop settlement

Two of the four platforms examined are Late Bronze Age and at least one of the other two is Roman Iron Age. This emphasises the difficulties in interpreting such a complex site in the absence of extensive excavation. Each of the periods of occupation revealed in the current excavation may subsume episodes of expansion and contraction of the settlement; and the role of the hilltop settlement may also have altered over time. This periodicity of settlement also calls into question previous scholars' estimates of the site's population (for example, Feachem 1966, 79).

A hiatus is indicated between the Late Bronze Age and the Roman Iron Age settlement of Hill North. This hiatus is contemporary with the gradual deterioration of climate in the Late Bronze Age, culminating in a period of unprecedented wetness between approximately 800 and 400 BC (Lamb 1982, 27–31; Lamb 1982a, 144–67). Such factors would have had an exaggerated effect on an exposed hilltop site such as Eildon and climate may have been a principal cause of the site's possible abandonment during the hiatus. However, future excavations elsewhere on the hilltop may demonstrate that other parts of the site were in fact occupied during this period.

Climatic constraints may have limited use of the hillfort to intermittent occupation. The notion that the house platforms were not necessarily intended for all-year round occupation is not new (Breeze 1982, 37), although there has been a more general assumption that permanent occupation was intended (Feachem 1966, 79; Harding 1976, 20). It has been generally assumed that the site is Iron Age in date and that it functioned as a tribal centre, or even an *oppidum* comparable with some

of the immense late La Tène sites on the Continent (*cf* Collis 1975). Within Scotland, fortified Iron age sites like the duns, brochs, *etc*, have prompted theories of a growing need in the Iron Age for refuges and strongholds for local populations and their cattle, or alternatively, of aristocratic centres of power. None of these theories preclude the possibility of impermanent use although this rather begs the question of where the population lived for the rest of the year. This issue must be addressed, for Eildon Hill, in the context of two, apparently distinct periods of settlement.

### The Late Bronze Age settlement

The pre-rampart hearth and Pits 1 and 2, together with the ninth-century BC house platforms (1, Episode 1; and 3) indicate a phase of settlement of the early first millennium BC whose full extent has yet to be identified by excavation. The radiocarbon dates indicate an approximate duration of, perhaps, some two to three centuries for excavated features of this period. Clearly it is not possible to gauge the extent of the Late Bronze Age settlement from the small areas under discussion here. However, it is noteworthy that features of this period have been found close to the summit (Platform 3) and 220 m downhill (Platform 1), while the pre-rampart hearth is *circa* 250 m downhill from Platform 3. Thus, Late Bronze Age features occur over at least one-eighth (roughly 4 acres) of the total area of the fort. Late Bronze Age features are, in fact, more numerous and more varied than Roman Iron Age features in the areas examined. Since the excavation areas were effectively randomly selected, there seems no reason not to assume that future excavators will locate a substantial Late Bronze Age hilltop settlement.

It is becoming clear that there was a general increase both in number and size of hilltop settlements in the Late Bronze Age throughout Britain, from the Welsh Marches (for example, Breiddin, Montgomeryshire: Musson 1976) through the Midlands (Mam Tor, Derbyshire: Coombs 1976) and to the North (Traprain Law, East Lothian: Jobey 1976). There is similar evidence from Ireland (Navan, Co. Armagh: Waterman 1970). A number of theories have been advanced for the causes of such developments, for instance climatic deterioration, population pressures and increased territorial organisation of arable and pastoral land (*cf* Avery 1976, esp. 54).

The extensive territory over which Eildon Hill is visible prompts the speculation that it may have served as a political centre even in the Late Bronze Age. This possibility has been commonly expounded for the assumed Iron Age fort on the basis of its size and apparent density of settlement, and by analogy with southern English *oppida*, like South Cadbury (Alcock 1972, 131–73) or Maiden Castle, Dorset which, Wheeler argues, had many of the characteristics of towns by the end of the Iron Age (1943, 68–72). Present indications are that the origins of large, centralised settlements lie in the Late Bronze Age. It is worth recalling here the quantity of Late Bronze Age material from Traprain Law (Burley 1955–6) which may indicate a similar situation on that hilltop (Jobey 1976, 193–5) to that postulated for Eildon Hill North.

Systematic field-work in recent years has located platform settlements in Peeblesshire (RCAHMS 1967) and Upper Clydesdale (RCAHMS 1978) and they are now considered a not uncommon feature of the hillsides of northern Britain (Feachem 1961, 79–85; Jobey 1980, 12–26). Additionally, they occur densely packed on other hilltops in the area (for example, Hownam Law, Yeavering Bell and Old Fawdon Camp). Different types of structures have been recorded on platforms, within the same fort. Thus, both timber and stone structures occurred on platforms at Yeavering Bell (Jobey 1965, 34). Unfortunately, traces of Late Bronze Age structures at Traprain cannot be substantiated beyond scant records of wattle and daub and occasional post-holes (Jobey 1976, 193). The nature of the structures on the Eildon Hill platforms also remains elusive, although the absence of coherent patterns of rock-cut post-holes may indicate that turf, earth and stone structures are more probable than free-standing wooden houses.

House platforms are such a simple and direct response to providing house stances on steeply sloping ground that the slight structural differences discerned between the excavated platforms appear insignificant. The use of perishable materials (probably some combination of turf, wood and wattle) for house construction was probably dictated by the problems of availability of materials and their transport to the hilltop. Turf would have provided a readily available, efficient, insulating material and would have served to protect and anchor wattle or timber walls against the elements, without leaving very much evidence for the archaeologist.

The curvilinear slot on Platform 3 is closely paralleled at the Unenclosed Platform Settlement of Green Knowe, Peeblesshire, by a feature on that site's Platform 5 termed a 'wall-groove' (Jobey 1980, 80–82, Figure 4). Here, some fragments of burnt wattle were recovered *in situ* and Jobey postulates a wattle-walled house *circa* 7.7 m in diameter. The Green Knowe settlement had its *floruit* in the second half of the second millennium BC. Its platforms parallel those on Eildon Hill North in their construction and in the nature of their overlying stratigraphy (which included levels interpreted as probable relict occupation and hearth areas); and also in their artefactual and ecofactual assemblages.

It is clear that a range of normal domestic functions were carried out on the Eildon Hill North, Late Bronze Age platforms, such as food preparation (namely the evidence of cooking vessels, carbonised barley grains, quernstones and rubbers and burnt bone fragments). More specialised activities also appear to have taken place, amongst which evidence survives for metalworking (namely crucible fragments and the bronze tool).

A group of seven, Late Bronze Age, socketed axes were discovered on Eildon Mid Hill in 1982 (O'Connor & Cowie 1985, 151–8), *circa* 1 km from Entrance 1 (Defensive System A) on Eildon Hill North. This hoard '. . . appears to represent part of a significant local concentration of Ewart Park phase axes around the Eildon Hills and of a regional concentration in the middle Tweed valley.' (*ibid*, 157). O'Connor and Cowie postulated that contemporaneous settlement might be discovered on Eildon Hill North and concluded that '. . . it would be no surprise if the earliest defences were eventually found to have been in existence by the seventh century BC' (*ibid*, 158). The current excavations have demonstrated the prescience of their speculation, at least to the extent that contemporaneous settlement has been found on Eildon Hill North, together with evidence for metalworking during this period. It is not unreasonable to suggest that Eildon Hill North is the source of the local Late Bronze Age industry and, at least, a contributor to the regional, mid-Tweed Valley concentration of bronzes.

Its status as a possible production centre in the Late Bronze Age militates against the site's interpretation as a seasonal, or transhumance, settlement, although not necessarily against it being an occasionally occupied centre for tribal ceremonies and business. The exposed conditions on the hilltop and its distance from cultivable land must always have presented problems for its occupants. Given the probable scale of the Late Bronze Age settlement, these logistical difficulties must have applied at this period, just as, it has been speculated, they did in the Iron Age (Breeze 1982, 37). From this, it might be inferred that the site had a relatively small, constant and static population, augmented intermittently by larger numbers of the local or regional populace. The large part of a pot, found *in situ* in the hearth of the Late Bronze Age House Platform 1 (Episode 1), might be interpreted as indicating that basic equipment necessary to hilltop existence, such as cooking vessels, was left in the house ready for use on a subsequent visit. Alternatively, these big, bucket-shaped pots may have been permanently embedded in the hearth, functioning like slow-cookers (P Hill, pers comm), in which case the survival of one here may represent a straightforward abandonment of the Late Bronze Age platform.

### An Unenclosed Platform Settlement or a Late Bronze Age hillfort?

Whether the Late Bronze Age settlement was enclosed or unenclosed cannot be determined with confidence from the excavated evidence. As noted above, the absence of soil formation over the hearth and Pits 1 and 2 beneath the rampart, and the spread nature of the rampart before House Platform 2 was emplaced, suggest that the rampart is closer in date to the Late Bronze Age than to the Roman Iron Age. In this context, it may be that a pit beneath a rampart at Broxmouth, East Lothian, containing a butchered ewe (P Hill, pers comm), provides a parallel for Pit 2 with its, apparent, partly cremated, horse burial; and even for Pit 1, with its high phosphate levels perhaps indicative of a further animal burial.

Animal special deposits are also known from other sites, notably Danebury hillfort, Hampshire, where 43 pits contained animal burials (of single or combinations of animals: horses, sheep, cattle, pigs, dogs, one goat and one cat) (Grant 1984, 533–43). At Farmoor, Oxfordshire, a pit comparable in size with Pit 2 at Eildon contained two horse skeletons of Romano-British date (Lambrick & Robinson 1979, 16, 130–32, Figure 8). The excavators suggest that this was a rubbish deposit or that it may have been a ritual deposit. It is thus conceivable that one or both of the Eildon pits may have been dedicatory in nature, a conjecture strengthened by the discovery of both beneath the rampart. On balance, then, the indications are that a Late Bronze Age rampart may have been erected at Eildon Hill North but, until more substantive evidence emerges, it is probably safer to return the appropriately Scottish verdict of 'not proven'.

A growing number of radiocarbon dates and contexted bronze artefacts tends to indicate that hilltops were commonly settled in the Late Bronze Age in Britain. Challis and Harding suggest that in the Trent-Tyne area '. . . the evidence of hill fortifications . . . is to be seen in a predominantly 1000–500 BC context' (1975, 124), although it should be added that it is by no means clear that the Late Bronze Age hilltop settlements were fortified. At Mam Tor, Derbyshire, for example, the defences were undatable, although apparently later than elements of the internal settlement dated to 1180 ± 132 BC and 1130 ± 115 BC (Coombs 1976). As Megaw and Simpson note (1984, 364), it is often difficult to relate occupation episodes to the construction of the defences.

In Scotland, Kaimes Hill, Midlothian, has a second phase, stone-faced rampart, radiocarbon dated to the fourth century BC, which succeeded a timber-laced rampart of unknown earlier date (Simpson 1969) and at Burnswark, Dumfriesshire, two radiocarbon dates indicate the existence of a 17 acre hilltop enclosure by the seventh to sixth century BC (Jobey 1970, 21). Jobey has grappled with the problem of the apparent extent of Late Bronze Age settlement on Traprain Law, East Lothian, and whether it was enclosed or not (1976, 193–8). Here, it had been conjectured (Burley 1956, 284ff; Feachem 1966, 77) that an open Late Bronze Age settlement may have been succeeded by a small palisaded enclosure, then by a series of more substantial defences, enclosing *circa* 40 acres at their maximum extent, all undated. As Jobey says:

'The difficulty is now obvious, since to accept the Late Bronze Age material as evidence of occupation by the seventh century BC, relate it to this proposed 30 acre enclosure, and yet maintain the proposed physical analysis, [that of a hillfort gradually expanding in size],

would entail at least one and possibly two enclosures being of earlier date. With the current dates from Dinorben hillfort and, indeed, others [Savory 1971], anything might seem possible . . .' (Jobey 1976, 197).

Of the *circa* 20-acre enclosed phase, he says its large size need not deter us from proposing such an early context (Jobey 1976, 1960). However, at the time at which he was writing, the possibility that a *circa* 30-acre hillfort had been established on Traprain Law in the Late Bronze Age seemed truly exceptional in a Scottish context; and he, wisely, concluded that the present evidence did not support such a hypothesis. In the light of a possible parallel situation on Eildon Hill North and the accumulating instances of sites dated to the Late Bronze Age throughout Britain, this possibility may now be advanced with somewhat more confidence.

Thus, there are precedents for Late Bronze Age hilltop settlements and, in one case, for Late Bronze Age defences. There are, however, no precedents for large-scale multivallate defensive systems like System A at Eildon. This does not, of course, rule out the possibility that a univallate Late Bronze Age rampart was converted to a multivallate system at a later date.

To summarise, two general interpretations are possible for the Late Bronze Age evidence from Eildon; either:
*a* there is a large unenclosed platform settlement, or;
*b* there is a platform settlement of that type and date, 39 acres in extent, enclosed by one or more of the triple ramparts of Defensive System A.

## Defensive systems

The defensive systems remain undated. The absence of a relative chronology for Defensive System A, B and C makes it impossible to determine whether the fort developed on the Hownam model (Piggott, C M 1948), or expanded with time, as suggested by the RCAHMS (1956); indeed, it is not inconceivable that the defensive systems are contemporaneous.

Even allowing for erosion and disturbance, the ramparts are little more than accentuations of natural lines of defence. The insubstantial nature of the System A rampart suggests that the defences may have been intended more as a territorial marker than as a defensive barrier. It is significant that there are five entrances, weak points in any defence, giving access to the hilltop. In this connection, the large area over which Eildon Hill North is visible may have been a significant factor in its selection. Hilltop occupation may be defensive merely by virtue of its location, but is not necessarily effectively defensible.

It is clear that a considerable labour force would have been necessary for the construction of System A. Even if it had been univallate originally, some 1.5 km of rampart was built; if the three circuits of System A are contemporaneous, the ramparts amount to almost 5 km in length. The differences in constructional details between the ramparts north and south of Entrance 2 are primarily due to the use of immediately available materials and exigencies of local topography. However, they may also represent the work of different 'work gangs' on either side of the entrance, perhaps testifying to a 'communal' nature of the construction work.

In type, the ramparts of Defensive System A demonstrate that the fort falls into the category of 'contour forts', although they are even less substantial than most parallels (*eg* The Dunion, this volume). Little can be added about the type of entrance and putative gateway structure since the evidence is so scanty. Other entrances, particularly Entrances 4 or 5, may reward future excavation with much fuller potential for reconstruction.

## The Roman Iron Age settlement

The Late Bronze Age hilltop settlement centre may not have been dissimilar to that of the Roman Iron Age, save only that the notion of the latter as a tribal centre is perhaps more familiar. There is little doubt that the Roman Iron Age settlement was enclosed, the defensive systems probably having been in place for some time. Indeed, a more pertinent question might be whether they had a perceived role in this period or had already fallen into disuse. It seems most likely that the interpretation of Defensive System A as a highly visible, territorial marker in the earlier period is equally applicable to the Roman Iron Age.

Although there is less evidence of all types from the excavated platforms of this period, the results imply that a similar range of activities took place within the fort as have been described for the earlier period. House Platform 2 was used for the preparation and cooking of various foodstuffs, while Platform 1 (Episode 2) was sited in the vicinity of a metalworking area. It is not suggested that bronze fibulae, such as [71], were being manufactured on the hilltop, although it is conceivable that waste Roman vessel glass was being worked into Romano-British armlets on the site (Henderson, above).

## Eildon Hill North and Newstead

A Roman fort and a series of marching camps are located near the north-east footslopes of Eildon Hill North, at Newstead (Curle 1911; RCAHMS 1956, *no* 604). The fort, identified by Roy (1793) as Ptolemy's *Trimontium*, covered 4.3 ha initially and was enlarged to 6 ha later. Established around AD 80, it was occupied in the Flavian and Antonine periods and probably continued in use until the first decade of the third century AD (Hartley 1972). The traces of a signal station on the summit of Eildon Hill North have been dated to *circa* ad 80 (Steer & Feachem 1952, 202–5), despite coin evidence which indicates use in the early decades of the second century AD.

The presence of Newstead and the signal station have guided previous scholars' interpretations of the relationship between the occupants of the hillfort and the Roman invaders, the theory being that the hillfort had been abandoned prior to or because of the establishment of Newstead and the signal station. The 1986 excavated evidence clearly indicates that this is not the case. House Platform 2 was almost certainly occupied during the second century AD by people who had access to first-, to second-century AD goods such as glass armlets. Platform 1 (Episode 2) may be of similar date and its users apparently had access to an unenamelled dragonesque fibula of likely mid-first-, to late second-century date. Against this background, the small assemblage of 1986 and unstratified earlier finds of Roman or Romano-British type, appear less likely to be casual losses by individual visitors, although no Roman pottery was found *in situ* on the excavated platforms.

The dating of House Platform 2, an apparently unexceptional platform which fulfilled common domestic functions, implies that at least some part of the hilltop continued in use by native peoples while the Roman fort at Newstead was garrisoned. Moreover, it is at least possible, if not probable, that the signal station was in use contemporaneously, indicating a workable co-existence between Romans and natives at Newstead and on Eildon Hill North. It should of course be noted that radiocarbon dating is not sufficiently precise to reflect fluctuating relations over the course of a century or more of Roman presence in the immediate area.

## Eildon Hill North, Traprain Law, and the native tribes

On Traprain Law, East Lothian, there is some evidence of Neolithic and Early Bronze Age activity on the hilltop (Jobey 1976, 192–3). More significantly, the artefactual evidence from Traprain convincingly indicates a strong Late Bronze Age presence which may be similar in nature and scale to that now postulated for Eildon Hill North (Burley 1956; Jobey 1976, 193–8). Moreover, the evidence indicates an hiatus in occupation at Traprain, between the Late Bronze Age and at least the first century BC, possibly the Roman Iron Age (Stevenson 1966, 20). Jobey (1976, 194–5) found this hiatus an unpalatable phenomenon, postulating that settlement dating to the apparent hiatus would be found in the unexcavated areas. The occurrence of an apparently similar hiatus in activities on Eildon Hill North increases the possibility that there truly is an abandonment of hilltop settlement on these two large sites, in the intervening centuries. It should however be noted that settlement continued throughout the period on smaller sites, like The Dunion and Gillies Hill (this volume).

Large numbers of Romano-British artefacts have been retrieved from Traprain Law (Jobey 1976, 198–203; Burley 1956), indicative of free access to Roman material between the first and fourth centuries AD. The comparative affluence of Traprain Law (seen against the general paucity of material from the smaller native settlements of the Borders) has prompted the suggestion that it was, perhaps, a trading centre linked with nearby *vicus* settlements, such as Inveresk (Jobey 1976, 201). A similar relationship may have existed between the native users of Eildon Hill North and the Romans at

Newstead, given the possible contemporaneity of native settlement and the use of the Roman signal station and the admittedly modest amounts of Roman material from the site.

Whatever their relationships with the Romans, there is little doubt that, in this period, both Traprain Law and Eildon Hill North represent tribal centres of some kind. The traditional identification of Eildon as the tribal centre of the Selgovae (for example, Feachem 1966, 79) has recently been questioned by Mann and Breeze (1987, 88–9) who, re-interpreting Ptolemy's map, suggest instead that the Selgovae were probably based in Dumfriesshire. They propose that *Trimontium* (the Roman fort of Newstead) lies in the territory of the Votadini, whose tribal centre has always been seen as Traprain Law. If correct, and if Ptolemy's map is assumed to correctly identify at least the main native tribes, then Eildon Hill North and Traprain Law both lie in Votadinian territory.

There are striking general similarities between the Traprain Law and Eildon Hill North forts. Both have traditions of centrality which extend back as far as the Late Bronze Age; they are similar to each other in scale and prominence, and are distinguished from most other forts in the area on those grounds; and they have, perhaps, parallel cultural assemblages. These observations indicate that the two sites should perhaps be regarded in some sense as 'sister' forts, functioning in parallel and serving the population in their hinterlands.

It is doubtful whether the identification of Traprain Law and/or Eildon Hill as Votadinian centres can be demonstrated by archaeological excavation. Certainly, the house platforms at Eildon do not preserve stone-built houses in Hill's 'Votadinian tradition' (1982a & c). There is, however, the danger of a circular argument here in that the houses prescribed 'Votadinian' are termed thus because their clearest manifestations occur in the area commonly attributed to the Votadini. Evidence for such structures is also lacking from the available accounts of the excavations at Traprain Law, although Jobey notes the occurrence of four or five superimposed, circular, stone foundations for either stone or turf walls, which might have borne 'Votadinian' houses (1976, 202). In general, the term Votadinian is used here, *sensu* Hill (1982c), to indicate a style of architecture.

To summarise, Mann and Breeze (1987) conclude that the Roman Iron Age fort on Eildon Hill North can no longer be associated with the Selgovae on historical evidence; it should, perhaps, be seen as a 'sister' fort to Traprain Law on archaeological evidence.

Most hillforts in southern Scotland are less than 6 acres in extent. Feachem identified a number of monuments (6 acres and larger) as minor *oppida*, including The Dunion (Rideout, this volume), and listed Eildon Hill North and Traprain Law as major *oppida* (Feachem 1966, 77–9). The use of this term in a southern Scottish context has come to seem increasingly inappropriate since it has been based almost exclusively on the criterion of size (Avery 1976, 41). Avery describes

an *oppidum* as a defended town with an economy largely dependent on semi-industrialised manufacturing and trade, whereas a hillfort would have been overwhelmingly dependent on agriculture and barter. The present material evidence from Eildon Hill North and Traprain Law does not indicate that they were *oppida* in the sense in which the term is applied to Manching, southern Germany (Kramer & Schubert 1970). Additionally, *oppida*, *sensu stricto*, are Late Iron Age phenomena, dating from roughly the first century BC and, as has been indicated, a significant part of the settlements on Eildon Hill North and Traprain Law may be Late Bronze Age in date.

These Scottish sites are long-lived tribal centres to which Late Iron Age continental comparisons may be of little relevance. That they were centres of some kind is demonstrated on archaeological evidence as well as on the grounds of their distinctively large size compared to other local hillforts.

### Conclusion

More than 99% of the Eildon Hill North platforms, almost all the defensive systems and four entrances are unexcavated. Consequently, the 1986 results are tentative and the glimpse that they have offered of the nature and date of the hilltop settlement may be radically altered and extended by further work. The most significant conclusions can be briefly summarised as follows.

*i* There is probably a large-scale Late Bronze Age hilltop settlement from the tenth or ninth centuries BC, which may have functioned as a local or regional centre.

*ii* No certain evidence was recovered of pre-Roman Iron Age activity or settlement on the hilltop.

*iii* At least the inner rampart (and perhaps all three rampart circuits) of Defensive System A is conceivably as early as Late Bronze Age in date.

*iv* There is no irrefutable evidence that Defensive System C exists, nor that the Defensive Systems represent a gradually expanding fort.

*v* There is probably a large-scale Roman Iron Age hilltop settlement which functioned similarly to the postulated Late Bronze Age centre. This may have co-existed with the Roman fort of Newstead whose signal station was sited on the summit of the native-occupied hill.

*vi* Eildon Hill North and Traprain Law may be, in some sense, 'sister' forts, fulfilling similar functions.

Given the oft-quoted interpretation of Eildon Hill North as the tribal centre of the Selgovae, it is important to emphasise here, following Mann and Breeze (1987), that there is no evidence to support this contention. Instead, Ptolemy may have intended to show that both Eildon Hill North and Traprain Law lie in the territory of the Votadini.

The 1986 project has demonstrated that, in spite of the poorly preserved archaeological stratigraphy and the scant nature of the structures, it is possible to retrieve dating and structural evidence from the platforms; and it is likely that the defensive systems and entrances are better preserved elsewhere on the hill than in those areas threatened in 1986. In the meantime, the unanticipated range of the radiocarbon dates from Eildon only serves to highlight how little can be said about the fort in its regional context. It remains a priority to build up a dating framework for southern Scottish hillforts and for other settlement types in the region.

## ACKNOWLEDGEMENTS

The author would like to thank the Buccleuch Estates for permission to excavate and especially, Mr N Campbell, the Factor, for his help and co-operation. Thanks are due to the people of Newtown St Boswells for their interest and practical help, especially Mrs Hunter of Hawkslee Farm, Mrs Pauline Tait of Briarbank, Mrs Dale of The Holmes, Mr Lindsay of Eildonbank and Mr Amos Adams.

The project would not have been possible without the commitment and enthusiasm of the site assistants, Michael Rains, Norman Emery, Valerie McLellan and Paul Sharman, and the good-humoured hard work of the excavators and student volunteers. The excavated areas were backfilled and reinstated by the Community Programme workforce, kindly organised by Mr Mackie of Borders Regional Council. Thanks are also due to Michael Rains and Valerie McLellan for invaluable post-excavation assistance, and Fionna Ashmore for research assistance. The advice and guidance of Gordon Barclay and Noel Fojut in the early stages of the project, and Patrick Ashmore latterly, are gratefully acknowledged.

The author is grateful to the many colleagues and friends who have discussed the site with her and offered information, but especially John Barber, David Breeze, Trevor Cowie, Peter Hill and Jim Rideout. John Barber and Finbar McCormick kindly commented on earlier drafts of this text; and the illustrations are all by Sylvia Stevenson. Figure 2.2 is reproduced by kind permission of the Royal Commission on the Ancient and Historical Monuments of Scotland; and Plate 2.1 is reproduced by kind permission of the National Galleries of Scotland.

# The Dunion, Roxburgh, Borders  *J S Rideout*

## Contributors

1961–1962 excavations *E V W Proudfoot*
Glass *J Henderson*
Querns *A MacSween · J S Rideout · D Dixon*
Stone axe *P R Ritchie*
Coarse stone *V J McLellan · G Collins · D Dixon*
Pottery *A MacSween · E Campbell*
Metalworking debris *R M Spearman*

Chipped stone *B Finlayson*
Bronze bell *D Caldwell*
Pollen *S Butler*
Macroplant remains *A D Fairweather*
Charcoal identification *R P J McCullagh*
Thermoluminescence dates *D C W Sanderson*
Line drawings *S Stevenson · J S Rideout*

## Abstract

*In 1961, gradual expansion of the quarry at The Dunion prompted investigation of a roundhouse and defensive walls. In a second season, in 1962, a second roundhouse was excavated.*

*In 1983, a group of scooped platforms, identified as an Unenclosed Platform Settlement to the north of the fort on The Dunion, Roxburghshire, were threatened by quarrying. A survey was followed by three seasons of excavation between March 1984 and June 1986. The scooped platforms were found to be Later Iron Age roundhouse stances within the fort. In all, seven houses were investigated as well as two lines of defence and contemporary roadways.*

The Dunion, also known as Dunion Hill, lies some 3 km south-west of Jedburgh and to the south of the B6358 Jedburgh to Denholm road (NGR NT 625 190; Figure 3.1). Originally rising to an altitude of *circa* 335 m OD, it has been an imposing landmark by virtue of its position among lower, more rounded, hills. It is now much reduced by quarrying for roadstone. The gradual expansion of The Dunion Quarry destroyed a number of known house platforms in the early 1980s and the remainder were threatened, prompting rescue excavation by Historic Buildings and Monuments (SDD), (now *Historic Scotland*). In the event, this threat was at least temporarily averted when The Dunion Quarry closed in April 1987 without having destroyed that part of the hill investigated by the CEU.

### GEOLOGY, GEOMORPHOLOGY AND SOILS

The Dunion is one of many hills in the Jedburgh area formed from volcanic intrusions of the Carboniferous period. The intrusions have cut through the surrounding Upper Old Red Sandstone (Devonian) sediments. The volcanic vents have plugs of basalt, agglomerate, or a mixture of both. The Dunion vent is filled with basalt while Lanton Hill, *circa* 1 km to the north, and Black Law, *circa* 1 km to the south-west, have plugs of agglomerate and basalt (Greig 1971, 88). Part of the quarry face in The Dunion, adjacent to the area investigated by the CEU, exposed the interface between the basalt plug and the soft, red, interbedded sandstone.

The upper part of the excavation area was situated over the basalt (Areas 3, 4, and 8, below), the lower part on soils overlying the sandstone (lower part of Area 1 and all other areas). House 3, in the upper part of Area 1, sat on the interface.

Of the three hills mentioned above, The Dunion is the most prominent. While Lanton Hill and Black Law have been eroded to form rounded conical hills, The Dunion has a steep-sided rocky summit with more gentle lower slopes to the north, east, and south. To the south-west it is connected to Black Law by a narrow shoulder. The rocky summit of The Dunion has been eroded by glacial action to form a summit-plateau with ridges and terraces falling away to the south-west and north-west, all aligned roughly north-west/south-east. The lower slopes, especially on the north-east, are of sandstone protected from glacial action by the harder basaltic plug, forming a slight crag-and-tail feature.

The sandstone of the lower slopes is overlain by pink glacial till with small inclusions of rotted stone. This was evident in the exposure along the quarry-face where the till proved to be roughly 1 m thick under House 2 but became thinner uphill, petering out short of the basalt plug. During the excavation similar till was found in crevices in level surfaces of the basalt. Most of the hill is covered by Darleith Series soils with Skeletal Darleith soils on the higher parts. The lowest parts of the north-west, north, north-east, east and south slopes are covered by soils of the Hobkirk Series while to the south-west (the shoulder between The Dunion and Black

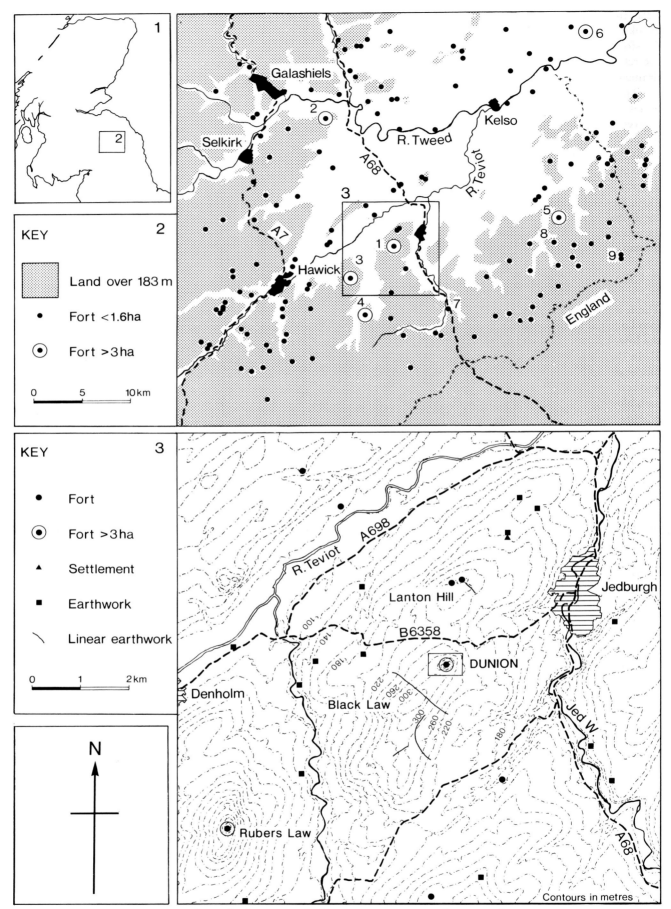

*Figure 3.1   Map composite to show the location of The Dunion. (Drawing by J S Rideout).*

Law) the soils belong to the Cessford Series of the Hobkirk Association. With the exception of the Cessford Series soils, which are poorly drained, the soils are relatively shallow (less than 1 m thick) and freely drained (Muir 1956).

The area investigated by the CEU lies on Darleith Series soils. These soils developed on parent material derived from basaltic rocks. The predominant parent material is a stony, loamy till, the remainder being screes or rock outcrops. The soils encountered during excavation, however, were somewhat different from the general profile description cited in the *Memoirs* (Muir 1956, 83–84), probably because of human activity since the Iron Age, at least. Few of the soil profiles in the excavated areas had developed naturally, without human disturbance.

## PRESENT VEGETATION

The lower slopes of The Dunion to the south-east fall into Land Capability Class 3, Division 1, and the rest of the lower slopes are Class 4, Division 1 (SSS 1982, sheet 7). In the former, the land is capable of producing a moderate range of crops including cereals, vegetables, and root crops in rotation with grass leys. Class 4 land is suitable for a narrower range of crops, mostly grass pasture but also forage crops and feed cereals. This is reflected in the present land boundaries in the area. The higher slopes of the hill are more or less enclosed by a headland dyke which separates the arable/pasture fields of the lower slopes from the rough pasture of the summit of The Dunion and from the wetter soils of the shoulder with Black Law (Class 5, Division 2). The higher slopes are, in the main, rocky and unsuitable for arable cultivation. No evidence of arable cultivation was noted on the less rocky north-east slope of the summit although a vertical aerial photograph taken in 1968 (OS/68/024V.033) shows narrow rig-and-furrow (*cf* Halliday 1982, 82) on an area of the north-east slope of Black Law, now partly drained and converted to arable/pasture use and partly under gorse scrub. The marks, however, could not be identified on the ground, and may be nothing more than relatively recent attempts at drainage.

The vegetation cover of the summit area is predominantly grass moorland but contains discrete areas of heather (*Calluna vulgaris*), especially to the north, downhill from the area excavated by the CEU. Bilberry (*Vaccinium myrtillus*) is also common. With the opening of the quarry the hill ceased to be used for sheep pasture and some scrubby trees have grown (mostly birch; *Betula* and rowan; and *Sorbus*), and human activity has led to an increase in invasive weeds of disturbed ground, such as rosebay willowherb (*Epilobium angustifolium*) and stinging nettle (*Urtica dioica*).

## ARCHAEOLOGICAL BACKGROUND

In the late nineteenth century it was noted that a fort occupied the summit of the hill. The date of discovery is not known; a list of Border forts published in 1884 makes no mention of the site (Geikie 1884) nor is it referred to in Christison's *Early Fortifications in Scotland*, although it is marked on his distribution map (Christison 1898, facing p 386). The earliest plan of the fort, unsigned and unpublished, currently rests in a solicitor's office in Jedburgh (see Figure 3.2a). Except for an outwork on the north-east side of the hill (marked X on Figure 3.2a) unnoted in later field-work, the plan is similar to that published in the Roxburghshire *Inventory* (RCAHMS 1956, Figure 96 and Figure 3.2). Here, the entry for The Dunion states that:

'The structural remains on the hill comprise the fragmentary ramparts of a fort, perhaps of Dark Age date; seven hut-circles, scattered over the west face of the hill, which are all later in date than the fort; and some later foundations and lengths of stone dyke . . . The main rampart of the fort, a massive drystone wall appears to have enclosed the whole summit of the hill . . . Tactically the weakest sides of the fort are on the north and north-west . . . To meet this threat additional ramparts have been erected on these sides. Two of these are drawn across a broad gully on the west . . . Both ramparts are pierced by a hollow track which leads up the centre of the gully and is bordered at one point by four upright stones; . . . A third outer rampart can be traced westwards for 50 yards from the north-east end of the summit-plateau to the edge of the quarry . . . Secondary occupation of the hill is attested by seven hut-circles, four of which – one blocking the main entrance of the fort and three lying outside the defences on the west – are patently later in date than the fort, while the remaining three . . . resemble the others and are presumably contemporary with them. . . . On the north-east flank of the hill . . . there is a group of four roughly circular scoops which may be either hut floors or quarry pits.' (*ibid*, 63–4).

In 1961 and 1962 two of the circular structures in the fort were excavated, and the defences investigated by E V W Proudfoot. The results of these excavations are summarised here; the full reports have been archived.

### Excavations at The Dunion 1961–1962
*E V W Proudfoot*

Edwina Proudfoot, at the invitation of the then Ministry of Public Buildings and Works, carried out limited excavations at The Dunion in August 1961 followed by a second season in April 1962. Four men were hired from

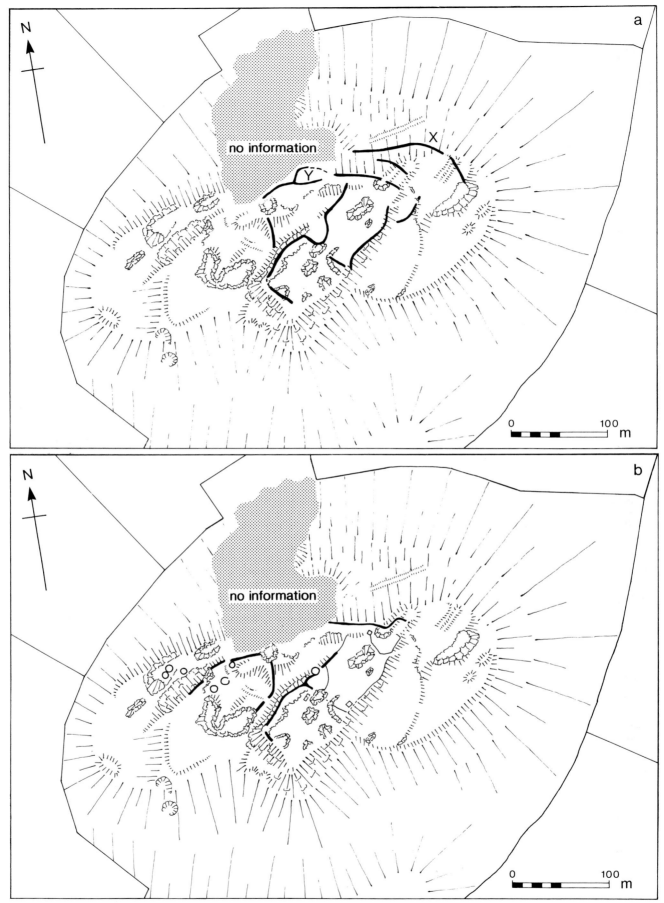

*Figure 3.2   Plans of the fort. a After an unpublished and undated plan. b After RCAHMS, planned 1939 and published 1956. (Drawing by J S Rideout).*

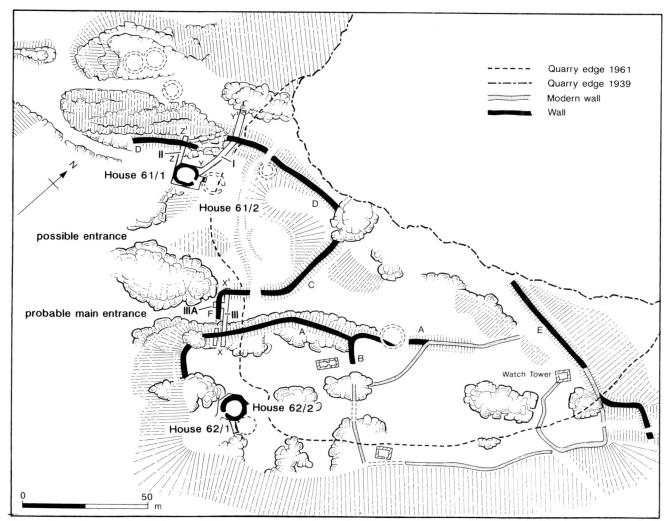

*Figure 3.3   Plan of the 1961 and 1962 excavations (after RCAHMS 1939). (Drawing by S Stevenson).*

the local Jedburgh Labour Exchange, and a small number of volunteers assisted in the excavation.

The areas selected for excavation in the first season, in August 1961, were the remains of House 61/1 and part of the surviving walling of a second house (House 61/2; Figure 3.3). Near the summit of the hill, most of the latter had already been destroyed by the quarry and only a small area was deemed safe to uncover, although more of the structure in fact survived towards the quarry edge, though too dangerous to reach.

A field survey by E V W Proudfoot of the hilltop located several additional houses and further wall fragments. These were planned with Feachem, for RCAHMS. Thereafter it was decided that a second very short season of excavation should be carried out, in April 1962, concentrating on the remains of another house on the summit-plateau, House 62/2. This was selected for excavation because its prominent position suggested it might be a primary structure and would shortly be destroyed by quarrying.

The small labour force and the short excavation seasons – three weeks in 1961 and two weeks in 1962 – did not allow time for a section through the house walls nor was it feasible to put a section through the house floors.

*1961 season*

*Defences (Figure 3.3 & 3.4)*   Wall A, around the summit-plateau, was sectioned at two points, *circa* 2 m apart in trenches *circa* 1.5 m wide. The northern trench continued downhill to section Wall C, and a side-extension extending in a south-westernly direction from this was cut to investigate the short length of hitherto unrecognised walling (Wall F) between Walls A and C. Two trenches, running roughly north and north-west from the trench opened over House 61/1, were cut to investigate Wall D.

Wall A (Figure 3.4, section X–X[1]; Plate 3.1) survived to a width of *circa* 4.5 m and a height of *circa* 0.5 m and consisted of a bank of soil and rubble. Wall-facing survived in places but no evidence for the use of timber was noted in the limited exposure. A piece of jet armlet [61/6], (Figure 3.23), was recovered from the wall-facing exposed in the smaller cutting and pieces of daub [61/12] were found throughout the lowest levels of the wall. In the northern trench, a sherd of pottery [61/2] was found at the edge of Wall A and another [61/3] at the interface of the wall with the bedrock.

Wall C (Figure 3.4, section X–X[1]) was of similar construction but was poorly preserved, surviving only as a single course of stones.

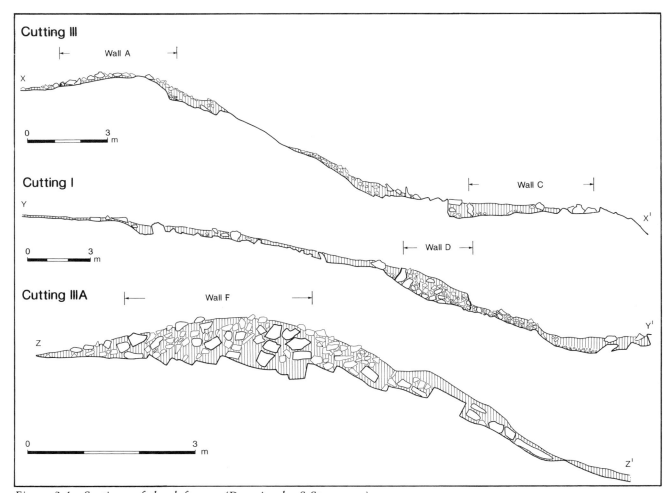

*Figure 3.4   Sections of the defences. (Drawing by S Stevenson).*

*Plate 3.1   Cutting through Wall A.*

*Plate 3.2   Cutting through Wall D, looking north-westwards across an entrance gully.*

The vestigial remains of Wall F, running between Walls A and C, survived to *circa* 1 m in height and *circa* 4 m in width. Like the other walls it was built of local stone, but there were pockets of earth within this. At the time of the excavation it was considered that there was no evidence for any use of timber in the construction, but on examination of the drawings and photographs it seems a reasonable assumption that timbers may have been present for which the soil pockets may be partial evidence.

One difference between Wall F and the other defences examined may support the above suggestion, notably that the wall appears to be leaning downhill. All the stones in the construction show a pronounced southward inclination. This could be caused by the steepness of the gully at this point, but it could also be the result of the loss of timber supports.

Wall D (Figure 3.4, sections Y–Y$^1$ and Z–Z$^1$; Plate 3.2), of similar but more substantial construction to Wall A, was spread to *circa* 4.8 m wide and survived to

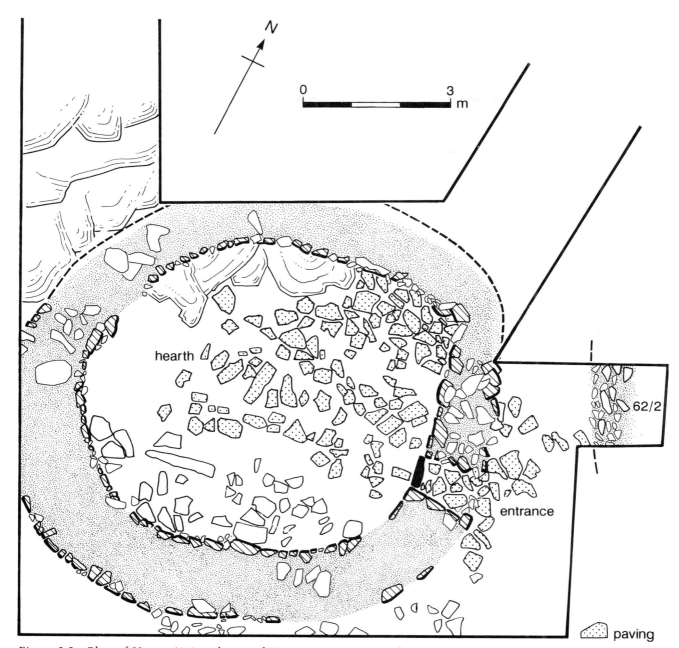

*Figure 3.5   Plan of House 61/1 and part of House 62/2. (Drawing by S Stevenson).*

*circa* 1 m high. Two small stone balls [61/10] were found in Wall D as were fragments of an unidentifiable iron object [61/15] (Appendix 17). Maximum use had been made of rock outcrops to emphasise the lines of the walls, so that they proved less substantial than they had at first appeared. Large amounts of rubble downslope from the defences suggested that they probably originally had been of some considerable height. No structural evidence, for example, of timber-lacing, was noted in the small exposures of the wall examined.

*House 61/1 (Figure 3.5 & Plate 3.3)*   A trench measuring a maximum of *circa* 13 m by *circa* 10 m was opened over house 61/1. Three narrow trenches extended from the main trench; two to investigate Wall D (above), the third to link up with House 61/2.

House 61/1 was roughly circular externally but internally it was sub-square, measuring *circa* 7.8 m by

7 m. Only the lowest course of stone facing survived, best preserved on the outer face to the south. It abutted a rock outcrop, to the west. The wall was 1.1 m to 1.9 m wide and varied from one to five courses high. The doorway, to the east, was 0.7 m to 1 m wide with a threshold stone on the inner edge.

The interior of the house was paved, the paving continuing through the entrance and into the area between House 61/1 and House 61/2.

Because the interior of House 61/1 was not excavated to bedrock and because the central baulk could not be removed, no evidence was uncovered for a central hearth or of any possible internal post settings. Trodden into the floor of House 61/1, however, were many charcoal flecks and also fragments of burnt bone. These were submitted for examination (charcoal: Botany Department, University of Edinburgh; bone: the

*Plate 3.3    House 61/1.*

*Plate 3.4    House 62/2.*

late Dr Ian Hodgson). In both cases no identifications were feasible because of the comminuted nature of the fragments and it was suggested that such tiny fragments were indicative of a hearth nearby.

There is a possible square hearth setting, visible in Plate 3.3, on the west of the site, though close to the wall. It is possible, however, that these and adjacent stones are indicative of internal stone arrangements.

Finds from House 61/1 included coarse pottery from the house floor [61/1, 61/16], a broken hollowed stone lamp fragment from the wall [61/9] and a flint flake found on the floor [61/8].

A stone disc was picked up from the hillside just above House 61/1 [61/11], but it is not diagnostic and is probably not related to the period when house 61/1 was in use.

*House 61/2 (Figure 3.5)*    House 61/2, on the quarry edge, survived only as a curved fragment of walling *circa* 0.5 m thick and up to 2.5 m long. Too little of the surviving walling was accessible to ascertain any features of this house or why the area between it and 61/1 was paved.

*1962 season*

*House 62/2 (Figure 3.6 & Plate 3.4)*    An irregular trench measuring roughly 12 m by 11 m was opened over House 62/2 on the summit-plateau. The house was similar in shape to House 61/1 but was more nearly circular, and measured internally *circa* 6.6 m north-north-west/south-south-east by 6.7 m transversely within a wall *circa* 1.1 m to 2.3 m thick. The wall, less well preserved than that of House 61/1, had been of stone, varying from one course to more than four in several places.

The entrance, to the south, was *circa* 1 m wide and was roughly paved, with a substantial threshold stone on the inner edge. The paving continued for a short distance into the interior, most of which was of earth and unpaved, though with many stones bedded into it. The floor-surface had inclusions of charcoal flecks, burnt bone, and pottery. A broken sandstone slab in the centre of the floor, and burnt material around it, formed the hearth. No internal post-ring was visible. A bank of rubble outside and to the east of House 62/2 probably represented another house, 62/1, recorded as a partial

feature on plans of The Dunion. The area between the two was paved in a manner similar to the paving between House 61/1 and House 61/2.

From under the end of the baulk – approximately opposite the entrance – a large group of sherds [62/11 & 62/13] were found under the wall. There was a distinct hollow in the wall at this point, like a cupboard, possibly the remains of a storage recess in the thickness of the wall. Part of the wall had to be removed to reach the rest of the pottery. Most of the sherds that could be examined *in situ* were placed outer side downwards, below three sloping groups of stones. They appeared to have been laid in this sloping position. The inference is probably that the wall collapsed onto the pots, hence the layered deposit.

Found with the coarse pottery were two other sherds, a rim sherd of finer pottery, possibly Roman in origin, and part of a small medieval strap handle. The presence of Roman or medieval sherds on The Dunion would not be unusual and such sherds could have been weathered or settled lower into the wall, resulting in an apparent association.

Other sherds of coarse ware [62/17] were found in the house floor, together with a flint point [62/18]. Two small stone balls [62/10] were also found in the floor, and a flint flake [62/9] was found in the entrance.

*Further comment*

Following the 1961 and 1962 excavations and field survey, it was noted in the interim reports that the results of this work indicated that The Dunion, as an *oppidum*, was proving to be of greater significance and earlier date than previous interpretation had indicated.

In particular it was reported that acceleration of the extraction by the quarry would affect the lower slopes, those areas where the greatest concentrations of the newly discovered house remains had been recorded. It was recommended that further excavation of those house remains should be undertaken as a matter of urgency in 1962. In addition, attention was drawn to the difference in nature between houses near the summit and those on the lower slopes, and it was recommended that it would be desirable to preserve some of these, at least on the back (*ie* on the east and south-east) of the hill. A further recommendation was for 'excavation on a

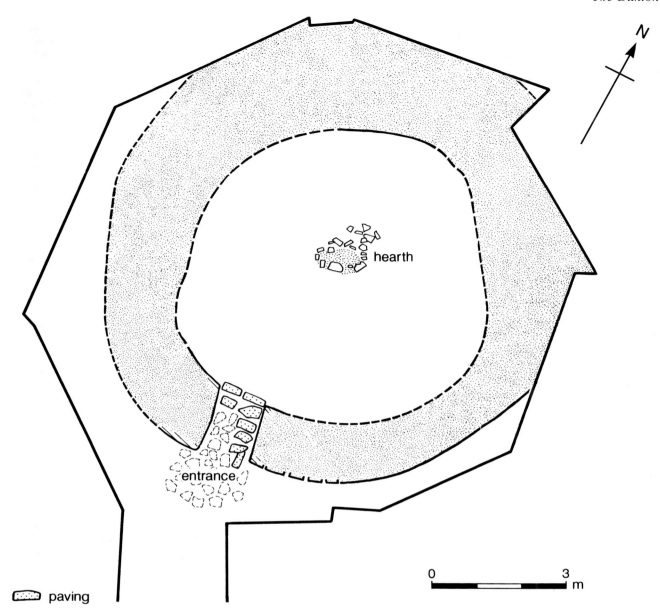

N

hearth

entrance

0        3
         m

paving

*Figure 3.6 Plan of House 62/2. (Drawing by S Stevenson).*

considerable scale', that is, not just one or two houses, but to open larger areas, and seek answers to some of the many questions raised by these two brief excavation seasons. This would have been an unusually large excavation at that date and was not, therefore, considered seriously.

It was only in 1984 that further work was carried out, by which date much of the hill itself had been quarried away, but enough of the houses discovered in 1961 and 1962 survived to show just how different they were from the stone built, nearly square houses on the summit.

*Acknowledgements*
The 1961 and 1962 excavations were carried out under the auspices of the then Ministry of Public Buildings and Works, now *Historic Scotland*.

Thanks are due to John Dunbar and Alastair McLaren, who assisted with planning this difficult site at very short notice, I am also indebted to R W Feachem who had been surveying The Dunion and with whom I was able to survey a number of new houses both in and outside the main part.

A number of friends provided support and manpower, Mike and Kit Whitfield, their late mother, Margaret, Rosemary Meldrum, Catherine Field, Bruce Proudfoot and the late Sue Notman. The local labour force proved most helpful, if somewhat bemused by the work. The quarry workers helped in a number of ways; in particular they looked for artefacts after blasting, and found the quernstones recorded here.

Finally, thanks are due to the present staff at *Historic Scotland* for funds and assistance, and the staff at *AOC (Scotland) Ltd* for making it possible to produce this long overdue account of an important excavation. It is most valuable that it can be published alongside the more recent excavations.

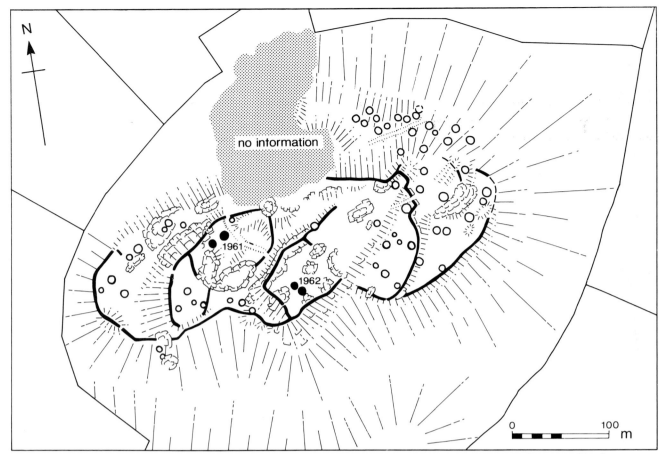

*Figure 3.7    Plan of the fort (after Feacham 1961). Houses excavated in 1961 and 1962 are shown in black. (Drawing by J S Rideout).*

### The Unenclosed Platform Settlement

Following field survey by R Feachem and E V W Proudfoot, the hill was re-surveyed by the Royal Commission. The unpublished plan shows a much larger fortification than had been revealed previously, with an additional rampart to the west and another to the east, enclosing more than forty circular structures with a further two outwith the defences to the south (RCAHMS RXD/86/3–7). This is reproduced here as Figure 3.7, by kind permission of RCAHMS. On the basis of this re-survey, Feachem identified The Dunion, *circa* 5.3 ha in extent, as a minor *oppidum* in his analysis of hillforts in northern Britain (Feachem 1966, 79).

The RCAHMS re-survey of 1961 also records seventeen house platforms lying outwith the fort on the north flank of the hill, amongst which, presumably, are the four mentioned in the *Inventory*. The Ordnance Survey records them as an Unenclosed Platform Settlement (UPS) but comprising fourteen, rather than seventeen, platforms (OS record card NT 61 north-west 22), and they were planned at 1:2500 (OS plan NT 6219).

#### Other structures

On the summit-plateau, rectangular structures and stone dykes were noted. The *Inventory* records them thus :

'At the extreme north-east end of the summit-plateau . . . a small oblong building measuring 19 ft by 15 ft over walls about 3 ½ ft thick built of rubble and mortar . . . The foundations of a second oblong structure of similar character, measuring 22 ft by 14 ¾ ft over walls 2 ft thick, appear about the centre of the south-east edge of the summit-plateau.' (RCAHMS 1956, 64).

The *Inventory* suggests that these structures may have served as a Border look-out post of the fifteenth or sixteenth centuries and refers to Lord Dacre's letter to Henry VIII, concerning a raid into Scotland. Lord Dacre reports that he 'came with a stale to a place called the Dungyon, a mile from Jedworth [Jedburgh]' (HMSO 1920, I pt. ii, 1079: the OED cites this reference as an example of the use of 'stale' to mean a body of armed men on ambush or scouting sortie). The smaller oblong structure is marked on the OS 1:10,000 map as a 'Watch Tower' (Figure 3.3). A third structure is recorded by the *Inventory* as:

'A cottage, of which the foundations can also be seen, seems to be of no antiquarian interest, and the lengths of stone dyke . . . may or may not be connected with this phase of the history of the hill-top.' (RCAHMS 1956, 64).

*Plate 3.5   The Dunion quarry from the air, looking south-westwards. Areas excavated during 1984–1986 are located immediately in front of the quarry.*

Stray finds from the hill include an inurned cremation from a field on the north slope of the hill (Anderson 1886, 98), two barbed and tanged arrowheads (*PSAS* 1888, 270), a stone axe (*PSAS* 1933, 9), and querns, three of which are recorded below (reports from quarry workers). A flat axe mould reported to have come from Rubers Law or The Dunion, (G Dorward, pers comm), is recorded elsewhere (Cowie, forthcoming b).

*Survey, excavation and methodology*
By the time of the CEU investigation the quarry had increased in size to such an extent that the hill survived as little more than a shell (Plate 3.5). Most of the fort, as recognised in 1961, had been removed and quarry roads obscured much of the remaining ramparts and houses. During the CEU survey season it was noted that the quarry had destroyed seven, and damaged one, of the platforms of the unenclosed settlement while the easternmost platform had been destroyed in the construction of a radio transmitter early in 1984 (Figure 3.8). This transmitter is the latest of a series constructed on the hill and all have caused damage to archaeological remains.

The survey concentrated on the area of the surviving platforms. Two additional platforms were located and a possible third, apparently partly obscured by a quarry track, was investigated. A trial trench, 1.5 m wide, was

opened across what appeared to be the apron of the platform, revealing two parallel lines of stones, the area between them filled with earth. This was later identified as a defensive rampart, Rampart 1.

The excavation was undertaken in three seasons (second to fourth seasons, the survey constituting the first season). In the second season work concentrated on the investigation of five platforms in three areas, later amalgamated into one area. In this season the defensive rampart was also investigated, in an extended trench (Area 2). This season, of eight weeks' duration, was found to be insufficient to complete the planned objectives of the excavation. A third season, of four weeks duration and shorter than planned, was undertaken in October 1985. The unexcavated strips between the three original areas were opened to create a single main area (Area 1) and work continued on the house platforms, a roadway (Roadway 1), and on Area 2. In the fourth season (eight weeks in April to June 1986) work was completed on the main area. Area 2 was extended to the east to locate an entrance through the rampart, and seven small trenches were opened on other parts of the hillside: three to investigate the course of the rampart (Rampart 1), one to investigate an inner rampart recorded on the 1961 plan (Rampart 2), and two to investigate anomalous features. The seventh trench, in House 7, was designed to locate dating material.

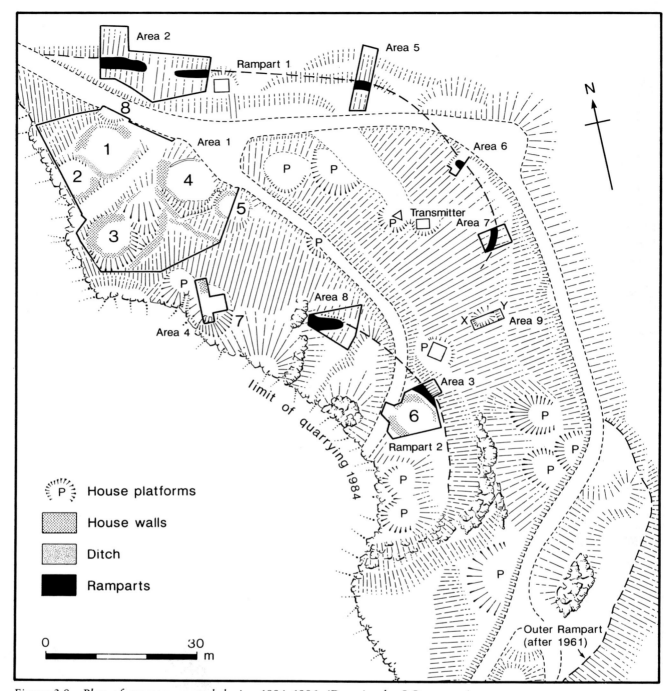

*Figure 3.8   Plan of areas excavated during 1984–1986. (Drawing by S Stevenson).*

In all trenches the turf and modern topsoils were removed by hand. The modern topsoils may have formed on archaeological deposits and so finds from these soils were three-dimensionally recorded. On the platforms, the house walls were identified and the interiors emptied before the wall and platform structures were investigated by the cutting of sections. All archaeological soils were sampled according to standard CEU practices (Appendix 10).

In all, nine areas and trenches were opened by the end of the three excavation seasons (Figure 3.2). Several structural elements were uncovered and recorded in the excavated areas.

*i* Two lines of defence were investigated; an outer

rampart (Rampart 1), and an inner rampart (Rampart 2) An entrance in Rampart 1 was excavated.
*ii* Eight houses were partially or totally excavated.
*iii* Walls and other features associated with the houses were excavated.
*iv* Contemporaneous roads were revealed and sectioned.

THE DEFENCES

**Rampart 1**

The line of the outer defence was investigated in four trenches (Figure 3.8, Areas 2, 5, 6, and 7). Unlike the

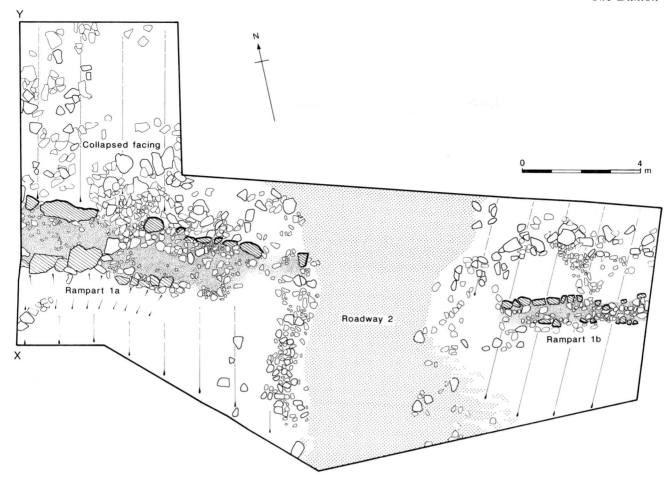

*Figure 3.9   Plan of Area 2, showing Rampart 1. (Drawing by S Stevenson).*

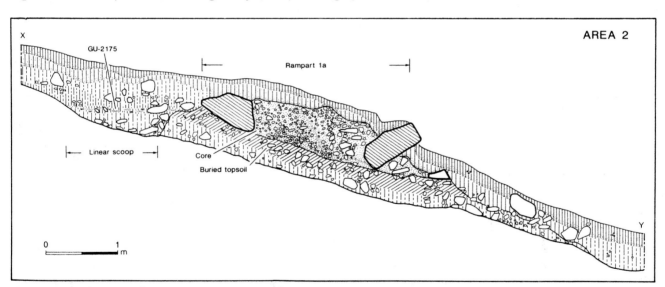

*Figure 3.10   Section of Rampart 1a. (Drawing by S Stevenson).*

other ramparts on the hill, it does not appear to have followed natural lines of defence although, for most of its course, it seems to have roughly followed the contour of the north-east flank of the hill. Unrecorded before the excavation of 1984, its west or south-west extent is unknown. Apart from that part of its course located by excavation, the only other source of information is from vertical aerial photographs of varying quality. These show that by 1948 quarrying had removed much of its

western sector and, by 1984, its west limit was defined by the quarry road, some 8 m west of Area 2.

### Area 2 (Figure 3.9 & 3.10)
This trench measured 22 m long by 10 m wide, with an extension running north from the north-west end of the main trench, measuring 5 m by 5 m (Figure 3.9). The shape and size of the trench was restricted by the quarry road to the south and south-south-west, and by a

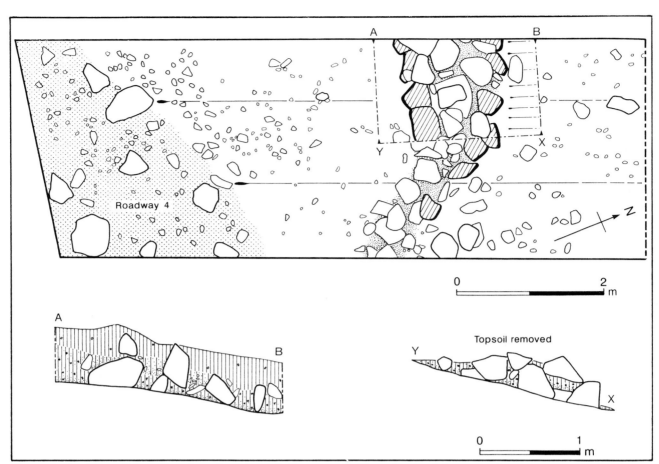

*Figure 3.11   Plan of Area 5 and section through Rampart 1. (Drawing by S Stevenson).*

modern platform for a shed to the south-east. The trench exposed three elements of the outermost defence; an entrance, a rampart to the west of the entrance (Rampart 1a), and a less substantial wall (Rampart 1b) to the east of the entrance.

Rampart 1a, to the west of the entrance, appears to have been constructed in two stages. At the west end of the trench, starting *circa* 6 m from the entrance and running into the west baulk, was a 3.5 m length of rampart. The outer face of the rampart consisted of a single course of massive boulders, averaging 1.0 m high. The inner face, of less substantial boulders, was also one course high. The core was made up of loam and small stones to cobble-size (Figure 3.10). The rampart was *circa* 2.5 m thick. The upper surfaces of the boulders forming the outer face were near-level, which would have provided a foundation for further courses of facing. The upper surfaces of the inner face were less regular but could also have supported higher courses.

The core-space appears to have been filled with topsoil derived from surface stripping, probably on areas downhill from the rampart. A quantity of small boulders and stones on the steep slope below the outer face, many of which had flat surfaces, may be collapsed upper courses of the outer facing. There was less collapsed material on the uphill side.

Underneath the rampart was a well-preserved old ground surface with relict A-, and B-horizons. This profile was sampled for pollen analysis. Beyond the

rampart, to both north and south, this profile survived for a short distance, although in a less well-preserved state. Behind the rampart was a linear scoop which had cut into the B-horizon. It was not possible to determine the function of the scoop. It had a lower fill of thin lenses of clean sand alternating with dark loam. The fairly homogeneous upper fill was a very dark brown loam with some charcoal inclusions. The charcoal consisted of hazel and birch roundwood, and gave a radiocarbon date of $2120 \pm 50$ bp (170 bc; GU-2175).

Between the earth-cored section of the rampart and the entrance, the defence's character changed. Here, the inner face was constructed of smaller stones, the core changed from earth to rubble, and the outer face was constructed of smaller boulders. This section of the rampart appeared somewhat more crudely built than the remainder.

To the east of the entrance Rampart 1b was very different to Rampart 1a, and was less well-preserved. Here, it consisted of a drystone wall, one course high, *circa* 0.75 m thick, comprising two wall faces with a core of earth in its eastern half and a core of rubble in its western half. A short distance in front of the wall was a single discontinuous line of small boulders which could not be related stratigraphically to the drystone wall. The wall was built on to an old ground surface.

The entrance was *circa* 4.5 m wide, between Rampart 1a to the west, and the drystone wall (Rampart 1b) to the east. A road (Roadway 2) running through the

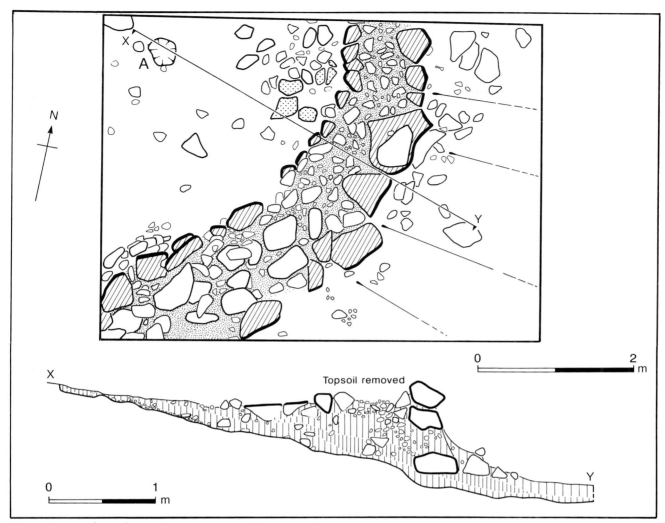

*Figure 3.12    Plan of Area 7 and section of the wall. (Drawing by J S Rideout).*

entrance and into the fort was defined by two
'hornworks' running uphill from the rampart terminals.
The east 'hornwork' consisted simply of two ill-defined
lines of stones while the west 'hornwork' was a low
bank of rubble *circa* 0.25 m high and 1 m wide. The
road was surfaced with rounded basalt brash, up to
three stones deep, which ran around behind both the
rampart and the wall, thinning out rapidly. Outside the
entrance, the brashy surface fanned out to the east and
west. A line of stone kerbing, curving westwards from
the west rampart terminal, formed an abrupt division
between the brashy road metalling and a triangular area
of stone-free soil between it and the front face of the
rampart. A short line of kerbing to the east of the
entrance, mirroring the line to the west, appears to have
served a similar function.

All of the finds from this area came from modern
topsoil horizons. These finds included chert cores [58,
59], four lumps of slag [52–55], a hammerstone [19], and
a crumb of pottery [46].

### Area 5 (Figure 3.11)
A long, narrow trench, measuring 13.5 m by 3 m was
cut roughly at right angles to, and north of, the later
quarry road to locate the continuation of Rampart 1b to

the east of Area 2. The wall ran through the trench 6 m
to the north of the road. It was constructed in a similar
manner to the length of wall at the east end of Area 2,
with two crude faces and a rubble core, and survived to
*circa* 1.5 m thick and 0.5 m high. A spindle whorl [13]
and some burnt bone were found amongst the wall
stones. At the south end of the trench a second feature
was noted. A scatter of large stones appeared to form
kerbing for a layer of small sub-rounded and sub-
angular stones in a loam matrix. The layer, similar to
the metalling in the entrance in Area 2 (Roadway 2) and
on the road in Area 1 (Roadway 1), may also be a
roadway (Roadway 4). A Neolithic stone axe [44] was
found under the stony layer.

### Area 6
A small trench was cut to the south of the later quarry
road, 25 m south-east from Area 5. The trench, little
more than a clean-up of a face originally exposed by
quarry traffic, located a band of rubble, probably part of
Rampart 1b as located in Areas 2 and 5.

### Area 7 (Figure 3.12)
A fourth trench cut to follow the line of Rampart 1b was
opened *circa* 14 m south of Area 6. The trench, 5.5 m by

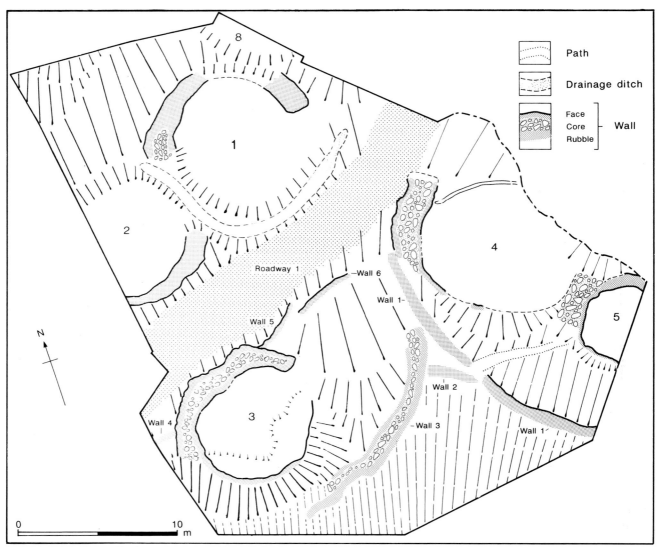

*Figure 3.13   Overall plan of Area 1, showing Houses 1–2 and 8, Walls 1–6 and Roadway 1. (Drawing by J S Rideout and S Stevenson).*

4 m, located the wall at a point where it turns south to run uphill towards the inner lines of defence. Because the hillslope was steeper at this point, the wall appears to have been built on a prepared platform. The wall, again crudely built, measured *circa* 1.6 m thick and survived to a height of *circa* 0.9 m. A shallow pit (Figure 3.12, A) was found *circa* 2 m to the west of the wall. A possibly utilised water-worn stone [29] was recovered from the topsoil.

**Rampart 2**

A second, inner line of defence was investigated in the final excavation season. The defence, noted by Feachem on the 1961 plan, was the only line of defence located in 1984, and its course was investigated by trenching in Areas 3 and 8. Rampart 2 was not unambiguously identifiable in Area 8 (see archive report for details).

*Area 3*
Before excavation only a short length of the inner wall could be identified. It showed as a short, turf-covered

bank at the top of a short steep slope, the latter affording a natural line of defence, and overlooking a house platform now bearing a modern brick shed. The rampart had apparently continued the strong natural line of defence of the cliff-top (Figure 3.8).

A small trench was opened over the turf-covered bank, locating the remains of Rampart 2, and the wall of a house, hitherto unrecognised. The trench was expanded to reveal most of the house (House 6, below) and more of the rampart (Figure 3.17). Rampart 2 survived as a spread bank of rubble in a matrix of humic loam. No structure was noted within the rubble and no *in situ* facings survived. However, House 6 has been built into the thickness of the rubble bank and may have been the cause of its destructuring.

**Houses and other structures: Area 1 (Figure 3.13)**

*House 1 (Figure 3.14 & Plate 3.6)*
The platform for House 1 was elliptical with its long axis, atypically for The Dunion houses, aligned at right angles to the slope. The platform was created by the

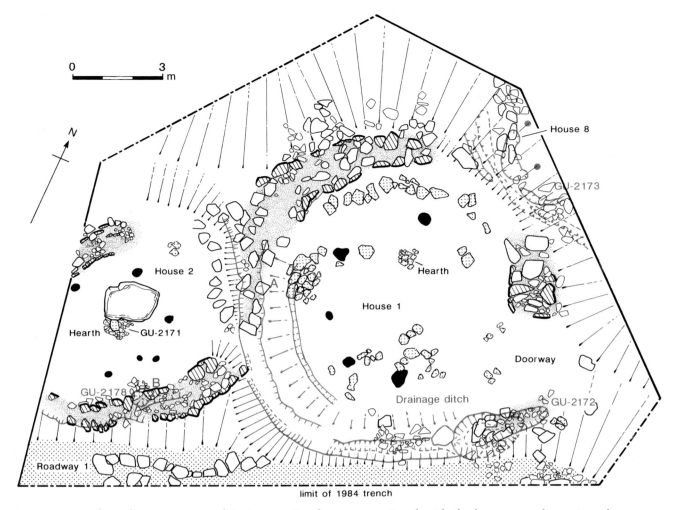

*Figure 3.14   Plan of Houses 1, 2 and 8, Area 1. Cut features associated with the houses are shown in red. (Drawing by S Stevenson).*

quarrying of a low scarp into the till subsoil and dumping the spoil downhill to form an apron. A break in slope at the level of the platform enhanced the apparent height of the apron. The platform sloped to the north-west, dropping *circa* 1 m from back to front. All the available platform space had been enclosed to form the interior of the house which measured *circa* 8.5 m by 8 m. The low apron and part of the natural slope below it were revetted by large irregular stones and boulders which rose to form the outer face of the front wall of the house. The inner face of the front wall was also crudely constructed and survived to more than one course only to the north-west. The wall ran from the west-north-west, where it met the natural hillslope, around the front of the apron, to end at a terminal, or door-jamb, to the east-north-east. The west segment of the wall consisted of the two wall faces with a soil core, a maximum of 1.7 m thick in all, while near the east terminal there was no soil core. Here the wall was *circa* 1.1 m thick. Between these two segments, the wall has collapsed downhill. Immediately inside the wall, and apparently following its course, were traces of a shallow wall-slot, *circa* 0.2 m wide. A similar, but more ephemeral, wall-slot was found around the back of the platform at the bottom of the scarp slope (Figure 3.14, A). It could not

be ascertained if, as seems likely, the two wall-slots joined to form a single feature. Inside the house were elements of an internal post-ring, measuring *circa* 5.2 m in diameter. This consisted of five, or possibly six, irregularly-spaced post-holes in the west half of the interior.

As noted above, the entrance was on the east-south-east. Only the stone-built right door-jamb survived. It is possible that the left jamb was formed by a terminal of the back wall-slot, rather than a stone wall. A line of edged stones at the inner edge of the doorway represents a threshold (not illustrated). The remains of an arc of paving ran from near the doorway, around the front of the house interior. Some paving stones overlay the front wall-slot. A scatter of paving-stones was also found at the back of the platform. A glass bead [1] was found between two of these paving stones. A broken flat slab of sandstone, blackened in places by fire, found north of the centre of the house, has been interpreted as a hearth-stone.

Above the scarp, and cut into the hillslope, was a crescentic ditch which ran from near the doorway, around the south of the scoop, to end to the west of the house. The east and west ends of the ditch were not terminals as such, but simply opened out onto the

*Plate 3.6   Houses 1 and 2, looking westwards.*

hillslope below. The ditch varied in depth and width, and was filled with a mixture of inwashed till and topsoil. The silted fill and the open ends suggest that it was a drainage ditch, cut to divert run-off from the hill around the house. To the south-east of the house, a short length of the ditch was considerably wider and the fill contained many large stones and boulders. This may have been a later pit cutting the ditch but this could not be proved stratigraphically. At the east end of the ditch, the fill contained a relatively high proportion of charcoal, some of it burnt hazelnut shell, and some burnt bone. The charcoal consisted of hazel and willow roundwood and gave a radiocarbon date of $2080 \pm 50$ bp (130 bc; GU-2172).

### House 8 *(Figure 3.14)*

Below and in front of House 1 was a scoop which may account for the damage to the front wall of the house. Investigation of the scoop was restricted by the quarry road to the north, but it appears to have been part of a house platform. The back scarp was cut into the steep slope in front of House 1. In front of the scarp was part of a level platform overlain by rubble. Under the rubble were remnants of paving, two lengths of possible wall-slot, a possible drainage ditch, and two post-holes. Hazel roundwood charcoal, from the putative drainage ditch, gave a date of $1910 \pm 120$ bp (ad 40; GU-2173).

### House 2 *(Figure 3.14 & Plate 3.6)*

The platform for House 2 was adjacent to, and west of, House 1. Because the hillslope at this point was relatively level the scoop was fairly shallow. A small scarp has been cut into the till subsoil and the apron was correspondingly low. The full shape of the platform was not ascertained, because some 50% of it has been removed by the quarry, but the surviving portion suggests that it was originally elliptical, some 6 m wide, and of unknown length. The short, steep slope in front of the platform appears to have been caused by scarping and is not a reflection of the apron which survived as a thin layer of re-deposited till and topsoil. Although House 2 was generally poorly preserved, the surviving evidence suggested that structures of two phases had occupied the scoop.

*Phase 1*   Phase 1 pre-dated the stone element. The surviving features of this phase are a wall-slot, patches of floor surface and, possibly, elements of a post-ring. The wall-slot survived around part of the south-west of the platform, at the bottom of the scarp, and was overlain by the later stone wall of Phase 2. It was a very shallow discontinuous groove, consisting of seven indentations measuring a maximum of *circa* 0.2 m wide and 0.05 m deep. Hazel roundwood charcoal from its fill was submitted for radiocarbon assay but the sample was found to be too small for dating. The remnant floor surface, surviving mostly under later stones, consisted of patches of compacted small stones and patches of concreted yellow B/C-horizon material, especially around a large basalt boulder located near the centre of the house. The boulder, naturally bedded in the till, protruded *circa* 0.25 m above the floor. The surviving elements of an internal post-ring comprised at least four post-holes. Because of the lack of stratigraphic relationships, it is impossible to identify the phase to which the post-ring belongs, although both phases may be represented. A pit (Figure 3.14, B), beside the house wall to the south-east, contained the upper stone of a beehive quern [2] (Plate 3.13) and sufficient charcoal for radiocarbon assay. The wood charcoal was hazel and willow roundwood and several seeds were also identified. The charcoal gave a date of 2000±55 bp (50 bc; GU-2178). The position of the quern in the pit, upside down, almost exactly fitting the shape of the lower part of the pit, and filling more than half of the volume, suggests that it may have been deliberately buried.

*Phase 1 abandonment* A shallow topsoil formed over the platform and floor surface before the construction of Phase 2 front wall. Hillwash soil had accumulated over the scarp and the back of the platform, together with a quantity of possible occupation debris in the form of charcoal-rich soil. Both of these layers were overlain by the back wall of the Phase 2 structure.

*Phase 2* This consisted of a stone wall, possibly elements of the post-ring, a hearth, a paved area, and a possible doorway. The wall survived best at the back of the platform. On the front it survived as two discontinuous wall-faces, one course high, representing the remains of a wall *circa* 1 m thick. Between the wall-faces were remnants of a core of brash and earth. Around the back of the platform, the wall was *circa* 1.2 m thick and mostly one course high, but at one point was four courses high. The inner face revetted the scarp but the wall rose above the height of the scarp and had an outer face, one course high. The wall core comprised brash and earth. A gap in the wall at the east side of the platform may have been a doorway but here the wall appears to have been damaged by the construction of House 1 and its drainage ditch, which removed most of the evidence. Internal paving survived in patches in the front half of the platform. The hearth overlay the floor of Phase 1 and consisted of a thin slab (now broken) of sandstone measuring *circa* 1 m by 0.6 m, abutting the south side of the large basalt boulder. The layer of floor surface under the hearth contained sufficient charcoal for radiocarbon assay. The charcoal, hazel roundwood, gave a date of 1970±80 bp (20 bc: GU-2171). The hearth-stone was sampled for thermoluminescence dating. The three samples produced a mean date of 70±190 BC (random error, RE), 210 (systematic error, SE).

## House 3 (Figure 3.15; Plate 3.7 & 3.8)

The platform of House 3 had been cut into a steep slope at the junction of the basalt plug with the sandstone.

The scarp, quarried into the basalt, was steep and high and the apron was correspondingly pronounced. The roughly circular platform sloped to the north-north-east with a drop of *circa* 1.25 m from back to front. The whole of the platform area was enclosed to form the interior of the house. The internal area was roughly circular but with the circumference built in more or less straight segments, each *circa* 2.5 m to 3 m long, giving the house a slightly polygonal plan.

The internal area measured *circa* 7.7 m by 6.5 m and was defined by a stone-faced bank integral with the apron's stone revetment at the front, a stone-faced scarp around the back, and unfaced scarp around the back to the south-east. The doorway was to the north-east. The front wall and apron were apparently constructed at the same time. The sloping outer face of the apron, revetted with large, irregular basalt boulders, rose to form the outer face of the wall, although this survived only in a short stretch to the right of the doorway. Most of the outer face of the wall and apron had collapsed onto the adjacent roadway (Roadway 1). The inner wall-face was more carefully constructed and survived to a height of *circa* 0.4 m to the north-west. The brashy soil core of the wall was indistinguishable from the main bulk of the apron material.

Despite careful investigation, no post or wall shadows were found within the soil core, which has been severely disturbed by roots. The wall varied in thickness from 1.0 m beside the doorway, to 1.7 m to the north-west. Smaller stones were used to construct the outer wall-face where it meets the hillslope. Also at this point was a short length of walling set within the wall-core, possibly as a reinforcement. From this point, the inner wall-face rose around the bottom of the scarp for a distance of *circa* 8 m, acting as facing for the irregular, jagged basalt surface. It survived to a maximum height of *circa* 0.4 m. The rest of the scarp, to the south-east, was smooth and near vertical. A short length of rough walling, with no obvious facing stones, at the east end of the scarp, formed the left side of the doorway. The right side of the doorway was better preserved. The doorway, *circa* 1.5 m wide, was not paved and no threshold stone was noted. Burnt bone was recovered from the doorway and outside of it in the soil on both the apron and Wall 5 (below).

The interior of the house was arranged into three annular divisions. An arc of paving, *circa* 1.5 m wide, ran for 6 m from within the doorway around the front of the house while, at the back, the platform had been quarried in such a way as to leave a raised platform which ran from the doorway to a point opposite it. Due to the nature of the basalt, the raised annulus had been roughly quarried and the resulting pitted surface had been infilled and levelled with brashy soil. Toward the doorway, the annulus dropped in a series of steps which were left unfilled. The central area of the house had no obvious surface. The sloping platform surface of trampled basalt, metamorphosed sandstone, sandstone and till, does not appear to have been the house floor. An obtrusive point of bedrock, and a small slab set on

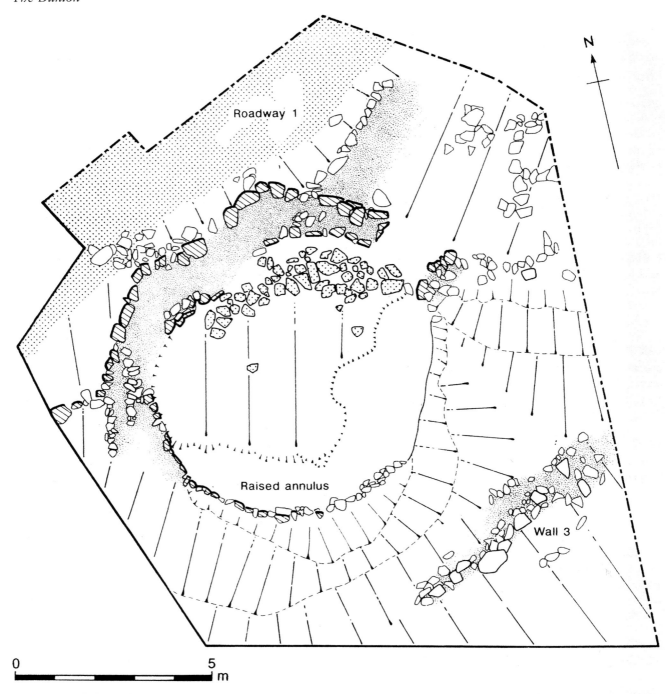

*Figure 3.15    Plan of House 3, Area 1. (Drawing by S Stevenson).*

edge, both beside the arc of paving, suggest that the central area was originally built up to form a level platform. Three layers of rubble filled the interior of the house and it is possible that the lowest represents this levelling. The upper rubble layers were associated respectively with the collapse of the house walls, and later gradual catchment of rocks from upslope. No internal post-ring was noted although it is possible that post settings may have remained undetected in the rubble in the front of the central area. Fragments of a burnt sandstone slab [43], probably the remains of the hearth-stone, and burnt bone were found within the lower rubble layer and sitting on the basalt bedrock.

*House 4 (Figure 3.16; Plate 3.9 & 3.10)*

The platform constructed for House 4 was at the bottom of a steep slope. The scarp had been cut into the slope and the material removed had been used to form a low apron, and hornworks to the north-west and south-east. The platform sloped toward the north-east and was elliptical in plan, measuring *circa* 10 m by 7.5 m. The quarry road has removed part of the apron and platform to the north-east.

The platform formed the internal area of the house which was defined by a variety of features. The inner face of the west hornwork was revetted with rough walling which increased in height to become facing for

*Plate 3.7  House 3, looking west-south-westwards. The entrance is located in the walling nearest to the foreground.*

*Plate 3.8  House 3, looking south-south-westwards. The apron and paving in the foreground show the extreme slope of the house floor.*

*Plate 3.9  House 4, looking south-westwards. The boulders on the eastern hornwork are on the extreme left, and the western hornwork is exposed on the right.*

the scarp. The preservation of the scarp facing was patchy but at one point, near the centre of the scarp, it survived to *circa* 1.7 m above the highest point of the platform. To the east was the second hornwork (Figure 3.16, X–Y). Here, no stone facing survived. The outer face of the west hornwork was also faced, the feature as a whole appearing as a broad stone-faced bank, *circa* 1.8 m wide and 6 m long, protruding from the hillside, with its upper surface dropping towards the north end.

The hornwork overlay Roadway 1 to the west. The front wall of the house was defined by a narrow, shallow wall-slot which ran around the front to meet the west hornwork *circa* 1.5 m from its terminal. The east end of the wall-slot (Plate 3.10) and the presumed doorway have been destroyed by the modern track.

Part of an internal post-ring survived (Plate 3.10). Its shape reflected the elliptical form of the house and it measured *circa* 5.5 m, north-south, by an estimated

*Plate 3.10  House 4, showing the hornworks, wall-slot and post-holes.*

6.5 m. At least seven post-holes survived, each *circa* 2 m apart, in the west part of the interior. During the occupation of the house, shallow gullies or hollows formed along the arc defined by the front wall-slot and the post-ring, and also from the presumed position of the doorway towards the centre of the house. These hollows were filled with dark, charcoal-stained loam which was subsequently overlain with flat paving-stones. The paving formed an incomplete arc running from the presumed doorway around the front of the house. A further area of paving survived between the post-ring and the west hornwork. Some of the paving stones overlay the wall-slot. A raised surface of compacted basaltic material ran around the back of the house between the post-ring and the faced scarp. No hearth was found, but patches of charcoal-flecked soil were noted on the house floor beside the west hornwork. This soil was interpreted as an occupation horizon. Charcoal from it, identified as hazel, oak, and various other species, was dated to $2090 \pm 150$ bp (140 bc; GU-2174).

After the abandonment of the house, the facing wall appears to have collapsed or been robbed, and the house floor was covered by a layer of stones and hillwash. Later disturbance, in the form of a crude 'cell', was built on this layer from stones presumably derived from the house walls. The cell was roughly U-shaped, faced internally with boulders, one course high, with an entrance to the south-east. Its use as a temporary shelter is indicated by layers of charcoal-stained soil and some burnt stone found within it.

### House 5 (Figure 3.16)

House 5 lay upslope, adjacent to House 4. Some 50% of the house and scoop was investigated. A steep scarp had been excavated and the material dumped to form a substantial apron. The north-west side of the scoop cut both the east hornwork of House 4 and a pathway (see Wall 1, below) associated with it. The front of the house was, like House 3, formed by a stone revetment of the apron which also served as the foundation of the outer face of the front wall. The inner face of the front wall survived to a maximum of two courses, and the space between the faces was filled with soil and rubble. The wall was *circa* 0.8 m thick. The inner face continued

around the internal area, facing the hornwork and scarp. Here, the facing was in the form of upright flat slabs. Gaps between the facing and the scarp were filled with soil and rubble.

The internal area appears to have been roughly D-shaped with the straight side formed by the scarp. The platform had a maximum observed width of *circa* 5 m and an estimated length of 7 m. It was probably totally surfaced with paving stones and rough cobbling. The back half of the platform was raised and mostly paved while the lower front half was crudely cobbled or 'pitched' with angular and sub-angular stones. The paving rested on a layer of re-deposited till, laid to provide a bed for the slabs and stones. Three post-holes were found after the paving was removed. It is not known if the posts protruded through the paving or if the paving was laid after the posts were removed. Like House 4, a layer of rubble and soil formed on the platform after its abandonment. A small hearth-like feature was built onto this layer but no hearth material was found.

### Peripheral features (Figure 3.13)

Walls and banks were found, in association with the houses (1 to 5, and 8) in Area 1. These appear to enclose, or partly enclose, houses or groups of houses, but poor preservation and the limited scale of excavation makes interpretation difficult. In some cases, relationships were established between walls, and between walls and other features.

*Wall 1 (Figure 3.13 & 3.16)*  This wall formed a boundary between the steep slope above Houses 4 and 5, and the less steep slope below House 7 (Figure 3.8). Both slopes appear to be natural although they have been altered to a limited extent by the occupation of the hill. The wall overlay the west hornwork of House 4 and Roadway 1 to the west-south-west of the house and ran from this point around the south of both Houses 4 and 5. It comprised a face or foundation course of boulders on the front edge, with rubble behind and on top of it. Behind the wall, and above House 5 and the east end of House 4, was a level pathway. A second pathway ran from House 5 to an entrance through Wall 1 at a point above House 4.

*Wall 2 (Figure 3.13 & 3.16)*  Wall 2, surviving as a short length of rubble bank, appears to block off the break in Wall 1, and is in turn overlain by Wall 3.

*Walls 3–6 (Figure 3.13 & 3.16)*  Wall 3, *circa* 1 m to 1.5 m thick, consisted of two faces of stones with an infill of brashy soil. It ran from a point near Wall 1 south-west of House 4, around and upslope of a scoop to the north-east of House 3, to die out above the scarp of House 3. This wall appears to have enclosed House 3 and the scoop to the north-east in conjunction with Wall 4–6. Wall 4 was noted to the west-north-west of House 3. It survived as a line of boulders, parallel to the roadway, and running from the front wall of House 3 to a point to the west-south-west where quarrying has removed it. Wall 5 is a bank of basalt rubble and brash, integral with the apron of House 3, and faced with a

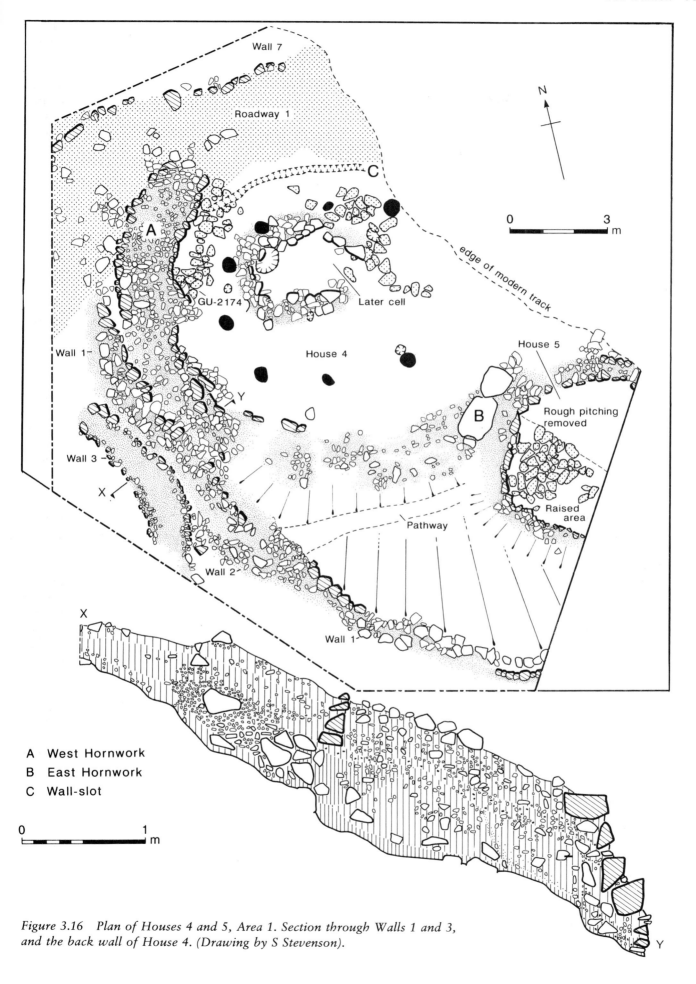

Wall 7

Roadway 1

N

0    3
m

C

A

edge of modern track

GU-2174

Later cell

Wall 1

House 4

House 5

Rough pitching removed

B

Y

Wall 3

Raised area

X

Wall 2

Pathway

Wall 1

X

A   West Hornwork
B   East Hornwork
C   Wall-slot

0    1
m

Y

*Figure 3.16   Plan of Houses 4 and 5, Area 1. Section through Walls 1 and 3, and the back wall of House 4. (Drawing by S Stevenson).*

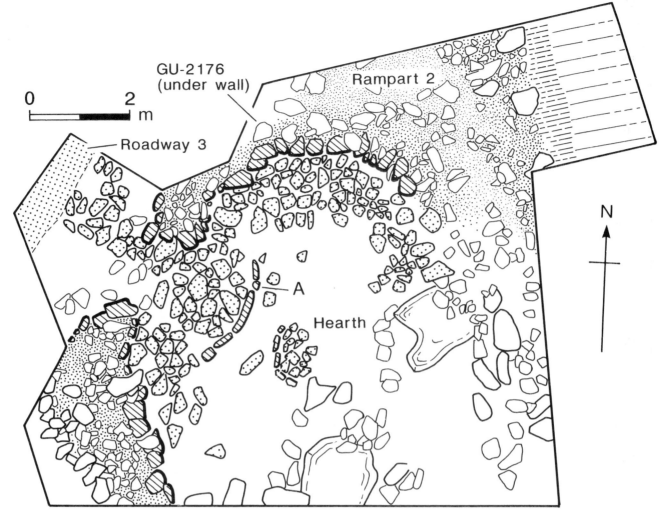

*Figure 3.17    Plan of House 6, Area 3. (Drawing by S Stevenson).*

single course of stones. It runs from the right of House 3 doorway and parallel to the roadway for a distance of *circa* 4 m. Wall 6, a single line of stones, appears to continue the line of Wall 5.

The scoop bounded by Wall 3, House 3, Walls 5 and 6, and the north end of Wall 1, has been quarried into the basalt plug. The quarried material appears to have been dumped downhill, behind Wall 6 and Wall 1, but no structure could be found in it. The scoop was filled with humic loam. In the bottom part of the fill some burnt bone was found.

*Wall 7 (Figure 3.16)*    This survived as a line of boulders overlying the north edge of Roadway 1 and behind House 2. Boulders in the wide part of the drainage ditch of House 1 may have originally continued this line along the road behind House 1. The wall was built on soil which had developed over the metalling of Roadway 1.

*Roadway 1*    The road ran between Houses 1 and 2 on its north side, and Houses 3 and 4 to the south. It consisted of a terrace rising across the hillside, surfaced with several layers and lenses of sub-rounded and rounded basalt pebbles in a matrix of humic loam. The pebble surfaces seem to result from attempts to prevent the surface of the road from becoming muddy. The

*Plate 3.11    House 6, looking north-westwards. The elliptical area of paving is to the left of the centre of the photograph.*

pebbles are unusual in that they only exist in any quantity on the road. It was noted, however, that basalt surfaces exposed during the excavation rapidly eroded due to frost action, and the resulting small angular stones quickly weathered to more rounded forms, giving a probable source for the road-stones. The relationship between the road and the houses was only clearly established in House 4, where the west hornwork and

*Table 3.1 Artefacts from Area 1.*

| context | coarse pottery | stone | | other |
|---|---|---|---|---|
| House 1 | | 67, 64, 56 | flint | 1 glass bead |
| | | 57 | flint scraper | |
| | | 24 | hammerstone | |
| | | 28 | notched | |
| | | 42 | water-worn | |
| House 2, interior | | 2 | beehive quern | 49 slag |
| | | 5 | small ball | |
| | | 18 | hammerstone | |
| | | 23 | water-worn | |
| House 2, exterior | | 11 | perforated disc | 70 bronze bell |
| House 3, interior | | 60, 65 | flint | |
| | | 8, 12, 10 | spindle whorls | |
| | | 21–22, 25–27 | hammerstones | |
| | | 15–16 | stone discs | |
| | | 3 | small ball | |
| | | 20, 31-41 | water-worn | |
| House 3, exterior | 45 | 62 | flint | |
| House 4, unstratified | | 7 | small ball | |
| | | 30 | hammerstone | |
| House 4, exterior | | 4 | small ball | |
| Wall 1 | | 9 | spindle whorl | 51 slag |
| Wall 3 | | 69 | quartz flake | 45 daub |
| Roadway 1 | | 61, 66 | flint blade | |
| | | 14, 17 | stone disc | |

Wall 1 overlay the road surface. Apron material from House 3 overlay the road but this could have been the result of slippage, while surfacing pebbles of the road overlapped the scoops of Houses 1 and 2; possibly also slippage.

*Artefacts*
Area 1 produced by far the greatest number of artefacts. These are presented in Table 3.1.

**Area 3 (Figure 3.17 & Plate 3.11)**

This trench was designed to investigate Rampart 2, the inner line of defence. It revealed not only the rampart but also the wall of House 6, and was then extended to investigate most of the house.

*House 6*
Unlike all other houses investigated, this house was constructed on a natural platform, obviating the need for quarrying. The platform was defined by a sharp drop in slope to the north and east, and a natural scarp of bedrock to the south. To the west was a narrow gully, the bottom of which was roughly level with the platform. The gully had functioned as a road (Roadway 3) during the occupation of the site, its surface metalled like Roadway 1. A natural and

convenient access, it was reused as the Upper Quarry Road, over the west of the house wall.

The house wall was poorly preserved. Where most complete, on the south-west, it survived as inner and outer arcs of boulders set on edge, with a core of soil and smaller stones. Elsewhere, the wall-line was marked by fallen facing stones, but on the south, beside the basalt scarp, none were found. Charcoal from a shallow negative feature beneath the wall, identified as alder, birch, and hazel roundwood, produced a date of $2120 \pm 110$ bp (170 bc; GU-2176). The house doorway, facing west-north-west, was identified from its paved floor; the door-jambs had not survived. The paving in the doorway continued outside the house for a short distance, to merge with the pebbled road surface. Inside the house, the paving was clearly defined. Here, the paving curved in towards the centre of the house, forming an elliptical platform, edged with upright stones on the south-east side (Figure 3.17, A). The rest of the house floor was lower and, apparently earthen, subsequently destructured by roots. A hearth was located *circa* 1 m from the widest part of the paving, near the centre of the house. It consisted of a sub-rectangular stone base, *circa* 1.2 m by 0.6 m, formed of small sandstone slabs kerbed with edged slabs on the north-west and south-west. The base slabs were sampled for thermoluminescence dating. Two of the three

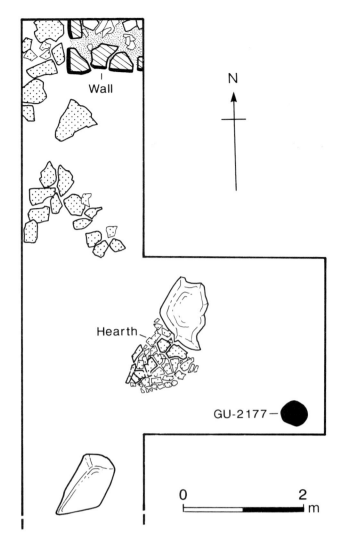

*Figure 3.18   Plan of House 7, Area 4. (Drawing by S Stevenson).*

samples (one was unsuitable for dating) produced a mean date of AD 60 ± 220 (RE), 220 (SE). Immediately to the south-south-west was a small outcrop of rock similar to, but smaller than, the one which protruded above the floor of House 2. A fragment of daub [47] and a burnt flint flake [68] were recovered from modern topsoil horizons. The negative feature under the house wall, which produced the radiocarbon date, contained some fragments of burnt bone and fragments of daub [48].

**Area 4 (Figure 3.18)**

*House 7 (Figure 3.18 & Plate 3.12)*
Before excavation, House 7 showed as one of a pair of house platforms beside the quarry edge to the south-west. The quarry had removed part of the scarp of the house. The trench in House 7 was designed solely to recover dating evidence from a presumed hearth. A trench 5 m by 3 m was opened in the centre of the platform. A hearth, similar to that in House 6, was located: 1.1 m long and 0.8 m wide, and of flat sandstone slabs edged by upright stones on the north-

*Plate 3.12   The hearth in House 7.*

west. The hearth-stones were sampled for thermoluminescence dating. Three samples produced a mean date of AD 180 ± 170 (RE), 180 (SE).

About 1.5 m to the south-east of the hearth was a single stone-packed post-hole. Charcoal from the post-hole, identified as oak from large diameter wood, produced a radiocarbon date of 4550 ± 100 bp (3600 bc; GU-2177). A trench, 2 m wide and 4 m long, was cut from the north-west corner of the original trench in an attempt to locate the house wall. Part of the left jamb of a door facing north, threshold paving and internal paving were found. A short trench running south from the south-west corner of the trench failed to locate a back wall.

Area 9

*Modern disturbance*
An unusual hollow was noted in a fairly steep slope on the north-east side of the hill *circa* 12 m south of Area 7. It lay outside the known limit of the fort and, on surface appearances, seemed to be a kiln or similar structure. A trench was opened over it, the north-west baulk serving as a half-section of the feature. This showed that it was a small narrow quarry with a level bottom, cut into the basalt bedrock, which had filled with rubble, brash, and brashy soil. No artefacts or other indications of its use were recovered. An anchor for a hawser, supporting a now dismantled radio mast, had been sunk into the fill.

ARTEFACTUAL EVIDENCE

The artefacts from the 1984–1986 seasons are discussed together with those recovered from the 1961–1962 excavations.

**Glass bead (Figure 3.19) *J Henderson***

There is a restricted amount of prehistoric glass from Scotland which derives from secure archaeological contexts. The glass bead from The Dunion [1] (Appendix 13), however, was found pressed into the platform surface of House 1, which has been dated to 130 ± 50 bc (GU-2172) by a radiocarbon date derived from a feature of the same phase on the site.

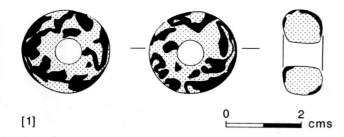

[1]

0 _____ 2 cms

*Figure 3.19 Glass bead. Areas shown in black represent yellow glass, and those shown stippled represent blue glass. (Drawing by S Stevenson).*

## Description and production technique

This annular bead has a translucent, bubbled, bottle-green coloured matrix with a random surface trailed decoration of opaque yellow glass. It measures 23.4 mm in diameter, 10 mm deep and is pierced by a hole 7.3 mm to 7.7 mm in diameter. The bubbles in the green glass are both circular and elongated, the latter radiating from the central hole. The combination of the regular bubble orientation and the regular cross-sectional profile of the bead indicates a specific technique of manufacture.

A rod of green glass was wound around a metal rod and joined to form a bead, the bead was re-heated to a semi-fluid state and possibly spun around on the metal rod. This would cause the bubbles to radiate from the metal rod/bead hole in the observed orientation and, at the same time, regularise the bead's shape. The opaque yellow glass was dropped onto the bead, possibly before it was spun. Some of the yellow glass extends into the hole where it has been flattened against the side of the hole. The yellow decoration has probably been marvered into the surface of the bead at a later stage.

The closest parallel for the bead is a type commonly found on the continent of Europe, dating from about the second century BC onwards (La Tène C2 and D1). The general type is described as being annular with spotted opaque decoration in contrasting colours (Guido 1978, group 1 and Haevernick 1960, group 24).

The Dunion bead is smaller than average. The transparent 'bottle green' colour of the bead matrix is also unusual for the type, since the bead matrices are normally translucent cobalt blue or translucent brown. The opaque yellow glass has been roughly applied; although it is of similar hue to that used for the decoration of continental examples, its chemical composition is distinctly different (see below). These factors indicate that The Dunion bead was made outside the main, central European, production areas.

## Scientific analysis (see Henderson p 43 for methodology)

The analytical results for both the opaque yellow and green glasses are given in Table 3.2. The most obvious difference in composition is the much higher level of lead oxide (PbO) (and correspondingly lower level of silica ($SiO_2$)) detected in the yellow glass (27.5%) than in the green glass. While this is typical of opaque yellow

*Table 3.2 Electron-probe microanalyses of the glass. Oxide weights are expressed as percentages.*

| matrix | opaque yellow decoration | translucent green |
|---|---|---|
| $Na_2O$ | 5.0 | 7.3 |
| MgO | 0.7 | 1.0 |
| $Al_2O_3$ | 3.0 | 5.4 |
| $SiO_2$ | 53.1 | 73.2 |
| $P_2O_5$ | ND | ND |
| $SO_3$ | 0.25 | 0.27 |
| Cl | 0.5 | 0.95 |
| $K_2O$ | 0.54 | 0.53 |
| CaO | 6.0 | 8.5 |
| $TiO_2$ | 0.1 | 0.19 |
| MnO | 0.7 | 1.2 |
| $Fe_2O_3$ | 0.79 | 1.0 |
| CoO | ND | MDL |
| NiO | ND | ND |
| CuO | ND | 0.09 |
| $As_2O_3$ | ND | MDL |
| $SnO_2$ | MDL | ND |
| $Sb_2O_3/Sb_2O_5$ | 2.0 | ND |
| PbO | 27.5 | 0.03 |
| totals | 101.24% | 99.82% |

ND   not detected
MDL   minimum detectable level

glasses which date as far back as the seventh century BC in Europe north of the Alps, the presence of a lead pyroantimonate ($Pb_2Sb_2O_7$) opacifier accompanied by 0.7% manganese oxide (MnO) is significant. The yellow lead pyroantimonate opacifier was used in the manufacture of yellow glass beads at Meare Lake Village, but at Meare the glass did not contain such a high level of MnO. A *terminus post quem* for the occurrence of MnO at the levels found in the opaque yellow The Dunion glass is the second century BC (Henderson & Warren 1983).

The yellow glass, used in decoration of continental beads of this type, is frequently opacified with a tin-rich compound ('$PbSnO_3$'), so The Dunion yellow glass is distinct from these. The composition of The Dunion yellow glass is most similar to glasses used in decorating beads from northern France and southern England (Guido 1978, class 5). Opaque yellow glass of a very similar composition is also used in the production of many of the beads found at Culbin Sands, Grampian

(Henderson 1989a and 1989b). Unfortunately the Culbin beads are very poorly provenanced, and possibly date to the first to second centuries AD.

The chemical composition of the transparent green matrix of the bead indicates that it is coloured by a combination of iron and manganese oxides. The relative contribution to the colour from each oxide is difficult to ascertain without using a technique such as ultraviolet-visible-infra-red spectroscopy analysis (Green & Hart 1987). The glass is otherwise of a soda-lime-silica composition, but with unusually high alumina and low soda contents.

*Discussion*

Although the bead is similar in type to those found in continental *oppida*, its colour, size and chemical composition distinguishes it from most other examples. It is radiocarbon dated to roughly the second to first century BC. A similar date range, perhaps extending into the first century AD, can be inferred from the compositional similarities of other Late Iron Age beads from Britain and Europe. Bearing in mind that the bead has important technical and typological differences from other related glass bead types and glass compositions, it can be classified as a variant from the more typical examples. It is possible that The Dunion bead was made in Scotland. However, there is no evidence that the putative manufacturing site at Culbin Sands, Grampian (Guido 1978 and Henderson 1989b) produced the type. It may have been a 'one-off' copy of extant examples. Another copy of a glass bead type which was in existence in Europe considerably earlier (*circa* fifth century BC), an opaque yellow annular bead, was derived from Culbin. This is of exactly the same type as examples excavated from Meare Lake Village, Somerset, but has a distinctly different chemical composition (Henderson 1987).

### Querns (Figure 3.20 & 3.21) A MacSween · J S Rideout *geological identification D Dixon*

Three upper stones of beehive querns, two complete and one half-stone, were recovered from The Dunion, together with a rough-out for a fourth upper stone (Appendix 14). All the finished stones fit into Curwen's (1937, 1941) southern Scottish 'Roman Legionary' type, having funnel-shaped hoppers, flat grinding surfaces and horizontal handle-holes which are not pierced through to the pipe. The circular cross-section of the perforation of the lower, pivot hole of quern [2], indicates that the upper stone was turned a full circle and not back and forwards through an arc.

MacKie (1971) and Caulfield (1977) have argued that beehive querns were introduced into Scotland prior to the Roman advance. Caulfield (1977, 106) has argued for the end of the first century AD as a *terminus ante quem* for the introduction of beehive querns into Scotland. The radiocarbon date from the pit containing quern [2] (Plate 3.13), (50±55 bc; GU-2178), does not contradict this hypothesis.

Plate 3.13  *The beehive quern [2] found inverted in Pit B inside House 2.*

Caulfield (*ibid*) has suggested that the southern querns appear, from their wide feed-pipes, to have been timber-mounted, while the narrow feed-pipes of the northern querns indicate that metal fittings were used (a wooden spindle slim enough to enable grain to pass down the pipe would not have supported the weight of the revolving top stone). That metal fittings were used is indicated by the survival, in quern [2] from The Dunion (Figure 3.21), of a small lump of material in the broken handle socket. It came away cleanly from the side of the slot and the crumbs were found to be magnetic (R Welander, pers comm). This probably represents the remains of a corroded iron handle.

The Dunion querns all appear to have been made in the vicinity of the site. The rock types, sandstone, LORS porphyry and vent agglomerate, can all be found locally. In addition, a rough-out for the top stone of a beehive quern was found on the site. The rough-out is a sandstone block, approximately bun-shaped in section, with a pecked hollow on the upper surface, a flattened lower surface, and the beginnings of a handle-hole in one side.

### Stone axe (Figure 3.22; Appendix 15) P R Ritchie

A small stone axe [44], sub-rectangular in shape, with an arc-shaped blade and a broad butt formed by three facets, was retrieved from beneath Roadway 4. The sides are curved and facetted, and there are scars along one

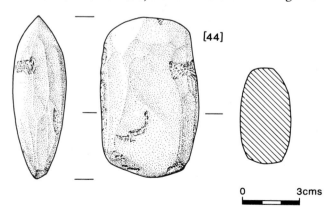

Figure 3.22  *Stone axe. (Drawing by S Stevenson).*

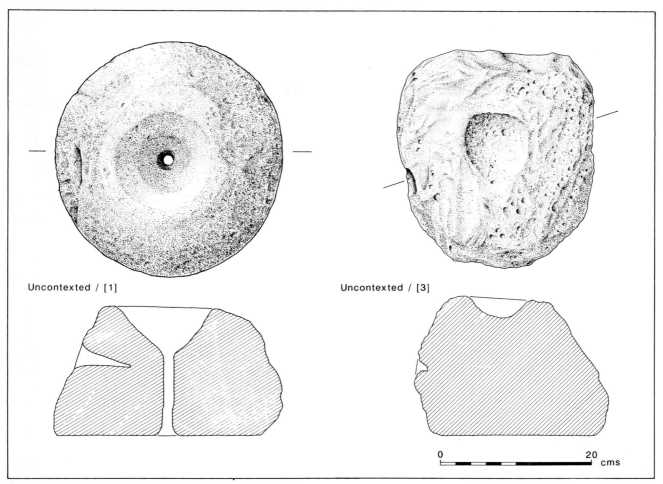

Uncontexted / [1]

Uncontexted / [3]

0           20
cms

*Figure 3.20 Beehive querns (uncontexted): complete [1] and roughed-out [3]. (Drawing by S Stevenson).*

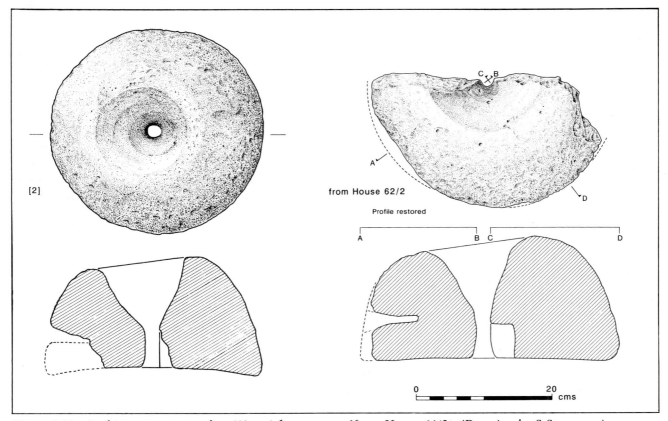

[2]

from House 62/2

Profile restored

0           20
cms

*Figure 3.21   Beehive querns: complete [2] and fragmentary [from House 62/2]. (Drawing by S Stevenson).*

side. The axe has a good overall polish, although some flake scars were not removed. Wear traces in the form of striations and edge chipping suggest that the axe was used, and it is probable from its shape that it was made from a larger axe. It was made from a fine-grained rock, light green in colour with small pale blebs. Thin-sectioning would be necessary to positively identify the rock type, but it appears to be fine-grained ash.

**Coarse stone (Appendix 15)** *V J McLellan · geological identification G Collins and D Dixon*

A total of fifty-seven coarse stone objects were recovered from The Dunion. These comprise fourteen manuports, fifteen utilised pebbles, five unperforated discs, four perforated discs, two discs with countersunk perforations, nine stone balls, a jet armlet fragment (Figure 3.23), a lamp fragment, a flat pebble with a depression on each face, and a carved 'cottage-loaf'-shaped stone [uncontexted/6]. Three querns and a quern rough-out are reported upon separately (above, and Appendix 14). There was no evidence for the use of any material which could not have been obtained locally.

Small stone balls have been found on various hillfort sites in south-east Scotland, and it has been suggested (Cool 1982, 95) that they were used as game-counters rather than as sling-stones, their traditional interpretation. The remainder of the coarse stone artefacts are chronologically insensitive. The 'cottage-loaf-shaped' stone was unstratified and its function is unclear. It is possible that a cloth was tied around it and that it was used as a vessel plug.

**Pottery (Appendix 16)** *A MacSween · geological identification E Campbell*

The pottery assemblage from The Dunion comprises over two hundred sherds, most from the 1962 excavations, representing at least fifteen vessels.

The majority of sherds are from hand-made, coil-constructed vessels, some (for example, [61/16], [62/3], [62/11]) with inverted rims, and one [62/11a] with a flat base. From the exterior and interior sooting on most of the sherds, it would seem that these were cooking vessels.

The vessels have been made from a very coarse clay, containing a high percentage of quartz sand, less frequent igneous inclusions and 'opaques', occasional mica and a 'mixed gravel' component, suggesting boulder clay as its most likely source. In most cases it appears that the natural clay provided sufficient 'opening material' to ensure that the vessels survived firing, but sometimes angular fragments of coarsely crushed rock were added, comprising up to 20% of the final clay body. Some vessels have disproportionately large inclusions. Vessel [62/11a], for example, has inclusions up to 20 mm long in walls 14 mm thick.

The rock fragments used for tempering the pottery from the 1961 and 1962 seasons were identified by

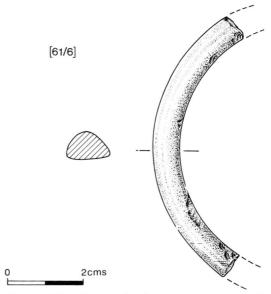

[61/6]

0    2cms

*Figure 3.23    Jet armlet fragment. (Drawing by S Stevenson).*

Ewan Campbell as micro-, and macro-porphyritic basalts with plagioclase feldspar phenocysts, known as Jedburgh and Markle type basalts. The fragments are weathered on all surfaces, and it is more likely that that their source was a local scree deposit possibly on The Dunion, rather than an alluvial deposit.

The sherds from The Dunion have parallels with pottery from other hillforts in south-east Scotland, notably from Hownam Rings (Piggott C M 1948) and Cool's Type I pottery from Broxmouth (Cool 1982). Cool notes that Type I pottery (large coarsely made vessels with inturned rims) regularly occurred along with small stone balls, and assigned it a date between 400 bc and 200 bc. However, the fragmentary nature of the pottery from The Dunion makes it difficult to ascertain whether or not the assemblage is restricted to vessels with inverted rims, and it is probably advisable to assign to it a more general 'late prehistoric' date.

Four sherds from the 1961–2 excavations stand out as different to these coarse vessels. [62/5b] is a fragment of an everted rim. Apart from being different in shape it is also different in fabric, being made from a fine clay with abundant quartz and black igneous inclusions. Due to the abraded nature of the sherd, it is not possible to tell if it was wheel-thrown, but it could be Roman in date.

Sherd [62/8] is a small sherd with a series of ridges and grooves on one side and a red slip on the other. It is possibly from the point of inflection of the neck and shoulder of a vessel. The clay is again fine with quartz sand and black igneous inclusions. Although abraded, there are very faint traces of what may have been a glaze on the ridged side. The sherd is most probably from a medieval vessel.

Two other sherds are differentiated by their fabrics. [62/6] is a fragment of a vessel made from very fine-grained clay. The sherd has numerous round voids, probably from burnt-out organics. [62/7] is from a similar clay, this time tempered with shell. The date and source of these sherds remain unknown.

The pottery was so fragile when found that it was sent to the Institute of Archaeology, London University for treatment with polyvinyl acetate, which has given it a heavy sheen. Black sooty deposits, probably cooking residues, are clearly visible on most of the sherds, but they are not now suitable for examination.

*Acknowledgement*
The author would like to thank Dr David Breeze for his comments on the later pottery.

## Metalworking debris (Appendix 17) *R M Spearman*

A small quantity of metalworking debris, from a variety of contexts, was examined at x10 magnification and checked for magnetic attraction. All was found to be iron-smelting debris from a bloomery furnace. The debris ranged from bloomery cinder to more vitreous run slags. While no furnace sites were recovered, it is likely that bloomery smelting had taken place at The Dunion. However, as the quantity of debris recovered was extremely small, the bloomery may be located at some distance from the excavation area. It should also be noted that such debris may be derived from bloomeries of any date from Iron Age to post-medieval times.

## Chipped stone (Appendix 18) *B Finlayson*

The sample consists of fourteen pieces, one of which, a quartz flake [69] is possibly natural in origin. The rest consists of ten pieces of flint and three pieces of chert. All three pieces of chert have been flaked, although only one [63] is truly a core, and then only a fragment. Five of the flint pieces have some retouch, but only two fit into typological categories. One [57] is a fine steep discoidal scraper, the other is a denticulate piece like Clarke's 'serrated flake' class (Clarke 1960). Little can be said about such an assemblage, both because of its small size and because of its composition (three chert cores, ten flint flakes).

## Bronze bell *D Caldwell*

A small cast bronze bell (H 58 mm; dia at lip 47 mm; Figure 3.24) was found in the topsoil overlying House 2. It is conical in shape with a suspension loop on its crown and a moulding wire just above an out-turned lip. In the interior corrosion at the top and side indicate that it originally had an iron clapper.

A comparison of its shape with tower bells, for example that from Kersmains near Roxburgh (Clouston 1976), suggests a twelfth-century date for it. Bells known to be later in date tend to have a convex profile and are often squatter. The Royal Museum of Scotland has five small cast bronze bells of similar size, only two of which

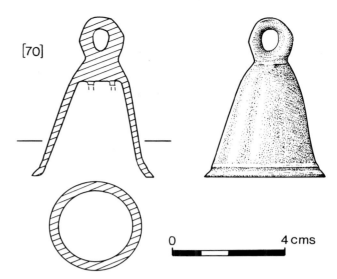

*Figure 3.24   Cast bronze bell. (Drawing by S Stevenson).*

have known Scottish provenances: one from Paisley, the other found near Linlithgow Palace. Both are likely to be later in date than the Dunion bell. Another similar bell was found at Houton Chapel in Orkney and is now in Tankerness House Museum, Kirkwall. Yet another, described as a 'small bronze bell, uninscribed and without ornament . . . rounded shoulders and a little ring-shaped handle at the top' was found underneath the Parish Church of Renfrew (*Palace of History* 1099, *no* 12).

Such bells might have served a liturgical purpose. They might equally well have been used as cattle-bells.

## ENVIRONMENTAL EVIDENCE

### Pollen *S Butler*

In the freshly cut section of Rampart 1a a thin dark line appeared to delimit the rampart material above from the *in situ* palaeosol beneath. It is thought that this darker material represents the land surface upon which the rampart was built: the A-horizon of the old soil with a leached A2-horizon beneath. Four small Kubiena tins were used to sample a stratigraphic column through the buried soil and the base of the rampart material. Three further samples were collected from the topmost one or 2 cm of other believed buried A-horizons. Two of the latter came from beneath boulders, one from the facing of Rampart 1a and one overlying Roadway 1, while the remaining sample came from beneath the apron of House 3. In the laboratory five contiguous samples from Kubiena tin number 2, containing the old land surface, plus the three additionally collected samples were all processed using the technique described in the Eildon pollen report (above).

*Results (Table 3.3)*
All five samples from under the core of Rampart 1a and the sample from beneath the apron of House 3 proved to

*Table 3.3   Pollen record. Values are expressed as percentages of total land pollen (TLP), which includes all trees, shrubs and herbs, and excludes spores. Spores: Pteridium, Polypodium, Filicales and Sphagnum. The pollen content of samples RED 0924(2) (0–8 cm) were insufficient for percentage calculations.*

| | raw pollen counts | | | | | | | | % TLP | |
| | rts | rys | HP3 | sample 0924 (2) sub-sample depths (cm) | | | | | rts | rys |
| | | | | 0–2 | 2–5 | 5–6 | 6–7 | 7–8 | | |
|---|---|---|---|---|---|---|---|---|---|---|
| Sample size (g) | 30 | 30 | 30 | 12 | 19 | 9 | 8 | 8 | | |
| *Pinus* | 2 | 0 | 2 | 0 | 0 | 1 | 0 | 0 | 0.7 | 0.0 |
| *Quercus* | 1 | 1 | 0 | 0 | 0 | 0 | 0 | 0 | 0.3 | 0.2 |
| *Betula* | 4 | 2 | 0 | 0 | 0 | 0 | 0 | 0 | 1.4 | 0.5 |
| *Alnus* | 12 | 13 | 0 | 0 | 8 | 0 | 0 | 0 | 4.0 | 3.0 |
| Coryloid | 28 | 39 | 0 | 1 | 12 | 1 | 1 | 1 | 9.6 | 9.0 |
| *Calluna* | 142 | 250 | 0 | 0 | 5 | 6 | 0 | 1 | 49.0 | 59.0 |
| Gramineae | 76 | 103 | 2 | 0 | 22 | 7 | 0 | 0 | 26.0 | 24.0 |
| cereal | 0 | 1 | 0 | 0 | 0 | 0 | 0 | 0 | 0.0 | 0.2 |
| *Plantago lanceolata* | 15 | 10 | 0 | 0 | 2 | 0 | 0 | 0 | 5.0 | 2.4 |
| Chenopodiaceae | 1 | 0 | 0 | 0 | 0 | 0 | 0 | 0 | 0.3 | 0.0 |
| Caryophyllaceae | 3 | 0 | 0 | 0 | 0 | 0 | 0 | 0 | 1.0 | 0.0 |
| Compositae tub | 3 | 2 | 0 | 0 | 0 | 0 | 0 | 0 | 1.0 | 0.5 |
| Compositae lig | 4 | 2 | 0 | 0 | 2 | 1 | 0 | 0 | 1.4 | 0.5 |
| *Pteridium* | 11 | 10 | 0 | 1 | 1 | 0 | 0 | 0 | 3.8 | 2.4 |
| *Polypodium* | 3 | 2 | 0 | 0 | 0 | 0 | 1 | 0 | 1.0 | 0.5 |
| Filicales | 600 | 75 | super-abundant | | | | | | 200.0 | 18.0 |
| *Sphagnum* | 3 | 5 | 0 | 0 | 2 | 1 | 0 | 0 | 1.0 | 1.2 |
| trees | 19 | 16 | | | | | | | 6.5 | 3.8 |
| shrubs | 28 | 39 | | | | | | | 9.6 | 9.0 |
| herbs | 244 | 370 | | | | | | | 84.0 | 87.0 |
| TLP | 291 | 425 | | | | | | | – | – |
| spores | 617 | 92 | | | | | | | 212.0 | 22.0 |

rts   rampart stone
rys   roadway stone

contain pollen spectra entirely dominated by fern spores. In contrast, the two samples from beneath boulders contained a much greater proportion of other pollen types, although fern spores were still present, and were indeed abundant under the rampart facing stone. Fern spores are noted for their resistance to decay (Dimbleby 1985, 29), and it is perhaps significant that other pollen and spore types have survived best only in those samples taken from beneath boulders. Thus it may be that large boulders have provided microenvironments at The

Dunion more conducive to pollen survival, perhaps by conserving soil moisture. The two pollen spectra from beneath boulders have therefore preserved more information about the past vegetation than the contexts buried by less protective material, such as the rampart fill. Whilst the condition of the pollen in these two samples was good, the evidence for soil leaching warns that post-depositional effects may have caused biases even in these contexts, but it is not possible to assess these without a detailed stratigraphic pollen profile. As essentially sealed contexts beneath boulders, there may have been little inwashing of younger pollen from above, but some pollen may have been lost to lower layers in the profile. The topmost 1 cm of these buried A-horizons was sampled, but the time period represented by these samples is not known; the pollen therefore represents an undefined duration of deposition but is likely to include pollen from the vegetation at time of burial.

Clear similarities exist between the two spectra. In both cases the best represented taxa are *Calluna vulgaris* (ling), Gramineae (grasses) and Filicales (ferns). This very likely represents a patchy heath-grass association growing on the shallow stony soil, while rocks and rocky outcrops were perhaps favoured by the ferns. The vegetation association could well have included as additionals many of the other taxa found in the pollen spectra, notably *Pteridium* (bracken), *Sphagnum* (bog moss) and Compositae species (daisy family). *Plantago lanceolata* (ribwort plantain) is strongly light-demanding and, as a local herb, its presence would suggest that the heathland association had plentiful open grassy places within it. The *Plantago lanceolata* pollen, which is often taken to signify pasturage or fallow land (see Behre 1981) might also suggest that this patchy heathland was used as rough grazing.

There are few trees and shrubs represented in the pollen spectra and there are no real grounds for postulating local tree or scrub growth. *Alnus* (alder) in particular, with its high moisture requirements, is unlikely to have favoured the well drained Dunion soils, and most of the arboreal pollen probably derives from 'regional' or 'extra-local' sources. Coryloid is the best represented taxon.

### Conclusion

Pollen analysis of believed A-horizons on The Dunion has been used to investigate the hillside vegetation prior to their burial. Locally, an open heathland mosaic of ling and grasses with ferns has been postulated. This could have provided rough pasturage prior to construction of the settlement on this part of the hill.

## Macroplant remains *A D Fairweather*

The bulk samples, and some dating samples, were floated without frothing agents, and the carbonised material collected in two mesh sizes (1 mm, 0.3 mm). Twelve samples were examined to assess the quality of the macroplant evidence. These samples were selected from contexts in Houses 1, 4, 5 and 6, judged likely to produce high levels of carbonised material. Cursory examination of the carbonised material suggested that few seeds were present. Two seeds, one leguminous and one unidentifiable, were retrieved from beneath the paving in House 4, while occupation material in House 4 yielded a range of seeds (Table 3.4). The other nine samples did not contain identifiable carbonised remains.

## Charcoal identification *R P J McCullagh*

Charcoal identification was undertaken on the nine samples submitted for radiocarbon dating, to identify and remove exotic species or other extraneous material that might bias the dates (Table 3.5). In most cases the samples were screened through a 2 mm sieve and the two fractions examined separately. Only when the fraction of smaller fragments contained identifiable specimens was it retained.

The carbonised material was identified using the CEU reference collections and the keys of Schweingruber (1978) and Bergren (1969, 1981). The nomenclature follows Clapham *et al* (1962).

All the charcoal, with the exception of the oak in GU-2177, came from small to very small diameter wood; no fragment derived from wood larger in diameter than 40 mm. It was highly fragmented, with few specimens retaining bark. Given the small size of the samples, the numbers of identified specimens are necessarily small. Identification was done in batches of ten specimens and ceased when no new species was encountered in a batch. Only wood charcoal was submitted for dating. Other remains noted in the samples are listed in Appendix 19.

Hazel was predominant in six samples (House 2 (wall-slot) GU-2178, GU-2171, GU-2172, GU-2173, GU-2175). Three specimens of willow and one of birch occurred in GU-2178; one specimen of willow was found in GU-2172; and three specimens of birch occurred in GU-2175. These seven specimens amount to only 10% of the total identified in these six samples.

Oak occurred in only two samples: as the sole species in one (GU-2177) and a minor component of the second (GU-2174). This charcoal was in all cases small radial fragments from timber of indeterminate diameter and in several cases the curvature of the growth rings was so slight that original diameters of at least 100 mm are indicated.

A greater diversity was recorded from the remaining sample (GU-2174) which contained charcoal of hazel, oak, and wild cherry (*Prunus avium*). This sample also contained small fragments of unidentifiable burnt bone, a few carbonised seeds and, in the fine fraction, an assemblage of small siliceous balls.

Little archaeological weight can be placed on these identifications because the sample yields were so low. However it is notable that hazel should occur almost exclusively in six of the samples. Hazel is among the commonest of roundwood types on prehistoric sites, presumably because it coppices so successfully.

The small siliceous balls, from sample GU-2174 (above), were no larger than 1.5 mm in diameter and were spherical. Several occurred as groups of spheres fused together. Their surfaces were deeply pitted and they were hollow. They were white or opaque. Two differed from this description in being more solid and the surface was flecked with red and grey. These latter spheres were magnetic.

*Table 3.4  Macroplant catalogue.*

| sample context | result |
|---|---|
| House 1, drainage ditch | no identifiable remains |
| House 1, drainage ditch | no identifiable remains |
| House 4, occupation layer under paving | no identifiable remains, siliceous ball (*cf* charcoal report) |
| House 4, occupation layer under paving | 1 seed, unidentifiable |
| House 4, occupation layer under paving | no identifiable remains, siliceous ball |
| House 4, occupation layer under paving | 1 leguminous seed, too damaged to be more specific |
| House 4, occupation material | no identifiable remains |
| House 4, occupation material | (see below) |
| House 4, raised annulus | no identifiable remains |
| House 4, secondary structure | no identifiable remains |
| House 5, platform levelling under paving | no identifiable remains |
| House 6, negative feature under wall | no identifiable remains |

Only one sample produced any quantity of significant remains (from occupation material in House 4), *viz* 19 grains of *Hordeum vulgare*, 12 fragments of *Hordeum* sp, 6 grains of *Avena*. The grain size of *Avena* could represent different species (most probably *A strigosa* or *A fatua*), or the smaller grains could be from secondary florets of the same species. There were not sufficient parts (*eg* fracture bases) to permit more certain identification.
2 fruits of *Polygonum cf persicaria/lapathifolium* type but fruits damaged.
1 achene of *Cirsium* sp.
3 caryopses of non-cereal Gramineae: 2 comparable to *Poa annua* (annual meadow grass) and 1 not further identifiable.
2 small seeds very abraded and not further identifiable.

*Table 3.5  Samples submitted for radiocarbon dating.*

| context | charcoal identifications | weight (g) | SURRC *no* |
|---|---|---|---|
| House 2, wall slot | hazel | 15.64 | * |
| House 2, quern pit | hazel, willow | 16.35 | GU-2178 |
| House 2, soil under hearth | hazel | 11.04 | GU-2171 |
| House 1, drainage ditch | hazel, willow | 46.08 | GU-2172 |
| House 8, drainage ditch | hazel | 10.72 | GU-2173 |
| House 4, occupation horizon | hazel, oak, wild cherry | 9.48 | GU-2174 |
| Fill of gully behind Rampart 1 | hazel, birch | 27.27 | GU-2175 |
| House 6, negative feature under wall | alder, birch, hazel | 10.15 | GU-2176 |
| House 7, post-hole | oak | 8.47 | GU-2177 |

## DATING

### Themoluminescence dates *D C W Sanderson*

Nine samples of heated stones taken from three hearths were collected for thermoluminescence (TL) dating at the Scottish Universities Research and Reactor Centre. The technique establishes the time elapsed since the last heating of the sample, which in the case of a domestic hearth-stone represents the *terminus ante quem* for the abandonment of the context. In view of the clarity of archaeological association, burned hearth-stones represent an important, and under-explored source of dating material. It was possible to obtain feldspar inclusion dates from eight of the samples. Taken together the TL dates imply that the occupation is most likely to have ended in the first century AD. See Appendix 20 for methodology and Table 3.6 for the results.

*Discussion and interpretation*
Of the samples examined, one proved to have been only partially zeroed by archaeological heating. This sample failed to give a plateau (*ie* a zone where the TL stored

Table 3.6  *Thermoluminescence (TL) dates.*

| sample | mineral type | density fraction | palaeodose P/Gy | intercept I/P | Slope ratio | plateau °C±% | stability (%) | total dose rate /mGy a-1 | age/ka BP |
|---|---|---|---|---|---|---|---|---|---|
| House 2, context F1031 | | | | | | | | | |
| SUTL41 | plagioclase | 2.62–2.74 | 5.77±.53 | .05±.15 | .88±.05 | 380–440±9 | .93±.03 | 2.55±.27 | 2.27±.32 |
| SUTL42 | Na feldspar | 2.58–2.62 | 4.07±.29 | .09±.09 | .98±.08 | 300–340±4 | .95±.03 | 2.01±.28 | 2.03±.32 |
| SUTL43 | K feldspar | 2.51–2.58 | 3.40±1.5 | -.3±.21 | .64±.26 | 330–430±19 | .72±.05 | 2.48±.23 | 1.37±.61 |
| House 6, context F9014 | | | | | | | | | |
| SUTL44 | K feldspar | 2.51–2.58 | failed plateau test: insufficiently heated | | | | | 2.73+.28 | —— |
| SUTL45 | Na feldspar | 2.58–2.62 | 3.63+.52 | -.1+.25 | .56+.15 | 350–450+8 | .99+.02 | 2.01+.30 | 1.08+.37 |
| SUTL | plagioclase | 2.62–2.74 | 5.72+1.5 | .12+.03 | .90+.08 | 400–430+7 | 1.06+.05 | 2.45+.27 | 2.33+.68 |
| House 7, context F12003 | | | | | | | | | |
| SUTL47 | K feldspar | 2.51–2.58 | 5.24±.31 | -.3±.4 | .75±.35 | 330–430±12 | .98±.02 | 2.01±.30 | 2.61±.42 |
| SUTL48 | Na feldspar | 2.58–2.62 | 4.10±.50 | -.04±.1 | 1.1±1.3 | 370–470±5 | .85±.03 | 2.22±.28 | 1.58±.32 |
| SUTL49 | polymineral | 2.51–2.74 | 3.42±.29 | -.31±2 | .93±.6 | 350–470±18 | 1.0±.01 | 2.22±.27 | 1.54±.23 |

The grain size was 90–125 and the water content 0.05 + 0.02 for all samples.

*Table 3.7   Weighted mean TL ages and dates for the hearths.*

| House | mean age | date |
|-------|----------|------|
| 2 | 2055 ± 190 | 70 BC ± 190, 210 |
| 6 | 1920 ± 220 | AD   60 ± 220, 220 |
| 7 | 1800 ± 170 | AD 180 ± 170, 180 |

dose is not dependent on glow curve temperature) and had a high and variable equivalent dose. Of the other eight samples measured, the most successful measurements came from Na feldspar extracts which had very acceptable plateaux and TL characteristics. The potassium feldspars and plagioclase extracts by contrast showed poorer reproducibility and produced ages with a high uncertainty. With the exception of samples SUTL43 and SUTL48 there was no significant fading of TL signal in the two-month laboratory storage test. In these other two cases the results have been corrected for observed fading which appears to be satisfactory at the level of precision achieved.

The individual results for each house refer to the same event and therefore the calculation of a mean result for each structure is justified. The weighted mean dates for each hearth are shown in Table 3.7 together with random and systematic error estimates at 1. The last heating of each hearth can be defined with a statistical precision of roughly two centuries at one sigma, spanning the period from the late first century BC to the second century AD. Although there is a suggestion that House 2 may have fallen out of use before House 7, they may have been contemporary. The overall mean date for all three structures, assuming contemporaneity, is ad 80 ± 120 (RE), 130 (SE).

**Radiocarbon dates** *J S Rideout*

Table 3.8 lists the radiocarbon dates from The Dunion giving their uncalibrated dates bp and the same calibrated using the computer program in *Radiocarbon* (Pearson & Stuiver 1986). The calibrated dates give only the extreme figures for dates with more than one intersection with the calibration curve.

**Taphonomy and relative reliability of the radiocarbon and thermoluminescence dates**

Nine charcoal samples were submitted to SURRC and, of these, eight proved of sufficient weight for radiocarbon assay. Since the excavations produced very little datable material in proportion to the area investigated and the number of structures uncovered, most of the samples were from less than ideal contexts. The following list considers the security of the contexts and the nature and validity of the radiocarbon dates. The sample which proved too small for dating after treatment (GU-2170) is omitted. Most of the charcoal samples were collected by flotation of soil samples taken

on site. Sample GU-2177, however, was hand-picked, on site, and samples GU-2174 and GU-2178 also contain some hand-picked material.

*House 7, post-hole: 3600 ± 100 bc (GU-2177)*
This date demonstrates the danger of using charcoal from post-holes. The position of the post-hole, near the back of a scooped platform (*ie* below the original ground surface) suggests that it has to be contemporary with the house (Figure 3.18). This was the only sample comprising oak alone, and the only wood of large diameter. One explanation of the very early date is that the charcoal could have been material from a Mesolithic/Neolithic fire (natural or anthropogenic) on the hill accidentally incorporated into the post-hole backfill. Alternatively, the timber could have been bog-oak, re-used in the Iron Age house (R McCullagh, pers comm).

*House 6, feature under wall: 170 ± 110 bc (GU-2176)*
The context was a small pit filled with material derived from occupation activities pre-dating the construction of House 6 (Figure 3.17). The hiatus between the filling of the pit and the construction of the house is of unknown duration, but the lack of a buried topsoil between the two may indicate a relatively short period. The date gives a *terminus post quem* for the construction of House 6 (see thermoluminescence dating report).

*Fill of hollow associated with Rampart 1: 170 ± 50 bc (GU-2175)*
The context was the fill of a linear scoop or worn gulley behind the rampart (Figure 3.10). The fill was derived from 'silting' and, given that it was not the lowest layer in the hollow, could include material associated with pre-, or post-fort activity as well as from activities contemporaneous with the use of the fort. However, this fill layer was rich in charcoal (unlike the other layers in the gully) and it is reasonable to interpret it as deriving from activities conducted when the gully was actively infilling, *ie* when the fort was occupied. The date provides a *terminus ante quem* for the construction of the rampart.

*House 4, occupation layer: 140 ± 150 bc (GU-2174)*
The context is secure: over the glacial till and under the paving (Figure 3.16). The sampled context and the paving relate to the occupation of the house. It is extremely improbable that the sampled deposit, rich in charcoal, was not a product of the day-to-day use of the house. Contamination by material from other sources is very unlikely and the assay dates the occupation of the house.

*House 1, drainage ditch: 130 ± 50 bc (GU-2172)*
This context was probably contemporaneous with the occupation of House 1. The source of the charcoal, however, was a deposit in the fill of the ditch (Figure 3.14) and, therefore, the material could have derived from relict pre-occupation material and from charcoal

*Table 3.8  Radiocarbon dates.*

| lab *no* GU- | context | uncalibrated date | calibrated date | |
|---|---|---|---|---|
| | | | 1 sigma | 2 sigma |
| 2177 | House 7, post-hole | 3600 bc ± 100 | 4500 BC–4340 BC | 4665 BC–4166 BC |
| 2176 | House 6, pre-house pit | 170 bc ± 110 | 366 BC–10 BC | 400 BC–AD 90 |
| 2175 | Hollow beside Rampart 1 | 170 bc ± 50 | 322 BC–100 BC | 363 BC–30 BC |
| 2174 | House 4, occupation layer | 140 bc ± 150 | 375 BC–AD 70 | 410 BC–AD 230 |
| 2172 | House 1, drainage ditch | 130 bc ± 50 | 178 BC–42 BC | 341 BC–AD 20 |
| 2178 | House 2, quern pit | 50 bc ± 55 | 94 BC–AD 62 | 161 BC–AD 110 |
| 2171 | House 2, floor | 20 bc ± 80 | 92 BC–AD 113 | 180 BC–AD 220 |
| 2173 | House 8, drainage gully | ad 40 ± 150 | 40 BC–AD 230 | 190 BC–AD 390 |

GU-2178 and GU-2171, both from House 2, are statistically indistinguishable. Their dates can, therefore, be averaged to produce: uncalibrated date 40.4 bc ± 45.3; calibrated dates 48 BC–AD 62 (1 sigma), 106 BC–AD (2 sigma).

produced during the occupation of House 1. Since the time taken for the ditch to fill is unknown, the sample could also contain post-occupation material. The date provides a *terminus ante quem* for the cutting of the ditch and, therefore, a broad date for the occupation of House 1.

*House 2, pit containing quern: 50±55 bc (GU-2178)*
The sample comprised charcoal and seeds from the rapid backfill of the pit (Figure 3.14). Although contamination by earlier charcoal cannot be wholly excluded, the nature of the material and its occurrence within the cleaned platform indicate that it probably derives from Phase 1 activity. The pit appears to have been prepared specifically for the burial of the quern, and it is therefore likely that the sample provides a general date for the 'legionary' type quern.

*House 2, Phase 1 floor: 20±80 bc (GU-2171)*
The context itself is securely stratified, over glacial till and under the Phase 2 hearth (Figure 3.14). It was interpreted as Phase 1 material because of its similarity to more secure Phase 1 floor material which predates the Phase 2 wall, hearth and paving. The charcoal probably derives from activities associated with the occupation of the house. The till surface was created by the removal of topsoil and till and it is, therefore, extremely unlikely that pre-occupation charcoal can have been a contaminant. Contamination of the sampled deposit with post-occupation charcoal is even more unlikely, because the deposit is sealed by the Phase 2 hearth-stone. The assay dates Phase 1 and provides a *terminus post quem* for the Phase 2 hearth, but see the TL dating report, above.

*House 8, drip gully: ad 40±120 (GU-2173)*
The fill of the context was assumed to be associated with a structure (Figure 3.14), probably a house (mostly obscured by the quarry road), later than House 1. The

security of this context is probably similar to that of the context which produced sample GU-2172. The charcoal may include material from the occupation of House 1 (or earlier), the occupation of House 8, or post-abandonment of House 8. The sample provides a general date for House 8.

*Thermoluminescence dates*
The security of the contexts which provided the thermoluminescence (TL) dating samples is better than that of most of the radiocarbon samples. The samples of the hearths in House 2 (Figure 3.14), House 6 (Figure 3.17) and House 7 (Figure 3.18) relate to the last re-heating of the hearth-stones and, by implication, to the abandonment of each house for normal domestic purposes (although they could have continued in use as auxiliary structures).

## 1984–1986 EXCAVATIONS: INTERPRETATION, DISCUSSION AND CONCLUSION

### Defences

Although the surviving length of Rampart 1 was poorly preserved, enough remained to permit some general interpretation. The rampart was constructed in two styles, with that part to the west of the entrance apparently of a more defensive nature than the rest. The use of the term 'rampart', even for this part, is a matter of convenience since it could be argued that a construction less than 3 m wide, and probably no more than 1.5 m high, could hardly be described as a defensive work. Its siting, however, at least in the area investigated, gave it an appearance of strength out of proportion to the size of the work itself. For this reason it seems logical to interpret Rampart 1 as a defensive construction.

The slighter rampart, to the east of the entrance, may have been constructed at a different, presumably

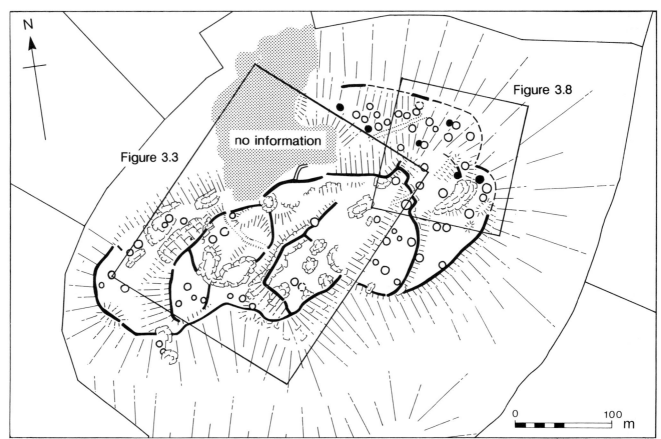

*Figure 3.25    Composite plan of the fort, with the positions of the areas shown at a larger scale in Figures 3.3 and 3.8. (Drawing by J S Rideout).*

later, date to the rampart to the west of the entrance. The western sector of the rampart, or at least that part with the massive facing stones and earth core, may have originally followed a different course, possibly turning uphill at about this point, to enclose a smaller area of the north flank of the hill. This, however, could not be demonstrated, since activity within the fort would have removed most, if not all, of the redundant length of rampart. This may also account for the change in rampart construction for the 6 m length immediately to the west of the entrance.

The fact that Rampart 1 to the east of the entrance was considerably slighter may indicate that the need for defense of the site had reduced by the time of its construction. Unlike the western sector, this part could never have appeared defensive. It runs, for the most part, across a gentle slope, and the width of the wall at its base suggests it could not have stood to any great height. Its very existence, however, indicates that the occupants continued to make a distinction between the settlement itself and the land beyond. That the site appears to have lost its defensive role by the time of the building of the drystone wall is also attested by the absence of a gateway structure in the entrance. The hornworks running inwards from the entrance do not appear to have performed such a function. Indeed, the eastern 'hornwork' had the appearance of randomly dumped stones along the edge of the metalled roadway, while the more substantial western 'hornwork' may be associated

with House 8. In all, the appearance of Rampart 1 suggests that it represents one or two late additions to a site already in existence. Indeed, most of the lines of defence shown on the composite plan (Figure 3.25), give the impression that the fort gradually expanded.

If this were the case, then Rampart 2 was also the boundary of an 'annexe'. However, its identification as a rampart on the 1961 plan (Figure 3.7) appears tentative and the remains uncovered in the latest excavations could be described as ambiguous. Its supposed position, however, along a natural line of defence for part of its route, and the fact that it was also noted by the original survey (Figure 3.7), tends to confirm its identification. In addition, the nature of the remains in Areas 3 and 8 suggests that they were originally defensive structures but, with the later addition of outer defences, fell into disrepair or were robbed for building material. The two possible entrances in Rampart 2, one to the west of House 6 and the other in the gully further west, line up with an entrance in an inner rampart, identified in 1961.

### Houses

As suggested above, this part of the fort seems to be an annexe which represents the movement from relatively level terrain on the summit-plateau and terraces onto a less suitable situation where the slope necessitated the construction of platforms to provide level sites for the houses. Most of the platform houses were elliptical, all but one (House 1) with the long axis of the ellipse set along the face of the hill. House 1, on the other hand, appears to have been constructed in a restricted space, its size and shape limited by the previously built House 2 to the west, and by Roadway 1 to the south and east. The result appears to have been an elliptical platform with its long axis projecting out from the hillside. The suggestion that there was pressure on the space available for house sites is also attested by House 3 which has been cut into a steep basalt slope, its location also restricted by Roadway 1, and by the basalt bedrock. Although only a small part was revealed by excavation, House 8 must have been restricted by Roadway 1 to the east, House 1 to the south, and by Rampart 1 to the north. This same pressure on space appears to have encouraged the maximisation of internal area by the enclosure of as much of the available platform space as possible by the house walls, resulting in rather variable house plans.

Of the seven platform houses, two (Houses 7 and 8) were investigated in trenches too small to permit structural analysis. The remainder, Houses 1–5, all had sloping platforms. Although this could be explained, at least in part, by apron subsidence, the evidence from House 3, and to a lesser extent, from House 4, suggests that a degree of slope may have been planned. In House 3 attempts had been made to provide a level raised annulus around the back, as well as a level paved annulus around the front. At the east and west the annulus would, of necessity, slope. In this house it was in the form of steps near the entrance and a smooth slope at the west. The sloping sub-circular inner area, however, appears not to have constituted the house floor and the suggestion was that this area was raised at the front, using rubble and brash, to form a third, intermediate level area. This was echoed in House 4 where a raised back annulus of brashy material appears to imitate that in House 3. Houses 4 and 1 both had lower front arcs of paving, and House 2 may have had a similar arrangement. The deliberate construction of split-level floors in, at least, Houses 3 and 4, is also seen in Houses 5 and 6, albeit in a slightly different form. The reason for having split-level floors is unclear, although they would be more practical than sloping floors if comfort and function are taken into consideration. The construction of completely level platforms on the hill was not impossible: the glacial till and sandstone under most of the house sites is easily worked, and even the surface of the basalt plug is sufficiently friable to be easily quarried.

Although this deliberate internal arrangement could simply be explained by the whim of the occupants, a more realistic reason would seem to be one of function, most notably drainage. Of the houses investigated, only House 1, and possibly House 8, had drainage ditches. The platform houses which did not, or could not, have such remedies must have had problems with water entering from upslope, the most extreme example being House 3. Sloping floors, or sloping tiered floors, might help to alleviate the problem by allowing water to run off quickly.

*Reconstructions*

Unlike houses which occupy level ground, it is difficult to understand how those on The Dunion were constructed (for an example of a house in a slight scoop, *cf* the reconstruction of Hut-circle I at Kilphedir, Sutherland (Fairhurst & Taylor 1971, 75, Figure 6). The slope of both platforms and hillside result in wall-tops that also slope, several degrees from horizontal. The most obvious example of this is House 3 where the surviving top of the front wall was below the level of the bottom of the facing of the back wall. The amount of rubble found around the houses with stone wall elements, the slight appearance of the walls themselves, and the unstable nature of the aprons on which they stood, suggest that the stone walls could not have stood to any great height. The front walls of House 1 and 3, for instance, are unlikely to have survived for any length of time, or to have provided much support for a roof, if they were originally much more than 1 m high above the paved part of the floor. Even at this height, the top of the front wall of House 3 would have been more or less level with the bottom of the back wall. The problems involved in reconstructing The Dunion houses are compounded where both stone and timber elements were used in combination.

*House 1*   The surviving evidence in House 1 indicates that two construction phases are represented. The evidence is tenuous but the paving which respects, and which is probably associated with, the stone wall overlay the traces of the wall-slot noted at both the back and the front of the platform. It seems reasonable to assume that the different lengths of slot identified were all parts of a single, oval wall-groove.

If the slot represents a first construction phase (superseded by the stone wall), then the house would not have been dissimilar to those found in lowland settlements or on the Unenclosed Platform Settlements excavated to date (*cf* Hayhope Knowe, Huts I & VII; Piggott C M 1949, Figures 3 & 4 and Platforms 2 & 5 at Green Knowe; Jobey 1980, Figures 3 & 4). The roof would have been supported, in the main, by the posts of the internal post-ring, the outer wall being set in the groove. For maximum stability, however, the front wall, and the posts of the post-ring, towards the front, must have been higher than those at the back. This would have provided a level wall-plate, on which the rafters of the roof would have sat.

The evidence for the Phase 2 building is ambiguous. The front wall was of stone, or stone and timber. The back could have been either the timber back wall of Phase 1 (or its replacement), or the roof could have rested on the back scarp, either above the drainage ditch, or on the 'wall' of till created between the drainage ditch and the lowest part of the scarp. Whichever formed the back wall, the most reasonable construction would involve a timber superstructure rising above the front wall to provide a level seating for the roof. A single post-hole under the west end of the front wall, found in a narrow trench cut to investigate the structure of the wall, may be part of such a superstructure.

A third possibility should be considered. Since the evidence for two phases was ambiguous, it is possible that the wall-groove and the stone wall were contemporary. The wall-groove was immediately inside the stone wall and concentric with it, and it is possible that the structure involved a timber outer wall supported and buttressed by the stone element as in Houses 1, 2, and 4 in the fort/settlement at Edgerston, *circa* 8.5 km south-east of The Dunion (RCAHMS 1956, 226–8, Figures 287 & 288).

*House 2*    The first phase of House 2 appears to have been similar to the first phase of House 1, although it lacks evidence for a timber wall-slot at the front. In the second phase, a stone wall was constructed around the platform. That the back wall rose above the height of the scarp, although probably not to any great height, suggests that the roof, possibly supported by the post-ring, rested on it. The platform of House 2 was less sloping than that of House 1, but similar problems of stability must have been encountered.

*House 3*    This exhibits the most extreme problems which would have been encountered in constructing a house in a restricted space, on a steep slope. Unlike Houses 1 and 2, it has only one construction phase and no internal post-ring was found. No post-ring would have been necessary (*cf* the reconstruction of the Conderton House in Reynolds 1982, 190–7). The lack of a post-ring means that the roof was probably supported by the external wall (it is not impossible that a post-ring was used which left no traces, *ie* the timber uprights rested on the floor and were not set in post-holes). The front wall of the house was slight and, if the roof simply rested on the wall-top, any lateral pressure would have led to collapse. One remedy for this, as shown in Figure 3.26, involves the setting of short timber uprights in the core of the wall (U Lee, pers comm). The roof beams could then be 'tied' to them to strengthen the structure. If timber uprights were used, however, it is reasonable to envisage them being long enough to provide a level seating for the roof. At the back of the house, the roof probably rested on the quarried scarp. The flimsy nature of the back wall facing, and the likelihood that it did not complete the wall circuit, suggests that it did not act as a roof support. A ledge in the bedrock scarp to the south-east may have served this function.

*House 4*    This appears to have been constructed using stone and timber. Like House 3, the roof probably rested on the back scarp, or on a ledge formed by the top of the stone facing and the packing soil behind it. The two hornworks may be an attempt to continue the scarp support out from the hillside. The east hornwork survived to the same height as the surviving wall-head at the back of the platform, while the top of the west hornwork was sloped. At the front, the wall was timber-built. The wall-slot stopped abruptly where it met the west hornwork. At this point the timber superstructure may have continued within the hornwork's core to provide a level roof seating. If the wall-head was level, the front wall would have been very high. The back wall survived to a height of *circa* 1.7 m, possibly close to the original height, which would have led to a front wall height of *circa* 3 m. The size of House 4 necessitated the use of an internal post-ring.

*House 5*    House 5 was probably similar to House 3.

*House 6*    Although not built on an artificial platform, House 6 appears to have been similarly constructed. While it is possible that here the roof simply rested on a low stone and earth wall, it is reasonable to assume that the walls could have served as foundations for a timber superstructure. No post-ring was necessary. The same can also be said for Houses 61/1 and 62/2, excavated in 1961–2.

## Other features

The traces of walls associated with the houses suggest a need for sub-division of space within the fort. However, a large part of the area covered by these enclosures was so steep as to preclude most forms of domestic activity. Wall 1 apparently enclosed an area of slope to the south of Houses 4 and 5. The slope consisted of the quarried scarps of both houses and part of the natural hillslope. Walls 3 to 6 enclosed the scarp of House 3 and part of the natural slope, as well as the scoop to the north-east. Since most of the enclosed areas were unusable, it is possible that the boundary walls simply protected the houses and activity areas around them from stones falling from uphill.

## Chronological relationships

Within Area 1 some stratigraphical relationships between structures were noted. Some were revealed in excavation while others can be inferred. For instance, it is inferred that the construction of House 1 post-dates that of House 2 because the drainage ditch of House 1 impinges on the east side of the latter. It is possible, however, that the drainage ditch represents a relatively late feature of the occupation of House 1 and that Houses 1 and 2 were originally contemporaneous, with House 2 abandoned before House 1.

Similarly, House 8 is seen to post-date House 1 because its scarp appears to have contributed to the collapse of the front wall of the latter. The collapse could have post-dated the abandonment of both structures. It is likely, however, that the three structures represent a period of occupation longer than the usable lifetime of one house. No relationship was established between the houses to the north of Roadway 1 and those to the south. Although House 4 proved to post-date the initial use of Roadway 1, the relationship between the latter and Houses 1 and 2 could not be established with any degree of certainty. Indeed, by their nature, roads are long-lived features, and it is possible that the use of Roadway 1 started before the presumed expansion of

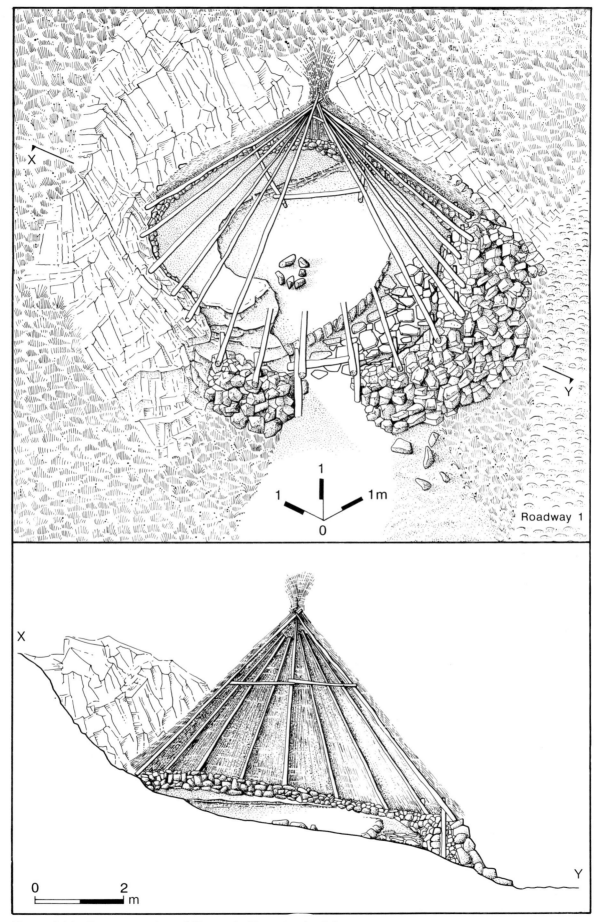

*Figure 3.26 Reconstruction of House 3. (Drawing by S Stevenson).*

the fort into this area, and ended after Houses 1–5 had been abandoned.

To the south of Roadway 1, the relationships between the houses are established by their relationships with the several walls in that area. Although the construction of House 5 was shown to post-date that of House 4, there was nothing to indicate that both houses were not occupied simultaneously. Indeed, the difference between the flooring of the two houses may indicate that House 4 was a domestic dwelling, while House 5 was an auxiliary building, possibly a byre or storehouse, built at a slightly later date. The north-east end of the pathway leading from the east hornwork of House 4 to the gap in Wall 1 was truncated by the construction of House 5, which suggests that Wall 1 predates the latter. In turn, Wall 1 post-dated House 4. Wall 3, which was probably integral with House 3, appears to have post-dated Wall 1, by virtue of its relationship with Wall 2 and the latter's relationship with Wall 1. While, again, this does not prove that House 3 is greatly different in date to Houses 4 and 5, it does suggest that the former was constructed at a later date. This may also be supported by the position of House 3, which is so unsuited to its function as to suggest that, by the time it was built upon, it was the only space left.

To summarise, the minimum duration of settlement on the site is one house 'generation'; the maximum, allowing for more than one phase of construction in Houses 1 and 2, is greater than six house 'generations'. However, there is no reason to suggest that the main occupation of this part of the hill was of any great duration.

### Settlement sequence

The evidence from the 1984–1986 excavations suggest the following general sequence.
*i* Sporadic pre-fort activity on the hill as shown by relict artefacts (Neolithic stone axe and flint artefacts). This is also suggested by the stray finds recovered in the last hundred years.
*ii* Presumed initial occupation of the hilltop by a fort. No features or artefacts from the area investigated can be definitely assigned to this period.
*iii* Occupation of the north flank of the hill by an extension of the fort.
*iv* Later activity, as shown by the later structures on Houses 4 and 5, possibly after the abandonment of the fort.
*v* Medieval and later occupation of the hill as shown by the 'Watch Tower' and other rectangular stone structures on the summit-plateau.

### Economy and environment

The lack of environmental information, as well as a shortage of artefacts and ecofacts, is not unusual for defended Iron Age sites in south-east Scotland. The small amount of information from The Dunion macroplant record, both seeds and charcoal,

accompanied by the small amount of burnt bone, suggests that the local economy was mixed. The presence of cereal grains and querns indicates that grain was ground on the site. The presence of fragments of burnt bone, mostly from domestic contexts, may represent animal bones burnt in hearths. The importance of hunting and gathering to the economy can only be guessed at; the fragments of burnt hazelnut shell from the drainage ditch of House 1 may indicate a reliance on woodland for more than timber and firewood.

It is possible, given that the settlement was so large, that a proportion of the food supply may have come from outside the immediate vicinity, perhaps from other, smaller settlements. If this were the case, then it is possible that The Dunion supplied goods to other sites. The evidence for industrial activity on the hill is slight; a handful of iron-smelting bloomery debris, mostly from insecure contexts but probably associated with the Iron Age occupation, may indicate production for domestic consumption. The siliceous balls, some magnetic, noted in the macroplant and dating samples from the occupation of House 4, may derive from such activity. The small quantity of slag, and the lack of bloomery sites, presumably means that the smelting was carried out elsewhere on the hill, probably upslope from the 1984–1986 excavations but possibly below the summit-plateau, since no slag was found there in 1962. No ironwork dating to the period of the fort's occupation was recovered.

### Artefacts

In common with sites of Iron Age date in southern Scotland, few artefacts were recovered from this excavation. With the exception of the glass bead from House 1, there were no exotic artefacts of the sort found on Traprain Law, Eildon Hill North or Edgerston. Few of the objects recovered as small finds from the site were from secure contexts, and fewer still from secure domestic contexts. House 1 produced the glass bead [1] and two pieces of flint [57, 67]. House 2 produced only quern [2]. House 3 had most finds, with contexts associated with its occupation producing two spindle whorls [8, 10] from immediately beside the raised annulus, one stone disc, one flint flake, one hammerstone, and eleven water-worn stones. The latter were recorded as small finds because they do not occur naturally on the site and must, therefore, have been carried to the houses from a nearby stream or similar source, that is, they were manuports. Less secure upper contexts, in House 3, relating to the abandonment and collapse of the house, also produced one small stone ball, one stone disc, two hammerstones, and one water-worn stone.

Artefacts from house aprons and walls, and from ramparts and boundary walls, may have been accidentally incorporated. This material, like the spindle whorls from both the apron of House 3, and the core of Rampart 1a in Area 5, is substantially the same as that from domestic contexts, Roadway 1, and post-abandonment contexts. The obvious exception to this is the stone axe [44] from under the possible road, Roadway 4.

The total assemblage from the 1984–1986 excavations comprises only nine artefact types, namely, small stone balls, spindle whorls, stone discs, hammerstones, chipped stone (flint), water-worn stones, querns, other worked stone, and a glass bead. The artefacts from the 1961–1962 excavations added pottery to the assemblage. None of these types, with the possible exception of the beehive querns, are particularly chronologically or culturally sensitive (*pace* Cool 1982).

## Dating

The fort on The Dunion was originally believed to be of Dark Age date by virtue of the superficial resemblance of the *Inventory* plan (RCAHMS 1956) to forts variously described as nuclear, citadel or defensive enclosures in general, and to the later of two forts on Peniel Heugh, *circa* 7.7 km north-north-east of the site. Indeed, the hut-circles on The Dunion have been interpreted as a later 'hut-village', possibly of the tenth century AD or later (RCAHMS 1956, 35). Artefacts from the excavations of 1961 and 1962, however, indicated a later prehistoric date for the fort. The original identification of the platforms on the north flank of the hill as an Unenclosed Platform Settlement (UPS) was effectively disproved in 1984 by the location of the outermost rampart (Rampart 1), although the possibility that a UPS was re-used as part of the fort, while improbable, has not been ruled out.

The later prehistoric date indicated by the 1961–1962 excavations was based on the artefact assemblage, and reinforced by the artefacts recovered in the CEU excavations. Indeed, the beehive quern from House 2 indicated a later pre-Roman Iron Age date for the site (Caulfield 1978, 106 & 124). Since none of the other find types are chronologically sensitive, the radiocarbon and thermoluminescence samples provide the only reliable dating evidence for the fort.

To summarise the dating of the areas investigated by the CEU, the evidence from the main structural elements is discussed below in the same order as in the excavation summary (above).

### Defences

Neither of the ramparts produced direct dating evidence. The date from the scoop behind Rampart 1 in Area 2 provides a *terminus ante quem* for its construction of 170±50 bc (GU-2175; 355 to 20 bc, at LCR). Rampart 2 produced no dating evidence. It was, however, earlier than House 6, which is TL dated to AD 60±220 (RE), 220 (SE).

### Houses

House 1 was in use at 130±50 bc (GU-2172; 235 BC to ad 70, at LCR) as the dated sample, from its drainage ditch, demonstrates. The glass bead from the house floor (platform surface) is similarly dated, to roughly the second century BC to first century ad, by similarities in chemical composition to other beads from Britain and Europe. House 8, adjacent to House 1 but probably constructed later than it, produced a date of ad 40±120 BC (GU-2173; 195 BC to ad 380, at LCR) from its probable drainage ditch. House 2 was probably contemporaneous with, or later than, House 1. The quern pit within House 2 was dated to 50±55 bc (GU-2178; 135 bc to ad 125, at LCR). The pit could belong to either of the two inferred occupation phases. The occupation material under the hearth-stone produced a date of 20±80 bc (GU-2171; 160 BC to ad 220, at LCR). The hearth-stone itself gave a mean TL date of 70±190 BC (RE), 210 (SE).

House 4 was radiocarbon dated to 140±150 bc (GU-2174; 465 BC to ad 215, at LCR) by a sample from the remains of an occupation horizon. House 3 and House 5 produced no useful dating evidence. While House 5 was stratigraphically earlier than House 4, and House 3 was stratigraphically later than House 4, all three were broadly contemporaneous.

House 6 has a *terminus post quem* of 170±110 bc (GU-2176; 400 BC to ad 110, at LCR) from a pit under the house wall. A date for its final use is supplied by a mean TL date from the hearth-stone of ad 60±220 (RE), 220 (SE). A House 7 hearth-stone was TL dated to mean AD 180±170 (RE), 180 (SE). The very early radiocarbon date from the post-hole in the house has been discounted. On the basis of the uncalibrated radiocarbon dates alone, there is a suggestion that the main structural elements (ramparts and houses) belong to a relatively short period. The central dates span a period of only 210 years (170 BC to ad 40). Unfortunately, the errors on a few of the dates means that at the 2σ level of confidence the overall range is 845 years (465 BC to ad 380). It is likely, however, that this date range is excessive and that the true range is probably more in the order of second century bc to first century ad.

One of the questions arising from the excavation is whether or not the site was occupied at the time of the Roman incursions and continued in occupation into the Roman period. The absolute TL dates suggest that this may be so. Unfortunately, the errors of about ±10% give a date range of more than six centuries, at the 1σ level of confidence. However, the date from House 7 suggests that the site may have been occupied into the Roman Iron Age. This is also suggested by the calibrated radiocarbon dates. At 1σ, the overall calibrated date range is 300 BC to AD 240. If the dates with the greatest errors (GU-2174 and GU-2173), as well as the pre-House 6 date (GU-2176), are discounted, the calibrated range is 200 BC to AD 125, which is probably a more realistic estimate of the date and duration of settlement in the part of the fort beyond Rampart 2.

## Discussion

### Defences

The defences on The Dunion appear, in the main, to have been sited to make maximum use of the local topography. Indeed, the hill was probably chosen for its defensiveness. The excavated evidence indicates that, where available, stone was used in the construction of the ramparts. However, they appear to be crudely constructed. The stones were set in a matrix of soil to form a rubble-, and soil-cored rampart with stone facings. The poor quality of the facings is probably due to the local stone which is generally unsuitable for drystone building. The inner defences, RCAHMS Walls A, C and D, and Rampart 2, contain more stone than Rampart 1, the latter constructed at a level where stone was less abundant and soil for the core was more readily available.

Although there are no excavated parallels for the very slight Rampart 1b, there are some similarities between the rest of the defences and other sites in south-east Scotland. The ramparts are not dissimilar to the inner rubble rampart (Phase III), or even the Phase II wall at Hownam Rings, *circa* 16.5 km to the east (Piggott C M 1948, 203, Figure 6).

The Hownam sequence (of palisade to single stone wall to multivallate enclosure to open settlement to homestead) has been promulgated as an ideal but seems rather too complicated to have had widespread currency. While the use of palisading may demonstrate choice of style and material (or the availability of suitable timber), the difference between Phases II and III at Hownam may be explained by nothing more than a strengthening of defences and not by a change in the choice of building material. Having used up most of the available surface stone for the construction of the Phase II wall, the builders were forced to collect spoil from shallow quarry ditches to strengthen the wall and thereby create the Phase III rampart. Thus, the quarry ditches were simply by-products of the process of rampart construction. The Phase II wall and the Phase III ramparts at Hownam Rings exhibit essentially the same construction style.

Also generally similar to The Dunion's walls, are Walls I, IA, and IB in Cutting 1 at Bonchester Hill, some 8 km to the south-south-west (Piggott C M 1950, Figure 5, 120), and Rampart 7 at Kaimes Hill, Midlothian (Simpson 1969, 12, Plate 2). All three forts fall into the category of contour forts and are chronologically complex. Phases II and III at Hownam Rings, and the earliest fort (Wall I) at Bonchester Hill may be broadly similar in date to The Dunion. The lower stone of a rotary quern was found in the Phase III blocking of the Phase II entrance at Hownam; the upper stone of a beehive quern was found under Wall I at Bonchester Hill. Probably earlier in date, by one or two centuries, but with similar rampart construction, is Gillies Hill (this volume). Here, and at The Dunion, the materials employed in the defences simply reflect local availability, and this, in turn, influences the architecture of the ramparts.

### Houses

In all, ten houses, including those from 1961–1962, were investigated in whole or in part. Two general types were represented: platform houses, and houses of the type often called hut-circles. As with the defences, the fabric of both of these basic forms arise from local conditions rather than deliberate choice, or strong architectural tradition.

The evidence from the site does not readily permit subdivision into distinct phases, but the dates span two or three of the periods identified at the fort of Broxmouth Hill (Hill 1982b, 141–88). Indeed, The Dunion houses are generally similar in appearance to the stone houses of Periods VI and VIII at Broxmouth (Hill 1982a, 16, Figure 4; Hill 1982b, 174, Figure 9), Period VI representing a transitional stone and timber Votadinian house (*sensu* Hill 1982c). Hill (1982c, 24–31), however, has proposed that the real difference between earlier Iron Age houses and the later Votadinian houses should be sought, not in the materials used, but in factors which indicate differences of use, and points to the apparent annular divisions of earlier houses as opposed to the radial division of houses of the Votadinian tradition, as well as to different uses for different structures. It could be argued, however, that the houses on The Dunion with annular paving, raised annulus at the back, or both, could fit equally well into either group. The combination of front paved annulus with raised back annulus could be seen as reflecting the penannular divisions in ring-ditch or double-ring roundhouses; alternatively, the two annuli and the level or sloping central area could be interpreted as three distinct zones.

Zonation may also be exhibited in House 5 with its split-level paving similar to that noted at Crock Cleuch Hut E1 (Steer & Keeney 1947, 145, Figure 3), and possibly by the raised area of paving in House 6. Another feature of Hill's Votadinian tradition, threshold stones, as seen at Crock Cleuch (*ibid*, Plate XVI) and Murton High Crags (Jobey & Jobey 1987, 171, Figure 8), were seen in The Dunion Houses 61/1 and 62/2 and House 1. All-over paving, peculiar to the same tradition, was seen in House 5, House 61/1, House 62/2 and possibly House 6. It could also be seen as similar to Stone House A at Tower Knowe, in the Upper Tyne Valley, Northumberland (Jobey 1973, Plate VII). The parallels at Crock Cleuch, Murton High Crags, and Tower Knowe, however, have all been assigned later dates than those suggested for The Dunion: Crock Cleuch to the later Roman/early Saxon period and Tower Knowe and Murton High Crags to early to mid Roman Iron Age. It seems, therefore, that the houses on The Dunion exhibit elements of both earlier Iron Age and later pre-Roman/Roman Iron Age traditions and could be seen as transitional in house style.

*Artefacts*

The artefact assemblage is basically similar to assemblages from other settlement sites of broadly Iron Age date in the area. At Bonchester hillfort, Piggott's second phase, dated to the late first century BC or first century AD, produced a beehive quern, coarse pottery, spindle whorls, and small stone balls (Piggott C M 1950, 121–3). Finds from Iron Age periods at Burnswark, in Annandale, included coarse pottery, part of a saddle quern, part of a beehive quern, a spindle whorl, a glass armlet, and glass beads (Jobey 1978, 82–96). Hownam Rings Phase II produced coarse pottery and slag; Phase III, possibly relict coarse pottery and a lower stone of a rotary quern; Phase IV, coarse pottery, Roman pottery, cobble tools, a spindle whorl, and a fragment of a rotary quern of flat type (Piggott C M 1948, 212–220). Similar assemblages, or similar elements of The Dunion assemblage, were also found at Kaimes Hillfort, Midlothian (Simpson 1969), Crock Cleuch homesteads, Roxburgh (Steer & Keeney 1947), and the forts at Braidwood, Midlothian (Stevenson 1949), Craig's Quarry, Dirleton, East Lothian (Piggott & Piggott 1952, Piggott S 1958b), and Castlelaw, Glencorse, Midlothian (Childe 1933).

*Fort*

Although little now remains of the site, the range of source material is better than might be expected. Three plans (four if the OS 1:2500 plan is included) and post-war aerial photographs, provide an insight into the overall plan of the fort. On a hill like The Dunion, with numerous rocky outcrops and terraces, and a tendency for moderate depths of topsoil to develop, identification of the defences and houses has obviously proved difficult. This has been compounded by the nature of the stone used in construction, which does not break into regular shapes and which has consequently proved relatively unsuitable for building. Walling, where it survives, appears crude and walled structures probably collapsed within a relatively short time after abandonment.

Notwithstanding the problems in identifying structure, the first three plans of the fort record several of the same features. The original plan and the published RCAHMS plan both record only part of the fort. It seems that, although the two plans are similar, some errors were made in the original survey. It did not distinguish between the prehistoric remains and some of the modern walls on the summit-plateau, and no house sites were noted. Also, part of the outer line of defence on the original appears to have been mistaken. This defence is shown as having an entrance. To the east of the entrance is the rampart investigated by the CEU (Rampart 2), which at this point appears to be genuine. To the west of the entrance, however, no rampart could be seen in 1986. Indeed, the line of this part of the rampart coincides with small natural landscape features and with House 7 and its neighbouring platform. It appears that these have misled the anonymous original

surveyor. The original plan, however, identifies a rampart and possible annexe to the north of it (Figure 3.2, Y) which had been destroyed before the second survey. The survey of 1962 expanded the first RCAHMS plan.

Figure 3.25 is a composite based on these early plans, with the addition of some topographical information from vertical aerial photographs, and archaeological detail from the 1984–1986 excavations. Information from the 1962 plan has been used as a base to which information from the original plan has been added. The stippled area represents that part of the hill for which no information is available, and the filled circles are houses discovered during the CEU involvement, either on-site or from aerial photographs.

The overall impression of the composite plan is one of a fort originally occupying the summit-plateau, which was subsequently expanded by the addition of annexes. The large number of lines of defence do not appear to have been designed for depth of defence, as might be expected with a multivallate fort. It is possible, however, that some of the annexes were original and that they may represent simple enclosures later occupied by houses. It is interesting to note that the fort as recognised in 1962 occupied all of the exposed part of the basalt plug.

The composite plan shows a total of sixty-six houses within the fort. The two houses (platform sites) outside the defences to the south-west tend to reinforce the possibility that the emphasis on defence, never strong, became weaker with the passage of time (as suggested by the slight section of Rampart 1). Since the houses in Area 1 appear to have been tightly packed into the available suitable spaces it is possible that there were many more on the terraces of the summit where there appears to be sufficient space for more than twice the number of houses recorded in the whole fort. The large empty spaces here may, therefore, have contained houses later obscured by soil development or by stone robbing during the later, medieval and modern, use of the hill. Indeed, House 62/2, set in the area of the later occupation, was more denuded than House 61/1, possibly for this very reason. House 62/2 and the possible structure beside it were discovered late in the history of the site, after most of the summit-plateau and other terraces had been removed by quarrying.

As mentioned above, Feachem identified The Dunion as a minor *oppidum* some 5.3 ha in extent. With the addition of the area bounded by Rampart 1, the total area enclosed would have been 6 to 6.5 ha. This falls within the size range of the other large forts in the Tweed Basin: Eildon Hill North (16 ha), Hownam Law (8.9 ha), Yeavering Bell (5.2 ha), Rubers Law (3.6 ha), White Meldon (3.5 ha), Hirsel Law (3.7 ha) and Whiteside Rig (2.6 ha). In basic form The Dunion resembles many of these larger forts. Feachem includes The Dunion in a list of large forts which 'All have a single wall and almost all still show abundant surface traces of timber houses.' (Feachem 1966, 79). Jobey also claims that The Dunion has a single rampart (Jobey 1965, 32).

It must be assumed that both are referring to the rampart surrounding the fort at its greatest extent, although this is, in fact, composite, parts having been constructed at different stages of the growth of the site (for example, part of the outer perimeter of the fort was part of the south-east side of the summit-plateau). A similar, but less complex example of a gradually expanding single-walled fort is Humbleton Hill, in the Till valley, a fort with a final extent of 3.6 ha after, apparently, two expansion phases (Jobey 1965, 35–6). Like The Dunion, Humbleton Hill also has a stronger defence in the early stage and weaker later lines of defence. Other minor *oppida* in the area, however, appear to have been large from the start. Yeavering Bell has only two small annexes to bring it to its final size (*op cit*, 33, Figure 7) and Hownam Law has none (RCAHMS 1956, 157–9).

Of the house sites in these forts (at least 130 at Yeavering Bell and 155 at Hownam Law) many are built on platforms. The Hownam house sites give no indication of house style, but at Yeavering Bell it seems that some houses may have been timber, others of stone (Jobey *ibid*, 34, Figure 8). At White Meldon, another expanded fort, in upper Tweeddale, all twenty-nine of the visible houses appear to have been of timber, their ring-grooves now showing in the turf (RCAHMS 1967, 151, Figure 143). It is interesting to note that the plans of some of the houses display the distinctive eyebrow/eyelash hachures of the platforms within the ring-grooves; a feature noted in other forts in the Peeblesshire *Inventory*. It is possible that these are the well-preserved surface remains of three-level houses like those excavated on The Dunion.

*Dating*

The calibrated radiocarbon dates suggest that at least that part of the fort investigated in 1984–1986 was occupied in the last two or three centuries BC and the first century AD. The TL dates tend to reinforce this date range but also suggest the possibility that the occupation continued into the Roman Iron Age. The artefact assemblage indicates a date for the site in the few centuries before the Roman Iron Age. The single small sherd of pottery which may be of Roman Iron Age origin from the 1961–1962 excavations does not necessarily indicate an occupation continuing into the second century AD. The sherd is very abraded and was found with an abraded sherd of medieval pottery. That the two sherds were found together alongside the coarse Iron Age pottery in House 2 suggests that this was simply the result of contamination. Despite the use of both radiocarbon and thermoluminescence dating techniques, combined with the, admittedly small, artefactual assemblage, the question of whether The Dunion spans the late pre-Roman Iron Age/early Roman Iron Age period remains unanswered.

Macinnes (1984, 241–244) suggests that before the Antonine period Roman material appeared in the south of Scotland only at a few important native sites such as brochs and at *oppida* like Traprain Law. Assuming that the excavated area of The Dunion represents the outer limit of the fort at its greatest extent, then the site appears to have been large enough to be considered of some importance in the area. It is reasonable to assume, therefore, that if The Dunion was occupied in the late first/early second centuries ad, some Roman material would have found its way there. Although only a small part of the fort has been excavated, no material of unquestionably Roman date has been found, even as stray finds. It is possible, therefore, that the site was abandoned some time in the second half of the first century ad at the latest, and was not used again until the later medieval period.

The abandonment of the hill need not have taken place before the Roman advance into what is now Scotland. Indeed, the impetus for the abandonment may have been the Roman incursion itself. That there was no evidence for violent destruction in the areas investigated does not preclude the latter possibility. Antipathy towards the advancing invaders may have precipitated a dispersal of populations of defended or defensive sites in much the same way that the tower-houses of the border lairds were abandoned in favour of more secluded hiding-places during the period of large-scale English incursions in the sixteenth century.

**Conclusion**

Since these excavations only investigated a small part of the site, the conclusions are necessarily tentative. The results of the 1984–1986 seasons only shed some light on the occupation of part of a site, which, by inference, was constructed towards the end of the site's lifespan. Sadly, questions raised by the excavation cannot be answered elsewhere on the site because it is largely destroyed.

What is suggested is that the site started as a small fort and gradually expanded into a larger fort, with a progressive reduction of emphasis on defensiveness. There is a little evidence to suggest that the fort continued to be occupied after its defensive function had become unimportant, possibly as a contracted settlement, before being abandoned and not re-occupied until the medieval period at the earliest.

The Iron Age occupation can only be dated by use of radiocarbon and thermoluminescence dates which lack the precision necessary to facilitate correlation with dated historical events. The results of the dating suggest that the part of the fort investigated in 1984–1986 was first occupied in the second or third centuries BC. By inference, the original core fort will probably fall into the middle of the first millennium BC. The site continued to be occupied into the first century ad and possibly even into the second century AD.

The poor survival of the structures in the fort, and the poverty of the artefact assemblages associated with them, raise some questions about the functions of minor *oppida* in south-east Scotland. In a footnote, Hill has argued that 'The period of these major sites must be critical to any comprehensive study of economic and social developments in the area' (1982a, 27). As things stand, the available information on such sites is limited. Some light has been shed on Eildon Hill North, and somewhat more on The Dunion; the other minor *oppida*, however, can be dated only by notoriously misleading stray finds, or finds from small-scale, poorly documented excavations. Until more, if not all, of these large sites are reliably dated little can be said about their role in the regional picture, or about the interrelations between the large forts. Without the same information from a reasonable sample of smaller forts and other sites of the Iron Age, little can be said of the relationship between these larger forts and the territories over which they may have exerted influence.

## ACKNOWLEDGEMENTS

The author is very grateful to Kings & Co for permission to excavate and, in particular, to Mr Penman, quarry manager, and the quarry workers for their help and patience during the four CEU seasons. Thanks are due to the site staff, Nick Tavener (Assistant Supervisor), Chris Russell-White and Eoin Halpin (Site Assistants), Myra Tolan (sample processing), and all the volunteers. Peter Hill and Annemarie Gibson carried out a plane-table survey of the surviving remains of Rampart 1, and their help is gratefully acknowledged. Thanks are also due to Mr George Dorward who brought the original site plan to the author's attention and who also allowed stray finds from the site to be examined by the CEU and the Royal Museum of Scotland in Queen Street, Edinburgh. With the exception of Figures 3.1, 3.2, 3.7, part of 3.13, and 3.25, the line drawings were prepared by Sylvia Stevenson. Figure 3.26 is based on an original reconstruction drawing by Una Lee. The radiocarbon dating was done by Gordon Cook and his staff at SURRC. The author is grateful to staff at RCAHMS for providing access to the 1961 plan and for other advice and assistance, in particular Strat Halliday and Leslie Ferguson. The extracts from the Roxburghshire *Inventory* and the 1962 plan are reproduced here by permission of RCAHMS. Peter Hill, John Barber and Olwyn Owen kindly read and commented on earlier drafts of this report.

# Harpercroft and Wardlaw Hill, Dundonald, Strathclyde

*E Halpin*

## Contributors

Chipped stone *B Finlayson*
Jet armlets *V J McLellan*

Pottery *A MacSween*
Line drawings *S Stevenson*

## Abstract

*Small areas were excavated on the adjacent summits of Harpercroft and Wardlaw Hill, Dundonald, in 1984, in advance of the erection and modernisation of radar installations. At Harpercroft, the innermost of two ramparts and two phases of truncated ring-grooves were examined. At Wardlaw Hill, examination of the two-phase rampart indicated intermittent use of the fort over a lengthy period.*

The adjacent summits of Harpercroft (NS 358 328) and Wardlaw Hill (NS 360 325) form the Dundonald Ridge, some 3.5 km from the sea (Figure 4.1b). From its summits there are commanding views of the coastline and the surrounding countryside. The ridge runs roughly north-south but is divided by a marshy gully in which a stream flows during wet weather. The southern summit, Harpercroft (143 m OD, Figure 4.1c), has steep sides, with a gently rounded top measuring approximately 300 m by 250 m. Harpercroft commands clear and uninterrupted views on all sides, a fact confirmed by the siting of a radar installation on this summit. The northern summit, Wardlaw Hill (145 m OD), is bounded on the north-east and south by steep slopes, which, to the north-east, form a vertical face some 3 m high. The remaining sides are bordered by less steeply inclined slopes. These features delimit a relatively large flat area of hilltop measuring some 120 m by 70 m.

A series of excavations was undertaken in 1984 in response to the proposed modernisation of the existing radar station on Harpercroft and the proposed construction of a second station near the summit of Wardlaw Hill.

## HARPERCROFT

The ramparts on Harpercroft consist of two concentric banks separated by 100 m of relatively level ground (Figure 4.1c). The outer bank encloses the entire hilltop, some 6.4 ha in extent. The construction of the outer bank on the line of a natural break in slope creates an impressively defensive monument, enclosing an oval area about 360 m by 240 m. Cultivation ridges and rectangular enclosures in the area between the two banks are visible on aerial photographs (RAF; F21.58.2712:0070–1) but no trace of them could be seen on the ground. The inner bank is well preserved, for the most part, although it has been badly mutilated to the north, where there may once have been an entrance, and

a modern track has been cut through the bank to the south-east (Figure 4.1e). The bank forms a stone-built rampart surviving as a scarp up to 1.5 m high and 3 m wide, enclosing an area some 105 m in diameter. An early survey provides evidence of structures and internal divisions within the inner bank, concentrated to the east of the enclosed area (Christison 1893, Plate VI, Figure 1), which are no longer visible on the ground. The ground within the inner enclosure was generally marshy with standing water in many places, particularly in the area immediately surrounding the radar installation.

A survey of the inner rampart, involving the recording of the surface profiles at various places across the earthwork, was also undertaken (Figure 4.2). The sections were broadly alike and showed the rampart to consist of a low, spread, earthen and stone bank some 5 m wide and at most 0.5 m in height.

### Excavation Area B (Figure 4.1e, 4.2 & 4.3)

An area 12 m by 9 m was machine-stripped down to archaeological levels and then trowelled clean to reveal a number of features. The depth of stratigraphy was a mere 0.3 m, measured from the bottom of the modern A-horizon to the top of the undisturbed natural which in places consisted of bedrock. Over the bedrock lay a thin, discontinuous deposit of glacial till. Above this was a layer of disturbed till, heavily mottled with a dark-brown, greasy soil.

A number of curvilinear features with dark fills had been cut into this deposit. It was not possible to estimate their horizontal extent or exact dimensions in the small area excavated. In section they proved to be shallow, round-bottomed ditches some 0.7 m across and at most 0.2 m deep. Two of them, at the north end of the area (Figure 4.3, Ditch A & Ditch B) appear in plan to be the butt ends of a penannular enclosure. However, examination of the section through them revealed that they represent two quite distinct and separate features.

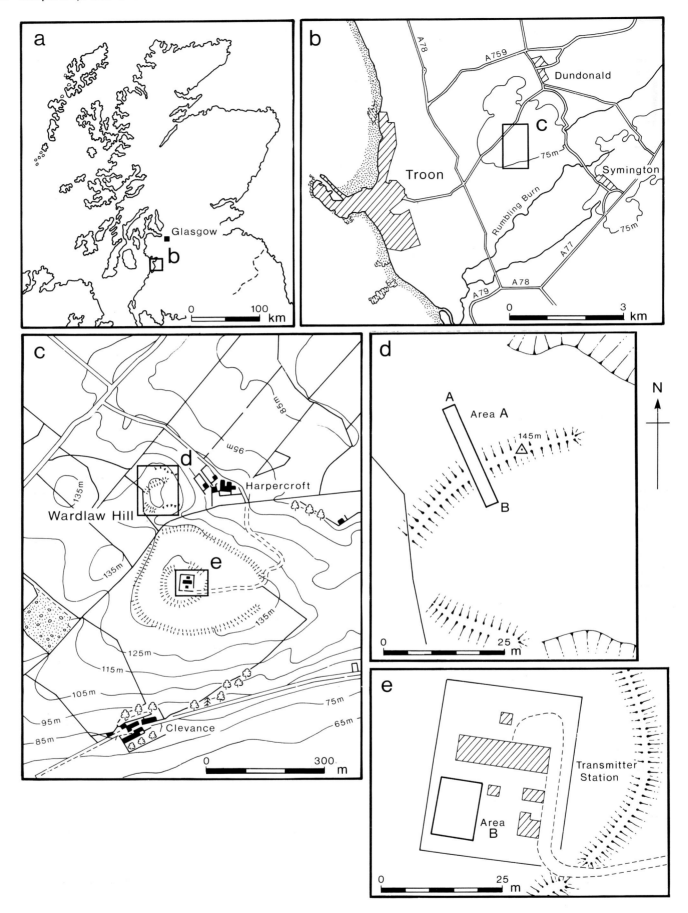

*Figure 4.1   Map and plan composite to show the location of Harpercroft and Wardlaw and the excavation areas.*

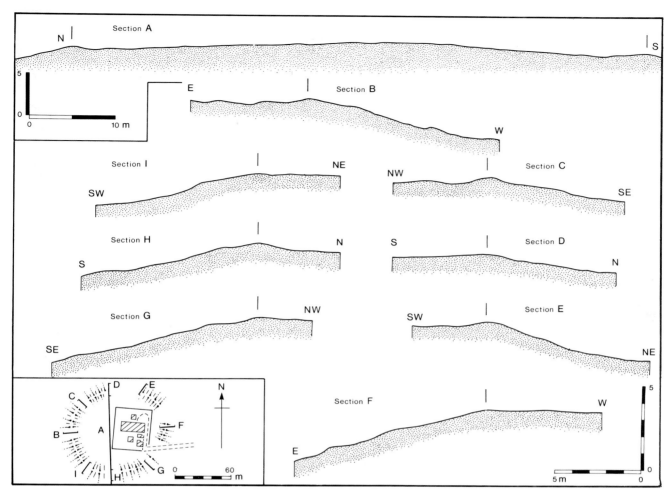

*Figure 4.2  Profiles surveyed across the rampart.*

The shorter length of ditch (Figure 4.3, Ditch B) is apparently earlier than the longer ditch segment (Ditch A). This interpretation is shown by the relationship between the ditches and a layer of dark grey/brown soil (F3 on Figure 4.3). This soil lies over Ditch B but is co-terminus with the inner edge of Ditch A. The majority of the artefacts recovered during excavation came from this layer; these included the remains of two pots, seven pieces of flint, and five fragments of at least three shale armlets. Two sections were cut across the linear features revealed at the south end of Area A (Figure 4.3, C & D). These features appeared in plan to be part of a penannular enclosure but it was not possible in the small area excavated to determine the relationship between the two. The final feature noted was a short stretch of kerbing, surviving to a maximum of only two courses (Figure 4.3, E), which sat in a shallow depression and curved from the north baulk round to the south-east for 1.50 m before disappearing. The kerb sat on the layer of disturbed glacial till through which Ditch A had been cut. This layer also overlay an area of very dark brown soil (F10) which was high in soil organic matter and when exposed gave off an unpleasant aroma. Similarly, a very dark, brown humic soil, the lowest fill of Ditch C (Figure 4.3), also gave off an unpleasant aroma when exposed. In both cases the level of waterlogging noted

during excavation coincided with the upper surfaces of these soils.

The finds recovered from topsoil contexts (F2) were limited to three types: shale, flint/chert and mudstone. The shale consisted of ten fragments of unworked stone. These fragments were found concentrated in the north-west corner of the area. The chipped stone recovered was distributed evenly about the area. It consisted of four unworked flint flakes, part of a plano-convex flint knife, and a chert core. All of the remaining finds came from F3. These include flint, shale and pottery. In all, seven flint flakes were recovered from F3.

The pieces of shale recovered from F3 and the topsoil may indicate that this material was worked on site, because they include both unworked pieces and finished articles.

### Chipped stone (Appendix 21) B Finlayson

The assemblage comprised six pieces from F2, five of flint and one of chert, and seven pieces from F3, all of flint. The cortex remaining on the flint pieces suggests it is originally from beach pebbles. None of the pieces from F3 has any secondary modification, although two have damaged edges, possibly from use. The one retouched piece from F2 is part of a plano-convex knife.

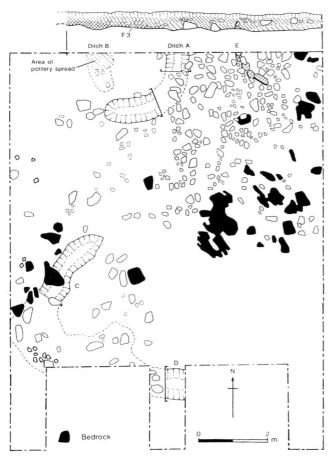

*Figure 4.3    Plan of Area B.*

### Jet armlets (Appendix 22) *V J McLellan*

Five fragments of at least three jet armlets were retrieved from soil layer F3. As has been stated above (Kemp, this volume) jet armlets are chronologically insensitive, spanning the Bronze Age to the post-Roman period. These examples add no further information to either typology or chronology.

### Pottery (Appendix 23) *A MacSween*

The pottery assemblage comprises seventy-seven sherds, the majority of which came from one vessel. The vessel has a flattened, slightly everted rim 320 mm in diameter at the mouth, widening out at the neck to a slight shoulder, then gradually narrowing again to a slightly footed base 180 mm in diameter. By projecting the line of the body from the basal angle (65°), the pot seems to have been 400 mm high. The vessel's colour varies but it is mainly red with a grey core. Its average thickness is *circa* 10 mm, excluding the flat part of the base which is 15 mm thick. The pot was hand-made (coil constructed), with the rim formed by neatening the top coil.

The fabric comprises a matrix of fine clay with very small quartz inclusions, tempered with 10% crushed rock fragments, measuring 5 mm to 8 mm. The inclusions were identified as biotite-augite-diorite (G

Collins, pers comm). With the use of such fine clay, addition of inclusions would have been necessary to prevent the pot cracking from steam build-up during firing, or from differential expansion of the exterior and interior during its probable use as a cooking vessel (sooted patches on the exterior and interior indicate that this was its function).

The second pot was represented by only two sherds (one rim and one body). The rim is plain but tapers, and seems to represent a vessel *circa* 260 mm in diameter at its lip, with walls 9 mm thick. The fabric is very similar to the previous vessel, but the inclusions comprise only 5% of the whole.

Due to the vessels' undiagnostic features and the lack of comparative material from similar sites in the area, it is not possible to date them with any confidence. Much of the later prehistoric pottery from lowland sites such as Broxmouth (Cool 1982) and Hownam Rings (Piggott C M 1948) is broadly similar, apart from having inturned, rather than everted, rims. The slightly shouldered profile of the Harpercroft pottery, and the find circumstances, tentatively indicate an early Iron Age date, possibly around the mid first millennium BC (T Cowie, pers comm). It should be stressed, however, that the undecorated shouldered pot with everted rim was a style of vessel which continued to be made in some regions of Scotland such as Orkney (Hunter 1984) well into the first half of the first millennium AD.

### Discussion

The archaeological deposits within the relatively small area excavated consisted for the most part of truncated features. Relationships were hard to define, partly because of outcropping bedrock, which also caused problems with drainage. Ditch B, representing an early phase of activity, was overlain by a phase represented by the digging of Ditch A, the deposition of F3 and the erection of the short length of kerbing.

The unpleasant aroma noted during the excavation of the lower fill of Ditch C and F10 was caused by the preservation of organic matter in both of these waterlogged, anaerobic deposits. The most puzzling aspect of the site was the origin of the two layers of dark, grey-brown soil, one found in association with Ditch A (F3) and the other found overlying bedrock (F10). Both were high in soil organic matter, evidenced by a weight loss of over 50% on ignition, and both were markedly acidic. Despite its similarity to the F3 soil, deposit F10 is a peaty formation which has survived due to waterlogging. It has become partly covered by a disturbed layer of glacial till as a result of human activity, possibly that associated with the digging of Ditch B (Figure 4.3). Layer F3, although similar to F10, is an archaeological deposit with anthropic components in the form of pieces of shale bracelet and pottery. The reasons for its survival are less obvious. The damp conditions would have affected the layer to a certain degree, but for a feature such as this to have survived it

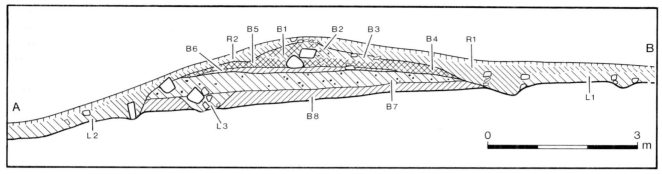

*Figure 4.4   Section of the rampart.*

would have needed to have been protected from normal soil processes. Christison mentions the existence of 'other obscure mounds' in this area, two of which coincide with the excavated area. These mounds may have afforded the necessary protection for the survival of F3 and indeed the other features. It must be concluded that the removal of these mounds has initiated the destruction of F3 and similar deposits in the area.

## WARDLAW HILL

The defensive aspect of this site was enhanced by the construction of a rampart along its most accessible sides. In its best preserved part, at the north end, the earthwork represents a stony, grass-covered rampart some 1.2 m high and spread to as much as 7 m wide (Figure 4.1d). It is first detectable to the north-east of the hilltop and runs south-west for 35 m, then turns south-east. It is much denuded in this area, being only barely traceable before disappearing down the hillslope at the south end. To the north of the rampart the terrain is some 1.5 m below the level of the ground enclosed by the rampart. A short stretch of rampart may be seen running round the rim of the hill to the south. This is a much denuded, collapsed bank, *circa* 55 m long, with some traces of what may be walling protruding through the grass. No evidence of ditches associated with the rampart were seen prior to excavation.

### Description and interpretation

In advance of the proposed installation of radar masts and other equipment close to the earthwork, an excavation was undertaken to determine the form and mode of construction of the bank and to ascertain whether a contemporaneous ditch lay to the north of it. A trench, measuring 2 m by 22 m, was cut through the bank (Figure 4.1d). No contemporary ditch existed to the north although shallow trench-like features were found both north and south of it, as well as one under the rampart. This last feature (L3 on Figure 4.4), which proved to be a small elongated pit, was found dug into a buried topsoil (B8) beneath the bank. Stones formed a large part of its fill but, although they may be packing stones of a post-hole, the function of the pit remains unknown.

The earthwork has two phases of construction. The earlier rampart (B7) was constructed by turf-stripping and surface quarrying on either side of the bank's intended course, burying an area of topsoil in the process. Material had been removed from a strip extending some 6 m to the south and 10 m to the north of the rampart, distances at which fully developed soil profiles were recognised. Closer to the rampart, both to the north and south, slope-wash and naturally accumulated soil directly overlay the glacial till (Figure 4.4, L1 and L2). Sufficient time had then elapsed to allow two events to occur: firstly, the original rampart had eroded and its constituents spread as deposits both north and south of its original limits (Figure 4.4, L1 & L2), and secondly, a soil horizon had developed on top of the primary bank (Figure 4.4; B6). This layer, which consisted of a light yellow-brown soil of relatively constant colour and texture, was interpreted as a continuous, *in situ*, topsoil rather than as a dumped deposit of discrete turves.

After an unknown interval the bank was rebuilt (B1–B5). This time large stones and boulders were piled on top of the now denuded primary bank as a core for the new rampart, and two narrow ditches were dug into the deposits washed from the original bank with the resulting material piled on top of the core. The ditches were stone-lined and may have held palisades, revetting the rampart. It was not possible to confirm this hypothesis in the limited area excavated.

## CONCLUSION

The series of small-scale excavations on the Dundonald Ridge were, in the main, successful, but as with most investigations of this size they posed more questions than they answered. This is certainly true of the area investigated on Harpercroft. Only very basic conclusions may be drawn. It is likely that the penannular features uncovered in the area coincide with those noted by Christison as 'obscure mounds'. The only apparently undisturbed deposit found, F3, produced nearly all the finds. Neither the pottery nor the shale objects are particularly chronologically sensitive but they do not rule out an Iron Age date for the site.

The two-phase rampart on Wardlaw Hill indicates that the site was used over a considerable period. The development of a soil profile over the primary bank indicates a period of disuse before the erection of the later rampart. No direct dating evidence was recovered from the excavation, and the soil organic matter of the buried A-horizon was insufficient for radiocarbon dating of the soil. In the absence of reliable chronological indicators, the original interpretation of this as an Iron Age site remains unchallenged.

## ACKNOWLEDGEMENTS

The author would like to thank Alan Duffy, site assistant, and thanks to all the volunteers for their hard work in often less than clement weather.

# Gillies Hill, Stirling, Central   *J S Rideout*

## Contributors

Artefacts *A J Barlow*
Charcoal identification *R P J McCullagh*

Line drawings *J S Rideout · M M B Kemp ·*
*S Stevenson*

## Abstract
*In 1984, the hillfort on Gillies Hill was threatened by the expansion of Murrayshall Quarry. A trench was opened over the defences to assess the archaeological potential of the site. Three ramparts were investigated.*

Gillies Hill is situated at the east end of the Gargunnock Hills about 4 km south-west of Stirling (NGR NS 768 917, Figure 5.1). It is formed by a sill of quartz-dolerite intruding through the surrounding limestone which has eroded to form a ridge with steep crags to the west and gentle slopes to the east. The gradual encroachment of Murrayshall Quarry on the fort on Gillies Hill prompted an exploratory excavation in September 1984.

The fort is sited on the edge of the crags at a point where they are interrupted by a gully, providing natural lines of defence to the west and south. When the RCAHMS investigators visited the site in 1957 it was covered by a plantation. Thus, only a general description and sketch plan are given in the *Inventory* (RCAHMS 1963, 70, Figure 9). The plan shows that the fort was defended to the north and east by three ramparts, which survive as low banks.

The plantation has since been cleared, leaving hummocky ground and uprooted tree stumps which have caused some damage both to the defences and to the interior of the fort. The Ordnance Survey records show that in 1973 there were '. . . only vague unsurveyable traces of a single rampart . . .' (OS record NS 79 south-east 60). A plane-table survey carried out by Peter Hill in April 1985 shows that the fort is roughly triangular in shape with the line of the defences less convex than suggested by the RCAHMS sketch plan. The outermost rampart (Rampart 3) is traceable for most of its circuit and fragmentary remains of the other two are also discernible (Figure 5.2). The possible entrance to the north-east (shown on the RCAHMS plan) is not visible, but the defences appear to stop short of both the gully and the cliff edge, suggesting that here are the positions of the original entrances. The site is named Gillies Hill because it was used as the campsite of retainers (gillies) on the eve of the Battle of Bannockburn in 1314.

## EXCAVATION

A trench, 39 m by 4 m, was opened over the defences and extended *circa* 13 m into the interior, near the junction of the ramparts with the gully (Figure 5.3). The remains of three ramparts were uncovered. The innermost rampart (Rampart 1) was *circa* 3 m wide and survived to a height of 0.5m (Figure 5.4). Its external stone face was crudely built while large stones along its inside edge indicated that it had been faced on both sides. The gritty, stony, loam core overlay a buried old ground surface. Most of the facing stones had tumbled forwards and a saddle-quern [9] was found within this rubble spread. Rampart 2, *circa* 4 m east of Rampart 1, was poorly preserved and only traces of the inner and outer facing remained (Figure 5.5). The core material, *circa* 3.5 m wide and 0.2 m high, was similar to that of Rampart 1 and produced a large quantity of pottery ([1] & [5]). Charcoal of alder and oak from the lowest part of the core produced a date of $2385 \pm 65$ bp (435 bc; GU-1909). Alder branch charcoal from within the outer facing was dated $2085 \pm 80$ bp (135 bc; GU-1910).

The outermost rampart (Rampart 3) was better preserved than the others. It was *circa* 3 m wide and 0.6 m high with rough stone facing on the inside and the remains of a facing on its outer edge (Figure 5.6). The core material was similar to that in Ramparts 1 and 2 and overlay a well-preserved buried A-horizon. The soil forming the rampart cores appears to have been obtained by stripping the ground surface between and beyond them. Behind Rampart 1 the soil had been stripped down to the bedrock for a distance of *circa* 8 m into the interior of the fort, leaving the original soil only in fissures in the rock. The soil had also been stripped to bedrock between Ramparts 1 and 2 while, between Ramparts 2 and 3, the rock itself had been quarried, probably for facing stone, creating a small scarp in front of Rampart 2. The quarrying seems to have been less complete beyond the defences, where more of the original soil survives.

An accumulation of dark humic soils containing charcoal, burnt bone [18] and pottery [6], [2], [4], a sherd of [3] and [7] overlay the bedrock behind Rampart 1. This soil seems to have built up against the back of the rampart during the occupation of the fort and represents the remains of domestic debris. Carbonised

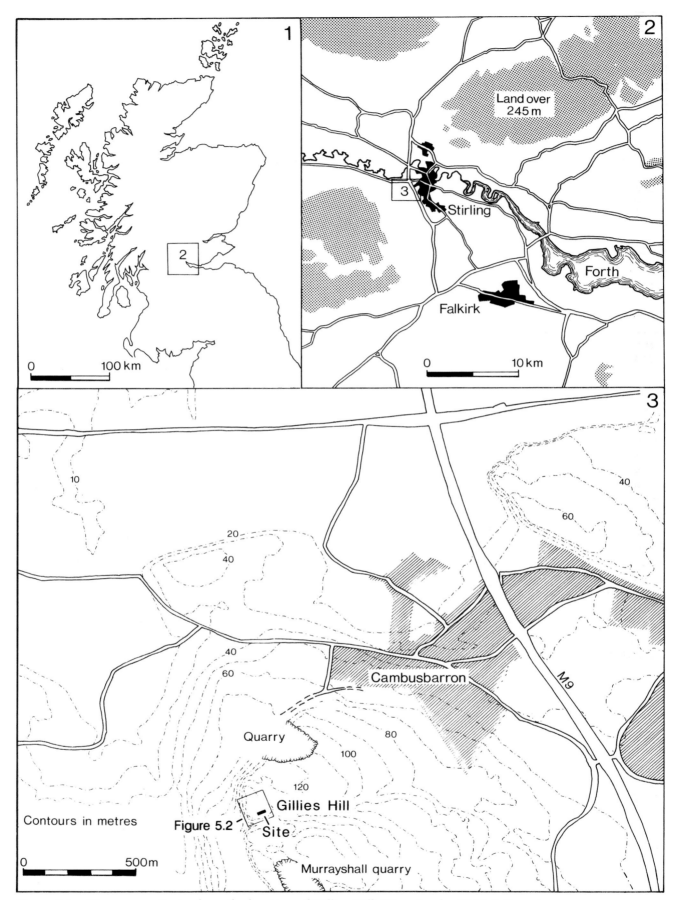

*Figure 5.1    Map composite to show the location of Gillies Hill. (Drawing by M M B Kemp).*

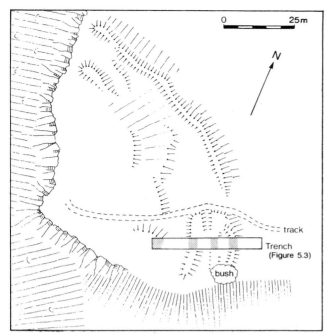

*Figure 5.2   Plan of the ramparts. (Drawing by P H Hill and J S Rideout).*

twigs of oak, hazel and alder from the lower part of this layer produced a date of 2310±55 bp (360 bc: GU-1911). The upper part of the occupation layer has been assimilated by root action into the present B2-horizon. The upper part of a late beaker [3] (Figure 5.7) was found embedded in a rock fissure near the inner edge of the occupation layer. The vessel had been inserted rim downwards, probably in a pit, and its base later disturbed by surface quarrying, probably for rampart construction. A sherd from the beaker was recovered from the occupation layer. Soil, presumably derived from the erosion of the ramparts, had accumulated beside and between them, forming a matrix for the collapsed facing stones. Parts of a stone armlet [8] and a rim sherd of beaker [2] were found within this soil and behind Rampart 3. A concentration of large stones at the west end of the trench appears to have been disturbed by the surface quarrying associated with Rampart 1. The

stones may have been part of a derelict cairn, but since the extent of this was not defined by excavation it has not been investigated further.

Bulk samples of all soil contexts were taken (20 kg per sample). All were floated and, as an assessment, the carbonised material from four contexts deemed most likely to produce cereal grains were examined. The samples, from the soil around the late beaker [3], the occupation accumulation behind Rampart 1, the buried topsoil under Rampart 1, and the buried topsoil under Rampart 3, contained no cereal grains. This absence of cereals, and the tiny amount of unidentifiable burnt bone from the occupation layer, means that no information has been retrieved which bears on the economy of the site.

## ARTEFACTS (Appendix 24–27) *A J Barlow*

The Gillies Hill pottery comprises two groups: a Late Neolithic/Early Bronze Age (LN/EBA) assemblage represented by two beakers and relict sherds of Neolithic character, and an Iron Age assemblage. Apart from the ceramic material, the only artefact of any but the most general chronological significance is the stone armlet [8].

The LN/EBA vessel [3] (Figure 5.7) belongs to a typologically late group of beakers; Clarke's (1970, 234) Final Southern British (S4) group, Lanting and van der Waals' (1972, 37, 39) Step 7. In decoration, it is most closely paralleled by a fragmentary beaker found under the final cairn at Balbirnie stone circle, Fife (Ritchie 1974, 7, 18). The Balbirnie vessel seems to have been displaced during the cairn's construction and an associated radiocarbon date from a mature tree gives it a *terminus ante quem* of 1338±90 bc.

Similar in size and form, both vessels exhibit 'Food Vessel characteristics': their flattened rims have been stabbed/impressed with a row of small rectangular pits. A zone of decoration 20 mm deep immediately below the rim is either borne on a narrow collar (Balbirnie), or contained by a cordon (Gillies Hill), the visual effect being virtually the same. Below this is a

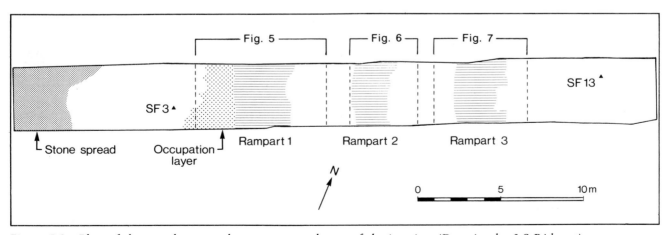

*Figure 5.3   Plan of the trench across the ramparts and part of the interior. (Drawing by J S Rideout).*

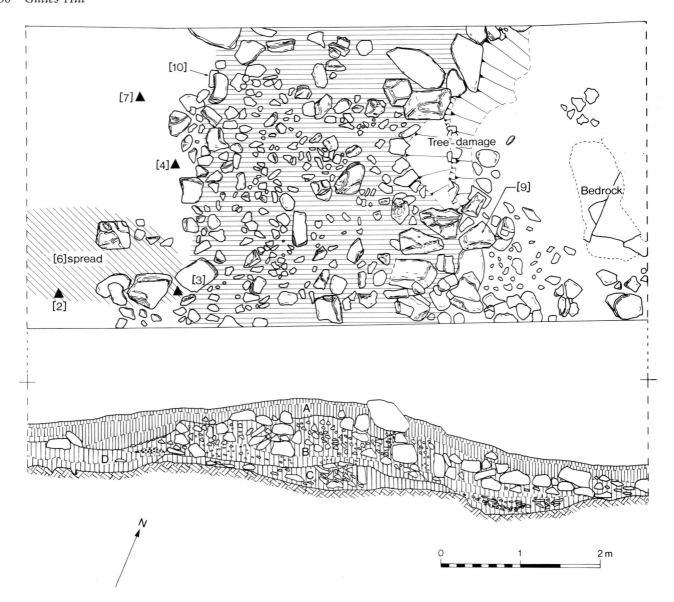

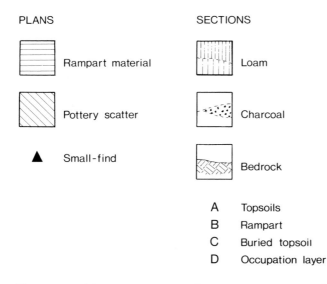

*Figure 5.4  Plan and section of Rampart 1. (Drawing by M M B Kemp).*

PLANS

| | Rampart material |

| | Pottery scatter |

▲  Small-find

SECTIONS

| | Loam |

| | Charcoal |

| | Bedrock |

A  Topsoils
B  Rampart
C  Buried topsoil
D  Occupation layer

*Key to graphic conventions used in Figure 5.4, 5.5 and 5.6.*

band of lozenges 'in reserve', formed by hatched triangles. Similar lozenges on the Balbirnie vessel interlock and are infilled with rows of horizontal jabs, the design continuing over the belly of the vessel. The Gillies Hill vessel has a blank zone (*circa* 20 mm deep) around it below the band of triangles. The reconstruction of the lower part of the Gillies Hill beaker is tentative because, apart from two flat basal sherds which fell into the cavity when the vessel was first disturbed, only one non-conjoining sherd scraped up during rampart construction survives from below the widest part of the body. This sherd, found *circa* 3 m south of the main part of the beaker, suggests that the zone of hatched triangles seen immmediately below the cordon was repeated.

A beaker from Kirkcaldy, Fife (Clarke 1970, 406, Figure 1014), assigned to Step 5, around 1700–1600 BC (Burgess 1980, 67, Figure 2.12), shares with the Gillies Hill pot both the cordon below the rim and a blank zone around the belly. Cordons below the rim in

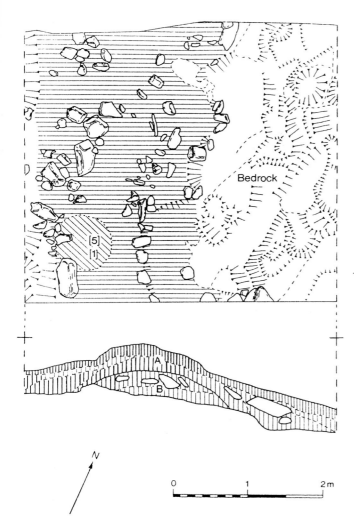

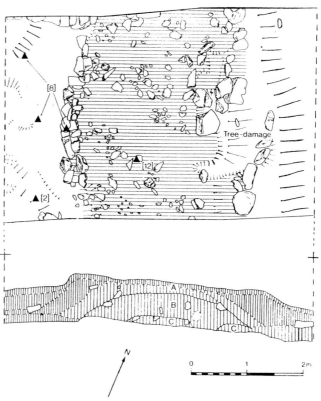

*Figure 5.6 Plan and section of Rampart 3. (Drawing by M M B Kemp).*

*Figure 5.5 Plan and section of Rampart 2. (Drawing by M M B Kemp).*

typologically late vessels are indicative of an affinity with elements of contemporary funerary pottery developed from indigenous Neolithic wares, the Food Vessels and Collared Urns (Clarke 1970, 236; Longworth 1961, 274, 276).

The position of the Gillies Hill beaker, apparently deliberately inverted in a small pit, is strongly suggestive of an urn cremation burial subsequently leached, demonstrating yet another aspect of the recuperation of the once-distinctive beaker type by other, parallel, funerary practices (Longworth, 1984, 79).

Two fragments of the second beaker [2] (Figure 5.7) were found as relict material in Iron Age contexts. The rim sherd, found on the bedrock in front of Rampart 2, indicated that the vessel had a smooth profile and a plain, possibly slightly beaded, everted, round rim. The exterior was decorated with opposed fingernail impressions comparable to a rim sherd from Hedderwick, East Lothian (Clarke 1970, 286, Figure 49a). This beaker may be as early as Steps 1–2.

The small thumb-pot [4] (Figure 5.7) was found in the occupation layer against the back face of the inner rampart. Its closest affinities, insofar as such an

elementary vessel might be said to have any, are with a slightly larger pinch-pot from Balloch Hill, Argyll (Yarrington, in Peltenberg 1982, 175–6), which it resembles in form and fabric, both being extremely coarsely-gritted. It could be argued that it is a crude crucible of the sort found at Foshigarry, North Uist (Callander, in Beveridge 1931, 342, 349) and other Hebridean Iron Age sites, or at Clumlie Broch, Shetland (NMA GA 397) and Finavon, Angus (Childe 1935, 71, 72, 74, Figures 14 & 16). However, the Gillies Hill vessel, like the Balloch example, does not appear to have been heavily fired and bears no traces of metal products. The fabric, cracked with large protruding grits, would militate against them being crucible fragments. It is improbable, therefore, that this is a crucible fragment. The fabric of the Gillies Hill thumb-pot resembles that of the two large Iron Age pots found on the site.

The two large vessels [5] and [6] are probably Iron Age in date. Less than half of [5] survives; it was incorporated in a horizon under Rampart 2, but a complete profile for this vessel can be reconstructed. The other Iron Age vessel [6] was represented by a single rim sherd and a few small body sherds, scattered throughout the occupation deposit in the area behind the inner rampart. Both vessels, as far as can be judged, were flat-based and bucket-shaped, with upright or inturned plain rims. The fabrics are coarsely gritted. According to Cool's (1982, 93) classification of pottery of this type from Broxmouth, East Lothian, the more complete Gillies Hill vessel [5] would belong to Class I on the basis of the fabric, while the other would possibly

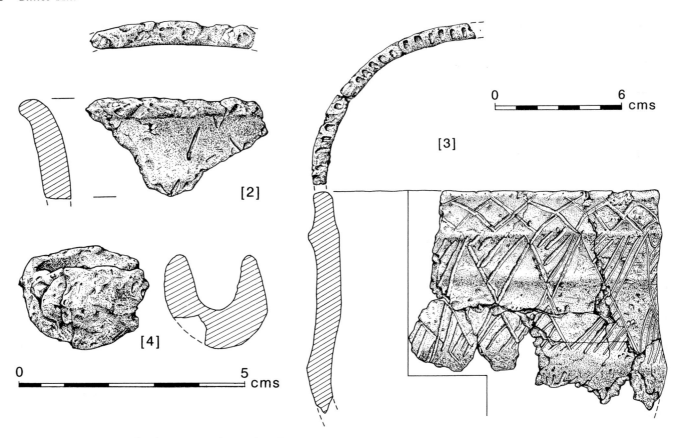

*Figure 5.7   Pottery: beakers [2] and [3]; thumb-pot [4]. (Drawing by S Stevenson).*

belong to Class II. Cool suggests dates of about the fifth to the second century BC for Class I and the second century BC to the end of the first century AD for Class II.

The stone armlet [8] (Figure 5.8) cannot be dated accurately. Shale, jet and jet-substitute armlets were first manufactured in the Late Bronze Age (Henshall 1956, 264; Burgess 1980, 280) and continued to be manufactured until the Early Christian Period. A fragment, found with coarse Iron Age pottery of the type discussed above, was found at Craig's Quarry, Dirleton, East Lothian (Piggott S 1958b, 70, 76), in a context now thought to date from the first century AD to '. . . several centuries earlier . . .' (Harding 1982, 2). At Broxmouth, shale-working seems to have been restricted to Period VI

(Cool, pers comm; Hill 1982, 161). The Gillies Hill armlet can be matched in cross-section and its external diameter can be matched in an example from Dun Mor Vaul, Tiree (MacKie 1974, 135, Figure 15, *no* 223), although the width and thickness of the latter are only half that of the Gillies Hill find. It was stratified with fragments of Roman glass and pottery which gave a *terminus post quem* of the second half of the second century AD.

RADIOCARBON DATES   *J S Rideout*

The identifications, by R P J McCullagh, of the carbonised material submitted to SURRC for radiocarbon assay are detailed in Table 5.1. The calibrated dates are listed in Table 5.2. The taphonomy of the samples is discussed below.

**Rampart 2, core: $2385 \pm 65$ bp (GU-1909)**

The sample was selected from the lowest part of the rampart core, immediately above the buried topsoil, and from the area of the pottery concentration [5] and [1]. Given that [5] was roughly half of a pot, broken *in situ* and untrampled, it is likely that material in this deposit derives from activities predating the construction of the rampart by a very short interval. The inclusion of earlier material cannot be ruled out, but remains only a slight possibility in this context. The assay provides a *terminus post quem* for the construction of the rampart.

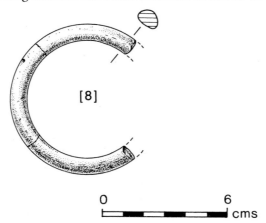

*Figure 5.8   Stone armlet. (Drawing by S Stevenson).*

Table 5.1  *Carbonised wood identifications.*

| lab *no* GU- | context | description |
|---|---|---|
| 1909 | rampart 2 core | Most of the sample consisted of fragments of a single piece of *Alnus glutinosa* (alder) with small fragments of *Quercus* species (oak). Final weight 14 g. |
| 1910 | rampart 2 facing | *Alnus glutinosa*. All fragments were from a single piece of wood with a diameter of about 6.8 cm. Final weight 10 g. |
| 1911 | occupation layer | 60% *Quercus* species, 30% *Corylus avellana* (hazel), 10% *Alnus glutinosa*. All specimens were from small diameter round and twig wood. Final weight 15 g. |

Table 5.2  *Radiocarbon dates.*

| lab *no* GU- | uncalibrated date | calibrated date | |
|---|---|---|---|
| | | 1 sigma | 2 sigma |
| 1909 | 435 BC±65 | 752 BC–395 BC | 770 BC–380 BC |
| 1911 | 360 BC±55 | 403 BC–376 BC | 510 BC–210 BC |
| 1910 | 135 BC±80 | 198 BC–5 BC | 370 BC–AD 80 |

**Rampart 2, revetment: 2085 ± 80 bp (GU-1910)**

The sample was a single branch of alder, from between the front revetment stones. Its position indicates that it had been inserted between the stones some time after the construction of the rampart. The assay provides a *terminus ante quem* for the construction of the rampart.

**Rampart 1, occupation material behind it: 2310 ± 55 bp (GU-1911)**

The charcoal for this assay came from a restricted area in the lower part of this deposit. It is not possible to say whether the charcoal derives from a single event or accumulated over a short period. Contamination from earlier material cannot be wholly ruled out, as indicated by the single beaker sherd from elsewhere in this deposit, but the assay is likely to date a period in the occupation of the fort, shortly after the construction of Rampart 1.

DISCUSSION  *J S Rideout*

The primary objective of the excavation was to establish the state of preservation of the fort and to assess its potential for future excavation. The trench was therefore located at a point where the defences were relatively well-preserved. The excavation showed that, although the upper levels of the stratigraphy have been degraded by root and animal activity to form the present topsoils, enough survives to permit a certain amount of interpretation of the features uncovered.

The excavated area was small and it was not possible to determine whether the defences were all of one build or were gradually strengthened, perhaps representing more than one period of occupation of the site. The latest plan shows that only the outermost rampart (Rampart 3) remains relatively intact for its full length. The others survive as short lengths of low bank obscured by uprooted trees. Indeed it is possible that the spread of stones encountered at the west end of the trench may be the last vestiges of a fourth, innermost rampart. Its appearance thus suggests that Rampart 3 may have been a later defence, either adding to or replacing existing defences. It is equally possible, however, that the inner defences have suffered from greater modern disturbance, so creating a false impression of non-contemporaneity.

There is no physical evidence of reconstruction in the excavated area and the significant difference between the radiocarbon dates from the core and facing of Rampart 2 cannot be explained by refurbishment of the revetment. The difference is more likely to be the result of contamination, since the charcoal from the revetment was a single piece of wood from a less secure context than that of the core. It may equally be the result of activity of a later date on probably ruinous defences. The uncalibrated dates from the core of Rampart 2 and the occupation layer, suggest that the fort was constructed in the fourth or fifth century bc. That the site may have continued in use for some centuries is possibly indicated by the date from the facing of Rampart 2. In addition, the finds, particularly the armlet, from the accumulation of soil between the ramparts, indicate activity at a time when the defences were dilapidated.

More accurate dating for the site is not possible from only three samples. When the dates are calibrated using

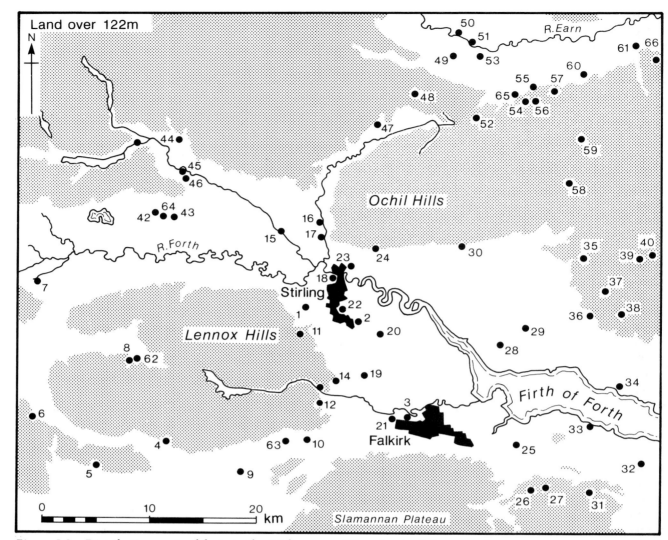

*Figure 5.9 Distribution map of forts in the Stirling area. (Drawing by S Stevenson).*

1 Gillies Hill NS768917
2 Bannockburn NS815904
3 Camelon NS863811
4 Meikle Reive NS639789
5 Craigmaddie NS575765
6 Quinloch Muir NS 515813
7 Gartclach NS519942
8 Dunmore NS605865
9 Castle Hill NS709761
10 Coney Park NS770792
11 Sauchie Craig NS763893
12 Myot Hill NS781825
13 Wester Barnego NS783839
14 Braes NS797847
15 Easter Row NS744990
16 Mill of Keir Bank NS781999
17 Gallow Hill NS782984
18 Mote Hill NS793944
19 Langlands NS782984
20 Cowie NS836892
21 Wester Carmuirs NT849810
22 Livilands NT800916
23 Abbey Craig NS809956
24 Dumyat NS832973
25 Avonbank NS 961786

26 Bowden Hill NS977744
27 Cockleroy NS989745
28 Keir Plantation NS946882
29 Castlehill Wood NS971899
30 Castle Craig, Tillicoutry NS911976
31 Peace Knowe NT030741
32 Craigton Hill NT076769
33 Stacks NT032801
34 Waulkmill, Crombie NT058842
35 Cult Hill NT024965
36 Cowstrand Burn NT030910
37 Easter Cairn, Saline NT042933
38 Craigluscar NT059910
39 Dumglow NT076965
40 Dummifarline NT088968
41 Dunmore, Bochastle NN601075
42 Tam na Falloch NN629008
43 Keir, Easter Borland NN645003
44 Auchenlaich NN649078
45 Mid Torrie, 'The Auld Knowe' NN652048
46 Easter Torrie NN657040
47 Grinnan Hill of Keir NN834093
48 Orchill NN868123
49 Machany NN 902158
50 South Mains, Innerpeffray NN907179

51 Craig Shot NN919171
52 Loaninghead NN924100
53 North Mains, Strathallan NN928158
54 Ogle Hill NN969115
55 Castle Craig, Pairney NN976127
56 Ben Effray NN980115
57 Rossie Law NN997124
58 Down Hill NO00103659 John's Hill NO002080

60 Dun Knock, Dunning NO023142
61 Jackschairs Wood NO072168
62 Dunbeg NS608866
63 Ruchill NS753785
64 Keir, Easter Torr NN637007
65 Thorn NN961120
66 Castle Law, Forgandenny NO099154

the program in *Radiocarbon* (Pearson & Stuiver 1986) it is clear that they fall into the problem area in the mid-first millennium BC. The date from the occupation layer calibrated at the 1σ level of confidence gives a remarkably narrow range, 403 BC to 376 BC, but at the 2σ level gives a three-century range. The calibrated date from Rampart 2 core is even less precise, with a three-, to four-century range at both 1σ and 2σ levels. Although this latter date falls into one of the 'disaster areas' in the calibration curve (Baillie & Pilcher 1983, 58–60), the narrow range of the former may indicate that Rampart 2 core construction belongs in the later end of the calibrated range (*ie* 500–400 BC).

Pre-defensive activity is attested by pottery representing at least three vessels identified as Late Neolithic, Early and Late Beaker. With the exception of the Late Beaker vessel, this material was residual and had been incorporated into the ramparts and occupation layer. The method of deposition of the Late Beaker vessel may, however, indicate Later Bronze Age funerary activity on the hill. The stone concentration at the west end of the trench may be the remains of a cairn much reduced by the Iron Age activity. The two large vessels, represented by sherds from the occupation layer and rampart core, are of a form commonly found in forts in south-east Scotland (Barlow, *passim*). The stone armlet, the saddle-quern and the thumb-pot are probably roughly contemporaneous and, while the other finds are mostly from disturbed contexts, they may also date to the same period. The only demonstrably late artefact is a single sherd of medieval pottery [7] (Appendix 25).

The sequence of events identified on Gillies Hill may be summarised as follows.
*i* Late Neolithic and Bronze Age activity, possibly funerary.
*ii* Ramparts constructed and fort occupied in the fifth century BC.
*iii* Fort abandoned at an unknown date.
*iv* Sporadic medieval activity on the hill.

Figure 5.9 shows the distribution of forts in an area 60 km east-west by 50 km north-south centred on Stirling. Gillies Hill is one of a concentration of about twenty forts in the immediate area of Stirling. The apparent isolation of this concentration can be explained in part by the unsuitability of the territory outwith it, notably the wet, low-lying Carse of Forth to the north-west and south-east, the high ground of the Ochil Hills to the north-east and the Lennox Hills to the west. However, there is a marked absence of forts on the northern fringes of both the Slamannan Plateau, to the

south of Falkirk, and the Campsie Fells; and there are only a few forts on the southern flanks of the latter.

With the exception of a few forts identified by the *Inventory* as being of later, Dark Age date, such as Dunmore (8) in the Central Campsie Fells, and the later phase at Dumyat (24) at the western end of the Ochil Hills, most of the forts are described in the *Inventory* for Stirlingshire as contour forts and promontory forts (RCAHMS 1963, 27). The contour forts have stone walls as defences, while the promontory type have ramparts and ditches. Gillies Hill was identified as a promontory fort, but excavation has shown that, insofar as the construction of its ramparts is concerned, it does not fall comfortably into either class. Although useful, the classification of forts into groups based on their topographical location takes no cognisance of the fact that the line of the defences only reflects the local terrain. The differing styles of defence construction probably results from the need to use the materials to hand.

Of the concentration of forts, only two, Lower Greenyards, Bannockburn (2; Rideout & Tavener forthcoming) and Camelon (3; Proudfoot 1978), have been investigated. Camelon, a small, strongly defended site on a low sand promontory, produced very few finds from contexts associated with the 'native' occupation. It is, however, similar in situation, internal dimensions and defence construction to the defended promontory at Bannockburn, *circa* 5 km east of Gillies Hill. The defensive period at Bannockburn accounts for only part of its span of occupation but radiocarbon dates suggest that it may have been defended contemporaneously with Gillies Hill (Rideout & Tavener, forthcoming). Post-excavation analysis of the data from Bannockburn is as yet incomplete which, together with the small scale of the investigation of Gillies Hill, makes detailed comparison between these sites difficult. However, the proximity of the two forts must have resulted in some interaction, the scale and extent of which remain unknown in the absence of further excavation at Gillies Hill.

Another excavated fort, Meikle Reive (4; Fairhurst 1956), lies outwith the concentration, some 18 km south-west of Gillies Hill. The defences of Meikle Reive are constructed in a similar way to those at Gillies Hill, with stone-revetted ramparts and shallow rock-cut ditches. Its situation differs only to the extent that there are no cliffs serving as natural defences. Although undated, Meikle Reive produced a few finds of the sort commonly found in earlier Iron Age forts, namely a stone disc, a small stone ball, a shale bracelet and sherds of coarse pottery. It may be broadly contemporary with Gillies Hill.

## ACKNOWLEDGEMENTS

Permission to excavate was kindly granted by Kings and Co, and A and R Brownlee Ltd permitted access to the site; the co-operation of both is gratefully acknowledged by the author. Thanks are also due to the site staff, Nick Tavener and Chris Russell-White, and to the volunteers for their hard work and good humour. The author is particularly grateful to Peter Hill, who undertook the plane-table survey of the site and was of great help in correcting the text, and also to Sylvia Stevenson and Mary Kemp for preparing the illustrations. Finally, the author is most grateful to Mike Spearman, Eoin Halpin, and Trevor Cowie for commenting on the finds.

3 Discussion *J S Rideout · with O A Owen*          139

# Discussion   *J S Rideout · with O A Owen*

This final discussion considers the group of excavated sites in their wider context, in Scottish and British archaeology.

On Eildon Hill North, the 1986 excavations have revealed the existence of a Late Bronze Age hilltop settlement. No incontrovertible evidence for an Early Iron Age occupation was retrieved. There is evidence for a probably large-scale settlement of Roman Iron Age date. These discoveries have highlighted the problems in interpreting a fort of this size, in the absence of large-scale excavations. It had been thought that Eildon was the tribal centre of the Selgovae, that it supported a population of several thousand and that it was abandoned before the construction of the Roman fort at Newstead in, roughly, AD 80. These assumptions now appear most improbable. Instead there seems to have been a hiatus in the use of the hilltop between the end of the Bronze Age and the Roman Iron Age, a hiatus it may share with Traprain Law. All three of the defensive systems (RCAHMS 1956, 306–10) were examined. Defensive System C was not located and its existence is now in doubt. Defensive Systems A and B were shown to be relatively slight constructions sited to take advantage of naturally defensive topographical features. The indications are that at least the inner rampart of Defensive System A is of Late Bronze Age date.

All three of the identified defensive systems on Eildon Hill North (RCAHMS 1956, 306–10) were investigated. The innermost, C, was not located and its existence must now be doubted; B was shown to be very slight and mostly reliant on naturally defensive topographical features. The outermost defensive system, A, enclosing *circa* 16 ha, also proved to be of slight construction.

The house platforms are devoid of architectural embellishment, implying that the structures they once carried were made from organic materials during both periods of use of the hilltop. This feature was noted in both phases of use of one platform (House Platform 1), separated by several hundred years. The series of radiocarbon dates indicate two main periods of occupation, one in the Later Bronze Age, the other in the Roman Iron Age, with no clear evidence of a pre-Roman Iron Age occupation.

The identification of The Dunion as an *oppidum* is a recent event. The monument had been identified as a Dark Age fort with later early medieval (and later) open settlement overlying it. The results of the 1961–1962 excavations produced finds which indicated a later prehistoric date and the re-survey of the hill by RCAHMS confirmed that the fort was much larger than had been suspected. In fact, it was large enough to be included in the short list of minor *oppida* (Feachem 1966, 79). The area investigated in 1984–1986 lay beyond the defences even of this *oppidum*, and was believed to be the site of an Unenclosed Platform Settlement (UPS). The excavation showed that the settlement was in fact a group of house platforms within an even larger fort of *circa* 6 ha to 6.5 ha. Like some other forts in the class, The Dunion was probably first constructed as a small fort and gradually expanded by the additions of annexes, tailored to the local topography. The area excavated by the CEU produced a series of radiocarbon dates which indicated that the occupation of this, the outermost annexe to the north, spanned the last two, or perhaps three, centuries BC and the first century AD. There are indications that the occupation of the hill continued into the Roman Iron Age. By implication, the original core-fort on the summit-plateau of the hill may have been constructed at least as early as the mid-first millennium BC.

The excavation at Gillies Hill, although small-scale, produced radiocarbon dates indicating that the fort was originally constructed around the middle of the first millennium BC and that it was occupied continuously or intermittently to the end of that millennium. The small excavations on the two adjacent summits of Harpercroft and Wardlaw Hill, unfortunately, indicated no more than a general Iron Age date for these forts.

The pollen analyses of the core from Blackpool Moss, and the samples from Eildon Hill North and The Dunion, have added to our understanding of the environmental impact of human settlement in south-east Scotland. The suggestion that Neolithic and Early Bronze Age activity had a considerable effect on the vegetation is, however, not borne out in the archaeological record (*cf* the introductions to the Roxburghshire and Selkirkshire *Inventories*: RCAHMS 1956, 10–15; RCAHMS 1957, 15–17), where settlement sites in particular are noticeably under-represented. That this will be corrected in due course is indicated by recent discoveries of Later Bronze Age settlement in the uplands surrounding the area, where dates in the second half of the second millennium BC have been recorded from unenclosed settlements. Thus a date of $1230 \pm 60$ bc (HAR-2414) has been returned from Bracken Rigg, Co. Durham (Coggins & Fairless 1984, 5) and a date of $1270 \pm 75$ bc (GU-1213) from Platform 5 at Green Knowe, Peeblesshire (Jobey 1980, 82).

The majority of artefacts from Eildon, The Dunion and Wardlaw Hill are either undiagnostic, or chronologically insensitive and can, therefore, provide only a general chronology for the occupation of the sites. However, Cool (1982), while summarising the problems inherent in the interpretation of later prehistoric assemblages from southern Scotland, has drawn attention to the potential for characterisation of total assemblages. She suggested that while individual artefact types may be of little use for chronology building, the relative proportions of types on a site may be more helpful. Thus, while of little consequence to these individual sites, the current assemblages incorporated into regional studies with materials from future excavations may contribute to the evolution of regional artefactual chronologies for southern Scotland.

The excavations of later prehistoric sites undertaken in the decade before the 1981 Edinburgh conference had generated much debate and, undoubtedly, their publication will revive and hopefully extend that debate. The results of those excavations have, in general, been interpreted very much in line with the Hownam model. Trends have been discerned leading from open settlement to simple enclosed settlements (palisades) and thence to more strongly defended settlements (forts) and finally to open settlement or enclosed non-defensive settlements in different areas at different times. Superimposed on this sequence is the further trend from timber construction to stone or earthworks.

The identification of such trends was both required and facilitated by the increasing number of radiocarbon dates. Sites of the later prehistoric period in southern Scotland are poor in diagnostic artefacts and, as a result, too much reliance has been placed on exotic find-types, often poorly provenanced. Increasing numbers of radiocarbon dates have reduced our reliance on exotica. This, in turn, has resulted in a downgrading of discussion of the artefacts and their cultural affinities. The conflict between site (radiocarbon) chronologies and artefactual (typological) chronologies has, in effect, led to the abandonment of the latter. Iron Age settlement excavation in general, and excavation of forts in particular, is now concentrated on the architecture and basic economic and environmental background of sites with a reduction of interest in questions of cultural associations (*cf* Harding 1982b). Furthermore, there has been a general rejection of diffusionist theories. In particular, the perceived drift of innovations of all sorts from southern Britain to Scotland has been rejected and the relevance of comparisons with other parts of the country has been questioned.

When the poorly provenanced exotic finds are necessarily dismissed from the reckoning, there are few potential links with the southern forts. Furthermore, the recent Scottish emphasis on structural and economic features of excavated and unexcavated sites has encouraged the beginnings of a regional model for forts. This model requires further study, excavation and dating evidence before an adequate basis for comparisons with similar studies in other areas can emerge.

Although increasing numbers of radiocarbon dates were becoming available, the small size of the sample of dated hillforts prompted the comment, at the 1981 conference, that '. . . there was an urgent need for a series of [radiocarbon] dates from key sites . . .' (Harding 1982a, 193). This deficiency was also noted by Cunliffe who warned against the improper use of the available dates (1983, 90). While conscious of the difficulties posed by small samples, by 1984 the indications were that in south and east Scotland occupation of forts began at least as early as the seventh century BC, (based on dates from Finavon, Angus; MacKie 1969: and Burnswark, Dumfriesshire; Jobey 1978). The results from Broxmouth, East Lothian, indicated that some forts may have lost their 'defensive' function before the end of the first millennium BC (Hill 1982b). Although its development was more complex than that of other excavated forts, Broxmouth did not contradict the trend of simple to complex defences identified at Hownam Rings and interpreted from the visible remains of many forts in south-eastern Scotland.

It is widely accepted that an understanding of the larger hillforts sites is a major aim of future researches (Hill 1982a, 27; Stevenson 1966, 28–30). It must be borne in mind, however, that the pursuit of an understanding of large forts alone, at the expense of the more common small forts and other settlements and homesteads, would be of limited value and probably doomed to failure.

Notwithstanding the potential errors engendered by the small scale of these excavations, the results suggest that the two larger sites differ in date and development. While The Dunion appears to have been a gradually expanding fort of the second half of the first millennium BC, Eildon, at its greatest extent, may belong to the Later Bronze Age. Whereas The Dunion seems to have declined before or during the Roman Iron Age, the evidence from Eildon attests to its importance during this period. The Dunion appears to have been densely occupied, at least during part of its history and with houses of some durability. The apparently dense concentration of platforms on Eildon may have resulted from two distinct settlement periods and perhaps from a shifting population occupying relatively flimsy structures. What is indicated, therefore, is that coherent patterns of construction, expansion, contraction and abandonment may not be detectable in the larger forts in anything short of very large area excavations.

These sites have a number of features in common, the most obvious being their size and their prominent siting on distinctive hills which provide a considerable degree of natural defence. However, their man-made defences are slight even where they do not follow natural lines of defence. On The Dunion, Rampart 1a was only *circa* 2.5 m thick and Rampart 1b little more than a drystane dyke. The ramparts on Traprain Law were of similar scale to Rampart 1a at The Dunion (*eg* Cruden 1940, Figure 3 & 6). The inner rampart of Defensive System A on Eildon consisted of a slight rampart with some scarping to enhance a natural break in the slope.

An earlier belief in a common house morphology (Hill 1982a, 27) has been shown by these excavations and, indeed by earlier field-work (Jobey 1965, 34, Figure 8) to be erroneous. House platforms are to be expected where houses are built on sloping ground. Apparent similarities in house densities must be treated with caution. In the case of Eildon, the apparently dense occupation may be the result of superimposition over a lengthy period of occupation or, at least, over two periods of occupation. At The Dunion, the dense concentration of houses seems to reflect genuinely high population figures.

*Oppida* appear to differ in their development. For instance, while The Dunion and Humbleton Hill appear to have become *oppida* after gradual expansion, Yeavering Bell and Hownam Law both appear to have been constructed as large forts, although the fort on Yeavering Bell was preceded by a small palisaded site. Eildon, originally thought to have expanded from a fort of 0.8 ha on the summit to a larger fort of 3.6 ha before a final expansion to *circa* 16 ha, may have started as a large fort. Indeed, the fort of 3.6 ha, if it existed at all, could just as easily represent a contraction of the site from the 16 ha fort. Rubers Law, a fort of 3.6 ha, was replaced by a smaller fort in the Dark Ages, while at Traprain Law the fort may have expanded in stages before contracting a little.

Differences or similarities in the architecture of the defences are probably of no importance in most cases. Where stone was locally plentiful, drystone walling has been used (for example, Hownam Law; RCAHMS 1956, 157–9; or some of the inner lines of defence on The Dunion). Where less stone was available stone-revetted ramparts have been used (such as Rampart 1a on The Dunion, Traprain Law [Cruden 1940, Figures 3 & 6], and Walls Hill, Renfrewshire [7.5 ha; Newall 1960, Figure 1]). Eildon is unusual, however, in that Defensive System A comprises three concentric lines of defence (ramparts/scarps poorly revetted with unsuitable stone), and differs from most others in being multivallate, at least in its final form. At Burnswark, a fort of *circa* 7 ha is defended by a single rampart on the north side and by twin ramparts on the south (Jobey 1978) where the main (inner) rampart was initially timber-revetted (Phase 1) and subsequently stone-revetted (Phase 2). It is clear, therefore, that despite having some elements in common, the large forts of southern Scotland probably do not form an architecturally coherent group.

Given their scale, the results of the CEU excavations cannot be expected to add much to our understanding of the functions of minor *oppida*. As noted above, the defences are, in the main, slight but designed to appear impressive to outsiders by exploiting natural features. The creation of the barrier, therefore, is probably more of a statement of intent rather than the strictly functional construction of a defensive barrier. Indeed, it would probably have been physically impossible to defend a fort the size of that on Eildon Hill North against an attacking force, although the scarped defences would have discouraged casual intrusions. The same is probably true of the defences of The Dunion at its greatest extent. The inner lines of defence on The Dunion would have proved a more effective barrier, but for reasons of topography rather than effective defence construction. The extreme example of slight defence at

The Dunion (Rampart 1b), however, was so slight that its function must have been merely to delimit an area of activity associated with the occupation of the site.

While it is possible that the sites for larger or more important forts were selected for their defensive characteristics, the fact that the chosen hills are obvious landmarks, visible over large areas, must have been of considerable importance. Whether this was for religious reasons as suggested by Hill (1987), for political as well as religious reasons (*cf* Bowden & McOmish 1987), or for even more complex reasons, may be resolved by further field-work.

The excavations on The Dunion and Eildon Hill North produced no obvious signs of specialisation in house types which might be taken to indicate differences in social status. Indeed, analysis of social organisation within minor *oppida* cannot be carried out without extensive excavation. The excavations at, for example, Moel y Gaer, Clwyd (Guilbert 1976) indicate the required scale (although for discussion of the potential for analysis of hillfort interiors see Guilbert 1981). The evidence from both The Dunion and Eildon shows that ordinary domestic and industrial activity was taking place, suggesting that the sites fulfilled at least some of the functions of later towns. The lack of evidence of solid structures on the platforms on Eildon Hill North has been seen as possibly the result of intermittent occupation of the site. The Dunion, where continuity of occupation is indicated, presents no such evidence and the inherent weakness of arguing from the absence of evidence suggests that the Eildon Hill North conclusion should be treated with caution.

It has been noted that ritual elements can be identified in hillforts (Bowden & McOmish 1987). Hill (1987), reinterpreting the evidence from Traprain Law, suggests that the hill was used for purely ritual purposes during the Roman Iron Age. He points to a possibly votive deposit in a pit at Broxmouth and also to the recovery of much of the small assemblage of late pre-Roman Iron Age/early Roman Iron Age artefacts from pits. It has also been suggested (above) that at The Dunion the upper stone of the beehive quern was deliberately, and therefore probably ritually, deposited in the pit in House 2. A possibly similar deposit, albeit richer, was recorded at Rathgall, Co. Wicklow, where a pit in a Late Bronze Age house was lined with organic deposits containing a gold ring and burnt human bone. The pit, mostly filled by a single boulder, was interpreted by the excavator as a ritual, foundation deposit (Raftery 1976, 342, Figure 2). Ritual deposition, on a somewhat more sumptuous scale, may account for the votive hoards of the Roman Iron Age at Blackburn Mill, Berwickshire, at Eckford, Roxburghshire and at Carlingwark Loch, Dumfriesshire (Piggott S 1953). It may also account for the hoard of Roman bronzes from Rubers Law (Curle 1905). Pit 2, and possibly Pit 1, at Eildon could be interpreted as the remains of deposits associated with foundation rituals. The horse teeth in Pit 2 may parallel deposits of goats' skulls and the lower jaws of boars, in post-holes of the Period 2 entrance on

Crickley Hill. There, the excavator noted that it is '. . . difficult to avoid the suggestion that some purpose such as conferring on the gates the vitality of the animals was here intended.' (Dixon 1977, 170). Other foundation rituals involve human rather than animal burials. Among these are the contracted burial of a young adult male in a pit beneath the ultimate pre-Roman Iron Age rampart at South Cadbury (Alcock 1970, 16–7, 23–4) and a contracted adult female in a pit under the counterscarp mound at Hod Hill (Richmond 1967, Vol 2, 16, Plates 6 & 7a).

The rarity of rich votive deposits from Scottish sites has almost certainly led to an under-representation of ritual features in the archaeological record for the area. The ritual elements of poorer deposits, especially those apparently lacking exotic inclusions, like the Broxmouth or The Dunion examples, are less easily or reliably identified. Post-depositional effects also militate against their identification, especially where soil acidity leads to a total loss of unburnt bone. The deposition of a largely defleshed child in four small pits under a wheelhouse at Hornish Point, South Uist (Barber *et al* 1989, 773–8), for example, would have gone unrecognised in the acid soils of most of lowland Scotland.

The Broxmouth results indicate abandonment of forts by the end of the first millennium bc, a conclusion that is somewhat at odds with the accepted view of hillforts. Some hillforts in southern Scotland have been ascribed to the native tribes listed by Ptolemy, namely, the identification of Traprain Law and Eildon Hill North as the tribal capitals of the Votadini and Selgovae, respectively. Eildon Hill North was thought to have been abandoned at the time of the Agricolan campaigns, while Traprain Law was believed to have continued in use by virtue of a 'special relationship' between the Votadini and the Romans. It was assumed, as noted above, that all other forts were abandoned following the arrival of the Romans.

Feachem has made popular the view that the fort on Eildon Hill North was the capital of the Selgovae tribe at the time of the Agricolan incursion into northern Britain. The location of the tribe, and others in southern Scotland/northern England, is understandably vague. Maps, all based originally on Ptolemy's *Geography*, locate the Selgovae in the central Southern Uplands. The OS Map of Roman Britain (3rd edition 1956), for instance, prints the name over the upper reaches of Annandale, Ewesdale, Liddesdale, and the Tyne. Eildon Hill North, The Dunion and Rubers Law sit in a void between this and the legend 'Votadini' which runs through central Berwickshire and north Northumberland. It has been generally accepted that the Selgovae occupied the upper half of the Tweed basin and spread across into Annandale (Feachem 1966, 78, Figure 13). This would place Eildon Hill North and The Dunion in the eastern borders of the territory of the Selgovae and very close to that of the Votadini. Mann and Breeze suggest that the Selgovae occupied Annandale and Nithsdale, while the Votadini occupied

the east coast plain from East Lothian to Northumberland, and Tweeddale (1987, 85–91).

The number of forts which can be reliably assigned to the first and second centuries AD are few, and the quality of information from them is variable. Yet this is presumably the period to which Ptolemy's map applies. In the Scottish Lowlands and Southern Uplands only sixteen forts have produced radiocarbon dates. Based solely on the radiocarbon dating evidence, four or five of these sixteen forts could be said to have been occupied in the first century ad; these are The Dunion, Eildon Hill North, Craigmarloch Wood (MacKie 1969, 18–19), Murton High Crags (Jobey and Jobey 1987), and Broxmouth, (Hill 1982b). As can be seen, these sites represent a tiny and well-dispersed sample. Craigmarloch Wood is possibly dated to this period by a date of $35 \pm 40$ bc (GaK-996, calibrated at $1\sigma$ to 40 BC–AD 63) from the core of a timber-laced rampart. At Murton High Crags occupation continued after timber-built phases dated to $180 \pm 80$ bc (HAR-6202, calibrated at $1\sigma$ to 358 BC–AD 91) and $110 \pm 100$ bc (HAR-6200, 200 BC–AD 51). Broxmouth produced a number of dates of this period from a post-defensive phase of the site. Eildon, definitely occupied later in the Roman Iron Age, may also have been occupied in the first century AD (date from House platform 1 of $50 \pm 130$ bc (GU-2371; calibrated to 180 BC–AD 120). Of the five sites, four, The Dunion, Eildon, Broxmouth and Murton, are in Votadinian territory, according to the Mann and Breeze scheme. While the four sites have some common elements, they display far from similar forms and settlement development patterns. It is difficult, therefore, to identify unifying traditions interpretable as tribal characteristics, whether Votadinian or Selgovian.

To try to assign areas to tribes reported to have existed in the first and second centuries AD, based only on a few second-, or third-hand sources, possibly all deriving their information from a single primary source, may in any event be futile. It can be little more than an intellectual exercise with little bearing on the information retrieved from the few excavated sites in southern Scotland.

The excavations on the smaller sites reported upon in this volume highlight some common problems in the archaeology of the Iron Age in southern Scotland. The results of rescue excavation vary in quantity and quality. Gillies Hill and the two Dundonald sites represent some of the more informative examples of small excavations undertaken on defended sites. Similar, or less useful information, has come from other projects such as Doon Hill, Kirkcudbrightshire (Crone 1982); Downlaw, Fife (D & E S 1988, 12); Rings Plantation, Roxburghshire (Rideout 1983); Tailburn, Dumfriesshire (Rideout 1989) and Allan Water, Roxburghshire (Rideout 1990).

Gillies Hill and the Dundonald sites lie on the overlapping margins of the distributions of hillforts, brochs and duns. The present excavations highlight the extent of our ignorance of the political and social interactions of the users of these sites. Indeed, on present evidence it is not even clear whether these site-types were occupied consecutively or contemporaneously. There is also a need to rectify a distinct lack of information from south-west Scotland, to the south of Dundonald and to the west of The Dunion and Eildon Hill North. Given that these excavations were rescue-generated and, therefore, to some extent random in selection, it is perhaps fortuitous that two projects were carried out on forts classified as minor *oppida*. Although this appellation is not currently in favour, it serves to describe a small group of forts in northern Britain, mostly in the Tyne-Forth area, of a size noticeably larger than the great majority of small forts. This can be illustrated, for instance, by looking at all forts in an area measuring 50 km east-west by 45 km north-south centred on The Dunion (Figure 2.1 & 3.1). Of the 120 forts of known area (147 in all), 114 are less than 1.6 ha in extent while six are more than 3.6 ha in extent. There are no forts between 1.6 ha and 3.6 ha. It has been suggested (*eg* Feachem 1966, 80) that the large forts were the result of a trend towards urbanisation. This may have been purely native in origin, representing the gradual centralisation of power, or stimulated by external pressures such as a sudden influx of population from outside the area at the time of the Agricolan incursion.

The proceedings of the 1981 conference on later prehistoric settlement in the south of Scotland identified a series of key issues, the investigation of which should form the next steps in the study of settlement of the period. Although of limited scale, the excavations reported upon here make significant contributions to some of these key issues. The dates from the two large forts should help to satisfy some of the perceived need for dates from key sites (Harding 1982a, 193). Similarly, Butler's palaeoenvironmental reports are a first contribution to meeting the '. . . urgent need for a programme of pollen sampling aimed at clarifying the environmental background to later settlement in south-east Scotland and the border regions.' (*ibid*, 194).

These excavations have shown that the current archaeological models for hillfort settlement are inadequate. The results have indicated a degree of chronological complexity and architectural diversity which was unanticipated in the current models. However, all of these excavations were conducted on such a small scale that insufficient evidence has been gathered to generate a new model. The true value of these excavations lies in their identification of the fact that we have yet to come to grips with the complexity, scale, date and duration of the several periods of settlement represented in southern Scottish hillforts.

# Appendices

Artefacts have been ordered into a single numbered sequence, which has been organised by material type (ie coarse stone 1 to n, chipped stone n + 1 to n + 100, etc). Within material types, the artefacts have been ordered by area, as follows: Defensive Systems A, B and C (DS-A, DS-B or DS-C); followed by House Platforms 1, 2 and 3 (HP-1, HP-2 and HP-3). Reports on and discussions of the artefacts can be found in the main text. The methodologies and results of any technological enquiries have been incorporated into the

text. All contributors' acknowledgements and references are incorporated in the text at the end of the reports.

Standard catalogue abbreviations have been used as follows:

L – length; W – width; D – depth; T – thickness; dia – diameter; H – height; mm – millimetres; g – grammes. All measurements are given in millimetres and all weights in grammes.

## EILDON HILL NORTH

### APPENDIX 1

**Coarse stone** A Clarke

*Flakes*

[1] HP-1
Regular inner flake of red sandstone.
L = 35 mm, W = 33 mm, T = 8 mm; 7.6 g.

[2] HP-3
Regular inner flake of soft black shale.
L = 16 mm, W = 31 mm, T = 8 mm; 2.0 g.

*Pounders/grinders*

[3] DS-A
Cobble of coarse grey sandstone. Worked over entire surface by pecking to form a sub-cylindrical shape with concave ends.
L = 66 mm, W = 76 mm, T = 71 mm; 620.6 g.

[4] HP-1
Regular cobble of coarse brown sandstone. Nine facets formed around perimeter through pecking and grinding.
L = 99 mm, W = 92 mm, T = 56 mm; 752.5 g.

[5] HP-1
Regular cobble of fine grey micaceous sandstone. Pecking and grinding around perimeter causing light faceting. Base made very smooth and flat by polishing.
L = 47 mm, W = 65 mm, T = 61 mm; 343.7 g.

[6] HP-3
Fragment of quartzite cobble. Burnt. Narrow band of pecking causing faceting. Truncated by breakage.
L = 64 mm, W = 47 mm, T = 50 mm; 168.9 g.

[7] HP-3
Lump of brown/pink quartzite. Pecked and ground at one end causing light faceting. Other end battered irregularly.
L = 117 mm, W = 68 mm, T = 57 mm; 656.3 g.

[8] HP-3
Irregular cobble of coarse brown sandstone. Pecked and ground on prominent edges and faces causing some faceting. Heavy pecking in a concave face.
L = 85 mm, W = 85 mm, T = 84 mm; 802.7 g.

*Whetstones*

[9] DS-A
Flat oval cobble of brown sandstone. Both edges lightly faceted through smoothing.
L = 120 mm, W = 55 mm, T = 27 mm; 297.7 g.

[10] DS-A
Long square-sectioned pebble of red sandstone. All faces quite smooth.
L = 139 mm, W = 24 mm, T = 16 mm; 88.6 g.

[11] HP-1
Flat oval cobble of grey sandstone. One edge lightly faceted through smoothing.
L = 153 mm, W = 62 mm, T = 31 mm; 430.3 g.

[12] HP-1
Flat oval cobble of fine-grained micaceous sandstone. Concave smoothed area along edge of one face.
L = 153 mm, W = 80 mm, T = 32 mm; 639.7 g

[13] HP-1
Long, square-sectioned pebble of laminated siltstone. Possibly heated. Smoothing around perimeter has caused a light polishing.
L = 95 mm, W = 26 mm, T = 6 mm; 70.2 g.

*Hammerstones*

[14] DS-A
Flat oval cobble of grey sandstone. Broken across width. Heavy pecking on proximal end.
L = 103 mm, W = 70 mm, T = 41 mm; 471.8 g.

[15] DS-A
Regular triangular cobble of fine-grained sandstone. Thick distal end is heavily pecked on prominent edges and corners. Proximal tip also pecked.
L = 92 mm, W = 72 mm, T = 40 mm; 378.5 g.

[16] DS-A
Elongated oval cobble of grey sandstone. Broken across width. Light pecking on proximal tip and possible areas of smoothing along length.
L = 135 mm, W = 45 mm, T = 28 mm; 299.0 g.

[17] HP-1
Fragment of sandstone cobble. Fractured by heating. Cortical surface exhibits light random score marks and

some pecking.
L = 62 mm, W = 47 mm, T = 23 mm; 94.2 g.

[18]   HP-1
Fragment of flat round cobble of brown sandstone. Some pecking and flaking on unbroken edge.
L = 63 mm, W = 87 mm, T = 22 mm; 167.0 g.

[19]   HP-3
Elongated oval pebble of grey sandstone. Worked on both ends with pecking and flaking.
L = 184 mm, W = 40 mm, T = 33 mm; 375.6 g.

[20]   HP-3
Flat oval cobble of sandstone. Broken across width. Worked on inner concave edge by battering and bifacial flaking. Also battering on distal end.
L = 131 mm, W = 78 mm, T = 34 mm; 491.5 g.

*Anvils*

[21]   HP-2
Flat oval cobble of coarse red sandstone. Random pecking on opposite faces.
L = 91 mm, W = 93 mm, T = 40 mm; 526.1 g.

[22]   HP-3
Flat cobble of red sandstone. Burnt. Area of light pecking on one face. On opposite face there is a striation running diagonally for 85 mm.
L = 146 mm, W = 84 mm, T = 38 mm; 839.7 g.

*Quern rubbers*

[23]   HP-3
Regular-shaped slab of igneous rock. Lower face very flat and smooth. Edge around base smoothed and rounded.
L = 270 mm, W = 160 mm, T = 40 mm; 3224.1 g.

[24]   HP-3
Regular-shaped slab of igneous rock. Lower face very flat and smooth. Edge around base smoothed and rounded.
L = 338 mm, W = 189 mm, T = 70 mm; 5243.1 g.

*Quern*

[25]   HP-3
Large fragment of coarse sandstone. Weathered. Base slightly concave and pecked. Upper convex face exhibits light grooves and pecks. ?Quern fragment.
L = 270 mm, W = 170 mm, T = 100 mm; 4760.7 g.

*Miscellaneous*

[26]   DS-A
Sub-circular pebble of coarse sandstone. Possibly pecked and smoothed into shape.
L = 29 mm, W = 23 mm, T = 22 mm; 24.3 g.

[27]   HP-1
Sub-circular pebble of coarse sandstone. Possibly pecked and smoothed into shape.
L = 22 mm, W = 18 mm, T = 17 mm; 10.6 g.

[28]   HP-1
Fragment of coarse sandstone. Light groove on one face running to edge. ?Sharpener.
L = 55 mm, W = 37 mm, T = 22 mm; groove: L = 16 and U-shaped; 71.3 g.

[29]   HP-3
Fragment of sandstone fractured by heating. Unbroken

surface extremely smooth, almost shiny. ?Polished stone.
L = 116 mm, W = 37 mm, T = 29 mm; 137 g.

[30]   HP-3
Fragment of brown sandstone. Part of one face very smooth and polished. ?Polished stone.
L = 52 mm, W = 48 mm, T = 18 mm; 72.2 g.

[31]   HP-3
Fragment of flat round sandstone cobble. Light pecking around perimeter. One face very flat and smoothed. ?Smoothing stone.
L = 90 mm, W = 58 mm, T = 26 mm; 184.5 g.

## APPENDIX 2

**Igneous rocks** *G Collins*

Several samples of igneous rock from below House Platforms 1 and 3 were submitted for examination to clarify the nature of such raw materials as were readily available on the hilltop. All samples were of trachyte, the name given to fine-grained igneous rocks of intermediate composition. These rocks are the fine-grained equivalent of the syenites. Ideally, they contain no quartz, which distinguishes them from the granites and rhyolites.

Both porphyritic and non-porphyritic varieties were present, the former distinguished by small pits or holes where crystals of sanidine have weathered out. One sample was cut by a thin vein of felsite. The samples from Hut Platform 3 were all rather weathered.

## APPENDIX 3

**Chipped stone** *S McCartan*

*Notes to the catalogue*

*i* During examination, all pieces are held dorsal face uppermost with the proximal end towards the observer.
*ii* Formal, ie retouched, tools are assigned a conventional typological term at the end of the entry. These terms are not intended to indicate function.
*iii* Length is measured along a line at 90° to the platform of the piece; width is in the same plane and 90° to the length along a line across the widest part of the flake; thickness is measured from the ventral to the highest point of the dorsal surface along a line perpendicular to both length and width. Only intact pieces are measured.
*iv* Chalcedony is the name given to compact varieties of silica, two of which are flint and chert (Hamilton *et al* 1974, 130). The term 'chalcedony' has been adopted here where the nature of the raw material cannot be accurately determined, but the parent material is known.
*v* Colour has been noted to illustrate variation.
*vi* Cortication refers to the matt discolouration of the piece; patination refers to the lustrous sheen that may subsequently develop (Shepherd 1972, 114–18).
*vii* A chunk has no ventral surface or platform.
*viii* Pebbles are noted as they are potential sources of raw material.
*ix* Macroscopic edge damage has been noted where apparent. This generally consists of the removal of small flakes and may be due to use, although this cannot be verified without the use of a high-powered microscope.

*Flint*

[32]   DS-A
Flint; grey; secondary chunk; frost-shattered.

[33]   DS-A
Flint; tan and red; secondary chunk; corticated.

[34] DS-A
Flint; tan and grey; inner chunk; partially corticated; frost-shattered.

[35] DS-A
Flint; grey; inner chunk; sporadic edge damage.

[36] DS-A
Flint; pale grey; inner chunk; corticated; partially patinated.

[37] DS-A
Flint; pale yellow and grey; secondary flake; step termination; small fragment missing on left lateral.

[38] DS-A
Flint; pale grey; inner flake; segment surviving; extensive edge damage on both sides; minor edge damage on broken ends.

[39] DS-A
Flint; dark grey; secondary chunk; corticated; partially patinated.

[40] DS-A
Flint; grey and pale yellow; inner chunk; corticated; partially patinated.

[41] HP-1
Flint; dark grey and white; secondary flake; corticated; partially patinated; cortical platform; edge damage on left lateral.
L = 12 mm, W = 9 mm, T = 2 mm.

[42] HP-1
Flint; dark grey; secondary chunk; partially corticated; partially patinated.

[43] HP-3
Flint; dark grey; secondary flake; partially corticated; broken platform; edge damage on right lateral; hinge termination.
L = 24 mm, W = 14 mm, T = 4 mm.

[44] HP-3
Flint; grey and pale yellow; inner chunk; corticated; partially patinated; sporadic edge damage.

[45] HP-3
Flint; grey and white; secondary flake; partially corticated; partially patinated; broken platform; hinge termination.
L = 9 mm, W = 12 mm, T = 3 mm.

[46] HP-3
Flint; brown and grey; inner chunk; burnt and crazed; corticated; patinated; sporadic edge damage.

## Chert

[47] DS-A
Chert; dark grey; inner flake; bifacially modified; with oblique and sub-parallel invasive retouch; pointed distal, 'square' barb; broken tang; left barb missing. Right edge angle 47; left edge angle 57. Barbed and tanged arrowhead.
L = 18 mm, W = 16 mm, T = 5 mm.

[48] DS-A
Chert; grey; inner chunk; sporadic edge damage.

[49] DS-C
Chert; black; inner flake; partially corticated; broken; segment surviving; fine, scalar retouch on one lateral; miscellaneous retouched piece.

[50] HP-1
Chert; pebble; heavily weathered and damaged.

[51] HP-1
Chert; grey and brown; inner flake; partially patinated; broken platform; fragment missing at distal end.

[52] HP-1
Chert; grey; inner flake; broken; right side surviving; irregular retouch on right lateral; edge damage on right lateral; miscellaneous retouched piece.

[53] HP-1
Chert; grey; inner flake; broken distal point; irregular retouch on sides converging to form point; edge damage on sides. Right edge angle 68; left edge angle 64. Broken awl.
L = 16 mm, W = 20 mm, T = 6 mm.

[54] HP-1
Chert; dark grey; split pebble; corticated.

[55] HP-3
Chert; grey and black; secondary chunk; corticated.

[56] HP-3
Chert; grey; pebble; extensively weathered.

[57] HP-3
Chert; brown, rust and yellow; secondary flake; corticated; platform broken.
L = 33 mm, W = 30 mm, T = 16 mm.

## Quartz

[58] DS-A
Milky quartz; pink and white; secondary flake; faceted platform; edge damage on sides; divergent outline.
L = 23 mm, W = 22 mm, T = 5 mm.

## Chalcedony

[59] HP-1
Chalcedony; grey and tan; inner irregular flake; corticated; partially patinated.
L = 13 mm, W = 15 mm, T = 1 mm.

[60] HP-3
Chalcedony; pink grey and white; inner flake; burnt; corticated; patinated; broken; segment surviving.

## APPENDIX 4

### Jet armlets *M M B Kemp*

[61] DS-A
One third of a D-sectioned armlet with an estimated diameter of 68 mm.
L = 70 mm, T = 7 mm.

[62] DS-A
Small fragment of armlet, both section and diameter cannot be estimated.
L = 12 mm.

[63] HP-2
Two joining fragments of a D-sectioned armlet with an estimated diameter of 84 mm.
L = 24 mm (joined fragments), T = 10 mm.

## APPENDIX 5

**Glass** *J Henderson · M M B Kemp*

*Note to the catalogue*
anal *no* chemical analysis number

[64] DS-A
Cylindrical, transparent green glass bead. Guido (1978), Roman bead cylindrical type, 208b; anal *no* 5.
L = 5 mm, dia = 5 mm, perforation dia 2 mm.

[65] DS-A
Fragment of an opaque white glass armlet. Kilbride-Jones (1938), type 3A; anal *no* 1.
L = 18 mm, T = 9 mm, estimated dia 52 mm.

[66] HP-1
Fragment of a transparent green glass armlet. Sub-triangular cross-section. Decorated with an opaque yellow blob along the apex. The fragment has a long air bubble in it. Kilbride-Jones (1938), type 3H; anal *nos* 2 and 3.
L = 15 mm, T = 8 mm, estimated dia 64 mm.

[67] HP-1
Fragment of an opaque blue glass object. Irregular shape in all facets. Apparently a chip subjected to re-heating, perhaps derived from an armlet(?) but the fragment is too damaged to be certain of its original character.
L = 10 mm, W = 6 mm, T = 2 mm.

[68] HP-2
Fragment of an opaque blue glass armlet. Sub-triangular cross section. Decorated with a thin, opaque yellow cordon along the apex. Kilbride-Jones (1938), type 3G; anal *no* 4.
L = 15 mm, T = 8 mm, estimated dia 80 mm.

## APPENDIX 6

**Metalwork** *O A Owen · F M Ashmore · X-ray fluorescence P Wilthew*

*Bronze artefacts (selected)*

[69] Below DS-A (top fill Pit 2)
Bronze tool. Good condition apart from slight surface corrosion and slight damage to end. Chisel-shaped implement, tanged at one end, curved working edge. Rectangular section, tapering to chisel end. Tool marks visible on tang.
XRF analysis: 44.0% Cu; 25.0% Sn; 30.0% Pb; 1.0% Sb.
L = 27 mm, W = 7 mm, T = 3.8 mm; 1.93 g.

[70] DS-A
Fragmentary bronze object. Very poor condition, surface heavily encrusted and pock-marked. Roughly rectangular fragment tapering at one end. Convex upper surface. Concave underside retains concreted infill and may have been burnt. The object appears to be a curved plate which perhaps originally encased a rounded shaft.
XRF analysis: 83.0% Cu; 14.0% Sn; 3.0% Pb.
L = 31 mm, W = 15 mm, T = 10 mm; 6.22 g.

[71] HP-1
Fragment of bronze unenamelled dragonesque fibula. Poor condition, broken edges friable and corroded. Central portion of S-shaped body is better preserved. Protruding neck and head have been bent at right angles to body section. Upper surface convex, reverse flat and plain.

XRF analysis: 87.0% Cu; 7.0% Sn; 6.0% Pb.
L = 30 mm, T = 3 mm; 3.76 g.

[72] HP-1
Fragment of bronze fibula pin. Poor condition, badly corroded surface, remains of hinge broken but corroded into place. Comprises top section of pin shank, circular in cross-section, hooked at top. Two triangular-shaped fragments of bronze sheet attached to top of pin probably represent the remains of a hinge.
XRF analysis: 87.0% Cu; 13.0% Sn.
L = 28 mm, W = 15 mm; 1.75 g.

[73] HP-1
A fragment of bronze sheet and other small particles. Poor condition and fragile, all edges broken. Thin sheet fragments.
Largest fragment: L = 13 mm, W = 6 mm. Total 0.3 g.

*Iron artefact*

[74] DS-A
Fragment of iron nail. Badly corroded, hollow internally. Remains of roughly circular nail head and small part of the top of the shank. Shank probably rectangular in section.
L = 21 mm, shank Y = 15 mm, nail head dia = 24 mm; 4.9 g.

## APPENDIX 7

**Metalworking and vitrified debris** *M Spearman · XRF analyses and comment P Wilthew*

*Ironworking debris*

| Cat *no* | Context | Description | Weight (g) |
|---|---|---|---|
| [75] | DS-A | Fe bloomery waste | 0.7 |
| [76] | DS-A | Fe bloomery waste | 4.7 |
| [77] | DS-A | Fe bloomery waste | 1.3 |
| [78] | HP-1 | Fe prill waste | 0.3 |
| [79] | HP-1 | Fe bloomery waste | 1.2 |
| [80] | HP-1 | Fe bloomery waste | 0.8 |
| [81] | HP-1 | Fe bloomery waste | 13.6 |
| [82] | HP-1 | Fe bloomery waste | 6.4 |

*Droplet and pieces of run copper alloy*

| | | | |
|---|---|---|---|
| [83] | HP-1 | Mass of run metal | 84.8 |
| [84] | HP-1 | Droplet of run metal | 2.1 |
| [85] | HP-1 | Mass of run metal | 31.1 |

*Crucible fragments retrieved from DS-A*

[86] Crucible rim (square). Straight-sided, base shallows to rim. Possible lip of crucible. Lightly baked externally; lightly vitrified internally.
XRF analysis: Cu, Pb, Sn and traces of Sb and Ni.
L = 46 mm, D = 35 mm, T = 8 mm at rim.

[87] Crucible rim (square). Lightly baked externally; lightly vitrified internally.
L = 20 mm, D = 20 mm, T = 12 mm at rim.

[88] Crucible rim (square). Lightly baked externally; lightly vitrified internally.
XRF analysis: Cu, Pb, Sn.
L = 30 mm, D = 24, T = 14 mm, internal dia = *circa* 70 mm, external dia = 105 mm.

[89] Crucible rim (square). Lightly baked externally; lightly vitrified internally.
XRF analysis: Cu, Pb, Sn and traces of Sb.

L = 41 mm, D = 25 mm, T = 18 mm, internal dia *circa* 70 mm, external dia 105 mm.

[90] Crucible rim (square). Straight-sided, base only begins at 35 mm. Lightly baked externally; lightly vitrified internally. XRF analysis: Cu, Pb, Sn and traces of Sb and Ni. L = 28 mm, D = 40 mm, T = 14 mm at rim, internal dia *circa* 70 mm, external dia *circa* 100 mm.

[91] Crucible 'tile', inverted lip to rim. Lightly baked externally; lightly vitrified internally. L = 48 mm, W = 23 mm, Y = 11 mm at edge.

[92] Crucible 'tile', body sherd. Lightly baked externally; lightly vitrified internally. XRF analysis: Cu, Pb, Sn and traces of Sb and Ni. L = 30 mm, W = 20 mm, T = 11 mm at edge.

[93] Crucible body, 3 fragments. Lightly baked externally; lightly vitrified internally.

[94] Crucible/pot fragment. 1.8 g.

[95] Crucible/pot fragment. 7.7 g.

[96] Crucible/pot fragment. 1.3 g.

[97] Crucible/pot fragment. 0.9 g.

[98] Crucible/pot fragment (dust). 1.5 g.

*Vitrified stone and miscellaneous*

| Cat *no* | Context | Description | Weight (g) |
|---|---|---|---|
| [99] | DS-A | Vitrified stone | 40.2 |
| [100] | DS-A | Vitrified stone | 0.9 |
| [101] | DS-A | Vitrified stone | 11.3 |
| [102] | DS-A | Vitrified stone | 6.4 |
| [103] | DS-A | Vitrified stone | 0.9 |
| [104] | HP-1 | Vitrified stone/clinker | 4.7 |
| [105] | HP-1 | Vitrified stone/clinker | 0.3 |
| [106] | HP-1 | Vitrified stone/clinker | 0.8 |
| [107] | HP-1 | Vitrified stone/clinker | 10.3 |
| [108] | HP-1 | Vitrified stone | 87.8 (Fe rich) |
| [109] | HP-1 | Vitrified stone | 2.5 |
| [110] | HP-1 | Vitrified stone | 13.7 |
| [111] | HP-1 | Vitrified stone | 2.9 |
| [112] | HP-1 | Vitrified stone | 2.1 |
| [113] | HP-1 | Vitrified stone | 5.3 |
| [114] | HP-1 | Vitrified stone | 4.7 |
| [115] | HP-1 | Vitrified stone | 11.5 |
| [116] | HP-1 | Vitrified stone | 23.4 |
| [117] | HP-1 | Vitrified stone | 0.6 |
| [118] | HP-1 | Baked clay lining | 2.6 |
| [119] | HP-3 | Vitrified stone | 14.3 |
| [120] | HP-3 | Vitrified stone/clinker | 0.9 |

APPENDIX 8

**Roman pottery** *J N Dore · thin section petrology J Senior*

[121] DS-A
Wall sherd, probably from a large narrow-mouthed jar. Pale grey, mid grey core, burnished dark grey surface with burnished undulating line decoration. Inclusions: up to 0.5 mm dia, quartz and black grains. 2nd–4th century AD.

[122] DS-A
Wall sherd from a similar vessel, if not the same vessel, as [121].

[123] HP-1
A heavily abraded fragment of a samian vessel. Almost certainly a Dr. 18/31; the fabric appears Central Gaulish. First half of 2nd century AD. Dia 180 mm.

[124] HP-3
Rim sherd from a small mortarium. Micaceous orange with pale grey core. Inclusions: up to 0.1 mm dia, black grains (?iron), and red iron ore; trituration grits sparse but mostly quartz. This was almost certainly produced in the Oxford region. The fabric falls within the limits stated by Young for Oxford products (1977, 123) and the type is similar to his type C100 (*ibid*, Figure 67). While the flange is perhaps not as ornate as those which he figures, the sharply delineated convex facet on the inside face of the bead is very similar and distinctive. A similar type in a red fabric was made in the New Forest area (Fulford 1975, type 81). There is another Oxford Ware vessel, also of Young's type C100, known from Scotland, from Traprain Law (Curle & Cree 1916). 4th century AD. Dia 240 mm.

*Pottery of uncertain origin*

[125] HP-1
Hand-made, black with well burnished outer surface; inner surface relatively unfinished, even allowing for possible considerable abrasion. Inclusions: angular, mostly under 0.5 mm dia, occasionally up to 2 mm dia. Examination of a thin-section revealed that the following minerals are present: quartz, small quantities only; feldspar, mostly orthoclase, some plagioclase; biotite mica; composite grains containing pyroxene and iron oxide.

The angularity of the inclusions, combined with the presence of biotite mica suggests that they were obtained by crushing rock. The minerals present are likely to have derived from an intermediate igneous rock, likely to be of non-local origin. Scandinavia is tentatively suggested as one possible source (J Senior, pers comm).

There are no features of the vessel which can be regarded as intrinsically 'Roman', though vessels of generally similar form are known from contexts of Roman period date at other sites (*eg* Murton High Crags: see Jobey & Jobey 1987, Figure 11, *nos* 12–14 and comments on the accompanying pages).

[126] HP-1
Wall sherd from a hand-made vessel. Black. Inclusions: up to 0.5 mm dia, calcareous, quartz, rock fragments and black vitreous grains.

[127] DS-C (?)
Wall sherd from a hand-made vessel. Grey/brown, black surface. Inclusions: up to 0.2 mm dia, quartz, mica, black grains and rock fragments.

APPENDIX 9

**Coarse wares** *V J McLellan*

*Methods*

*On-, and off-site recording*   Pottery was recorded three-dimensionally and allocated a small find number as it was found, either per individual sherd or per group of associated, adjacent sherds. Where pot sherds were not recognised on site but had been placed in finds trays, they were recorded as general finds by context. Additionally, other sherds (usually crumbs and fragments) were found in soil samples during post-excavation sorting. Thus, all pot sherds were recorded by context but received either a small find, or a general find, or a sample number.

*Post-excavation analysis*   The assemblage was sorted by area (DS-A, HP-1, HP-2, HP-3) and, within areas, by fabric type (1–4 and other). Groups of sherds were sorted into individual vessels or parts thereof. All other sherds were treated as individual finds. Catalogue numbers were then allocated *a* by area and *b* by fabric type, regardless of the number of sherds per catalogue entry.

On House Platform 1, the most prolific area in terms of pottery retrieval, a group of sherds comprising a vessel or part-vessel may have originated from two or three recorded contexts. In these cases, the several contexts usually relate solely to the Episode 1 use of the platform: HP-1 (1). Of the handful of sherds found in Episode 2 contexts (*circa* 10), all but two physically join vessel sherds from the pottery-rich Episode 1 levels. In the catalogue (below), an identified part-vessel comprising sherds retrieved predominantly from Episode 1 contexts, but including a sherd(s) from Episode 2 contexts, is designated HP-1 (1–2). The two Episode 2 sherds which do not join vessels from Episode 1 are designated, as they were recorded on site, from HP-1 (2).

*Notes to the catalogue*
sherd: an individual piece no less than 20 mm square and with both surfaces remaining;
fragment: an individual piece less than 20 mm square and/or a sherd less than 30 mm square with one or no surfaces surviving;
crumb: an individual piece less than 10 mm square with or without surfaces;
FT: Fabric Type (1–4; other).
   A measurement for the thickness of a sherd has been given only if both the internal and the external surfaces survived. All dimensions are in millimetres and weights in grammes.

[128]   DS-A
1 rim sherd; FT 1. Upright, slightly obliquely flattened top. Coil-built and with an external encrustation. Abraded. Gritted throughout.
T = 11 mm, grits 2-6 mm; 13.77 g.

[129]   DS-A
1 rim fragment? 2 body sherds; FT 1. Either a rim or a break along a coil. Slightly everted and round-topped. Grey fabric throughout.
T = 10 mm, grits 2-7 mm; 2.81 g, 5.96 g, 8.60 g.

[130]   DS-A
1 crumb; FT 1. Abraded, with grey core, buff interior and exterior.
Grits 2–4 mm; 0.83 g.

[131]   DS-A
1 fragment, 1 crumb; FT 1. Abraded sherd with grey core, buff exterior. Angular grits break the surface.
Grits 2–8 mm; 6.54 g, 0.60 g.

[132]   DS-A
1 rim sherd; FT 1. Flat-topped and very slightly everted. Coil-built, generally well finished, although some angular grits break the surface. External encrustation. Grey core, dark exterior, pinkish interior.
T = 11 mm, grits 2–7 mm; 11.50 g.

[133]   DS-A
1 body sherd, 1 fragment, 1 crumb; FT 1. Bright orange exterior, pinkish buff interior and core. Tempered with angular grits.
T = 14 mm, grits 2 mm; 1.08 g, 4.07 g, 3.64 g.

[134]   DS-A
Rounded, everted coil-built rim; FT 1. Slightly abraded. Well finished with sooting on the exterior.
T = 13 mm, grits 2–7 mm; 15.3 g.
interior of the rim. Angular grits break both surfaces which in general are very coarse, knobbly and abraded. Bluish grey core, buff exterior, yellowish to grey interior.
T = 11–16 mm, grits 2–7 mm; total 135.63 g.

[158]   HP-1 (2)
1 body sherd; FT 2. Very abraded sherd tempered with angular grits which break the surfaces. Blue/grey core, buff interior and exterior.
T = 13 mm, grits 2–7 mm; 4.70 g.

[159]   HP-1 (1)
One rim sherd, 1 ?base sherd, 5 body sherds, 18 fragments and 4 crumbs; FT 2. The rim is flat-topped and slightly everted. The fabric is smooth and heavily tempered with small angular grits, some of which break the surface. The colour throughout the sherd is a uniform pale bluish grey. All the sherds have an abraded appearance.
T = 7–12 mm, grits 2–7 mm; total 69.33 g.

[160]   HP-1 (1)
1 body sherd; FT other. Abraded, reddish orange, soft fabric, slightly sandy texture. No grits visible.
T = 6–8 mm; 1.50 g.

[161]   HP-1 (1)
1 fragment; FT other. Abraded soft orange fabric. Perhaps baked clay? No grits visible.
2.92 g.

[162]   HP-1 (1)
1 body sherd; FT other. Abraded surfaces and evenly tempered with angular grits. 'Chalky' to the touch. Grey core, yellowish pink surfaces.
T = 16 mm; 9.24 g.

[163]   HP-2 (platform preparation)
1 rim sherd; FT 1. Simple, round-topped, coil-built, slightly inturned rim with internal residue. Angular grits break the surface. Grey core, pink/buff exterior, brown interior.
T = 11 mm, grits 2–6 mm; 29.89 g.

[164]   HP-2 (platform preparation)
1 body sherd; FT 1. Abraded sherd with pink/buff core and interior, grey exterior. Tempered with angular grits. Sooted exterior.
T = 11 mm, grits 2–6 mm; 7.38 g.

[165]   HP-2 (glacial till?)
1 fragment; FT 1. Abraded. Grey core is all that remains.
2.18 g.

[166]   HP-3
1 rim sherd, 2 rim fragments, 5 body sherds, 9 fragments, 10 crumbs; FT 3. Fabric is hard and gritty to the touch and evenly tempered with small angular grits. Some sherds are abraded and others have internal residues. Grey core with brown/buff surfaces. T = 12 mm, grits 2–4 mm; total 121.09 g.

[167] HP-3
5 body sherds, 7 fragments, 2 crumbs; FT other. Abraded 'chalky' fabric. Grey interior and core, ash grey to buff exterior. No grits visible.
T = *circa* 11 mm; total 42.74 g.

[168] HP-3
1 crumb; FT other. Abraded crumb of soft fabric. Bright orange exterior, buff core and interior. No grits visible.
1.29 g.

[169] HP-3
6 ?base sherds; FT other. Soft, abraded fabric which contains mica. Rough exterior with angular grits. Grey core and interior, orange/biscuit exterior.
T = 12 mm, grits 2–12 mm; total 71.65 g.

[170] HP-3
1 body sherd; FT other. Tempered with crumbly white grits protruding through the surface. Grey core, brown/buff surfaces. Abraded.
T = 10 mm, grits 2–6 mm; 6.75 g.

## APPENDIX 10

### Routine soil analyses *S Carter*

#### Methods

A soil sample was collected from each excavated soil context and analysed for pH, Loss on Ignition and phosphorus. In addition, more detailed analyses of phosphorus content were carried out on a limited number of samples by the Department of Soil Fertility, Macaulay Land Use Research Institute.

In post-excavation, each routine soil sample was air-dried and passed through a 2 mm mesh sieve. pH was determined in both 0.01M CaCl2 and distilled water using a 1:20 weight:volume suspension. Loss on Ignition (LOI) was determined with *circa* 10 g of oven-dry soil (105°C) heated to 400°C for 4 hours. Phosphorus analysis for all samples used a Spot Test for easily available phosphate (Hamond 1983, 55). Samples were rated on a three-point scale (Hamond 1983, 57) using the time taken for a blue colour to develop following the addition of the two reagents to the sample, a shorter time indicating a higher phosphate content.

| Time for colour to develop (seconds) | Phosphate rating |
|---|---|
| 0–30 | High (H) |
| 30–90 | Medium (M) |
| 90 + | Low (L) |

Phosphorus analyses undertaken at the Macaulay Land Use Research Institute used either an acetic acid extraction or a total phosphorous extraction.

## APPENDIX 11

### Animal bone *F McCormick*

Burnt bone fragments were hand-picked on site where they were large enough. The assemblage is therefore incomplete; additionally, retrieval rates between excavators are likely to have varied. To test the hypothesis that retrieval rates represent only a small fraction of what was present, 20 kg of material from the dispersed hearth on House Platform 2 was sieved for burnt bone. Much greater quantities of burnt bone were recovered (below). Given that most bone from the site has, in any case, decayed away, no further work was undertaken.

#### Defensive System A

Pre-rampart hearth, at Entrance 2
163 unidentifiable burnt fragments

Rampart cores, at Entrance 2
26 unidentifiable burnt fragments
3 cattle teeth (1 fragmented)

Rampart core, adjacent to HP-2
1 cattle tooth

Pit 2, beneath DS-A, adjacent to HP-2
159 unidentifiable burnt fragments
107 unidentifiable unburnt fragments
10 horse teeth

#### House Platform 1

Episode 1, lower 'floor' level
90 unidentifiable burnt fragments
2 fragmented ?cattle teeth

Episode 1, dispersed hearth
101 unidentifiable burnt fragments
Episode 1, upper 'floor' level/abandonment
17 unidentifiable burnt fragments

Episode 2, mixed, lower 'floor' level
41 unidentifiable burnt fragments

House Platform 2

Platform preparation/redeposited till
5 unidentifiable burnt fragments

Floor level
28 unidentifiable burnt fragments

Dispersed hearth
1595 unidentifiable burnt fragments

House Platform 3 Floor level
10 unidentified burnt fragments

## APPENDIX 12

### Thermoluminescence dates *D C W Sanderson*

The gamma ray dose rates from a number of contexts at Eildon Hill North were recorded on site, using a portable NaI scintillation counter, to evaluate the prospects for thermoluminescent dating. Somewhat unusually, the ambient radioactivity was both high and rather variable; $4\pi\gamma$ dose rates ranging from 1 to 2 mGya. Given the likelihood of an internal matrix dose rate of 2 mGya from typical ceramic samples, the relative dose contributions on this site would range from about 30–50% of the total radiation dose. It was also noted during the site visit that few contexts had a complete 20–30 cm overburden of soil, due to natural erosion; and that many of the artefacts came from residual contexts. Under this combination of circumstances, it is unlikely that the actual $\gamma$ dose rate experienced by a sample could be defined with better than 25% precision. This in turn would lead to uncertainties of 10–15% in the thermoluminescence dates, purely from this source (*ie* several centuries for 2000 year old samples).

Finally, it was not possible to identify samples from contexts which could provide useful chronometric information relating to site evolution; accordingly, the persuance of a thermoluminescence dating programme was not recommended.

*On-site $\gamma$ dosimetry (Eildon Hill North; 11.9.86)*

| Reading | Context | $4\pi$ dose geometry | Rate\mGya |
|---|---|---|---|
| GS1/103 | Entrance 2, bedrock | 2 | 1.5 ± 0.15 |
| GS1/104 | DS-A, S rampart terminal | 3.2 | 1.18 ± 0.15 |
| GS1/105 | HP-1, bedrock | 2.5 | 2.05 ± 0.15 |

| GS1/106 | Spoilheap adj. to HP-1 | 3.5 | 1.0 ± 0.15 |
| GS1/106a | Spoilheap adj. to HP-2 | 3.5 | 1.1 ± 0.15 |
| GS1/107 | HP-1, post-aband. level | 3 | 1.6 ± 0.2 |
| GS1/108 | HP-1, Episode 1 floor | 3 | 1.66 ± 0.15 |
| GS1/109 | HP-3, hearth base | 2 | 1.27 ± 0.15 |

Mean + standard deviation: 1.42 ± 0.34 mGya

## THE DUNION

### APPENDIX 13

**Glass bead** *J Henderson*

[1]   Annular glass bead with a translucent bubbled 'bottle green' coloured matrix with a random surface decoration of opaque yellow glass.
dia = 23.4 mm, D 10 mm, perforation dia 7.7 mm.

### APPENDIX 14

**Querns** *A MacSween · J S Rideout*

*Note to the catalogue*
ORS   Old Red Sandstone

*1984–1986 excavations*

[2]   Top stone of a beehive quern with a concave grinding surface and a central perforation for the spindle. Between its top and bottom end the perforation is misaligned, possibly deliberately. The misalignment would allow a more direct feed of grain to the grinding surfaces. A portion of the under surface is missing where the stone has split across the handle-socket, possibly during removal of the handle. Sandstone.
max dia = 313 mm, max H = 200 mm; hopper dia = 127 mm, D = 98 mm; perforation dia = 22 mm, D = 102 mm; handle socket H above base = 52 mm, D = 63 mm, outer end L = 52 mm, inner end L = 52 mm.

Uncontexted/[1]
Top stone of a beehive quern with a slightly concave grinding surface and a central, misaligned perforation (by around 10 mm). At one side of the stone is a tongue-shaped handle socket. LORS porphyry.
max dia = 300 mm, max H = 175 mm; hopper dia = 130–135 mm, depth = 71 mm; perforation dia = 20 mm, D = 120 mm; handle socket H above base = 90 mm, D = 72 mm, outer end L = 52 mm (H = 29 mm), inner end L = 15 mm (H = 3 mm).

*1961–1962 excavations*

From House 62/2
Almost half of the upper stone of a beehive quern with a slightly concave grinding surface and a central perforation. Vent agglomerate.
max dia = 342 mm, max H = 164 mm; hopper dia = 146 mm, D = 104 mm; perforation dia = 22 mm, D = 74 mm; handle socket H above base = 46 mm, D = 68 mm, outer end L = 69 mm (H = 33 mm), inner end L = 35 mm (H = 13 mm).

Uncontexted/[3]
Rough-out for the upper stone of a beehive quern. The lower surface has been pecked flat, and on one of the long sides is a shallow slot, probably to mark the position of the handle-socket. On the top surface is a pecked sub-circular depression, the beginnings of the hopper. Sandstone.
max L = 288 mm, max W = 265 mm, max T = 194 mm;
hopper depression max dia = 95 mm, max D = 23 mm; handle slot max H above base = 77 mm, max L = 40 mm, H = 14 mm, D = 23 mm.

### APPENDIX 15

**Coarse stone and miscellaneous** *V J McLellan · geological identifications G Collins (1984–1986 excavations) and D Dixon (1984–1986 and 1961–1962 excavations)*

*Notes to the catalogue*
ORS   Old Red Sandstone

*1984–1986 excavations*

[3]   House 3, topsoil
Pecked stone ball. Almost spherical except for a slight facet. Greenish micaceous sandstone, probably ORS.
min dia = 26 mm, max dia = 30 mm.

[4]   Outside House 4, unstratified
Almost perfectly spherical. Pecked surface, under which the facets are only just noticeable. Brownish sandstone, possibly ORS.
min dia = 42 mm, max dia = 43 mm.

[5]   House 2, topsoil
Stone ball in the making. Faceting visible and pecking initiated. Greenish sandstone, possibly ORS.
min dia = 29 mm, max dia = 30 mm.

[6]   House 3, upper rubble
Stone ball in the making. Rubbed down facets and peckmarks visible. Brown sandstone, possibly ORS.
min dia = 26 mm, max dia = 29 mm.

[7]   House 4, unstratified
Slightly discoid in shape, looks to have been rubbed down, facets still just visible. Buff-coloured sandstone, possibly ORS.
min dia = 28 mm, max dia = 30 mm.

[8]   House 3, lower rubble
Disc with countersunk perforation, edges rubbed down to form a rough circle. Greenish micaceous sandstone, probably ORS.
dia = 54 mm, T = 15 mm, perforation dia = 6 mm.

[9]   Wall 1, rubble
Disc with countersunk perforation, edges rubbed down to form a rough circle. Brown micaceous sandstone, probably ORS.
dia = 53 mm, T = 10 mm, perforation dia = 5 mm.

[10]   House 3, lower rubble
Disc with countersunk lower rubble perforation, edges rubbed down to form a rough circle. Brown micaceous sandstone, possibly ORS.
dia = 52 mm, T = 18 mm, perforation dia = 6 mm.

[11]   Outside House 2, topsoil
As above. Siltstone.
dia = 22 mm, T = 5 mm, perforation dia = 3 mm.

[12]   House 3, apron 5
As above. Brown material sandstone, possibly ORS.
dia = 51 mm, T = 11 mm, perforation dia = 5 mm.

[13]   Area 5, Rampart 1 core as above. Green sandstone, possibly ORS.
dia = 61 mm, T = 10 mm, perforation dia = 5 mm.

[14] Roadway 1, topsoil
Edge rubbed to form rough disc. Brown micaceous siltstone.
dia = 21 mm, T = 7 mm.

[15] House 3, upper rubble
As above. Red sandstone, ORS.
dia = 49 mm, T = 13 mm.

[16] House 3, doorway
Flaked into a discoidal shape. Possibly trachyte.
dia = 59 mm, T = 15 mm.

[17] Roadway 1, metalling
Just the beginning of a central countersunk perforation. Brown sandstone, possibly ORS.
dia = 75 mm, T = 19 mm.

[18] House 2, topsoil
Quartz pebble with batter marks at either end. Vein quartz, slightly iron-stained.

[19] Area 2, topsoil
End fragment from quartz pounder. Batter marks visible. Vein quartz, some iron-rich siltstone. ORS.

[20] House 3, upper
Naturally flat stone with score marks rubble on one side, some are deeper than others. Greenish siltstone.

[21–22] House 3, lower rubble
Two water-worn stones which have some batter marks. LORS.

[23] House 2, topsoil
Small, rounded pebble with polished area – possible polisher. Quartz.

[24] House 1, wall tumble
Ovoid river pebble with flake damage at one end. Green sandstone, ORS.

[25] House 3, upper rubble
End fragment from quartz hammerstone. Vein quartz.

[26] House 3, upper rubble
Quartz pebble with batter marks at each end. Vein quartz, heavily iron-stained, probably ORS.

[27] House 3, doorway
Elongated stone with batter marks and flake damage at each end. Greenish micaceous sandstone, probably ORS.

[28] House 1, wall core
Fragment of tool. Notched on either side; roughly triangular in section. There are parallel striations at the tip, not unlike those observed on ards. Green and brown sandstone, possibly ORS.

[29] Area 7, topsoil
Flat, flanged shaped stone, both ends broken. Possible implement. Siltstone, probably Lower Palaeozoic.

[30] House 4, unstratified
River pebble with clear areas of battering at each end. Veined quartz.

[31] House 3, upper rubble
River pebble. Iron-stained sandstone, possibly UORS.

[32] House 3, lower rubble
River pebble. Quartzite sandstone, possibly Lower Palaeozoic.

[33] House 3, lower rubble
River pebble. Quartzite sandstone, possibly Lower Palaeozoic.

[34] House 3, lower rubble
River pebble, broken. Quartz.

[35–37] House 3, lower rubble
3 river pebbles. UORS and LORS.

[38] House 3, lower rubble
River pebble, broken. Quartzite.

[39] House 3, bedrock surface
Waterworn stone, broken. Possibly trachyte.

[40–41] House 3, soil on platform
2 water-worn stones. One possibly trachyte, other iron-stained and weathered greywacke.

[42] House 1, topsoil
River pebble. Siltstone, probably Lower Palaeozoic.

[43] House 3, lower rubble
Fire-reddened and heat-cracked red sandstone, ORS.

[44] Under Roadway 4
Small stone axe.
L = 87 mm, W = 52 mm, T = 28 mm

*Miscellaneous*

Uncontexted/[2]
Cobble tool – flat pebble. Greenish sandstone. Pecked around the edges with a shallow depression showing traces of wear polish in the centre of each side.
L = 103 mm, W = 89 mm, T = 27 mm.

*1961–1962 excavations (geological identifications D Dixon)*

[61/6] Wall A face, on E
Armlet fragment. Jet. D-shaped in section. At one end is an incised groove suggesting secondary use, possibly bead-making.
dia = 70-80 mm.

[61/9] House 61/1, in wall
Stone lamp of buff sandstone. One half of an oval-shaped stone with a pecked depression on its upper side.
Overall L = 105 mm, W = 80 mm, T = 53 mm; depression L = 60 mm, W = 51 mm, T = 27 mm.

[61/10a] Wall D
Stone ball, almost spherical. Sandstone. Pecked surface.
dia = 24 mm.

[61/10b] Wall D
Stone ball, possibly unfinished. Sandstone. Pitted surface with traces of facets.
dia = 29 mm.

[61/11] House 61/1
Stone disc, probably a water-worn pebble, with scratches on both sides, possibly as a result of use as a sharpening stone.
Siltstone, Lower Palaeozoic.
dia = 45 mm, T = 4 mm.

[62/10a] House 62/2, floor
Stone ball. Sandstone. Pitted surface with traces of facets.
dia = 28 mm.

[62/10b] House 62/2, floor
Stone ball. Sandstone. Pitted surface.
dia = 25 mm.

[62/22b] House 62/2
Manuport, fragment of quartz crystal, possibly detached from 62/23.

[62/23] House 62/2, wall west of entrance
Manuport, composite crystal of quartz.
L = 30 mm.

Uncontexted/[4] 1962 season
Rubber, probably Old Red Sandstone. Pebble with traces of polishing on one face.
L = 83 mm, W = 75 mm, T = 46 mm.

Uncontexted/[5] 1962 season
Rubber, sandstone. Pebble with traces of polishing on one face.
L = 90 mm, W = 72 mm, T = 76 mm.

Uncontexted/[6]
Carved stone (found by quarry). Stone carved in the shape of a 'cottage loaf'. Old Red Sandstone. From the indentations at the top and bottom it appears that the stone may have been turned. A shallow groove separates the top and bottom sections. It is possible that cloth was tied around it and that it was used as a vessel plug.
H = 49 mm, max W = 78 mm.

## APPENDIX 16

**Pottery** *A MacSween · V J McLellan*

Each entry in the catalogue begins with a note of the find number and context, followed by the number and type of sherds in the find, their average thickness and weight. If a rim or basal sherd is included, its type is described and, where possible, its diameter is estimated. Colour is recorded across the section of the sherd, and is only described in very general terms. The fabric description begins with a list of the components of the clay matrix. Any inclusions are then noted, the description including the percentage of inclusions present, their angularity and the length of the largest inclusion. 'N' denotes that the inclusions are probably natural to the clay.

*1984–1986 excavations*

[45]    House 3, rubble on apron
1 lump burnt clay (20 g) rubble on red fabric; clay has abundant quartz and opaques, occasional igneous inclusions.

[46]    Area 2, topsoil
1 abraded body sherd (0.7 g) red fabric, soft; very occasional quartz and opaques.

[47]    Area 3, topsoil
Fragments of burnt clay. Red fabric, quartz and opaques.

[48]    House 6, pit under wall
1 lump burnt clay (20 g). Red fabric, quartz and opaques, occasional igneous.

*1961–1962 excavations*

[61/1]   House 61/1, floor
1 body sherd, 10 mm thick (11.5 g). Red fabric with grey patches, hard; clay has abundant quartz and opaques; igneous inclusions (5%, 1 mm, N).

[61/2]   Wall A
1 abraded body sherd, 8 mm thick (4.4 g). Red fabric, soft; clay has abundant quartz sand. Coil-constructed, N-shaped junction.

[61/3]   Wall A
1 abraded body sherd 17 mm thick (4.4 g). Red exterior, grey interior. Fabric soft; clay has abundant quartz sand and less frequent igneous inclusions. Mixed gravel component (5%, 5 mm, angular and round, N).

[61/12]  Wall A, lowest layer
12 abraded fragments of daub or dried clay (44 g). Red fabric soft; clay has abundant quartz sand.

[61/16]  House 61/1, floor
1 rim sherd, 3 body sherds, 11 abraded fragments, 13 mm thick (139 g). Plain rim, slightly inverted, 160 mm diameter. Grey with red exterior and interior margins. Fabric hard; clay has abundant quartz sand, frequent opaques and occasional mica. Mixed gravel component (5%, 5 mm, angular and round, N). May be same vessel as 61/3.

[62/1]   Uncontexted
3 body sherds, 120 mm thick (28 g). Red exterior, grey interior. Fabric hard; clay has abundant quartz and igneous inclusions. Mixed gravel component (10%, 16 mm, angular, N). Coil-constructed. Interior sooting.

[62/2]   Uncontexted
1 rim sherd, 2 body sherds. Rim probably slightly inverted. Fabric hard; clay has abundant quartz, and occasional black igneous inclusions. Mixed gravel component (10%, 10 mm, round and angular, N). Coil-constructed, N-shaped junctions. Interior and exterior sooted, possibly same vessel as 62/11 and 62/11a.
T = 15 mm; 38 g.

[62/3]   Uncontexted
5 rims, all from the same vessel. Inverted rim. Grey. Fabric hard; clay has quartz and igneous inclusions. Large inclusions of crushed (probably igneous) rock (10%, 12 mm, angular). Coil-constructed; top coil folded to the interior. Interior and exterior sooted.
T = 10 mm, dia = 220 mm; 62 g.

[62/5b]  Uncontexted
1 rim. Everted, probably from a globular vessel. Brown. Fabric hard; fine clay with abundant quartz and black igneous.
T = 6 mm; 8 g.

[62/6]   Uncontexted
1 body sherd in two fragments. Brown exterior, black interior, brown interior surface. Fabric very hard; fine clay with few quartz inclusions. Organic tempering round voids, possibly heather. Exterior sooted.
T = 11 mm; 4 g.

[62/7]   Uncontexted
1 body sherd. Black. Fabric hard; fine clay with occasional quartz. Shell temper. Exterior and interior sooted.
T = 7 mm; 1.5 g.

[62/8]   Hut 2, hollow in wall
1 body sherd. From the point of inflection at the neck or shoulder. Series of ridges and grooves on one face. This face also has faint traces of a brown glaze or slip. Grey with a red slip on one surface (surface abraded). Fabric hard; clay has quartz and black igneous inclusions.
T = 3 mm; 6 g.

[62/11] Hut 2, debris of hut wall at north
5 rims, 2 bases, 137 body sherds and abraded fragments. Possibly from more than one vessel, but extent of abrasion, burning and variation in thickness and temper makes it impossible to be certain. Rim slightly inverted. Base plain, slightly angled. Red exterior, grey interior. Fabric hard; clay has quartz and opaques. Large (?igneous) inclusions (10–20%, 20 mm thick, angular). Interior and exterior sooted. Possibly same vessel as 62/2 and 62/11a.
T = 14 mm, rim dia = 13 mm; 1560 g.

[62/11a] House 62/2, 'recess in wall'
8 rims, 2 bases, 150 body sherds and abraded fragments. Possibly from more than one vessel, but extent of abrasion, burning, and variation in thickness and temper makes it impossible to be certain. Rim slightly inverted, 130 mm diameter. Base plain, slightly angled. Red exterior, grey interior. Fabric hard; clay has quartz and opaques. Large (?igneous) inclusions (10–20%, 20 mm, angular). Interior and exterior sooted. Possibly the same vessel as 62/2 and 62/11a.
T = 14 mm; 1778 g.

[62/11b] House 62/2, 'recess in wall'
3 rim sherds, 1 body sherd. Tapered rim with H-shaped coil junction fixing it onto body of pot. Fabric very distorted, a waster. Probably over-fired. Red fabric, very hard; clay has abundant quartz sand.
T = 20 mm; 23 g.

[62/11c] House 62/2, 'recess in wall'
3 body sherds. Red exterior, grey interior. Fabric hard; clay has abundant quartz and igneous inclusions. Mixed gravel component (10%, 16 mm, angular, N). Coil-constructed. Interior sooting.
T = 12 mm; 28 g.

[62/11d] House 62/2, 'recess in wall'
5 rims, all from the same vessel. Inverted rim, 220 mm diameter. Grey fabric, hard; clay has quartz and igneous inclusions. Large inclusions of crushed (probably igneous) rock (10%, 12 mm, angular). Coil-constructed, top coil is folded to the interior. Interior and exterior sooted.
T = 10 mm; 62 g.

[62/11e] House 62/2, 'recess' in wall
1 rim. Everted rim, probably from a globular vessel. Brown. Fabric hard; fine clay with abundant quartz and black igneous inclusions.
T = 6 mm; 8 g.

[62/11f] House 62/2, 'recess' in wall
1 body sherd in two fragments. Brown exterior, black interior, brown interior surface. Fabric very hard; fine clay with few quartz inclusions. Organic tempering round voids, possibly from heather. Exterior sooted.
T = 11 mm; 4g

[62/11g] House 62/2 'recess' in wall
1 body sherd. Black fabric, hard; fine clay with occasional quartz. Shell temper. Exterior and interior sooted.
T = 7 mm; 1.5 g.

[62/11h] House 62/2 'recess' in wall
1 body sherd. From point of inflection at neck or shoulder. Series of ridges and grooves on one face. This face also has traces of brown glaze or slip. Grey with a red slip on one surface (surface abraded). Fabric hard; clay has quartz and black igneous inclusions.
T = 3 mm; 6 g.

[62/13] House 62/2 'recess' in wall
1 body sherd. Grey with red exterior surface. Fabric hard; clay has abundant quartz and opaques; mixed gravel component (10%, 10 mm, round and angular, N). Coil-constructed. Interior sooted.
T = 10 mm; 16 g.

[62/14] House 62/2, base of wall
1 body sherd. Grey with red margins. Fabric hard; clay has abundant quartz and opaques; mixed gravel component (10%, 4 mm, round and angular, N).
T = 15 mm; 31 g.

[62/17] House 62/2, floor
2 body sherds. Grey with red exterior margin. Fabric hard; clay has abundant quartz and opaques; mixed gravel component (10%, 10 mm, round and angular, N).
T = 18 mm; 100 g.

## APPENDIX 17

**Metalworking debris** *R M Spearman*

*Bloomery debris distribution (1984–1986 excavations)*

| Find *no* | Context | Debris weight |
|-----------|---------|---------------|
| [49] | House 2, topsoil | 70.5 g |
| [50] | House 1, layer on platform | 244.8 g |
| [51] | Wall 1, rubble | 45.6 g |
| [52] | Area 2, topsoil | 53.8 g |
| [53] | Area 6, topsoil | 90.3 g |
| | Total | 988.1 g |

*Iron artefact (1961–1962 excavations)*

| Find *no* | Context | Description |
|-----------|---------|-------------|
| [61/15] | Wall D | Fragments of a non-identifiable iron object |

## APPENDIX 18

**Chipped stone** *B Finlayson*

*1984-1986 excavations*

[56] House 1, topsoil
Flint, secondary, irregular flake, patinated.
L = 20 mm, W = 11 mm, T = 5 mm.

[57] House 1, layer on platform
Flint (grey), inner, irregular flake, retouched, steep discoidal scraper.
L = 27 mm, W = 27 mm, T = 14 mm.

[58] Area 2, topsoil
Chert, secondary chunk, weathered (making identification difficult), an attempt has been made to use the piece as a core.
L = 43 mm, W = 22 mm, T = 19 mm.

[59] Area 2, topsoil
Chert(?), secondary chunk, weathered (making identification difficult), used as a core.
L = 74 mm, W = 37 mm, T = 18 mm.

[60] House 3, soil associated with hearth
Flint (grey), inner, regular flake, irregular shallow retouch

along one edge.
L = 40 mm, W = 34 mm, T = 12 mm.

[61]  Soil under roadway 1
Flint (grey), inner, regular flake.
L = 129 mm, W = 24 mm, T = 4 mm.

[62]  House 3, soil on apron
Flint, inner, irregular flake, burnt.
L = 20 mm, W = 12 mm, T = 6 mm.

[63]  House 3 area, unstratified
Flint (grey), fragment of an amorphous core.
L = 30 mm, W = 30 mm, T = 17 mm.

[64]  House 1, topsoil
Flint, inner, irregular flake.
L = 40 mm, W = 23 mm, T = 8 mm.

[65]  House 3, buried topsoil under apron
Flint, inner, irregular flake, patinated.
L = 11 mm, W = 5 mm, T = 4 mm.

[66]  Roadway 1, metalling
Flint (brown), inner regular flake, retouched, possible blade segment, denticulated along one side, the break probably occurring after the retouching. A 'serrated flake' in Clarke's terminology (Clarke 1960).

[67]  House 1, scarp surface
Flint(?), inner irregular flake, patinated (the material has numerous quartz crystals and while a chalcedony is possibly not flint), retouched to form a rough notch.
L = 36 mm, W = 33 mm, T = 13 mm.

[68]  House 6, topsoil
Flint, inner, irregular flake, burnt, fragment of abruptly retouched point.
L = 17 mm, W = 10 mm, T = 4 mm.

[69]  Soil above Wall 3
Quartz, flake, possibly not man-made.
L = 15 mm, W = 17 mm, T = 4 mm.

*1961–1962 excavations*

[61/8]  House 61/1, just above floor
Tertiary flake of grey chert. Retouched along left and right. Fire-cracked.
L = 35 mm, W = 27 mm, T = 6 mm.

[62/9]  House 62/2, entrance
Secondary flake of reddish-brown chert.
L = 42 mm, W = 38 mm, T = 19 mm.

[62/18]  House 62/2, floor
Tertiary flake of brown chert. Retouched along one edge.
L = 27 mm, W = 12 mm, T = 6 mm.

APPENDIX 19

**Charcoal identification (Table 3.9)** *R P J McCullagh*

APPENDIX 20

**Thermoluminescence dating of the hearth-stones** *D Sanderson*

*Summary*
Nine samples of heated stones taken from three hearths were collected for thermoluminescence (TL) dating at the Scottish Universities Research and Reactor Centre. The technique establishes the time elapsed since the last heating of the sample, which in the case of a domestic hearth-stone represents the *terminus ante quem* for the abandonment of the context. In view of the clarity of archaeological association, burned hearth-stones represent an important and under-explored source of dating material. It was possible to obtain feldspar inclusion dates from 8 of the samples. Taken together, these imply that the occupation is most likely to have ended in the first century AD.

*Potential and problems*
Hearth-stones present special problems relating to the effectiveness of the zeroing event, and to the heterogeneity of their TL characteristics. Exposure to temperatures of above 300°C for only a few minutes is sufficient to zero the dating signals from feldspars.

Although domestic fires reach temperatures well in excess of 500°C locally, it was not initially clear whether this would be expected to provide zeroing of TL at depth. The temperature gradient in an infinitely large slab of material heated from one side can be calculated (Carslaw & Jaeger 1959) using typical values of diffusivity for rocks. Results of such calculations suggest that a layer 5 cm beneath the surface of a sandstone slab heated at 500°C would reach 115°C after 15 minutes, 380°C after 3 hours, and 450°C only after 12 hours of heating. Therefore, while it is reasonable to expect that domestic fires are capable of resetting TL signals, there will almost certainly be thermal gradients across the stones, and care is needed to ensure that bulk samples have been adequately zeroed.

The TL characteristics of minerals are known to be sensitive to diagenetic origins, thermal history, and trace element composition. For hearths made from sedimentary rocks, diagenesis and mineralogy are prone to variation with depth simply as a consequence of crossing bedding planes. The additional effects of thermal gradients within the sample may also give rise to a heterogeneous TL response, which is likely to limit the reproducibility of TL readings. The extent to which either of these factors would limit the value of TL dates from The Dunion was unknown at the outset. In view of the scarcity of alternative dating material from the site and the overall importance of burned stones as a dating resource, it was decided to attempt to date samples from the hearths in three houses.

*The samples*
The hearths of Houses 2, 6, and 7 comprised cracked and slumped slabs of sandstone of Old Red Sandstone date approximately 7 cm thick. Triplicate samples from Houses 6 and 7 were collected on 11 September 1986, the contexts having been protected by temporary covers since the end of the excavation some weeks earlier. Gamma ray dose rates were recorded from each of these contexts and also

Table 3.9  *Other remains noted during preparation of charcoal for radiocarbon dating. NB Wood charcoal only was submitted for dating.*

| Context | Carbonised seeds | Other notable remains | SURC sample *no* for charcoal |
|---|---|---|---|
| House 2, quern pit | *Polygonum persicaria* (3) *Polygonum aviculare* (3) *Rumex* cf *acetosella* (4) *Hordeum* sp (4) | None | GU-2178 |
| House 1, drainage ditch | None | Hazelnut shell fragment | GU-2172 |
| House 4, occupation horizon | *Polygonum* cf *persicaria* (2) *Carex* sp (1) | Burnt bone fragments Small silicious balls | GU-2174 |

from the hearth in House 2 using a 2x2" NaI scintillation counter coupled to a Bichron portable scalar-ratemeter. Samples from House 2 had been removed from the site and were forwarded to the laboratory shortly after the visit.

*Measurements*
The samples were subjected to a standard feldspar inclusion dating procedure, similar to that developed for vitrified forts (Sanderson *et al* 1985, 1988). 30 g portions of each sample were carefully cut from the bulk using a water-cooled diamond saw under safelight conditions, and then transferred to the TL preparation laboratory. Saturated water contents were measured by soaking the samples, weighing them, and drying them for 2 days in a laboratory oven at 50°C before re-weighing. In all cases the saturated water content was 5%, which is quite typical for sandstones. It was assumed that the actual water contents during burial ranged between 60% and 100% saturation.

The dried samples were next disaggregated, infinite matrix beta dose rates measured by thick source beta counting (Sanderson 1988) and passed through a set of geological sieves to separate the grain size fraction 90–125 microns. Examination confirmed that the sample contained significant alkali and plagioclase feldspars which were separated into enriched fractions by heavy liquid separation with a centrifuge. The non-toxic sodium polytungstate liquids were used for this purpose, mixed to densities of 2.51, 2.58, 2.62, and 2.74 g cm$^3$. Feldspar separates thus extracted were subject to acid treatment comprising 30 minutes HCl and 10 minutes of 10% HF to remove residual carbonates and clean the grain surfaces.

Eight separate aliquots of each sample were dispensed onto 0.25 mm thick stainless steel discs which had been coated with a layer of outgassed silicone grease for TL measurement. A series of 64 separate glow measurements was then executed to determine the first and second glow growth characteristics, the reproducibility of specific TL, and the stability of the high temperature TL signal. Calibrated radiation doses were administered using a 90Sr beta source similar to that described by Sanderson and Chambers (1985) and samples were preheated for 16 hours at 120°C to attempt to avert short term fading of high temperature TL (Sanderson 1988b). Stored doses were calculated using a regression model (Scott & Sanderson 1988) along with quality control parameters describing the variation with temperature (plateau quality), fractional second glow intercept correction, first/second glow sensitisation, and stability over a two month storage test. These data and the corresponding TL ages calculated using standard microdosimetric models are shown in Table 3.6 (see main text).

*Discussion and interpretation*
Of the samples examined, one proved to have been only partially zeroed by archaeological heating. This sample failed to give a plateau (*ie* a zone where the TL stored dose is not dependent on glow curve temperature) and had a high and variable equivalent dose. Of the other 8 samples measured, the most successful measurements came from Na feldspar extracts which had very acceptable plateau and TL characteristics. The potassium feldspars and plagioclase extracts, by contrast, showed poorer reproducibility and produced ages with a high uncertainty. With the exception of samples SUTL43 and SUTL48, there was no significant fading of TL signal in the two month laboratory storage test. In these other two cases the results have been corrected for observed fading which appears to be satisfactory at the level of precision achieved.

The individual results for each house refer to the same event and therefore the calculation of a mean result for each structure is justified. The weighted mean dates for each hearth are shown in Table 3.10 together with random and systematic error estimates at 1σ. The last heating of each hearth can be defined with a statistical precision of roughly two centuries at one sigma, spanning the period from the late first century BC to the second century AD. Although there is a suggestion that House 2 may have fallen out of use before House 7, they may easily have been contemporary. The overall mean date for all three structures, assuming contemporaneity, is AD 80±120, 130.

*Table 3.10   Weighted mean ages and dates for the hearths*

| House | Mean Age | Date |
|---|---|---|
| 2 | 2055±190 | 70 BC±190, 210 |
| 6 | 1920±220 | AD 60±220, 220 |
| 7 | 1800±170 | AD 180±170, 180 |

Overall Mean 1910±120 AD 80±120, 130

*Conclusion*
The results, based on triplicate measurements of different mineral phases from the hearths of three houses, indicate abandonment of the site in the later Iron Age; most probably in the Roman period.

## HARPERCROFT AND WARDLAW HILL

### APPENDIX 21

**Chipped stone** *B Finlayson*

[8]   F2
Flint, primary, irregular flake, cortex is smooth and rounded.
L = 40 mm, W = 20 mm, T = 7 mm.

[9]   F2
Flint, secondary, irregular flake, cortex is smooth (but battered) and rounded.
L = 24 mm, W = 28 mm, T = 13 mm.

[10]   F2
Flint, secondary, regular flake, retouched, invasive shallow retouch along both sides not completely covering the dorsal surface, piece probably broken across middle, plano-convex knife fragment.
L = 33 mm, W = 28 mm, T = 6 mm.

[11]   F2
Flint, secondary, irregular flake, burnt.
L = 17 mm, W = 10 mm, T = 6 mm.

[12]   F2
Flint, inner, irregular flake, corticated.
L = 19 mm, W = 14 mm, T = 3 mm.

[13]   F2
Chert, amorphous core or core fragment.
L = 38 mm, W = 25 mm, T = 24 mm.

[14]   F4
Flint, secondary chunk.
L = 22 mm, W = 27 mm, T = 12 mm.

[15]   F4
Flint, primary, irregular flake.
L = 38 mm, W = 29 mm, T = 12 mm.

[16]   F4
Flint, secondary, regular flake.
L = 43 mm, W = 30 mm, T = 15 mm.

[17]   F4
Flint, inner, regular flake, blade-like flake bilaterally edge damaged.
L = 19 mm, W = 11 mm, T = 3 mm.

[18]   F4
Flint, secondary, regular blade, naturally backed.
L = 24 mm, W = 8 mm, T = 4 mm.

[19]    F4
Flint, inner, regular flake, blade-like flake.
L = 22 mm, W = 12 mm, T = 4 mm.

[20]    F4
Flint, inner, regular blade, edge damaged.
L = 21 mm, W = 10 mm, T = 4 mm.

## APPENDIX 22

**Jet armlets** *V J McLellan*

[1]    About half of an armlet. It is D-shaped in section and finely
finished with very few tool-marks surviving. Joins [4].
T = 15 mm, estimated internal dia 72 mm.

[2]    Probable section from an armlet. It shows striations and
honing marks which suggest secondary working. One end
has been whittled and rubbed to form a crude cone-shape,
and the other end bears rubbing striations. The fragment is
rectangular in section.
L = *circa* 52 mm, T = 15 mm.

[3]    Armlet fragment, oval in section. The surface is highly
polished, but shows signs of chipping, wear and tear.
L = *circa* 46 mm, T = 9 mm.

[4]    Surface sliver or flake which joins [1].

[5]    Small section of armlet circa 22 mm long. Sub-rounded in
section. The interior is slightly flattened, forming a ridge.
Striated on the surface. L = *circa* 22 mm, T = 9 mm.

## APPENDIX 23

**Pottery** *A MacSween*

[6]    12 rim sherds, 55 body sherds and 10 basal fragments from
a flat-based vessel with an everted rim and slight shoulder.
Red with grey core. Coil-constructed. Fine clay fabric,
tempered with 10% angular rock fragments.
T = 11–15 mm, rim dia = 320 mm, base dia 180 mm,
H = 400 mm.

[7]    1 rim and 1 body sherd, plain rim, grey with brown
surfaces. Fine clay fabric, with 5% angular rock fragments.
T = 9 mm, dia = 260 mm.

## GILLIES HILL

## APPENDIX 24

**Prehistoric pottery** *A Barlow*

[1]    Rampart 2 core
Three small body sherds from fairly large, relatively thin-
walled vessel of dense hard red ware, externally burnished
to gloss. These sherds are possibly Neolithic, possibly early,
or 'domestic beaker', McInnes (1966, 49 52–4) Class III.
estimated dia 200 mm.

[2]    Rampart 3
One rim sherd from primary silting behind Rampart 3 and
one sherd from the occupation material. Both sherds appear
to be parts of an early Beaker, possibly Steps 1–2.

[3]    Presumed pit
29 conjoining sherds plus one non-conjoining body sherd
from the occupation layer, all decorated; 3 undecorated
body sherds, and 3 base sherds, also undecorated. 2
externally decorated fragments, and 3 undecorated
fragments; 10 crumbs. The upper part of an incomplete
later beaker.
dia 150 mm.

[4]    B2 horizon over occupation layer
A small, irregular, broken but fairly complete 'thumb-pot',
wanting one small sherd from the rim where it has broken
away above a large grit, and some small 'base' fragments.
D 22, 13. The large, angular grits and general coloration
are suggestive of a similarity in fabric with the Late Bronze
Age/Early Iron Age ware found on the site (5 and 6); the
coarseness of grit argues against it being a very small
(unused) crucible.

[5]    Rampart 2 core
11 rim sherds, *circa* 100 body sherds, 2 base angle sherds,
many fragments and crumbs of a large flat-based vessel.
Not more than half of a large (?cooking) pot of Late
Bronze Age/Early Iron Age type, unweathered when
deposited, fairly fragile. Comparable with [6].
dia *circa* 320 mm.

[6]    B2 horizon and occupation layer behind Rampart 1
Rim sherd and thirteen scattered sherds and fragments of
the same fabric are probably from the same vessel, a large
Late Bronze Age/Early Iron Age cooking or storage pot of
typical form, flat-based, flaring towards mouth, then the
profile curving in more or less sharply to the rim, as
represented by [5].

## APPENDIX 25

**Medieval pottery** *J S Rideout*

[7]    B-horizon
Small body sherd, light brown with spots of yellow to
green glaze, of a medieval vessel.

## APPENDIX 26

**Stone** *A J Barlow · J S Rideout*

[8]    Silting behind Rampart 3
3 pieces of a stone armlet, conjoining, of fine-grained, but
not obviously laminar, sedimentary rock. Approximately
three-quarters of the object were found. *A Barlow*

[9]    Rampart 1 revetment
Large quartz-dolerite rock, weathered edges. Upper surface
triangular, concave. Probably a saddle-quern. *J S Rideout*

[10]   B2-horizon
Block of sandstone, rectangular, with upper surface smooth
but ends rough, slightly concave. Whetstone. *J S Rideout*

[11]   A-horizon
Quartzite cobble, edges roughened by repeated striking.
Hammerstone/pounder. *J S Rideout*

[12]   Rampart 3 core
Outer flake of rounded quartzite pebble, no obvious
striking platform or working. Probably natural, or
hammerstone fragment? *A Barlow*.

## APPENDIX 27

**Daub** *A Barlow · J S Rideout*

[13]   Topsoil
Fragment of daub or soft brick-like material, with sub-
rounded grits of an unidentified rock. Kiln or furnace wall
fragment (interior). M Spearman (pers comm) suggests that
it is a piece of sintered daub, the poor quality of the glaze
suggestive of a low metal content, probably iron derived
from the clay, which does not immediately suggest a
metalworking context such as a furnace interior. The

evenness and lack of inclusions and contamination of the surface tend to weigh against its being from a fired building or other frame and daub structure. It is possible that this is a manuport to the site. *A J Barlow*

[14]   Tumbled facing between Ramparts 1 and 2
       A single fragment of daub. *J S Rideout*

[15]   'Silting' layer between Ramparts 1 and 2
       A single fragment of daub. *J S Rideout*

[16]   Unstratified
       A single fragment of daub. *J S Rideout*

[17]   A-horizon
       A single fragment of daub. *J S Rideout*

APPENDIX 28

**Bone** *E Halpin*

[18]   Occupation layer
       Fragments of burnt bone from the occupation layer. The fragments are too small to identify precisely.

# References

Alcock, L 1970 — 'Excavations at South Cadbury Castle, 1969', *Antiq J*, 50 (1970), 14–25.

Alcock, L 1972 — *By South Cadbury is that Camelot . . . excavations at Cadbury Castle 1966–70.* London.

Andersen, S T 1979 — 'Identification of wild grass and cereal pollen', *Danm Geol Unders Yearbook*, (1978), 69–92. Copenhagen.

Anderson, J 1886 — 'Notices of recent discoveries of cists, or burials with urns', *Proc Soc Antiq Scot*, 20 (1885–6), 97–101.

Andrew, R 1984 — *A practical pollen guide to the British flora.* Technical Guide 1. Cambridge: Quaternary Research Association.

Avery, M 1976 — 'Hillforts of the British Isles; a student's introduction', *in* Harding, D W (ed) 1979, 1–58.

Baillie, M G L and Pilcher J R 1983 — 'Some observations on the High Precision Calibration of routine dates', *in* Ottaway, B S (ed) 1982, *Archaeology, dendrochronology and the radiocarbon calibration curve*, Edinburgh, 51–63. (University of Edinburgh Occ Paper, No 9).

Barber, J, Halstead, P, James, H and Lee, F 1989 — 'An unusual Iron Age burial at Hornish Point, South Uist', *Antiquity*, 63 (1989), 73–8.

Behre, K-E 1981 — 'The interpretation of anthropogenic indicators in pollen diagrams', *Pollen et Spores*, XXIII, 2 (1981), 225–245.

Bergren, G 1969 — *Atlas of seeds*, Part 2. Stockholm.

Bergren, G 1981 — *Atlas of seeds*, Part 3. Stockholm.

Beveridge, E 1931 — 'Excavation of an earth-house at Foshigarry, and a fort, Dun Thomaidh, in North Uist', *Proc Soc Antiq Scot*, 65 (1930–1), 299–357.

Birks, H J B 1989 — 'Holocene isochrone maps and patterns of tree-spreading in the British Isles', *J Biogeogr*, 16 (1989), 503–540.

Birse, E L 1980 — 'An introduction to the phytosociology of the Whitlaw Mosses Nature Reserve', *Trans Bot Soc Edin*, 43 (1980), 221–234.

Bowden, M and McOmish, D 1987 — 'The required barrier', *Scot Archaeol Rev*, 4 (1987), 76–84.

Breeze, D J 1982 — *The northern frontiers of Roman Britain.* London: Batsford.

Brewster, T C M 1963 — *The excavation of Staple Howe.* Scarborough.

Britton, D and Longworth I H 1968 — 'Late Bronze Age finds in the Heathery Burn Cave, County Durham', *Inventoria Archaeologia*, GB 5.

Brown, C J and Shipley, M 1982 — *Soil and land capability for agriculture, south-east Scotland.* Aberdeen: Soil Survey Handbook, sheet 7.

Bryant, V M Jr, and Holloway, R G 1983 — 'The role of palynology in archaeology', *in* Schiffer, M B (ed), *Advances In Archaeological Method and Theory*, 6, New York: Academic Press, 191–224.

Buckland, P C and Edwards, K J 1984 — 'The longevity of pastoral episodes of clearance activity in pollen diagrams: the role of post-occupation grazing', *J Biogeogr*, 11 (1984), 243–249.

Bulmer, W 1938 — 'Dragonesque brooches and their development', *Antiq J*, 18 (1938), 146–53.

Burgess, C B 1980 — *The age of Stonehenge.* London: Dent.

Burley, E 1956 — 'A catalogue and survey of the metalwork from Traprain Law', *Proc Soc Antiq Scot*, 89 (1956), 118–226.

Callander, J G 1916 — 'Notice of a jet necklace found in a cist in a Bronze Age cemetery, discovered on Burgie Lodge Farm, Morayshire, with notes on Scottish prehistoric jet ornaments', *Proc Soc Antiq Scot*, 50 (1915–16), 201–40.

Callander, J G 1931 — 'Notes on the structures and the relics found in them', *in* Beveridge, E (1930–31), 322–356.

Carslaw, H S and Jaeger, J C 1959 — *Conduction of heat in solids.* 2nd ed. Oxford.

Caseldine, C J 1979 — 'Early land clearance in south-east Perthshire', *in* Thoms, L M (ed), 'Early man in the Scottish landscape', *Scot Archaeol Forum*, 9 (1979), 1–15.

Caseldine, C J 1982 — 'Palynological evidence for early cereal cultivation in Strathearn', *Proc Soc Antiq Scot*, 112 (1982), 39–47.

Caulfield, S 1977 — 'The beehive quern in Ireland', *J Roy Soc Antiq Ir*, 107–8 (1977–8), 104–38.

Challis, A J and Harding D W 1975 — *Late prehistory from the Trent to the Tyne*. Oxford. (Brit Archaeol Rep Brit Ser, 20, 2 vols).

Chalmers, G 1807 — *Caledonia, an account, historical and topographical of north Britain*. London.

Chapman, J C and Mytum, H C (eds) 1983 — *Settlement in north Britain 1000 BC–1000 AD*. Oxford. (Brit Archaeol Rep Brit Ser, 118).

Childe, V G 1933 — 'Excavations at Castlelaw Fort, Midlothian', *Proc Soc Antiq Scot*, 67 (1932–3), 362–88.

Childe, V G 1935 — *The prehistory of Scotland*. London: Kegan Paul, Trench, Trubner and Co.

Childe, V G 1941a — 'Examination of the prehistoric fort on Cairngryffe Hill, near Lanark', *Proc Soc Antiq Scot*, 75 (1940–1), 213–18.

Childe, V G 1941b — 'The defences of Kaimes hillfort, Midlothian', *Proc Soc Antiq Scot*, 75 (1940–1), 43–54.

Childe, V G and Forde, C D 1932 — 'Excavations in two Iron Age forts at Earn's Heugh, near Coldingham', *Proc Soc Antiq Scot*, 66 (1931–2), 152–83.

Christison, D 1887 — 'The prehistoric forts of Peeblesshire. With plans and sketches', *Proc Soc Antiq Scot*, 21 (1886–7), 13–83.

Christison, D 1888 — 'Notice of ancient remains in Manor Parish and other districts of Peeblesshire', *Proc Soc Antiq Scot*, 22 (1887–8), 192–210.

Christison, D 1890 — 'Forts, camps, and motes of the Upper Ward of Lanarkshire', *Proc Soc Antiq Scot*, 24 (1889–90), 281–352.

Christison, D 1893 — 'The prehistoric forts of Ayrshire', *Proc Soc Antiq Scot*, 27 (1892–3), 381–406.

Christison, D 1894 — 'The prehistoric fortresses of Treceiri, Carnarvon; and Eildon, Roxburgh', *Proc Soc Antiq Scot*, 28 (1893–4), 100–19.

Christison, D 1895 — 'The forts of Selkirk, the Gala Water, the southern slopes of the Lammermuirs, and the north of Roxburgh', *Proc Soc Antiq Scot*, 29 (1894–5), 108–79.

Christison, D 1898 — *Early fortifications in Scotland*. Edinburgh: W Blackwood and Sons.

Clapham, A R, Tutin, T G and Warburg, E F 1962 — *Flora of the British Isles*. Cambridge: Cambridge University Press.

Clarke, D L 1970 — *Beaker Pottery in Great Britain and Ireland*. Cambridge: Cambridge University Press, 2 vols.

Clarke, J G D 1960 — 'Excavations at the neolithic site at Hurst Fen, Mildenhall, Suffolk', *Proc Prehist Soc*, 26 (1960), 202–45.

Clouston, R W M 1976 — 'Kersmains Bell', *Proc Soc Antiq Scot*, 107 (1975–6), 275–8.

Coggins, D and Fairless, K J 1984 — 'The Bronze Age settlement site of Bracken Rigg, Upper Teesdale, Co. Durham', *Durham Archaeol J*, 1 (1984), 5–21.

Coles, J M 1960 — 'Scottish Late Bronze Age metalwork: typology, distribution and chronology', *Proc Soc Antiq Scot*, 93 (1959–60), 16–135.

Collingwood, R G and Richmond, I 1969 — *The archaeology of northern Britain*. London: Methuen.

Collis, J R 1975 — *Defended sites of the late La Tène in central and western Europe*. Oxford. (Brit Archaeol Rep Suppl Ser, 2).

Cool, H E M 1982 — 'The artefact record: some possibilities', *in* Harding D W (ed) 1982a, 92–100.

Coombs, D G 1976 — 'Excavation at Mam Tor, Derbyshire 1965–69', *in* Harding, D W (ed) 1976, 147–52.

Cormack, W F 1963 — 'Burial site at Kirkburn, Lockerbie', *Proc Soc Antiq Scot*, 96 (1962–3), 107–35.

Cowie, T (forthcoming a) — 'Carwinning Hillfort'.

Cowie, T (forthcoming b) — 'A bronze flat axe mould'.

Cree, J E 1923 — 'Account of the excavations on Traprain Law during the summer of 1922', *Proc Soc Antiq Scot*, 57 (1922–3), 180–225.

Cree, J E 1924 — 'Account of the excavations on Traprain Law during the summer of 1923', *Proc Soc Antiq Scot*, 58 (1923–4), 241–85.

Cree, J E and Curle, A O 1922 — 'Account of excavations on Traprain Law during the summer of 1921', *Proc Soc Antiq Scot*, 56 (1921–2), 189–259.

Crone, B A 1982 — 'Doon Hill Hillfort, Balig', *Trans Dumfriesshire Galloway Natur Hist Antiq Soc*, 57 (1982), 85–6.

Cruden, S H 1940     'The ramparts of Traprain Law: excavations in 1939', *Proc Soc Antiq Scot*, 74 (1939–40), 48–59.

Cunliffe, B 1983     'The Iron Age of northern Britain: a view from the south', *in* Chapman, J C and Mytum, H C (eds) 1983, *Settlement in north Britain 1000 BC–1000 AD*, Oxford, 83–102. (Brit Archaeol Rep Brit Ser, 118, 83–102).

Curle, A O 1907     'Note of excavations on Rubers Law, Roxburghshire, supplementary to the description of the fortifications thereon', *Proc Soc Antiq Scot*, 41 (1906–7), 451–3.

Curle, A O 1910     'Notice of some excavation on the fort occupying the summit of Bonchester Hill, Parish of Hobkirk, Roxburghshire', *Proc Soc Antiq Scot*, 44 (1909–10), 225–36.

Curle, A O 1911     *A Roman frontier and its people*. Glasgow.

Curle, A O 1915     'Account of excavations on Traprain Law in the Parish of Prestonkirk, County of Haddington, in 1914', *Proc Soc Antiq Scot*, 49 (1914–5), 139–202.

Curle, A O 1920     'Report of the excavation on Traprain Law in the summer of 1919', *Proc Soc Antiq Scot*, 54 (1919–20), 54–123.

Curle, A O and Cree, J E 1916     'Account of excavations on Traprain Law in the Parish of Prestonkirk, County of Haddington, in 1915', *Proc Soc Antiq Scot*, 50 (1915–6), 64–144.

Curle, A O and Cree, J E 1921     'Account of the excavations on Traprain Law during the summer of 1920', *Proc Soc Antiq Scot*, 55 (1920–1), 153–206.

Curle, C L 1982     *Pictish and Norse finds from the Brough of Birsay, 1934–74*. Edinburgh. (Scot Antiq Soc Monogr Ser, 1).

Curwen, E C 1937     'Querns', *Antiquity*, 11 (1937), 133–51.

Curwen, E C 1941     'More about querns', *Antiquity*, 15 (1941), 15–32.

Cwynar, L C, Burden, E and McAndrews, J H 1979     'An inexpensive sieving method for concentrating pollen and spores from fine-grained sediments', *Canadian Journal of Earth Sciences*, 16 (1979), 1115–1120.

Dalland, M M 1984     'A procedure for use in stratigraphic analysis', *Scot Archaeol Review*, 3, 2 (1984), 116–127.

Dalland, M M (forthcoming)     'A programme for calibration of radiocarbon dates with procedures for the analysis of age differences and adjusting for stratigraphical data'.

Davies, G and Turner, J 1979     'Pollen diagrams from Northumberland', *New Phytol*, 82 (1979), 783–804.

Dimbleby, G W 1985     *The palynology of archaeological sites*. London: Academic Press.

Dixon, P 1977     *Crickley Hill and Gloucestershire prehistory*. Gloucester: Gloucestershire County Council for Crickley Hill Trust.

Duncan H B 1982     *Aspects of the early historic period in Scotland*, Glas Univ M.Lit thesis (unpublished).

Dundas J 1866     'Notes on the excavation of an ancient building at Tappock in the Torwood, Parish of Dunipace, County of Stirling', *Proc Soc Antiq Scot*, 6 (1864–6), 259–66.

Edwards, K J 1982     'The separation of *Corylus* and *Myrica* pollen in modern and fossil samples', *Pollen et Spores*, 23 (1982), 205–218.

Evans, A T and Moore, P D 1985     'Surface pollen studies of *Calluna vulagaris* (L) hull and their relevance to the interpretation of bog and moorland pollen diagrams', *Circaea*, 3, 3 (1985), 173–8.

Faegri, K and Iversen, J 1975     *Textbook of pollen analysis*. London: Blackwell.

Fairhurst, H 1956     'The Meikle Reive – a hill-fort on the Campsies', *Trans Glasgow Archaeol Soc*, 14 (1956), 64–89.

Fairhurst, H and Taylor, D B 1971     'A hut-circle settlement at Kilphedir, Sutherland', *Proc Soc Antiq Scot*, 103 (1970–1), 65–99.

Feachem, R W 1951     'Dragonesque fibulae', *Antiq J*, 31 (1951), 32–44.

Feachem, R W 1957     'Castlehill Wood Dun, Stirlingshire', *Proc Soc Antiq Scot*, 90 (1956–7), 24–51.

Feachem, R W 1959     'Glenachan Rig Homestead, Cardon, Peeblesshire'. *Proc Soc Antiq Scot*, 92 (1958–9), 15–24.

Feachem, R W 1961     'Unenclosed platform settlements', *Proc Soc Antiq Scot*, 94 (1960–1), 79–85.

Feachem, R W 1966     'The hill-forts of northern Britain', *in* Rivet, A L F (ed) 1966, 59–87.

Fulford, M G 1975     *New Forest roman pottery*. Oxford.

| | |
|---|---|
| Funkhouser, J W and Evitt, W R 1959 | 'Preparation techniques for acid insoluble microfossils', *Micropalaeontology*, 5 (1959), 369–395. |
| Geikie, J 1884 | 'List of hill-forts, intrenched camps etc, in Roxburghshire on the Scotch side of the Cheviots', *Hist Berwickshire Natur Club*, 10 (1882–4), 139–48. |
| Godwin, H 1975 | *The history of the British flora.* Cambridge: Cambridge University Press. |
| Goudie, A 1981 | *Geomorphological technique*, edited for the geomorphological reserch group. London: Allen and Unwin. |
| Grant, A 1984 | 'Animal husbandry', *in* Cunliffe, B 1984, *Danebury: an Iron Age hill-fort in Hampshire*, 496–548. (Counc Brit Archaeol Res Rep, 52). |
| Green, H S 1980 | *Flint arrowheads of the British Isles: a detailed study of material from England and Wales with comparisons from Scotland.* Oxford. (Brit Archaeol Rep, 75). |
| Green, L R and Hart, F A 1987 | 'Colour and composition in ancient glass: an examination of some Roman and Wealden glass by means of ultraviolet-visible-infra-red spectroscopy and electron microprobe analysis', *J Archaeol Sci*, 14 (1987), 271–82. |
| Greig, D C 1971 | *British regional geology: the south of Scotland.* 3rd ed. Edinburgh: HMSO. |
| Groenman-van Waateringe, W 1986 | 'Grazing possibilities in the Neolithic of the Netherlands based on palynological data', *in* Behre, K-E (ed), *Anthropogenic indicators in pollen diagrams*, Balkema, 187–203. |
| Guido, C M 1978 | *The glass beads of the prehistoric and Roman periods in Britain and Ireland.* London. (Soc Antiq London Res Rep, 35). |
| Guilbert, G 1976 | 'Moel y Gaer (Rhosesmor) 1972–1973: an area excavation in the interior', *in* Harding, D W (ed) 1976, 303–17. |
| Guilbert, G 1981 | 'Hillfort functions and populations: a sceptical viewpoint *in* Guilbert, G (ed), *Hillfort Studies*, 104–21, Leicester: Leicester University Press. |
| Haevernick, T E 1960 | *Die glasarmringe und ringperlen der mittelund spatlatenezeit auf dem Europaischen Festland.* Bonn. |
| Halliday, S 1982 | 'Later prehistoric farming in south-east Scotland', *in* Harding, D W (ed) 1982a, 75–91. |
| Hamilton, J R C 1956 | *Excavations at Jarlshof, Shetland.* Edinburgh: HMSO. |
| Hamond, F W 1983 | 'Phosphate analysis of archaeological sediments', *in* Reeves-Smyth, T and Hamond, F W, *Landscape archaeology in Ireland.* Oxford. (Brit Archaeol Rep Int Ser, 116). |
| Harding, D W (ed) 1976 | *Hillforts: later prehistoric earthworks in Britain and Ireland.* London. |
| Harding, D W (ed) 1982a | *Later prehistoric settlement in south-east Scotland*, Edinburgh, 1–3. (University of Edinburgh Department of Archaeology Occasional Paper, 8). |
| Harding, D W 1982b | 'Later prehistoric settlement in south-east Scotland: retrospect and prospect' *in* Harding, D W (ed) 1982a. |
| Hartley, B R 1972 | 'The Roman occupation of Scotland: the evidence of Samian Ware', *Britannia*, 3 (1972), 1–55. |
| Hawkes, C F C 1959 | 'The ABC of the British Iron Age', *Antiquity*, 33 (1959), 170–82. |
| Henderson, J 1985 | 'The raw materials of early glass production', *Oxford Journal of Archaeology* 4, 3 (1985), 267–292. |
| Henderson, J 1987 | 'The archaeology and technology of glass from Meare Village East', *in* Coles, J M 1987, *Somerset Levels*, 13, 170–182. |
| Henderson, J 1988 | 'Electron-probe microanalysis of mixed-alkali glass from Ireland and France', *Archaeometry* 30, 1 (1988), 77–91. |
| Henderson, J 1989a | 'The scientific analysis of ancient glass and its archaeological interpretation', Chapter 2 *in* Henderson, J (ed), *Scientific analysis in archaeology and its interpretation.* University of Oxford Committee on Archaeology Monograph 19, and UCLA Institute of Archaeology, Archaeological Research Tools 5. |
| Henderson, J 1989b | 'The evidence for Regional production of Iron Age glass in Britain. Chapter 5 *in* Feugère, M (ed), *Le verre préromain en Europe occidentale.* Libraire Montagnac. |
| Henderson, J (in press) | 'The archaeological interpretation of ancient glass analysis', *in* Henderson, J (ed), *Scientific analysis in archaeology and its interpretation.* Oxford. (University of Oxford Committee on Archaeology Monograph). |
| Henderson, J and Warren, S E 1983 | 'Analysis of prehistoric lead glass' *in* Aspinall, A and Warren, S E 1983, *Proceedings of the 22nd international symposium on archaeometry, Bradford 30th March–3rd April 1982*, 168–80. |
| Henshall, A S 1956 | 'The long cist cemetery of Lasswade, Midlothian', *Proc Soc Antiq Scot*, 84 (1955–6), 252–83. |

Hibbert, F A and Switzur, V R 1976 · 'Radiocarbon dating and Flandrian pollen zones in Wales and northern England', *New Phytol* 77 (1976), 793–807.

Hill, P H 1982a · 'Settlement and chronology', *in* Harding, D W (ed) 1982a, 4–43.

Hill, P H 1982b · 'Broxmouth Hillfort excavations, 1977–78: an interim report', *in* Harding, D W (ed) 1982a, 141–88.

Hill, P H 1982c · 'Towards a new classification of early houses', *Scot Archaeol Review*, 1 (1981c), 24–31.

Hill, P H 1987 · 'Traprain Law : the Votadini and the Romans', *Scot Archeol Review*, 4 (1987), 85–91.

HMSO, 1920 · *Letters and papers foreign and domestic of the reign of Henry VIII.* 2nd ed. London.

Hogg, A H A 1979 · *British hill-forts.* Oxford. (Brit Archaeol Rep Brit Ser, 62).

Holloway, R G and Bryant, V M Jr 1986 · 'New directions of palynology in ethnobiology', *Journal of Ethnobiology*, 6, 1 (1986), 47–65.

Hulme, P D and Shirriffs, J 1985 · 'Pollen analysis of a radiocarbon dated core from North Mains, Strathallan, Perthshire', *Proc Soc Antiq Scot*, 115 (1985), 105–113.

Hunt, C 1985 · 'Recent advances in pollen extraction techniques: a brief review', *in* Fieller, N R J (ed), *Palaeobiological investigations: research design, methods and data analysis*, Oxford, 181–8. (Brit Archaeol Rep Int Ser, 266).

Hunter, D M 1949 · 'Note on excavations at the broch of Tappoch in the Tor Wood, Stirlingshire', *Proc Soc Antiq Scot*, 83 (1948–9), 233–5.

Jacobson, G L and Bradshaw, R H W 1981 · 'The selection of sites for palaeovegetational studies', *Quaternary Research*, 16 (1981), 80–96.

Jobey, G 1965 · 'Hillforts and settlements in Northumberland', *Archaeol Aeliana 5 ser*, 43 (1965), 21–64.

Jobey, G 1966 · 'A field survey in Northumberland', *in* Rivet A L F 1966, 89–109.

Jobey, G 1970 · 'Early settlement and topography in the Border counties', *Scot Archaeol Forum*, 2 (1970), 73–84.

Jobey, G 1971 · 'Excavations at Brough Law and Ingram Hill', *Archaeol Aeliana 5 ser*, 49 (1971), 71–94.

Jobey, G 1973 · 'A Romano-British settlement at Tower Knowe, Wellhaugh, Northumberland, 1972', *Archaeol Aeliana 5 ser*, 1 (1973), 55–80.

Jobey, G 1976 · 'Traprain Law: a summary', *in* Harding, D W(ed) 1976, 191–204.

Jobey, G 1977 · 'Iron Age and later farmsteads on Belling Law, Northhumberland', *Archaeol Aeliana 5 ser*, 5 (1977), 1–38.

Jobey, G 1978 · 'Burnswark Hill', *Trans Dumfriesshire Galloway Natur Hist Antiq Soc*, 53 (1978), 57–104.

Jobey, G 1980 · 'Green Knowe, an unenclosed platform settlement and Harehope cairn Peebleshire', *Proc Soc Antiq Scot*, 110 (1980), 72–113.

Jobey, I and Jobey, G 1987 · 'Prehistoric, Romano-British and later remains on Murton High Crags, Northumberland', *Archaeol Aeliana 5 ser*, 43 (1987), 151–98.

Keef, P A M 1946 · 'Excavations at Chester Hillfort, Hundleshope, in Manor Parish, 1939', *Proc Soc Antiq Scot*, 80 (1945–6), 66–72.

Kilbride-Jones, H E 1938 · 'Excavation of a native settlement at Milking Gap, Northumberland', *Archaeol Aeliana 4 ser 15* (1938), 303–50.

Kramer, W and Schubert, F 1970 · *Die ausgrabungen in Manching 1955–61: ein fuhrund und fundstellenubersicht.* Romanisch-Germanische kommission des Deutchen Archaologischen Instituts-Wiesbachen. Steiver.

Lamb, H H 1982a · *Climate history and the modern world.* London: Methuen.

Lamb, H H 1982b · 'Reconstruction on the course of post-glacial climate over the world', *in* Harding, D W (ed) 1982a, 11–32.

Lambrick, G and Robinson, M 1979 · 'Iron Age and Roman riverside settlements at Farmoor, Oxfordshire' (Council Brit Archaeol Res Rep, 32).

Lane, A 1986 · 'An Iron Age enclosure at Candyburn, Tweeddale', *Trans Dumfriesshire Galloway Natur Hist Antiq Soc*, 61 (1986), 41–54.

Lanting, J N and van der Waals, J D 1972 · 'British Beakers as seen from the Continent', *Helinium*, 12 (1972), 20–46.

Longworth, I H 1961 · 'The origins and development of the Primary Series in the Collared Urn tradition in England and Wales', *Proc Prehist Soc* 27 (1961), 263–306.

Longworth, I H 1967 · 'Further discoveries at Brackmont Mill and Tentsmuir, Fife', *Proc Soc Antiq Scot*, 99 (1966–7), 60–92.

Longworth, I H 1984    *Collared Urns of the Bronze Age in Great Britain and Ireland.* Cambridge: Cambridge University Press.

MacInnes, I J 1964    'The Neolithic and Early Bronze Age pottery from Luce Sands, Wigtonshire', *Proc Soc Antiq Scot*, 97 (1963–4), 40–81.

MacInnes, L 1984    'Brochs and the Roman occupation of lowland Scotland', *Proc Soc Antiq Scot*, 114 (1984), 235–50.

MacKie, E W 1969    'Radiocarbon dates and the Scottish Iron Age', *Antiquity*, XLIII (1969), 15–26.

MacKie, E W 1971    'English migrants and Scottish brochs', *Glasgow Archaeol J*, 2 (1971), 39–71.

MacKie, E W 1974    *Dun Mor Vaul; an Iron Age broch on Tiree.* Glasgow: University of Glasgow Press.

MacKie, E W 1982    'The Leckie Broch, Stirlingshire: an interim report', *Glasgow Archaeol J*, 9 (1982), 60–72.

MacLaren, A 1958    'Excavations at Keir Hill, Gargunnock', *Proc Soc Antiq Scot*, 91 (1957–8), 78–83.

Main, L 1978    'Excavation at the Fairy Knowe, Buchlyvie, Stirlingshire, 1975–78', *Forth Naturalist and Historian*, 3 (1978), 99–111.

Mann, J C and Breeze, D J 1987    'Ptolemy, Tacitus and the tribes of north Britain', *Proc Soc Antiq Scot*, 117 (1987), 85–91.

Mannion, A M 1978a    'Late Quaternary deposits from Linton Loch, south-east Scotland', *J Biogeogr*, 5 (1978a), 193–206.

Mannion, A M 1978b    'A pollen-analytical investigation at Threepwood Moss', *Trans Bot Soc Edin*, 43 (1978b), 105–114.

Maryon, H 1938    'Some prehistoric metalworkers' tools', *Antiq J*, 18 (1938), 243–250.

McCormick, F 1988    'Animal bones from Haughey's fort', *Emania*, 4 (1988), 24–27.

Mears, J B 1937    'Urn burials of the Bronze Age at Brackmont Mill, Leuchars, Fife', *Proc Soc Antiq Scot*, 71 (1936–7), 252–78.

Megaw, J V S and Simpson, D D A 1984    *An introduction to British prehistory.* 3rd ed. Leicester: Leicester University Press.

Milne, A 1768    *A description of the parish of Melrose in answer to Mr Maitland's queries, sent to each parish of the kingdom*, 2. Edinburgh: Blackwood.

Mook, W G and Waterbolk, H T 1985    *Radiocarbon dating.* Handbooks for archaeologists, 3. European Science Foundation.

Moore, P D and Webb, J A 1978    *An Illustrated guide to pollen analysis.* London: Hodder and Stoughton.

Morrison, I A 1983    'Prehistoric Scotland', *in* Whyte, I and Whittington, G (eds), *A historical geography of Scotland*, 1–23, London: Academic Press.

Muir, J W 1956    *The soils round Jedburgh and Morebattle.* Memoirs of the Soil Survey of Great Britain. Edinburgh.

Munro, R 1882    *Ancient Scottish lake dwellings or crannogs.* Edinburgh.

Musson, C R 1976    'Excavations at the Breiddin 1969–73', *in* Harding, D W (ed) 1976, 293–302.

Newall, F 1960    *Excavations at Walls Hill, Renfrewshire.* Paisley: Public Library, Museum and Art Galleries.

NSA, 1845    *The new statistical account of Scotland.* Blackwood.

O'Connor, B and Cowie, T 1985    'A group of bronze socketed axes from Eildon Mid Hill, near Melrose, Roxburghshire', *Proc Soc Antiq Scot*, 115 (1985), 151–158.

O'Kelly, M J 1964    'Two ring-forts at Garryduff, Co. Cork', *Proc Roy Ir Acad*, 63 (1964), 17–125.

O'Riordain, S P 1942    'The excavation of a large earthern ring-fort at Garrones, Co. Cork', *Proc Roy Ir Acad*, 47C (1942), 77–150.

Ohnuma, K and Bergman, C 1982    'Experimental studies and the determination of the flaking mode', *Bull Inst Archaeol Univ London*, 19 (1982), 161–170.

Oldfield, F 1988    *in* Goudie, A, *Geomorphological techniques.*

Olsson, I U 1986    'Radiometric dating', *in* Berglund, B E (ed), *Handbook of Holocene palaeoecology and palaeohydrology*, Chichester: Wiley, 273–313.

Palace of history 1911    *Official historical catalogue to the Scottish exhibition.* Glasgow: Dalross Ltd.

Pearsall, D M 1989    *Palaeoethnobotany: a handbook of procedures.* Academic Press.

Pearson, G W, Pilcher, J R, Baillie, M G L, Corbett D M, and Qua, F 1986    'High precision 14C measurment of Irish oaks to show the natural 14C variations from AD 1840–5210 BC', *Radiocarbon*, 25, 2B (1986), 911–34.

Pearson, G W and Stuiver, M 1986    'High-precision calibration of the radiocarbon time scale 500–2500 BC', *in* Stuiver, M and Kra, R S 1986, 839–62.

| | |
|---|---|
| Pennington, W 1979 | 'The origins of pollen in lake sediment: an enclosed lake compared with one receiving inflow streams', *New Phytol*, 83 (1979), 189–213. |
| Piggott C M 1948 | 'The Excavations at Hownam Rings, Roxburghshire, 1948', *Proc Soc Antiq Scot*, 82 (1947–8), 193–225. |
| Piggott, C M 1949 | 'The Iron Age settlement at Hayhope Knowe, Roxburghshire: excavations, 1949', *Proc Soc Antiq Scot*, 83 (1948–9), 45–67. |
| Piggott, C M 1950 | 'The excavations at Bonchester Hill, 1950', *Proc Soc Antiq Scot*, 84 (1949–50), 113–36. |
| Piggott, S 1951 | 'Excavations in the broch and hillfort of Torwoodlee, Selkirkshire, 1950', *Proc Soc Antiq Scot*, 85 (1950–1), 92–116. |
| Piggott, S 1953 | 'Three metalwork hoards of the Roman period from southern Scotland', *Proc Soc Antiq Scot*, 87 (1952–3), 68–123. |
| Piggott, S 1958a | 'Native economies and the Roman occupation of north Britain', *in* Richmond, I A (ed), *Roman and native in north Britain*, 1–27. |
| Piggott, S 1958b | 'Excavations at Braidwood Fort, Midlothian and Craig's Quarry, Dirleton, East Lothian', *Proc Soc Antiq Scot*, 91 (1957–8), 61–77. |
| Piggott, S 1966 | 'A scheme for the Scottish Iron Age', *in* Rivet, A L F (ed) 1966, 1–15. |
| Piggott, S and Piggott, C M 1952 | 'Excavations at Castle Law, Glencorse, and at Craig's Quarry, Dirleton, 1948–9', *Proc Soc Antiq Scot*, 86 (1951–2), 191–6. |
| Pitts, M W and Jacobi, R M 1979 | 'Some aspects of change in the Mesolithic and Neolithic in southern Britain', *J Archaeol Sci*, 6, 163–177. |
| Price, J 1988 | 'Romano-British glass bangles from East Yorkshire', *in* Price, J and Wilson, P R with Briggs, C S and Hardman, S J (eds), *Recent research in Roman Yorkshire, studies in honour of Mary Kitson Clark*, 339–366, Oxford. (Brit Archaeol Rep, 193). |
| Proudfoot, E V W 1978 | 'Camelon native site', *Proc Soc Antiq Scot*, 109 (1977–8), 112–128. |
| PSAS 1888 | 'Purchases to the museum', *Proc Soc Antiq Scot*, 22 (1887–8), 270. |
| PSAS 1933 | 'Exhibition of relics Monday 12th Dec 1932', *Proc Soc Antiq Scot*, 67 (1932–3), 9–10. |
| PSAS 1967 | 'Donations and purchases for the museum', *Proc Soc Antiq Scot*, 99 (1966–7), 266. |
| Ptolemy | *Geographica* Bk II, Ch II. |
| Rackham, O 1976 | *Trees and woodland in the British landscape*. London: J M Dent and Sons. |
| Rackham, O 1988 | 'Wildwood', *in* Jones, M (ed), *Archaeology and the flora of the British Isles*. Oxford: Oxford Comittee for Archaeology, 3–6. |
| Raftery, B 1976 | 'Rathgall and Irish hill-fort problems', *in* Harding, D W (ed) 1976, 339–57. |
| Ragg J M 1960 | *The soils of the country round Kelso and Lauder*. Memoirs of the Soil Survey of Great Britain. Edinburgh: HMSO. |
| RCHM(E) 1962 | *Inventory of the historical monuments in the city of York: volume 1, Eburacum, Roman York*. London. |
| RCAHMS 1915 | *Sixth report and inventory of monuments and constructions in the County of Berwick*. Edinburgh: HMSO. |
| RCAHMS 1924 | *Eighth report with inventory of monuments and constructions in the County of East Lothian*. Edinburgh: HMSO. |
| RCAHMS 1929 | *Inventory of the monuments and constructions in the Counties of Midlothian and West Lothian*. Edinburgh: HMSO. |
| RCAHMS 1956 | *Inventory of the ancient and historical monuments of Roxburghshire*. Edinburgh: HMSO. |
| RCAHMS 1957 | *Inventory of the ancient and historical monuments of Selkirkshire*. Edinburgh: HMSO. |
| RCAHMS 1963 | *Inventory of the ancient and historical monuments of Stirlingshire*. Edinburgh: HMSO. |
| RCAHMS 1967 | *Peeblesshire: an inventory of the ancient monuments*. Edinburgh: HMSO. |
| RCAHMS 1978 | *Inventory of the prehistoric and Roman monuments of Lanarkshire*. Edinburgh: HMSO. |
| RCAHMS 1980 | *The archaeological sites and monuments of Berwickshire District, Borders Region*, Society of Antiquaries of Scotland Field Survey. Edinburgh. |
| RCAHMS 1988 | *The archaeological sites and monuments of Midlothian (prehistoric to early historic), Midlothian District, Lothian Region*. Edinburgh: HMSO. |

Reynolds, P J 1982 — 'Substructure to superstructure', *in* Drury, P J (ed), *Structural reconstruction.* Oxford, 173–98. (Brit Archaeol Rep Brit Ser, 110).

Richmond, I A 1967 — *Hodhill.* London.

Richmond, I A (ed) 1958 — *Roman and native in north Britain.* Edinburgh: Studies in History and Archaeology.

Richmond, I and Jacobi, R M 1979 — 'Excavations at Woden Law, 1950', *Proc Soc Antiq Scot*, 112 (1982), 277–84.

Rideout, J S 1983 — 'Excavation at Ring's Plantation, Yetholm, Roxburghshire, 1983', *Glasgow Archaeol J*, 10 (1983), 157–9.

Rideout, J S 1988 — 'Tailburn Earthwork: excavation 1987', *Trans Dumfriesshire Galloway Natur Hist Antiq Soc*, 63 (1987), 5–12.

Rideout, J S 1989 — 'An excavation at Allan Water earthworks, Roxburgh District, Borders Region', *Trans Dumfriesshire Galloway Natur Hist Antiq Soc*, 64 (1989), 1–6.

Rideout, J S (forthcoming) — 'Craighead'.

Rideout, J S and Tavener, P N (forthcoming) — 'Excavations on a promontory fort, and a palisaded homestead, at Lower Greenyards, Bannockburn, Stirling District, Central Region, 1982–5'.

Ritchie, J N G 1974 — 'Excavation of the stone-circle and cairn at Balbirnie, Fife', *Archaeol J*, 131 (1974), 1–32.

Rivet, A L F (ed) 1966 — *The Iron Age in northern Britain.* Edinburgh: University Press.

Robertson, A S 1970 — 'Roman finds from non-Roman sites in Scotland', *Britannia*, 1 (1970), 198–226.

Roy, W 1744 — *Military map*, map no. 8/3.

Roy, W 1793 — *The military antiquities of the Romans in north Britain.* London: Society of Antiquaries.

Russell-White, C J 1988 — 'Downlaw, Fife', *Discovery Excav Scot.*

Sanderson, D C W 1988a — 'Thick source beta counting (TSBC): a rapid method for measuring beta dose rates', *Nuclear Tracks*, 14 (1988a), (1–2), 203–6.

Sanderson, D C W 1988b — 'Fading of thermoluminescence in feldspars: characteristics and corrections', *Nuclear Tracks*, 14 (1988b), (1–2), 155–61.

Sanderson, D C W and Chambers, D A 1985 — 'An automatic Sr90 irradiator for TL dating', *Ancient TL*, 3 (1985), 26–9.

Sanderson, D C W, Placido, F and Tate, J O 1985 — 'Scottish vitrified-forts: background and potential for TL dating', *Nuclear Tracks*, 10 (1985), 799–810.

Sanderson, D C W, Placido, F and Tate, J O 1988 — 'Scottish vitrified-forts: TL results from six study sites', *Nuclear Tracks*, 14, 1–2 (1988), 307–16.

Savory, H N 1971 — 'A Welsh Iron Age hill-fort', *Antiquity*, 45 (1971), 51–261.

Schoenwetter, J 1987 — 'Review of Dimbleby, G W, *The Palynology of archaeological sites*', *American Antiquity*, 52, 1 (1987), 204–206.

Shennan, I and Innes, J B 1987 — 'Late Devensian and Flandrian environmental changes at the Dod, Borders Region', *Scottish Archaeol Review*, 4, 1 (1987), 17–26.

Schweingruber, F H 1978 — *Microscopic wood anatomy.* Birmensdorf.

Scott, E M and Sanderson, D C W 1988 — 'Statistics and the additive dose method in TL dating', *Nuclear Tracks*, 14, 1–2 (1988), 345–54.

Shepherd, W 1972 — *Flint: its origin, properties and uses.* London: Faber and Faber.

Simpson, D D A 1969 — 'Excavations at Kaimes Hillfort, Midlothian, 1964–1968', *Glasgow Archaeol J*, 1 (1969), 7–28.

Spearman, R M (forthcoming) — 'Metalworking and burnt material from Castle Green, Portnockie', *in* Ralston, I (forthcoming), 'Excavations at Castle Green, Portnockie', *Proc Soc Antiq Scot.*

Steer, K A 1956 — 'The Early Iron Age homestead at West Plean', *Proc Soc Antiq Scot*, 89 (1955–6), 227–51.

Steer, K A and Feacham, R W 1952 — 'A Roman signal station on Eildon Hill North, Roxburghshire', *Proc Scot Antiq Soc*, 85 (1951–2), 202–5.

Steer, K A and Keeney, G S 1947 — 'Excavations in two homesteads at Crock Cleuch, Roxburghshire', *Proc Soc Antiq Scot*, 81 (1946–7), 138–57.

Stevenson, R B K 1949 — 'Braidwood Fort, Midlothian: the exploration of two huts', *Proc Soc Antiq Scot*, 83 (1948–9), 1–11.

Stevenson, R B K 1954 — 'Native bangles and Roman glass', *Proc Soc Antiq Scot*, 88 (1954), 208–221.

Stevenson, R B K 1966 — 'Metalwork and some other objects in Scotland and their cultural affinities', *in* Rivet, A L F (ed) 1966, 17–44.

| | |
|---|---|
| Stevenson, R B K 1976 | 'Romano-British glass bangles', *Glasgow Archaeol J*, 4 (1976), 44–54. |
| Stuiver, M and Kra, R S 1986 | 'Proceedings of the twelfth international radiocarbon conference, June 24–28 1985, Trondheim, Norway', *Radiocarbon* 28 (1986), 839–62. |
| Stuiver, M and Reimer, P 1986 | 'Computer program for radiocarbon age calibration', *Radiocarbon*, 28(2b) (1986), 1022–1030. |
| Taylor, J A 1985 | 'The relationship between land-use change and variations in bracken encroachment rates in Britain', *in* Smith, R T (ed), *The biogeographical impact of land use change: collected essays*, Leeds, 19–28. (Leeds Univ Biogeog Monog, 2). |
| Thomson, G 1845 | *New Statistical Account* Vol III, 55. |
| Thomson, J K 1969 | 'Wallstale Dun, Polmaise, Stirling', *Proc Soc Antiq Scot*, 101 (1968–9), 119–21. |
| Thorneycroft, W 1933 | 'Observations on hut-circles near the eastern border of Perthshire, north of Blairgowrie', *Proc Soc Antiq Scot*, 67 (1932–33), 187–208. |
| Triscott, J 1982 | 'Excavations at Dryburn Bridge, East Lothian, 1978–1979', *in* Harding, D W (ed) 1982a, 117–24. |
| Turner, J 1965 | 'A contribution to the history of forest clearance', *Proc Royal Soc London*, 161, B (1965), 343–354. |
| Turner, J 1979 | 'The environment of north-east England during Roman times as shown by pollen analysis', *Journal of Archaeol Sci*, 6 (1979), 285–290. |
| Turner, J 1983 | 'Some pollen evidence for the environment of northern Britain 1000 BC–1000 AD', *in* Chapman, J C and Mytum, H C (eds), *Settlement in North Britain*, Oxford, 3–27. (Brit Archaeol Rep Brit Ser, 118). |
| Tylecote, R F 1986 | *The prehistory of metallurgy in the British Isles*. London: Institute of Metals. |
| Venclova, N 1985 | 'Collection of glass from Stradonice in Bohemia', *in* Nancy 1983, *Proceedings of the 9th International Association for the History of Glass*, 65–75. |
| Waterman, D 1970 | 'Navan Fort', *Cur Archaeol*, 22 (1970), 308–11. |
| Vourela, I 1973 | 'Relative pollen rain around cultivated fields', *Acta Botanica Fennica*, 102 (1973), 2–27. |
| Webb, J A and Moore, P D 1982 | 'The Late Devensian vegetational history of the Whitlaw Mosses, south-east Scotland', *New Phytol*, 91 (1982), 341–398. |
| Wheeler, R E M 1943 | *Maiden Castle, Dorset*. Oxford. (Oxford Soc Antiq Res Rep, 12). |
| Whittington, G 1980 | 'Prehistoric activity and its effect on the Scottish landscape', in Parry, M L and Slater, T R (eds), *The making of the Scottish countryside* 23–44. London: Croom-Helm. |
| Whittow, J B 1977 | *Geology and scenery in southern Scotland*. |
| Wickham-Jones, C and Collins, G H 1978 | 'The sources of flint and chert in northern Britain', *Proc Soc Antiq Scot*, 109 (1978), 7–22. |
| Wilson, D 1983 | 'Pollen analysis and settlement archaeology of the first millennium bc from north-east England', *in* Chapman, J C and Mytum, H C (eds), *Settlement in north Britain*, Oxford, 29–47. (Brit Archaeol Rep, 118). |
| Yarrington, C H 1982 | 'Small finds: pottery' *in* Peltenberg, E J, 'Excavations at Balloch Hill, Argyll', *Proc Soc Antiq Scot*, 112 (1982), 142–214. |
| Young, C J 1977 | *Oxfordshire Roman pottery*. Oxford. |
| Young, R 1987 | 'Barrows, clearance and land use: some suggestions from the north-east of England', *Landscape History*, 9 (1987), 27–34. |

# *Index*